NANCY L. COHEN

DELIRIUM

HOW THE SEXUAL COUNTERREVOLUTION IS
POLARIZING AMERICA

COUNTERPOINT | BERKELEY

FOR
Jonathan

Library of Congress Cataloging-in-Publication Data is available.

ISBN 978-1-58243-801-6

Cover design by BriarMade

Counterpoint
1919 Fifth Street
Berkeley, CA 94710
www.counterpointpress.com

Distributed by Publishers Group West
Printed in the United States of America

10 9 8 7 6 5 4 3 2 1

CONTENTS

INTRODUCTION

As baseball-sized hailstones rain down on Kansas and tornadoes touch down a few hundred miles south of Washington, D.C., Republicans nearly shut down the federal government over funding for birth control. When the Obama administration announces that it will not defend the Defense of Marriage Act because the Justice Department has concluded the law is unconstitutional, Republicans vote to spend taxpayer dollars to have Congress take over the appeal. Ten days into the controversial military operation to aid the Libyan rebellion against Muammar el-Qaddafi, the House Armed Services subcommittee calls the nation's military leaders to appear at a hearing about the recent repeal of Don't Ask, Don't Tell. The officials testify that there have been "no issues or problems" and the transition is going smoothly. Republican congressmen claim that allowing gays to serve openly in the armed forces will wreak devastation on troop morale and national security.

In the first weeks of summer, as Congressional Republicans play a game of brinksmanship with the nation's credit, wildfires sweep through Texas and 140 million Americans swelter under life-threatening heat. Minnesota Representative Michele Bachmann surges into second place in the 2012 Republican presidential race. Bachmann is the founder of the House Tea Party Caucus and promises to be a voice for "constitutional conservatism" and "limited government." She has also called homosexuality "personal enslavement" and told voters she follows the biblical admonition, "Wives, be submissive to your husbands."

Bad economies are treacherous to incumbents, and just two and a half years after the advent of the Age of Obama, the Republican Party has a remarkable opportunity to make Barack Obama a one-term president. The frontrunner, Mitt Romney, has the résumé of a Republican president-to-be, but inspires little love. Sarah Palin, who evokes passionate support among many Republicans, won't say whether she'll run or not, but still attracts a crush of fans and a media swarm wherever she ventures. The unusually large field of Republican candidates includes Newt Gingrich, the former House Speaker who commanded an earlier Republican revolution against a Democratic president. It includes Herman Cain, who believes God has chosen him to be president and that gays choose to be gay. Also among the Republican candidates is a former U.S. senator, Rick Santorum, who once compared homosexuality to "man on dog" sex. On the campaign trail, he likens preschool to Fascist youth brigades and warns parents that early childhood education is a government plot to "indoctrinate your children."

The Republican establishment, concerned that Romney is not conservative enough to survive the primary and that Bachmann's extremism will alienate mainstream voters in the general election, looks to Texas Governor Rick Perry for electoral salvation. Perry's sponsorship of "a day of Christian prayer and fasting," complicates the plan. One of the rally's sponsors, after all, is leading a boycott of *Glee* because the show "glamorizes homosexual behavior." Another had been a leader of Yes on Prop 8, the referendum campaign that changed the California constitution in order to end gay marriage in the state.

Why, when the United States is mired in its worst economic downturn since the Great Depression, would birth control, abortion, and the rights of gays and women top the agenda of the Republican Party? How could this obsession with sex and family matters be squared with the pledge by Tea Party Republicans that they would put Americans back to work and be true to the principles of limited government, personal liberty, and the constitution of the founding fathers?

"It wasn't supposed to happen like this," *New York Times* columnist Charles Blow wrote after the Republicans assumed control of the House following their 2010 midterm victory. "Judging by the lead-up to those elections, one could have easily concluded that the first

Obama took to saying, his views were "evolving." Even though only a small number of Democratic leaders have ever endorsed the agenda of the right-wing sexual counterrevolution, many others have tacitly advanced it—by evasion, passive acquiescence, or capitulation.

Were it true that turning right on the so-called hot-button issues was the way to win the hearts and votes of the American people, it would be hard to fault Democratic leaders for demanding everyone face up to the facts of majority rule. But, as we'll see, such claims are false. The notion that Democrats lose by being culturally progressive is a fiction, a narrative born of the delirium of defeat. The Democratic Party has repeatedly snatched defeat from the jaws of victory by its propensity to overreact and misinterpret the message being sent by voters.

Delirium IS A history of our current political dysfunction. First, let me state clearly and unambiguously that *the sexual counterrevolution is not the only source or cause of how American politics came to be the way it is in our time.* Race, war, money in politics, class, and competing ideas about American identity are also main determinants of the course of politics over the last few decades. Nonetheless, the sexual counterrevolution is one of the few key dynamics driving contemporary American politics. Seocond, my goal has been to uncover a missing piece of our history, *Delirium* is not intended to be a comprehensive political history of the last forty years. Third, much of the evidence that convinced me of the importance of the sexual counterrevolution is statistical. Unlike most books on current politics and culture, many of my specific conclusions are based on numbers: the raw data of public opinion surveys, and the work of experts and scholars who run the data through complex statistical analyses. The reader who is interested in the technical methods used in these studies or in the experts' debates can find citations to scholarly articles and links to publicly accessible databases on public opinion and voting behavior in the Notes section at the end of this book.

Finally, because this book covers unexplored ground, I have had the need to adapt some common political terms and to coin others. One of these is "sexual counterrevolution"—meaning the political reaction against the changes ushered in by the sexual revolution. (See

order of business on Republicans' agendas would be a laserlike focus on job creation and deficit reductions to the exclusion of all else. Not the case."

If the history of the sexual counterrevolution were better known, no one would have been surprised.

WELCOME TO THE sexual counterrevolution, the great untold story behind America's plunge into political delirium. To understand how we got from Barack Obama's historic victory in 2008 to the Republican resurgence just two years later, look no further.

Delirium investigates a shadow movement that has polarized our country. One of the leading forces fueling America's political wars has been the reaction against the sexual revolution and the progressive movements that emerged from it: feminism and gay rights. Here I tell the story of this shadow movement, how conflicts about sex, women's rights and women's roles, gay civil rights, and family drove Americans into irreconcilable warring camps, shattered and remade the political parties, and unhinged the nation. The sexual counterrevolution was not just a passing backlash. It was an ideologically powered, strategically organized, and well-financed political movement that persists to this day.

The sexual counterrevolution has played a leading role in determining who has won and who has lost in American politics over the last forty years. It has powerfully influenced what the winners do, or won't or can't do, once they find themselves in power. The surprising resilience of the sexual counterrevolution was one critical source of the paralyzing divisions that contributed to the Democrats' 2010 defeat. It is, as well, the subterranean force driving the race to the far right by the 2012 Republican candidates for the presidency of the United States.

WE KNOW, OF course, that the Republican Party has staked its electoral fortunes on promises to outlaw abortion, rewrite the U.S. Constitution to ban gay marriage, and resurrect the traditional family by legislative and judicial fiat.

We've grown so accustomed to a Republican Party consumed with gays and abortion that many Americans likely do not know it was ever any other way. In fact, in an earlier time, the highest-ranking woman in the GOP was a pro-choice feminist. Barry Goldwater, the 1964 Republican nominee, was an ultraconservative who supported women's right to abortion and thought Americans "had a constitutional right to be gay." Students for Goldwater in one Ohio high school was chaired by a young Republican named Hillary Rodham. President George W. Bush's grandfather, investment banker and Republican Senator Prescott Bush, was an active member of Planned Parenthood.

The GOP as we know it today was born in the 1970s, as ordinary conservative American women became community organizers in order to turn back the sexual revolution, feminism, and gay rights. These pioneering women, the original sexual counterrevolutionaries, launched successful political campaigns to kill the Equal Rights Amendment, federally financed child care, sex education, and gay civil rights. (Abortion, it is rather crucial to note, was not one of their early preoccupations.) In doing so, they galvanized Protestant fundamentalists to vote, created the Christian Right, and over the course of several decades, forged it into the largest, most powerful bloc of voters within the Republican Party. Over the last forty years, the GOP has been remade from within as a party of the Right, by the Right, and for the Right. But the Right had absolutely no mass popular support, no so-called base, before it followed the ladies in their crusade to stuff the genie of modern American sex back in the bottle of heterosexual marriage and the traditional nuclear family.

From the perspective of the Republican Party, the partnership with Christian Right sexual counterrevolutionaries has been a decidedly mixed blessing. Such voters have buoyed Republicans to a few big victories—not least the Republican takeover of the House in 2010. The GOP's problem is that these voters make up a small minority of the electorate, just 15 to 20 percent of potential voters in a national election. The majority of the American public rejects the sexual puritanicalism and religious dogmatism of the sexual counterrevolutionaries and tends to desert the Republican ticket when they sense it has, so to speak, gotten into bed with the sexual fundamentalists. Senator John McCain understands this perhaps better than anyone else. In his

first run for president, McCain denounced the preachers of the Christian Right as "agents of intolerance." Republica voters promptly ran McCain out of the race. In 2008, Mc a different tack toward the base of his party. He chose as his mate an evangelical fundamentalist who opposed gay civil ri education, and abortion: Sarah Palin. He won the sexual coun lutionaries but lost the election by 9.5 million votes.

YET THIS IS not a tale about the Republican Party only. It turn that the sexual counterrevolution has been a bipartisan affair.

The birth of the sexual counterrevolution in the Democratic P coincided with the kickoff of the Democrats' self-defeating inner c war. When George McGovern, the 1972 Democratic nominee, lc the presidential election by a landslide, Democratic politicians an opinion leaders attributed the loss to the radicalism of McGovern's sup porters. Gays, feminists, multiculturalists, and elitist college students, they claimed, had alienated Middle America by flouting its traditional values. And unless they were stopped, the cultural elitists would destroy the Democratic Party. Each time fortune turned against the party, as it did so often in the decades following, Democratic leaders would dust off this death-by-McGovernik narrative and deploy it against their brothers and sisters in the battle for the soul of the party.

The Democratic Party's reputation as the more progressive one is deserved, of course. Yet as we will see, many Democratic leaders have been reluctant to embrace this identity; to openly affirm their beliefs in cultural tolerance, diversity, and a live-and-let-live attitude about sex, sexuality, and personal relationships; to own the values of cultural progressivism held today by a good majority of all voters— not just self-identified Democrats. Some Democrats have hesitated to stand up for progressive values out of political calculation. They have been quick to accede to whatever compromise they have deemed expedient for victory, often with little regard to whose fundamental interests have been bartered away. Other Democrats have been consumed with a search for the Holy Grail, that sweet spot of moderation on the fabled middle ground. So, for example, supporting gay civil unions is a matter of simple justice. Gay marriage? Well, as President notes to this chapter for some others.) I want to particularly clarify what I mean by "fundamentalism," especially since it's often linked to sex, as in the term "sexual fundamentalism." I use "fundamentalism," lower-cased, *not* as a reference to Protestant fundamentalists, but rather as a term about a politics characterized by cultural traditionalism and an orthodox belief in the literal rules issued by some higher authority. Most of the sexual fundamentalists who appear here are indeed orthodox religious traditionalists, a group that includes some, but not all, Mormons, Catholics, Pentecostalists, and Charismatics, in addition to conservative Protestants who adhere to a belief that the bible is the literal, unerring word of God. I caution strongly against reading any mention of "fundamentalism" as a blanket statement about all evangelicals, all Christians, or even all fundamentalists. Fewer than a third of Catholics and mainline Protestants, and fewer than a quarter of African American evangelicals share the political views of the sexual fundamentalists. Even among white evangelicals, about four in ten vote Democratic or do not vote at all. Indeed, a sizable minority of evangelical Christians are politically and culturally progressive.

AS I WRITE, one in six Americans can't find enough work, and 46 million Americans, more than ever before, are living below the official poverty line. The Great Recession casts a dark shadow over the nation. I realize that in this moment it is counterintuitive, perverse even, to suggest that understanding the sexual counterrevolution is a key to solving our political and economic problems. But history does not proceed in a straight or logical line. Its path is winding and unpredictable. The Tea Party, our economic anxiety and political demoralization, even the irrational hostility some Americans harbor against our first African American president, are symptoms of our political crisis, not its cause. The wellspring of our political fever lies deeper in the American psyche; the roots of our political disorders are buried further back in time. How we got here, and why, is the story of this book.

1

SEX AND REVOLUTION

PERHAPS IF THE Pill had not been invented, American politics
would be very different today.

Enovid, the first birth control pill, went on the market in
1960. Unlike any other previously available form of contraception,
the Pill was both reliable and controlled by a woman herself, requiring
neither the consent nor the knowledge of her sexual partner. "I don't
confess that I take the Pill," said one Catholic mother after the Vatican reaffirmed its doctrine against the use of birth control, "because
I don't believe it is a sin." Within five years, 6 million American
women were on the Pill. With one quick visit to a doctor, a woman
immediately gained sole and exclusive power over her fertility, a
power that had eluded her sex since . . . well, since forever.

The Pill made possible the sexual revolution of the 1960s. The
true warriors in that revolution were young, single women, who,
with the help of this new contraception, took their sexuality into
their own hands. If not for women's self-determined sexual liberation, the sexual revolution might have been another unremarkable
episode in the long and varied sexual history of humankind. Instead,
with the impetus the sexual revolution gave to a new feminism and a

movement for gay liberation, it became one of the major catalysts of America's ongoing political delirium.

MEN CERTAINLY BENEFITED from the new sexual freedom, but for them, it was hardly an innovation. Although religious doctrine and public mores told them chastity and marital fidelity applied equally to men and women, the practical moral code included an important loophole: the double standard. Single men had always been able to avail themselves of sexual relations outside marriage, even at the pinnacle of American sexual puritanism in the waning days of the nineteenth century. For men, the sexual revolution changed things by making sex relatively cost-free. Women were now liberated, and the Pill steeply lowered the risks of accidental fatherhood and unwanted marriage.

For women, likewise, the sexual revolution concerned the rules of engagement, rather than the act of sex itself. Premarital virginity had been going out of fashion for decades before the declaration of sexual liberation. It started in the 1920s, as middle-class Americans converted from Victorianism to Freudianism and began to accept that a desirous woman was perhaps not so depraved after all. Thereafter doctors and psychologists counseled America's women that a happy marriage was sustained by mutual sexual satisfaction. Experts encouraged women to explore their natural desires, but to start the journey in the marital bed. Women accepted the prescription and ignored the fine print. At the high noon of fifties traditionalism, 40 percent of women had sex before they married—compared to just 10 percent who did in the reputedly Roaring Twenties.

Yet sex before marriage, like any act of civil disobedience, entailed risk. Each and every time an unmarried woman had intercourse, she risked pregnancy, and with it a limited number of unsavory life-changing options: an illegal abortion of doubtful safety, a shotgun wedding, forced adoption, or single motherhood of a child whose birth certificate would be stamped for posterity with the word "illegitimate." With rare exceptions, all known human cultures have policed the sexual behavior of girls and women, and America, circa 1959, was no different. Before women obtained the power to control their fertility, they had compelling reasons to comply with whatever arbitrary double standard their society imposed. The Pill permanently changed women's age-old pragmatic calculus. With a little pharmaceutical ingenuity, the double standard relaxed its clawing grip on female humanity.

Still, birth control remained illegal in some states, and the grip of the law also had to be pried loose before women could take full advantage of the new opportunity for sexual liberation. In the late nineteenth century, purity crusaders had succeeded in passing a spate of national and state laws criminalizing the sale, distribution, or even discussion of birth control. In 1965, the Supreme Court ruled Connecticut's 1879 anti-contraception statute—originally written by circus impresario P. T. Barnum—to be unconstitutional. In that case, Connecticut had convicted Estelle Griswold and Dr. C. Lee Buxton of the Planned Parenthood League of Connecticut for providing birth control to a married couple. (They had been fined $100.) In *Griswold v. Connecticut*, the Court ruled that the law, and any other restrictions on access to contraception for married couples, violated the marital right to privacy, and were thus unconstitutional. Seven years later, the Supreme Court effectively extended the right to obtain birth control to unmarried men and women, in *Eisenstadt v. Baird.* In that case, the state of Massachusetts had charged William Baird with a felony for giving away vaginal foam to an unmarried college student who attended one of his lectures on birth control and overpopulation. Justice William J. Brennan, Jr., wrote in his opinion for the court: "If the right of privacy means anything, it is the right of the individual, married or single, to be free from unwarranted governmental intrusion into matters so fundamentally affecting a person as the decision to whether to bear or beget a child."

Those who hoped to preserve the pre-Pill cultural norms now had only the power of persuasion at their service. It helped them little. The rapidity of change in women's sexual behavior was dizzying, and it suggests how much the old order had been preserved by cultural coercion rather than willing consent. In the 1950s, six in ten women were virgins at marriage and 87 percent of American women believed that it was wrong for a woman to engage in premarital sex, even with "a man she is going to marry." By the time girls born during the sexual revolution came of age, the double standard—in practice, if not exactly in the minds of teenage boys—had been obliterated. Only two in ten of them would be virgins at marriage. Teenagers, in particular, shed the old ways. In 1960, half of unmarried 19-year-old women had not yet had sex. In the late 1980s, half of all American girls engaged in sexual intercourse by the age of 17, two-thirds by the age of 18, and the difference between teenage male and female sexual experience had narrowed from 50 points to single digits.

As Americans settled into the new normal of open heterosexual sexuality, even more profound changes were afoot. The Pill allowed American women to delay marriage and motherhood, while remaining sexually active. Women took advantage of these added carefree years to improve their position in the labor market. According to the economists Claudia Goldin and Lawrence Katz, the surge in women's professional education occurred at the exact moment the Pill became legally available to college-aged women. "A virtually fool-proof, easy-to-use, and female-controlled contraceptive having low health risks, little pain, and few annoyances does appear to have been important in promoting real change in the economic status of women." They concluded, "The Pill lowered the cost of pursuing a career through its direct effect on the cost of having sex and its indirect effect of increasing the age at first marriage generally." The Supreme Court's 1973 decision in *Roe v. Wade* provided women with even greater control of their own fertility, a goal that had eluded them while abortion remained illegal. (In the years after the Pill went on the market and before abortion became legal, about 1 million illegal abortions took place per year.) In 1978, the first test-tube baby was born, marking the beginning of the age of assisted, sex-free reproduction.

Before the revolution, the whims of men determined the reputation, if not the fate, of women; female desire was contained within the closet of marriage; and men retained their traditional sexual privileges and discreetly enjoyed their sexual liberties. After the revolution, women, if they so chose, could dispense with men, or with marriage altogether, without giving up sex or children or a lifetime loving relationship. Of course, most women continued to love men, marry men, and have children with men. The point, however, was that for the first time in human history, women had a choice.

IN A DESPERATE effort to stop cultural change in its tracks, the critics of the new sexual order accused the sexual revolutionaries of destroying the traditional American family. They had their cause and effect reversed. By the time the revolution in sexual mores gained steam, the nuclear family was already in an advanced state of fission from the reactive force of its soul-bending emotional demands and outdated economic arrangements. Deprived of the coercive power of the law and public opinion, the sexual traditionalists took refuge in a myth.

The so-called traditional family of midcentury America was itself an invented tradition, with only a spotty historical pedigree. All proper families, according to this ideal, were made up of a working father, a homemaking child-focused mother, and two to four children, preferably residing in a suburban single-family home. Pets were common, grandparents and extended family less so. In previous eras, only the urban, educated, Protestant upper class could afford to live by this ideal.

Postwar prosperity, however, underwrote nuclear family proliferation for all—or almost all. The twenty years after the end of the Second World War in America were utterly unique in world history. Never before had the masses of ordinary people lived in such material comfort; never before had families in the midst of their child-rearing years had disposable income; never before could they look forward to an old age of plenty and security. A white working man generally earned enough to buy a house, support his wife to stay at home minding the kids and running the appliances, send the boys and even the girls to college, and pay for vacations, all while allowing him to retire while he still had his wits and strength about him. (African American families, because of legal segregation in the South and de facto segregation in the North, were left out of the postwar nuclear family compact. The wages of black men remained low, and black wives and mothers typically worked for wages as well. Poor Americans, of which there were millions, were left out as well.) In 1960,

62 percent of Americans owned their own homes. Two-thirds of all white women—not just those with children at home—did not work outside the home. Families were large, larger than they had been since the nineteenth century. Elderly parents retired on their Social Security checks, instead of inside the homes of their adult children. *Father Knows Best* wasn't quite reality TV, but for white middle-class Americans, it wasn't that far off.

After experiencing fifteen years of economic depression and war, most men and women were more than happy to sign up for the new traditionalism, the suburban lifestyle, and female domesticity. Still, politicians, teachers, medical experts, business leaders, journalists, and intellectuals worked hard to make sure the offer was one few women would refuse. In 1957, nine out of ten Americans thought any person who chose not to marry was either "sick," "neurotic," or "immoral." A national best seller made the case that it was dangerous to allow single women to teach young children and called for a nationwide ban on their employment. More than half of American women were married by the middle of their twentieth year; those that were not married by the age of twenty-five were viewed as damaged goods, to be avoided or pitied. Employers paid women less than men and refused to hire them in jobs considered men's work, in a practice that was perfectly legal because it was presumed to be perfectly natural. Even in cases in which a job was theoretically open to women, American women were grossly ill-prepared for most of those well-paying ones. In 1961, only 8 percent of women were college graduates. Only 2 percent of law degrees, 4 percent of MBAs, and 6 percent of medical degrees were conferred on women. In the year President John F. Kennedy announced the nation would put a man on the moon, most young American women dreamed of marrying by age twenty-one, quitting work, and having four children.

The long-term survival of the nuclear family depended on each sex's willingness to fulfill its prescribed role. Men were to be dutiful to their corporate employers and to financially support their families, but to leave the daily tasks—and the pleasures—of raising children to their wives. Women were to seek fulfillment in their roles as wife, mother, and homemaker. By the late 1950s, some Cassandras were raising the alarm that American life had become a real-life invasion of the body snatchers. Sociologists diagnosed the disease of the company man, while Hugh Hefner offered men relief with *Playboy,* the nation's first mass circulation porn magazine. Even before the 1963 publication of Betty Friedan's best-selling and wildly influential *The Feminine Mystique,* the placid mothers of the fifties were telling pollsters they wanted their daughters to graduate from college, go to work, and wait to get married—in other words, to *not* follow in their own footsteps.

The nuclear family order also depended on the ability of husbands and wives to sustain the arrangement economically. Whatever chance there might have been for it to survive the eruption of the sexual revolution, there was little hope for the model to withstand the whipsaw of the American economy and the rude return of insecurity brought on by the post-1973 economic troubles.

In the late 1940s, only one-third of all American women, single as well as married, worked outside the home, and women constituted only 29 percent of the nation's labor force. By the early 1960s, women had steadily increased their numbers in the workforce. College-educated daughters chose to delay marriage and pursue careers, while their mothers, who were availing themselves of the new birth control technologies, went back to work after their children left home.

What started as a choice, for more spending money or for broader horizons, became for many women a necessity by the late 1970s. When income growth stagnated after the oil shock of 1973, women flooded into the paid labor force in an effort to maintain the family income. As far as the nuclear family was concerned, the change that reverberated most powerfully was the move of married women with children still at home into the workforce. In the mid-1970s, fewer than half of all women with children and teenagers at home worked. By 2000, 79 percent of American mothers with school-age children were working outside the home. A typical middle-class mother was putting in about thirteen weeks more of full-time work in the first decade of the 21st century than her counterpart had in 1979. Among two-parent families, a stay-at-home mother was on the scene in only one of every four homes.

The changes in the American economy after 1973 combined with other monumental social changes—the Pill, the sexual revolution, feminism, increased levels of education among women and men—to revolutionize the American family. American men and women began to marry later, have fewer children, and divorce more frequently. In the year the Pill went on the market, most Americans lived in nuclear families, the average married couple had four children, and mothers stayed home. By 2000, the average family had two children, one out of two marriages ended in divorce, and almost a third of American children were being raised by a single parent or an unmarried couple.

The 1950s neotraditional domestic ideal had been a fragile creation, a hothouse flower of Cold War culture, coaxed into bloom by long-deferred dreams of stability, hiring practices that discriminated against women, and the pseudoscience of pop psychology. Its prospects for longevity were always slim. Viewed dispassionately, the 1950s ideal of the nuclear family set itself against almost every demographic trend of the modern world, and Americans were, if anything, modern. From 1900 to World War II, women had been increasing their labor force participation, marrying at a later age, attending college in greater numbers, having premarital sex more commonly, bearing fewer children, and divorcing at higher rates. These trends, briefly, were reversed from the end of World War II until 1961; after the mid-1970s, they reasserted themselves with a vengeance.

The nuclear family perished of natural causes after barely more than a decade of moderately good health. When this invented domestic ideal met the headwinds of the sexual revolution and economic crisis, a mass historical amnesia about the real history of the American family would set in. In the aftermath of its demise, the nuclear family would be resurrected as an age-old American tradition, as the endpoint of a desired return to the way we never were, and the source of political warfare about sex and women couched in the appealing yet deceptive brand of family values.

IT WAS INEVITABLE that relations between men and women would change as a result of the sexual revolution, women's mass exodus from the home into the workforce, and women's rapid educational advance. It was not inevitable that the new relations would take the form they did. The ultimate result was in good part the handiwork of the American women's movement of the 1960s and 1970s.

In the 1960s, a small group of women and men picked up where earlier women's rights movement had left off in the campaign to achieve equal treatment of the sexes in politics, law, and the economy. One of their first surprise victories piggybacked on the advancing tide of the civil rights movement. An opportunity presented itself when a southern congressman, Howard Smith, put forward an amendment to ban sex discrimination in employment in the Civil Rights Act of 1964. Smith, though himself a supporter of the Equal Rights Amendment, intended his amendment to function as a poison pill—a provision that would kill the whole bill. Given that almost everyone at the time considered it absurd to pretend the sexes had equal capabilities and aspirations, Smith knew the ban on sex discrimination could give cover to northern Congressmen to vote against black civil rights, while allowing them to avoid being charged with racism. Savvy lobbying by women's rights advocates foiled Smith's design, and the provision survived into the final version of the bill. The Civil Rights Act passed, but for reasons having nothing to do with women's rights.

There have been few pieces of legislation that have had a greater effect on the daily lives of Americans than that one clause of the Civil Rights Act of 1964. Title VII made it illegal for employers to discriminate against any individual on the basis of "race, color, religion, sex, or national origin."

Many men, however, didn't quite appreciate the historic momentousness of the act. The head of the Equal Employment Opportunity Commission, the agency created to enforce Title VII, called the ban on sex discrimination "a fluke . . . conceived out of wedlock." Clever wordplay. Over the next two years he blithely ignored the thousands of complaints of discrimination women sent to his office. The liberal *New Republic,* which had been appalled by Southern resistance to black equality, commended the EEOC's nullification of a national law: "Why should a mischievous joke perpetrated on the floor of the House of Representatives be treated by a responsible administrative body with this kind of seriousness?" Other bastions of the elite press became obsessed with the problem the new law posed for clients of

Playboy Bunnies. The *Wall Street Journal* worried for the well-being of businessmen who might encounter "a shapeless, knobby-kneed male 'bunny'" at their local gentlemen's club. The press started to refer to the sex discrimination clause in shorthand as "the Bunny Law." A glib *New York Times* editorial joked, "The Rockettes may become bi-sexual, and a pity, too . . . Bunny Problem, indeed! This is a revolution, chaos. You can't even safely advertise for a wife anymore."

The hue and cry over sex discrimination offers a revealing look inside the hearts of powerful men compelled to contemplate a world in which the sexes would be equal. The volcanic potential of these subterranean emotions becomes clearer once we consider the contrast between America before and America after the women's rights movement of these years. Before, it was perfectly legal to discriminate against women in employment; married women in many states could not get credit in their own name; states routinely treated men and women differently in family matters; state governments set different standards for the duties of citizenship; and sexual violence against women was routinely tolerated. Florida exempted women from jury duty, leaving women defendants to be tried by a jury of their all-male peers. Oklahoma set the legal drinking age for women at 18 and men at 21, so as not to inconvenience the young wives out on a date with their older husbands. Michigan deemed it improper and illegal for a woman to be a bartender, unless she was the wife or daughter of the bar's owner. Ohio compelled pregnant teachers to go on unpaid leave. North Carolina only allowed virgins to file rape charges, and Maryland had no provision in its laws to allow a wife to sue the husband who had beaten her to a pulp.

As men in power continued to make sport of women's equality, veterans of the battles over equal employment decided women needed a civil rights organization of their own. In 1966, they founded the National Organization for Women (NOW). Its statement of purpose declared that "the time has come for a new movement toward true equality for all women in America, and toward a fully equal partnership of the sexes." Between 1966 and 1976, NOW and its allies won campaigns to enforce the laws against wage and employment discrimination; to outlaw discrimination against pregnant women; to end discrimination against women in education; to provide equal funding for women in public education; to reform divorce law; to prohibit sexual harassment in the workplace; and—almost—to ratify the Equal Rights Amendment.

Today, equal rights, protected by laws banning discrimination on the basis of sex, are so ingrained that most Americans under the age of 50 hardly know it was ever any different. So, if self-declared feminists were the ones who achieved these gains for all American women, why and how did feminism get such an awful reputation? It did so because, at the very moment NOW and its allies tackled legal institutional discrimination, a new kind of activist entered the scene, proposing a more provocative theory about how women were kept down. Women's liberation offered Americans a new way to look at themselves in the world, wrapped up nicely in a four word slogan: *The personal is political.*

How was it that personal issues, private matters, had anything to do with politics? At its core, politics is about power, about who rules whom. A nation born in revolution well understood the script of protest and resistance. According to the logic of American politics, one that activists of every shade and opinion share, the oppressed eventually rise up to claim their rights, their interests, and their due. Indeed the two women who first turned the women's movement onto the women's liberation track were American Christian reformers, not angry man-hating radicals so prominent in the antifeminist imagination. Mary King was the daughter of a southern Methodist minister who came to politics via the YWCA; Sandra "Casey" Cason Hayden was a Texan, the daughter of a single mother, who had also gotten her initiation into activism in the YWCA. After several years working in the civil rights movement in the South with other student activists, King and Hayden simply asked, who was exercising power over women? Their answer, explained in a widely circulated memo written in the fall of 1965, would send shock waves through American society for the next decade. Of course, distant politicians and presumptuous bosses kept women down, but that was the least of their troubles. Nearer to home, Hayden and King suggested, women met their oppressors—fathers, husbands, lovers, brothers, and male friends—face-to-face. Intimacy and oppression, all wrapped into one. Their memo went viral among women under the age of 30.

The idea that the personal is political soon got even more personal. The budding feminists in the student and radical movements of the 1960s were also the advance guard of the sexual revolution. They quickly came to see that they could apply their new consciousness not only to politics and the workplace, not only to family relationships, but also to sex itself. Although there has always existed a strain of sexual radicalism in America—from the Free Love movement of the 1860s to the Greenwich Village Bohemians of the 1910s—it had always been held in check by the failure rate of birth control. (Sex for sex's sake simply doesn't mix well with pregnancy and the care of infants.) Feminists doubted that women could ever attain full equality, or the practical ability to realize their individual potential, if they were not free to decide if they wanted to have children.

While the Pill was more effective than other forms of birth control, women remained at the mercy of biology as long as abortion was illegal. These young women activists joined the movement for abortion law reform and reframed the issue. They declared abortion to be an issue of a woman's right to control her body on her own, with no man, church, or state having the power to tell her what she ought to do in such private matters of conscience. Feminists held public speak-outs in which they recounted their ordeals of illegal abortions in unsafe conditions. Men might have been able to take heart that at least they were needed by the newly sexually liberated women, except that these women had also redefined sex, or at least good sex. In 1970, in an influential essay, "The Myth of the Vaginal Orgasm," a founder of New York Radical Feminists claimed men had sold women a bill of goods about their own desires and biology. She declared women's right to sexual pleasure, told men they had been doing it wrong forever, and pronounced that women actually didn't need men for sex at all.

An even more radical challenge to sexual norms was emerging in the nascent gay liberation movement. On Friday night, June 27, 1969, the New York City police raided the Stonewall Inn, a gay and lesbian bar in Manhattan. Police raids of gay bars were common, but that night, a lesbian refused to go peacefully, and as crowds gathered in the streets of Greenwich Village, the patrons of Stonewall fought back. That night and throughout the weekend, New York gays and lesbians battled the NYPD in the streets. The Stonewall Riot, coming at the height of the antiwar movement, the black power movement, and a radical turn in the women's movement, immediately sparked a new social movement of gays and lesbians. Within a few weeks the Gay Liberation Front had been founded and spread quickly throughout the nation's thriving gay urban communities. The GLF quickly transformed the existing gay rights movement, previously focused on mounting legal challenges to discriminatory laws, much as the young feminists had redirected the women's movement from legal reform to cultural change. The GLF's manifesto declared, "We are a revolutionary homosexual group of men and women formed with the realization that complete sexual liberation for all people cannot come about unless existing social institutions are abolished." Influenced by all the radical identity movements of the time to take a "revolutionary" stand, the GLF had the greatest kinship with radical feminism. The two groups shared the belief that the proscribed gender roles of American society were oppressive to individuals, and they also shared a visceral suspicion of the nuclear family. "The family is the primary means by which this restricted sexuality is created and enforced," one GLF member wrote. "In a free society everyone will be gay."

Lesbians and gays claiming heterosexuality wasn't just optional but tyrannical and women talking openly about the pleasures of sex and the graphic details of illegal abortion made a lot of Americans queasy. Women asserting their right to all the perks previously enjoyed only by men alerted men that their own privileges would likely get renegotiated in the coming era. Many Americans were angered on a gut level by these feminists and gays, by their rejection of convention, by their disdain for classic femininity and masculinity, by their political radicalism and sexual experimentation.

But this phase of "liberation" lasted only a few years. It involved at most a couple tens of thousands of women and men in a nation of 205 million people. So, although it is easy to grasp why "women's lib" and gays coming out of the closet might have ticked off a lot of people, it is hard to imagine how it could have sparked the delirium that has consumed American politics for four decades.

But that is what feminism and, to a lesser extent, gay liberation did. Not because a handful of women refused to shave or put on makeup or associate with men. Or even because some men and women retreated into a gay subculture removed from mainstream society. The two social movements sparked resistance because their proponents claimed to have exposed the family as a petty tyranny, a site of sexual repression, gender inequality, and cultural oppression, the place where our ambitions and our desires went to die.

Such a notion of the false promise of family life set itself against fundamental assumptions about American culture. That the nation was sustained by the selfless domestic labors of wives and mothers, that the goodness of the nation was secured by their superior virtue, that men needed to assume their natural role at the head of the family and serve as its representative in the public world. Dating as it did from pre–Civil War America, the ideal bore an exceedingly remote relation to present reality. American womanhood was like the insect trapped in the amber gem, precious when preserved in its ancient casement, ugly and disturbingly menacing in its liberated form. The creation of a politically polarized America, of a nation divided between enraged Republicans and beleaguered Democrats, can never be understood without first acknowledging that many people interpreted sexual self-determination, economic self-sufficiency, and political power for living women as a lethal attack on the American way.

2

THE MORNING AFTER

SIX WEEKS BEFORE the 1972 presidential election, the man who was thought to control the votes of the Democratic Party's largest constituency stood before a roomful of steelworkers in a Las Vegas hotel and informed them that their party had been taken over by "abortionists," boys who want to marry boys, and "people who look like Jacks, acted like Jills, and had the odors of Johns about them."

George Meany, the president of the 13-million–member AFL-CIO, America's national labor federation, had actively supported every Democratic presidential candidate since 1936. In 1972, the 78-year-old, white-haired, cigar-chomping union boss spent election season golfing with Republican President Richard Nixon and ordering unionized working men and women to cease and desist campaigning for George McGovern, the Democratic candidate for president of the United States.

When McGovern went down to a landslide defeat, Meany and other Democratic leaders pinned the blame on young men and women, newly empowered in the Democratic Party, who were known to exhibit countercultural tendencies. Elitist cultural extremists, their logic went, had hijacked the party from its rightful owners. The exotic enthusiasms of the few had alienated mainstream America.

Meany and his comrades in fact knew better, for they themselves had thrown the election. After they failed to defeat McGovern in the primaries, a small group of Democratic powerbrokers connived to deprive McGovern of the presidential nomination. Among the conspirators were Meany, the elected leader of the unionized working class, the backbone of the Democratic electoral coalition; Hubert Humphrey, an eminent liberal and the party's 1968 nominee; and one future president, Jimmy Carter.

Despite the well reported existence of their plot and ample evidence disproving their theory of McGovern's defeat, their allegation that feminists, gays, and other cultural radicals were to blame for the Democratic Party's collapse acquired the status of unquestioned truth. This death-by-McGovernik theory would reverberate through the years, to be invoked each time Democrats lost an election. And thus the sexual counterrevolution within the Democratic Party was born.

ON NOVEMBER 7, 1972, Americans reelected President Richard M. Nixon. Nixon's 23-point margin of victory over McGovern surpassed even that of Democrat Lyndon B. Johnson's 1964 annihilation of the ultraconservative Republican candidate, Arizona Senator Barry Goldwater. Indeed, only three presidential candidates in all of American history had fared worse in an election than McGovern. It was a humiliating defeat for the Democratic Party. A catastrophe.

Post-election spin quickly and decisively concluded that McGovern "lost the election at Miami," where the Democrats had held their party convention in July. As one of these veterans saw it, "The American people made an association between McGovern and gay lib, and welfare rights, and pot-smoking, and black militants, and women's lib, and wise college kids, and everything else that they saw as threatening their value systems." The televised proceedings of the extremists' antics, so the theory went, inspired lifelong Democrats to vote against McGovern. The verdict was nearly unanimous that the convention carryings-on of these "kooks" and "freaks" had appalled the American people. Regular Americans, watching the convention from their living rooms, were repulsed by the cultural extremism of McGovern's supporters.

This death-by-McGovernik notion was first floated in the days after the November election, when the Democratic candidates McGovern had crushed in the primaries earlier that year were pleased to share their sage analysis with any journalist who asked. Former vice president Humphrey, a four-time loser in the presidential contest, pronounced, "unless we become acceptable to middle America, we've had it." Another 1972 contender, Washington Senator Henry "Scoop" Jackson, whose positions on the Vietnam War and America's nuclear arsenal were slightly to the right of Nixon's, scolded McGovern for ignoring the sentiments of the Democratic base. His ally, the intrepid Governor Carter, had already appointed himself the chief of party reconstruction; Carter assured worried voters that McGovern's people would not be "in charge of the invitation lists." George Wallace, the onetime segregationist and 1972's white backlash candidate, predicted the Democratic Party's future lay with "the average man," whom he represented, "not with the elitist group that took over in Miami."

In many ways, these Democrats were parroting their Republican opponents. At the GOP convention, held in August 1972, party leaders predicted Americans would spurn McGovern's extremist fellow travelers. California governor and future president Ronald Reagan had joked about the funny smell wafting out of the Democrats' "smoke-filled rooms." Goldwater, who famously claimed that "extremism in the defense of liberty is no vice [and] moderation in the pursuit of justice is no virtue," likened Democratic radicals to the bloodthirsty coyotes of his native Arizona, who lay in wait for the moment when they could "tear something down or destroy part of America." Future Indiana Senator Richard Lugar invited the "millions of Democrats deserted by McGovern and his extremists" into the GOP. *Time* approvingly quoted Republican strategist Kevin Phillips for his foresight in predicting the outcome. "The Democratic Party is going to pay heavily," wrote Phillips, "for having become the party of affluent professionals, knowledgeable industry executives, social-cause activists and minorities of various sexual, racial, chronological and other hues." Sexual and chronological *hues*? He apparently meant women, young people, and gays and lesbians.

These Republican talking points, recycled by resentful Democrats, soon hardened into conventional wisdom. Years later, even McGovern's chief campaign strategists confessed that they too had been seduced and led astray by their far-out supporters. Gary Hart, whose own 1984 presidential bid would be derailed by an old-school sex scandal, blamed the extremists for the fact that McGovern, the laconic South Dakota populist, became vilified as a radical. Their behavior, he recounted, "was just bizarre. The more we responded to their demands, the more extreme the campaign looked."

The notion that McGovern lost the election because cultural extremists alienated real Democrats eventually became enshrined in Democratic Party lore and fixed in the historical record. The idea was so pervasive that even the talented author Rick Perlstein interpreted the behavior of the McGoverniks at the Miami convention as a pivotal moment in Democratic decline. Men kissed men in the aisles of Miami, Perlstein wrote in his best-selling *Nixonland*. Braless women publicly debated abortion on national television. With the license of a novelist, Perlstein filled in the thought bubbles of the TV watching voters. "All of these people had given the Democrats a landslide in 1964. They had trusted the Democratic Party. In the interim they had seen America plunged into chaos. And then they looked at this convention and thought, *'Here are the people who are responsible for this chaos.'*"

BUT WAS IT really the optics of flamboyant radicalism that killed the Democratic Party and drove voters away from McGovern? Did the American people recoil in horror after witnessing the takeover of the Democratic convention by cultural radicals? The historical record does not support the myths that have accumulated around the McGovern campaign.

"The speculations were for a ranting mob, an 'unruly zoo' one prognosticator called them. If there was, television did not show it," Cecil Smith, the *Los Angeles Times* television critic, wrote in July while the convention was airing on national television. "It showed the young, the eager, the blacks, the Chicanos, the women. It showed a lot of frustrated elders. But it mostly showed order and attention and dignity." Given that past conventions were primarily occasions to reward party operatives with free vacations and free booze, *that* was the telltale sign that the delegates "must be amateurs." Smith did observe one freakish-looking character on the convention floor: a woman dressed as Alice in Wonderland. She was an NBC reporter.

What had prompted the speculations of anarchy in the first place? Of the 3,100 delegates elected to the Democratic convention, over 2,700 had never attended a party nominating convention before. In the party's first-ever open and free primary election, more than 1,200 women won election as delegates to the Democratic convention— three times as many as had ever been chosen before. African Americans, young people, Hispanics, Native Americans, and gays were also present in record numbers. Twenty percent of the delegates in 1972 were under the age of 30. In 1968, the last presidential election in which 21 had been the minimum legal voting age, hardly any young people had been delegates. The percentage of African American delegates had increased from 6 percent in 1968 to 16 percent. For the first time ever in the party's history, women, young adults, African Americans, and other minorities outnumbered party officials, politicians, and union men by nine to one. For these delegates and the people who had elected them, such an opening of the political process was a cause to celebrate.

Veteran journalists and political commentators agreed that the anticipated circus had failed to materialize. The rookies weren't kooks and freaks, they observed, but savvy pragmatists. "McGovern's legions," according to *Time*, "are some of the soberest and most serious practitioners of politics in the U.S. today." The convention "struck many onlookers as unusually serious," observed R. W. Apple of the *New York Times*, "as unusually courteous and nondisruptive." Reports were consistent that women, the group of delegates with the least experience of insider party politics, had massed the most disciplined and effective caucus of the year. "Those who muttered about wild-haired 'freaks' and 'kooks' taking over this convention have been dumfounded. It is, almost everybody says, the freshest, most attractive, most diverse national political convention they have seen," wrote a rare female reporter for the *New York Times*, Nan Robertson. She had been sent to cover fashion but instead turned in an

analysis of women's political ascension. Yes, some women wore pants
suits, miniskirts, and bell bottoms—prompting one male delegate to
declare he had never seen so many beautiful women under one roof—
but no one "doubted the women's seriousness of purpose and goals."
They were there to put women's concerns on the party's front burner.
Catherine Duggan, a white, 24-year-old, stay-at-home mother, came
to the convention to fight for comprehensive child care—not for herself, but for the poor, single mothers in her neighborhood. Duggan
had saved up her food stamps in order to hold a spaghetti dinner
fundraiser to pay her way to Miami. Gloria Steinem, the editor of *Ms.*
magazine and an elected Democratic delegate, encouraged women
to play hardball politics. Steinem reminded women delegates that
their work would not be done until they were "in those smoke-filled
rooms where the decisions are going to be made."

Was there other evidence that some Americans perceived
McGovern to be too radical? One influential group apparently did.
"We're scared to death of him," a senior partner at Goldman Sachs
told the *New York Times*. "We don't think he knows what he's talking
about." Wall Street, convinced that McGovern had radical economic
ideas, withheld campaign contributions. The stock market fell every
single day of the Democratic convention.

It was the case that McGovern's platform, even when compared
to those of Democratic liberals such as Franklin Delano Roosevelt,
Harry Truman, John F. Kennedy, and Lyndon Johnson, was extraor-
dinarily liberal on economic issues. When McGovern's Democratic
critics charged the candidate and his progressive supporters with
excessive radicalism, however, they weren't referring to his support for
labor rights and guaranteed jobs and incomes for the poor. They had
women's rights, feminism, abortion, and gay rights on their mind.

Women did score some victories at the convention, ones that
would have been inconceivable just four years earlier. They won
the party's renewed endorsement of the Equal Rights Amendment
(ERA)—a commitment that had been dropped in 1956 at the behest
of conservatives and organized labor. Since Congress had finally
passed the ERA and sent it to the states for ratification that March,
this was a fight that mattered. In two firsts for the Democratic Party,
the rookie delegates negotiated a 15-point statement on women's

rights to be included in the party's platform and elected a woman to head the Democratic National Committee. More controversially, feminists and gays made an unsuccessful bid to commit the party to gay civil rights and legal abortion.

Abortion was still illegal in two-thirds of the states in 1972, and abortion law reform was one of the highest political priorities for the women's movement. (*Roe v. Wade* was issued by the Supreme Court the following January. The decision surprised both sides.) On the platform committee, feminists had introduced a plank that stated, "in matters relating to human reproduction, each person's right to privacy, freedom of choice and individual conscience should be fully respected consistent with relevant Supreme Court decisions." The plank was defeated in committee, but it won enough votes to allow it to be brought to a floor vote before the full convention.

On the second night of the Democratic convention, live, on television, Democrats debated the question of abortion. Some people thought that was suicidal. "It was madness to confront the country with it at the convention," according to David Riesman, an eminent sociologist. It is "an issue of great importance to liberated women— and others of course—but think of the unliberated women. For many of them the right to get an abortion simply means that they have no way of holding on to their men when they get pregnant."

Riesman's expert ruminations, however, were contradicted by a Gallup poll on the subject. "It may be that both candidates—whatever their moral scruples—are miscalculating the issue's political reverberations," a *Time* report of the poll observed. Gallup's August survey "found that 64 percent of all Americans are actually in favor of legalized abortions, with Republicans more in favor (68 percent) than independents (67 percent) or Democrats (59 percent). Even Catholics in the sample approved by 56 percent."

Of course few voters even knew Democrats had spent two emotional hours of their convention arguing about abortion. McGovern's floor managers ensured that most viewers would be asleep when it happened, and the plank was defeated. The debate about gay civil rights, which candidate McGovern had promised to support, was shunted even farther into the predawn hours. That plank was defeated with a resounding voice vote—usefully leaving no record of an individual opinion to follow the ambitious delegates through their political careers. Few print outlets gave the two controversial debates more than a few-words mention in their voluminous convention coverage. That was because most reporters understood the more significant fault lines in the Democratic Party. Could McGovern's lieutenants assuage business if they fended off planks in favor of a guaranteed income for all Americans? Would McGovern's belated support for a strong pro-Israel plank win back skeptical Jewish voters? Would George Wallace's last stand for the white Right over busing in northern cities split the Democratic Party? He had, after all, won 13.5 percent of the popular vote running as a third-party candidate in 1968. Bitter conflicts over school busing to achieve racial desegregation, Israel, and taxes were all viewed by Americans in prime time. That the Michigan delegation joined the South in support of Wallace's anti-busing plank was probably the most ominous indicator of McGovern's prospects in the general election.

Did Americans see McGovern as a radical because of his association at the Miami convention with feminists, the counterculture, or gay sexual radicals? Public opinion surveys and the eyewitness reports of experienced journalists are not exact sciences, but together the evidence from these two sources powerfully indicate that the answer is no. Back in the spring, most voters had seen McGovern as a strong liberal. (This was considered a compliment in 1972.) Between the opening of the Democratic convention on July 10 and late August, on the eve of the Republican convention, the percentage of Democrats who viewed McGovern as a radical rose from 10 percent to 14 percent. This was an uptick surely, but hardly career shattering in a nation in which more than a third of white conservatives identified themselves as Democrats.

Eventually almost a third of Americans came to view McGovern as a radical. The radical label finally stuck to McGovern not because he cavorted with feminists, abortionists, and gays but primarily because voters associated him with the antiwar movement and its lack of patriotism. And, importantly, voters didn't come to this conclusion based on the Democratic convention, but only after the August Republican convention. In a September poll conducted by Daniel Yankelovich for *Time,* which showed that almost a third of voters viewed McGovern as a radical, 75 percent said yes to the question, are you "sick and tired of hearing people attack patriotism and American values?" Even 59 percent of voters who intended to vote for McGovern felt so.

That one-third of voters perceived McGovern as a radical was a relatively minor matter, considering what the majority felt about him: three-quarters of all voters viewed McGovern as weak and indecisive. A majority rated Nixon best able to end the Vietnam War and fix the economy, their two top issues. They felt Nixon cared more than McGovern for "the little man." By two to one, voters thought Nixon would run a more open and trustworthy administration.

The Democrats had not produced such an economically progressive platform since the New Deal, but Nixon was rated better on the economy. The nation had turned overwhelmingly against the Vietnam War, and McGovern had led Senate efforts to curtail Nixon's ability to wage the war. But Nixon was thought to be more likely to end the war. The young *Washington Post* reporters Bob Woodward and Carl Bernstein were already starting to trace the break-in at Democratic Party headquarters in the Watergate Hotel back to top officials in the Nixon administration, but voters didn't trust McGovern. "Such results seem to fly in the face of logic," *Time* couldn't help marveling.

McGovern had turned the election into a popularity contest, and against the notorious Tricky Dick, he was losing. How could this have happened? Granted, Nixon ruthlessly (and illegally) exploited the power of the presidency and manipulated public opinion, but McGovern had a hand in his own unmaking. Although nearly everyone thought McGovern was a good man with integrity, the heartland senator alienated a lot of regular folk. "He comes on like a soft-spoken preacher from South Dakota," worried Barbara Mikulski, a pro-McGovern Polish American councilwoman from Baltimore (who would go on to become the first woman elected in her own right to the U.S. Senate as a Democrat). "That style is hard to comprehend in a working-class neighborhood." There was an obstinacy there too. In the important New York primary, on a televised campaign stop to a Jewish deli to shore up his flagging support among Jewish voters, McGovern insisted on ordering milk with his chopped liver sandwich, even though the waitress kindly warned him that wasn't kosher.

Things got much worse for McGovern in the fall, as Nixon opened up a 39-point lead in the polls. The soft-spoken preacher-like politician began to channel his father, the strict fundamentalist minister of the harsh South Dakota plains. Young George had been forbidden to dance or listen to music, and he had long ago rejected his fundamentalist upbringing for a more broad-minded religiosity. But something about Nixon's impunity and the public's apathy summoned in him the lapsed absolutist. McGovern lacerated Americans for allowing the slaughter of innocents in Vietnam and for turning a blind eye to America's poor and oppressed. He lost his temper on the campaign trail and told a voter to kiss his ass. Meanwhile Nixon, one of the most troubled souls to have ever occupied the oval office, beguiled Americans with a soaring vision of American benevolence and peace—through strength—on earth.

By the end of the campaign, Americans perceived McGovern to be self-righteous, weak, and unpatriotic—a fatal combination of traits for any politician at any time in the history of the United States. Some voters by the end of the campaign also saw him as a radical for his opposition to the war. But there is little evidence for the election postmortem that McGovern earned that title because he empowered the cultural radicals—the women, the blacks, the young, and the gays—who had provided him with the votes to win the Democratic nomination and had made up the majority of elected delegates to the Democratic convention.

So where did the story of death-by-cultural-radicalism originate? With the Democratic Party's own leaders, kingmakers, and operatives, who had been defeated by McGovern in the party's first open, democratic, and fair presidential primary and who had tried to overturn that election through tried-and-tested tricks of machine politics. "We lost the election at Miami," turned out to be true, just not exactly according to the story that has been passed down by conventional wisdom.

A FEW HOURS before McGovern's plane touched down in Miami for the Democratic convention, George Meany held his own press conference on the tarmac. "We've made it quite plain we don't like McGovern."

In the thirty-four days between the decisive California primary and the Democratic convention, the defeated Democratic candidates and their old-guard allies schemed to strip McGovern of the presidential nomination. In those weeks, McGovern should have been selecting a running mate. He should have been planning his general election campaign against Nixon, whose popularity ratings had risen from a pre-primary low of 40 percent to a nearly invincible 61 percent. Instead, he and his staff were consumed with fending off a widely reported but secretive conspiracy to derail his candidacy.

Meany was widely recognized as the mastermind of the Stop McGovern operation, in close association with Chicago Mayor Richard Daley. Joining them were McGovern's defeated rivals: Humphrey, Scoop Jackson, Edmund Muskie, George Wallace, and the political allies and campaign aides they brought in. Also in on the attempted fix were a handful of powerful southern senators. The scheme involved preventing McGovern from winning the nomination during the first two rounds of delegate voting, and thus tarring him with the unelectable label. They would then step in with a consensus candidate who would save the party from disaster. Meany, Daley, and their lieutenants were plotting for Humphrey. Muskie, who had been anointed the frontrunner by the pundits before the primaries and who hadn't broken into double digits in the primary vote, inexplicably seemed to have thought he would emerge as the nominee. "It was the old politics of sheer political power: changing the rules after the game had been played," *Time* explained in its report on the machinations.

The Stop-McGovernites no doubt expected that it would be easy to foil the naïve political rookies massed by McGovern. They were mistaken. On the first night of the convention, July 10, the pro-McGovern delegation from Illinois led by the Reverend Jesse Jackson bested Daley's own delegation. Although McGovern and Jackson had offered a compromise that would have seated part of the Daley delegation, Daley demanded all or nothing. He got nothing. (His slate had violated the rules for holding delegate elections.) McGovern survived a potentially fatal challenge to his California delegation through brilliant parliamentary maneuvering orchestrated by the twenty somethings in his inner circle. The first all-night session of the convention ended at 5:20 am the next morning, with McGovern's nomination assured. At that point Muskie conceded and pledged his support for McGovern, but Humphrey and others threw their delegates to Scoop Jackson. Wallace stayed in the race for himself. (In the finale of the failed plot, Jimmy Carter made the speech putting Jackson's name in nomination.) Even after McGovern won the presidential nomination two days later on the first ballot, a few Stop-McGovern conspirators refused to accept reality and immediately set to work plotting their post-election moves against McGovern and his allies. The *New York Times* columnist Tom Wicker spotted "the barons of labor" in the hotel lobby bar after McGovern's triumph, "mumbling threats and recriminations around their fraying cigars—elephants on the way to the boneyard, determined to take their party with them."

MCGOVERN'S TROUBLES WITH the Democratic Party establishment were the paradoxical result of the advantage they had unwittingly handed him four years earlier. Before 1972, Democrats anointed their nominee through closed caucuses, secret meetings, and backroom deals. Through a particularly adroit manipulation of this system, in 1968, Meany and Daley had delivered the Democratic presidential nomination to Humphrey, even though he had won only 2 percent of the primary vote. Then at the Chicago Democratic convention that year, Daley sanctioned a police riot against antiwar protesters and assorted establishment Democrats. When delegates elected to support the antiwar candidates, the late Robert F. Kennedy and Eugene McCarthy, protested against the heavy-handed tactics, Daley ordered the convention center crew to cut power to their microphones and his cops to expel them from the hall. In a paltry effort to heal party divisions, the convention voted to create a commission to review the presidential nomination process. McGovern was chosen to head the effort because he had ties to the regulars and the insurgents alike.

Supporters of the reform commission looked to it to democratize the party and make it more inclusive. But experienced politicians know that commissions are created to evade inconvenient problems, not to solve them, and the party regulars quickly stopped paying attention. Imagine their surprise when they discovered the reform commission chaired by McGovern had stripped them of power simply by rewriting the rules for choosing the party's nominee. Thanks to the commission, from 1972 on, Democratic presidential hopefuls were required to compete for actual voters in open and transparent elections. Today's system of primaries and caucuses, with modest changes, is the product of these reforms.

In the old clubby system, McGovern had been unelectable. He was the junior senator of a tiny, rural, Republican-leaning state, where few members of the Democrats' traditional base lived. In the new system, a candidate could circumvent the old established party apparatus—controlled by labor leaders, big-city mayors, party officials, and senior politicians—and go directly to the people. McGovern, with aides hired directly from the reform commission staff, planned to wring every possible advantage out of the new nomination process, especially in states using the poorly understood caucus system. Not until Barack Obama felled the House of Clinton would a longshot again run the primary horse race so brilliantly.

McGovern's route to the nomination, mapped by his aides and dubbed the "left-centrist" strategy, called for him to run as the candidate of the Left in the early primaries. Formulated with the new competitive primary system in mind, it was as much the result of political calculation as of principle. With no incumbent or obvious Democratic leader in the race, many ambitious but unremarkable men would be game to enter. McGovern first had to knock out all the other liberal antiwar candidates by, in the words of Gary Hart, his campaign manager "co-opt[ing] the left." After winning sufficient delegates to clinch the nomination, McGovern would tack back to the center to bring the party leaders on board. The go-left step of the strategy fit the times. The Twenty-sixth Amendment had given 18-to-21-year-olds the right to vote, and the Vietnam War, and the antiwar protests, continued. McGovern's antiwar bona fides were as strong as anyone's, but opposition to the Vietnam War was no longer enough. RFK had charmed the Left in 1968 by denouncing the war, praising the civil rights movement, and lending the Kennedy stamp of approval to the United Farm Workers. But he never had to state his opinion about women's rights, abortion, or gays, because no one was asking. In 1972, any Democratic candidate who pursued the vote of the young and the Left had to answer new questions about women, sex, and culture. Still, victory would hinge on step two.

Co-opting the Left, as Hart cynically put it, therefore called for a nimble touch, particularly because those who formerly did not have a seat at the table had taken advantage of the opportunity presented by party reform. Exactly one year before the 1972 Democratic convention was scheduled to begin, several hundred women gathered to form the bipartisan National Women's Political Caucus (NWPC). Convened by Gloria Steinem, Betty Friedan (author of *The Feminine Mystique*), Republicans such as the feminist head of the Republican Federation of Women, and three of the twelve women representatives in the U.S. Congress—Patsy Mink, Bella Abzug, and Shirley Chisholm—the NWPC decided their first goal would be to gain proportional representation of women at presidential conventions. They had not been impressed when the Democratic reform commission announced it would require state delegations to include African Americans, people under the age of thirty, and women "in reasonable relation to their presence in the state as a whole." That language seemed to depend too much on the kindness of men. Democratic women lobbied the commission and won new language specifying a target of 40 percent female representation. (Republican women in the NWPC extracted a similar commitment from their party.)

With this deft move, women suddenly became the most important of the Left constituencies to be won by a non-establishment candidate. Not only would women potentially constitute the largest single bloc of voters at the convention, but the women's movement was also the only movement on the Left that could still mount effective political campaigns. (The antiwar movement and the black civil rights movement had both by 1972 been weakened by infighting.) Thus when Shirley Chisholm, a New York Congresswoman, a feminist, an African American, and a civil rights veteran, announced she was running for president, McGovern scrambled to steal her thunder with women. In the fall of 1971, McGovern's team at headquarters told local campaign staffers to send word to state chapters of the NWPC expressing McGovern's "full support for their goal of political equality" and asking for their endorsement. In a bid for women's votes, McGovern publicly threatened to participate in the boycott of an airline for its "tasteless and suggestive 'I'm Cheryl, fly me to Miami'" ad campaign. He forced his Illinois supporters to change their slate of delegates when he discovered it was disproportionately composed of older white men.

Step one, go left, worked. Although many women activists felt a sentimental kinship with Chisholm, most decided to fall in for McGovern, the candidate they thought was electable, even though he continued to resist their requests to support abortion law reform. McGovern had similar success wooing antiwar voters, no doubt because he was in fact the strongest antiwar candidate in the field. (His only real challenge would have come from Senator Edward M. Kennedy, who took himself out of contention in 1969 when he drove off a Chappaquiddick bridge.) McGovern also became the first Democratic candidate ever to pledge his support for making discrimination against homosexuals illegal (albeit, his pledge was issued privately in evasive language). By early April, just a little more than a month into the primaries, McGovern had indeed locked down the Left and was surging ahead in the delegate count. According to plan, the moment to pivot from left to center had arrived. With a commanding lead, surely the old party warhorses would come around, unwilling to repeat the split between the grassroots movements and the party regulars that had cost Democrats the presidency in 1968. The moment of inevitability was here.

That was when McGovern discovered he had no exit from his go-left strategy.

In early April, the influential *Washington Post* columnists Rowland Evans and Robert Novak labeled McGovern "the Barry Goldwater of the Left," and quoted an unnamed Democratic senator on McGovern's secret liabilities: "McGovern is for amnesty, abortion, and legalization of pot . . . Once middle America—Catholic middle America in particular—finds this out, he's dead." (Thus originated the GOP's infamous general election slogan labeling McGovern "the candidate of the three A's: amnesty, abortion, and acid.") Humphrey, the last remaining viable candidate in the race, decided to borrow a page from Evans and Novak. Although he and McGovern were old friends whose children had grown up together in the capital, this was his fourth and probably last shot at the presidency, and this was politics. In Omaha, Nebraska, home to a large population of Catholic Democrats, Humphrey placed an ad in a Catholic newspaper recycling Evans and Novak's charge. As the candidates headed into the home stretch for the California primary, Humphrey's radical-baiting, in the words of a reporter for *Time* magazine, became "sulfurous."

The attacks misfired, and on June 6, 1972, McGovern wrapped up the Democratic Party presidential nomination with a victory in California. With delegates gained in the few remaining contests that month, McGovern was poised to enter the Democratic convention with a commanding lead, controlling more than 1,300 of the 1,509 delegates needed to win the nomination.

Democratic voters had spoken. McGovern's opponents in the Democratic Party decided that was irrelevant. With no chance left to win the nomination honestly, Humphrey, Meany, and Daley reverted to their old ways. They would attempt through intrigue what they had accomplished openly and brazenly in 1968: fix the delegate vote so as to deliver the nomination to one of their own, the voters be damned.

The true casualty of that failed gambit was the Democratic Party itself. Conventions typically give the nominee a boost in the polls, but McGovern ended his with only a 2 percent bump, and he trailed Nixon badly, as he had since the end of the primary campaign. Immediately after the convention, Meany engineered a vote in the AFL-CIO to prevent a McGovern endorsement, over the strenuous objections of many other heads of national labor unions. Formally, the federation remained neutral, but Meany stacked the deck. He very publicly refused to even talk to McGovern, while he showed up in public with Nixon over and over again. Daley and Humphrey did campaign for McGovern, but with a notable lack of enthusiasm. Carter, with Daley, Meany, Jackson, and some of Humphrey's aides, looked to the future. They spent their time during the height of election season plotting the ouster of McGovern's choice for party chair, the first woman ever elected to the post; their preferred candidate was a close ally of John Connally, the Texas Democrat running the Democrats for Nixon campaign. Party officials "didn't do squat" to help elect their party's nominee, one McGovern staffer remembered.

It was hard to imagine how McGovern had any chance against Nixon when so many party leaders continued to scheme against him.

WHY DID THEY do it? The Stop-McGovern conspirators undoubtedly would have retorted, Who, really, betrayed whom? If you were to take their word for it, they had valiantly strived to save the Democratic Party from itself.

The McGovernik extremists, in their view, were so consumed by their own far-out cultural obsessions that they ignored the Democratic Party's most loyal voters and neglected the party's traditional bread-and-butter issues. "How could any one candidate alienate labor, the religious groups, the South and others in one election?" Scoop Jackson asked rhetorically. "Nixon would have been beaten," he insisted, by someone who could have held the party together. In Humphrey's estimation, working and middle-class voters who had favored Democrats since the New Deal felt ignored, disgusted, and abandoned. The Democratic "leadership must be closely related by word and deed to the working people, to the small town, Main Street people and the man in the shops," Humphrey warned. "Unless we become acceptable to this middle America, we've had it." And Wallace spelled it out bluntly: the party had been taken over by "elitists." The McGoverniks had to be stopped, or they would lead the party into extinction.

Let's look then at the real-Democrats-betrayed theory. The most convincing evidence seems to be the scope of the landslide itself. After all, in 1968, Humphrey had come within 1 percent of Nixon in the popular vote. The 1972 election is difficult to compare to any normal presidential election, however, as it was the only time in American history that the sitting president masterminded a criminal conspiracy in an attempt to fix an election. Nevertheless, the change in the Democratic vote over the two elections does reveal deeper shifts that had little to do with the Watergate conspiracy. In 1972, support for McGovern among traditional Democratic groups collapsed. In 1968, Humphrey had won a majority from Catholics, union families, urban residents, African Americans, and Jews. Only white southerners among the historic Democratic constituencies did not give Humphrey more than 50 percent of their votes. McGovern, however, lost not only southerners, but also Catholics and union families.

Humphrey's image of strength, however, was a mirage of Wallace's making. When Johnson signed the 1964 Civil Rights Act, he remarked, "We have lost the South for a generation." By 1968 Johnson's prediction had already come true. Humphrey won only 39 percent of white southerners—19 points less than Johnson had and only 3 points more than McGovern would win in 1972. This was no small concern, given that white southerners had historically voted for Democrats by a 10-point margin and provided, on average, about a quarter of all Democratic votes. In 1968, Wallace had won five southern states, including two by more than 60 percent. Had Wallace not run in 1968, the overwhelming majority of his supporters would have voted for Nixon, just as they did in 1972. Absent Wallace, Nixon's margin of victory over Humphrey could have been as large as 15 points, rather than merely one point. Without Wallace in the race, it is likely Nixon, not Humphrey, would have won Michigan. In short, Democrats lost the South well before the so-called cultural elitists captured the Democratic party and allegedly betrayed ordinary Democrats.

But perhaps the groups in the Democratic coalition most affected by McGovern's out-of-the-mainstream cultural radicalism were religious and ethnic voters. Although McGovern won a majority of African Americans, Jews, and secular Americans, and Catholics voted relatively pro-Democratic, each group voted less Democratic than they had in 1968. Yet these groups encompass the most culturally progressive voters—Jews and nonreligious Americans—and some of the most culturally conservative ones—black Protestants and white Catholics. What these groups shared was neither values nor cultural beliefs but the fact that they were all minorities within America's white Protestant majority. McGovern's poor showing with each of these groups suggests that many lifelong Democrats, as scores of anecdotes during the campaign attested, were indeed alienated by McGovern's rural, fundamentalist Protestant cultural style. His weakness was aggravated by the fact that, as the senator of North Dakota, he had no preexisting political ties to these constituencies.

Moreover, from the perspective of the many fiercely patriotic descendants of immigrants in these groups, McGovern's principled stance against the Vietnam War suggested he was insufficiently patriotic.

It becomes difficult to credit the Stop-McGovernites' charge that Democrats abandoned McGovern because they felt betrayed by the McGovernik cultural extremists, when voters had such an abundance of reasons to reject McGovern. The 1972 election was a perfect storm for McGovern and the Democratic Party. Nixon's criminal manipulation of the electoral system, his savvy and perfectly legal priming of the economy to mask its structural weakness, the continuing white backlash, Democratic divisions about the war and the meaning of patriotism, and the inclusion of women and other new political actors in the party, all came together to drive traditionally Democratic voters into the arms of the GOP or away from the voting booth altogether. Overshadowing all was the negative perception of the Democratic party candidate. Voters felt more negative toward McGovern than toward any other Democratic candidate since pollsters began asking Americans their opinions on the subject; they believed Nixon could better handle the war and the economy, the two issues that mattered most to them. With all these factors, it is not surprising the election was a rout.

WHETHER OR NOT there was a Democratic candidate who could have won in these circumstances, the question remains, why were McGovern's opponents willing to essentially throw the election to Nixon rather than work with Democratic women, young people, and cultural progressives to put their own troubled party back in power? As is true for most betrayals, self-interest and principle commingled. Humphrey, Muskie, and Scoop Jackson wanted to be president, the cost be damned. Many other politicians surely felt their pain. Rookies had defeated 249 Democratic representatives and senators in the open delegate elections. Among the losers were the Democratic majority whip, Thomas P. (Tip) O'Neill, six current and former governors, and countless lower-level elected officials and party hands. Meany, who spent the convention in his hotel room, complained that his men were treated like "second-class citizens" in Miami. The *New*

York Times editorial postmortem captured the bigger picture: "Men accustomed to viewing politics as a masculine game rather like professional football do not like to be told they have to allot half of the delegation to women. Dominant factions do not like to share their power with blacks or Chicanos . . . There is no such thing as a painless revolution."

"To the victors go the spoils" is one of the oldest unwritten rules in American democracy. When women, in the wake of the feminist movement, finally claimed an independent role for themselves in the Democratic Party, it became impossible to ignore that their demands threatened the privileges that powerful Democratic men had long taken for granted. Politics offers perks to those in power, and it is typically a zero-sum game.

Yet, as much as thwarted ambition and crass self-interest motivated those colluding in McGovern's demise, there was also something deeper going on. *New York Times* columnist Anthony Lewis pinpointed the dilemma from his front-row seat at the Stop-McGovern conspiracy. "The Democratic Party has no historic choice but to be the instrument of change, and there is no place on earth changing as fast as America today."

And nothing was changing as fast in America as relations between the sexes, sex, and gender roles. So fast, in fact, that the word "gender" was not even yet in use.

Feminism, at its self-confident peak in 1972, presented an especially acute challenge for the Democratic Party and to the principles for which it stood. The party was still proud to call itself liberal, but during their several decades-long run as the dominant political party in the United States, Democrats had done precious little to open opportunities to women or to bring American sex laws out of the dark ages. The most powerful party constituency, namely organized labor, had put up the biggest roadblocks to women attaining parity at work. The AFL-CIO opposed equal pay legislation until the early 1960s; it only passed after they finally signed on. The federation formally opposed the Equal Rights Amendment until 1973—a year after it had passed Congress and seemed on its way to swift ratification. The laws of the land finally changed, not because Democratic leaders realized that discrimination against women and prying into people's sex lives contradicted the party's liberal values but because two mass social movements compelled the federal and state governments to rewrite their laws. Many men joined women and gays in these movements for civil rights and equality; the Democratic Party establishment, not so much.

Most feminists and cultural progressives viewed the Democratic Party, which claimed to be the party of fairness, justice, equality, and cultural tolerance, as their natural political home. They were the ones who forced Democrats to take their first giant step toward recognizing women's rights in the party's core principles. They were the ones who tried (without success) to put the Democratic Party on record against legally sanctioned discrimination against individuals on the basis of whom they liked to have sex with. It was these people who, again unsuccessfully, hoped the Democratic Party would sign on to the idea that having a child is a decision best left to the individual, not to the government, acting to impose the particular morality of one religion or another.

To be blunt, the Democratic Party before 1972 was astonishingly retrograde on many matters that the majority of Americans today consider no-brainers. It would be no simple matter to merge the post-sixties new progressivism of women's rights, youth empowerment, sexual liberalism, multiculturalism, and cultural openness with the conventional New Deal liberalism of economic populism. Not because of the new cultural progressives—opinion surveys from then up to the present tend to show these new groups, especially women, to be the most supportive of traditional New Deal Democratic liberalism. Rather, it was difficult because it required men like Meany, Daley, and Humphrey to surrender some of their power, share it with others, and reach agreement with women, gays, and blacks on a common party agenda.

How difficult that would be brings us back to Las Vegas on a hot September day and Meany's fulminations about how his party had been hijacked that summer in Miami.

"We listened for three days to the speakers who were approved to speak by the powers-that-be at the convention," Meany detailed in his deep Bronx accent.

"We listened to the gay lib people—you know, the people who want to legalize marriages between boys and boys and legalize marriages between girls and girls . . . We heard from the abortionists, and we heard from the people who look like Jacks, acted like Jills, and had the odors of Johns about them."

Meany's delirious reaction to the idea of sharing his Democratic Party is a good place to start if we want to understand how some Americans reacted to the changes ushered in by the sexual revolution. Abortion, gay marriage, and the other concerns of feminists, gays, and young cultural progressives were utterly alien to a man like Meany. The 78-year-old devout Irish Catholic had entered adulthood as a 16-year-old high school dropout and plumber, nine years before American women had even won the right to vote. In the year he turned his back on the Democratic Party, Meany had run the most powerful group of working Americans ever organized in the history of the nation for nearly two decades, and the AFL-CIO still had hardly any women members.

What did the sexual revolution, feminism, and gay liberation have to offer men like Meany? Sexual liberation for their granddaughters? Sharing housework with their wives? Affirmative action for women in union jobs in a shrinking economy? As Meany conjured terrifying images of abortionists and sexual freaks, just 47 percent of Americans believed women should have an equal role in society. Among men *and* women Meany's age, two-thirds believed a woman's place was in the home.

The irony, however, was that Meany was a quintessential liberal— at least in the way that was understood before the sexual revolution changed everything. As much as anyone, he could claim credit for many liberal achievements. Without him, Medicare might never have passed in 1965. He was an early supporter of black civil rights, and he lavished AFL-CIO resources on the fight to pass the Civil Rights and the Voting Rights Acts. And he had even helped FDR win reelection in 1936, the year corporate America first tried to undo the work of a Democratic president trying to right a broken economy and make change.

This is what real change looks like from the other side, the side that didn't ask for it and didn't want it. It looks like George Meany, king-maker of twentieth-century American liberalism, suddenly stripped of power, place, and influence, seething in anger in a hotel room as he watches a political convention that he can no longer control.

Within a few years, Meany would be dead, the Democratic Party would write abortion rights into its platform, and long hair would be a badge of manly cool, sported by politicians, corporate executives, and blue-collar union men alike. But the first draft of history belonged to Meany and his generation. The Democratic Party, so it went, had been taken over by cultural elitists, who had betrayed real Democrats, diverted attention from what really mattered, and led the party down the road to ruin. But women, feminists, gays, cultural progressives, and young people, contrary to the charges leveled against them, did not deserve the primary blame for McGovern's defeat. There were many determinants of McGovern's loss, not least the conspiracy against him by those most responsible for peddling the death-by-McGovernik narrative. No matter. Democratic men would pick up Meany's loaded charge of cultural extremism and hurl it back at their fellow party members for the next forty years.

3

THE RISE OF THE SEXUAL
FUNDAMENTALISTS

THREE DAYS BEFORE Democrats arrived in Miami to enlist in their inner civil war, Phyllis Schlafly and a handful of Republican women met in a hotel room at Chicago's O'Hare Airport to plot how to stop women's equality from being written into the U.S. Constitution.

Earlier that year, in March 1972, the Equal Rights Amendment had been passed out of Congress, more than half a century after it was first introduced. The amendment read, "Equality of rights under the law shall not be denied or abridged by the United States or by any State on account of sex." Twenty-five minutes after the U.S. Senate voted 84 to 8 to pass the ERA, the Hawaii state Senate voted unanimously to ratify the amendment. During the next 72 hours, Delaware, Nebraska, New Hampshire, Idaho, and Iowa unanimously ratified the ERA. Among the states that considered the ERA in these first weeks, only Oklahoma had hesitated. Ann Patterson, a Sunday school teacher and wife of a defeated Republican Senate candidate, was in Chicago to tell Schlafly's allies how she had stopped the Oklahoma legislature from voting, as it intended, to ratify the ERA.

Schlafly, a trim, 47-year-old with a square-set jaw and hard, unsmiling eyes, was notorious in Republican circles. An orthodox Catholic, mother of six, and wife of a well-to-do St. Louis corporate lawyer fifteen years her senior, Schlafly had been active in right-wing politics since the 1940s. By the mid-1960s, she had founded a Catholic anti-communist foundation with her husband, Fred, run for Congress as an ordinary "housewife," and self-published a book that had helped to shatter the Republican Party.

That short book was the 1964 pro-Goldwater tract *A Choice, Not an Echo*, in which Schlafly accused establishment Republicans of betrayal and called for a virtual electoral insurrection by the Right to "take back" the GOP. A master publicist from the heartland in the golden age of *Mad Men*, Schlafly had placed her book into the hands of every GOP delegate and just about every right-wing activist in the nation. She had not been shy about taking credit for Goldwater's nomination to be the Republican standard-bearer in the 1964 presidential election. Goldwater lost by one of the largest margins ever in U.S. history.

The Republican Party establishment agreed with Schlafly's estimation of her own influence. To them, she was one of the reckless, out-of-the-mainstream agitators who had foisted on the party an unelectable extremist—one of those right-wingers the eminent historian Richard Hofstadter called pseudo-conservatives in his classic essay on the paranoid style in American politics. Looking to stop Schlafly from doing any more damage, the Republican Party tried to oust her from her base of power in the National Federation of Republican Women, the volunteer women's auxiliary that performed much of the grunt work of fundraising and envelope stuffing for the party. Schlafly was president of the Illinois chapter, a national vice president, and the beloved leader of the far-right minority faction among the rank and file.

Schlafly struck back. In 1967, she declared she would run for the Federation presidency, in defiance of the party leadership. She would be going up against Gladys O'Donnell, a pioneering aviator, a feminist, and the favored candidate of the majority of the Federation's members and the party's large contingent of feminists. Before the election, the outgoing Federation leader warned Republican Party leaders, "The nut fringe is beautifully organized."

Despite the Republican Party's considerable effort to defeat Schlafly, she lost by only a few hundred votes. She refused to accept the vote count and accused her fellow Republicans of sexism, fraud, and conspiracy. She marched a thousand of her supporters out of the room and threatened to bolt the Federation, take her followers with her, and create her own "grass-roots organization made up of just plain old American women and mothers who believe in the cause of constitutional government and freedom."

Thus wrapping her far-right mission in the mantle of motherhood, freedom, and the Constitution, Schlafly asked her supporters "to think about it, pray about it, and then write me what you want to do." After a few days cooling off, Schlafly thought better of a total break with the Republican Party and instead set up parallel institutions through which she could cultivate her women supporters for future action. She began writing and publishing a monthly newsletter, the *Phyllis Schlafly Report*. She established the Eagle Trust Fund, a way of circumventing the Republican Party to raise money directly from her supporters to be dedicated to the uses she determined. She began to convene a yearly gathering, where she trained those "plain old American women and mothers" in the basics of political organizing, communications, and lobbying.

The women who met with Schlafly in the summer of 1972 were leaders in the network of about two to three thousand conservative Republican women Schlafly had forged since starting her own political enterprise four years earlier. In September 1972, they convened a larger meeting, for a few hundred women, and formally chartered the organization "Stop Taking Our Privileges," otherwise known as STOP ERA. Stopping the ERA seemed a fool's errand, given that the amendment was sailing through ratification. One year after it was sent to the states, thirty states had ratified it, just eight shy of the three-fourths required to ratify a constitutional amendment. Two years later, when Gallup asked Americans if they had the chance, would they vote in favor of the ERA, 74 percent said they would, and three more states ratified the amendment that year.

Schlafly would likely have remained an obscure political agitator had it not been for the opportunity the ERA offered for a profitable alliance between her tiny faction of right-wing Republican women and America's vast reservoir of apolitical Protestant fundamentalist women. If it had not been for the right-wing women's movement to defeat the ERA, the U.S. Constitution would now in all likelihood include a guarantee of equal rights for women.

SCHLAFLY'S CLOSEST FUNDAMENTALIST ally was Lottie Beth Hobbs. One of ten children raised on a farm in Texas, Hobbs had worked in an arms plant during World War II and graduated from Abilene Christian College. She had never married, and she supported herself by working as a secretary in her church in Forth Worth, teaching ladies' Bible study classes, writing inspirational books for fundamentalist women, and traveling around the South speaking exclusively to ladies' groups. Hobbs was giving a talk to a group of church ladies one day when she noticed a leaflet about the ERA that changed her life. That ERA pamphlet sent her to the library to check out books about feminism and the women's movement. "They were all so awful," she recounted twenty-five years later, "that I put them under the bed so my nieces and nephews wouldn't see them."

"The feminists weren't proud to be women," Hobbs believed. "They put down women and wanted to be equal with men." She soon began working with her friend Becky Tilotta to alert other fundamentalist women about the horrors of the ERA. This was a matter of principle for Hobbs and Tilotta, both of whom were members of the Fort Worth Church of Christ. Like all fundamentalist churches, the Churches of Christ hold that the Bible contains only the literal truth, and that God ordained women to submit to their husbands and male authority. The Churches of Christ went further than many fundamentalist churches. They prohibited mixed-sex Bible study, taking to heart the New Testament passage, "I suffer not a woman to teach, nor to usurp authority over the man, but to be in silence." Hobbs and Tilotta named their new group "Women Who Want to Be Women."

Hobbs was too modest to put her own name on her organization, so it is probably not surprising that her role as one of the foremothers of the Christian Right and a key leader of the anti-ERA movement is rarely credited. Her signature contribution to the anti-ERA campaign was the so called Pink Sheet, a hand-typed, mimeographed pamphlet printed on pink paper, which circulated widely in the South and inspired many fundamentalist women to become politically active to kill the ERA.

"God created you and gave you a beautiful and exalted place to fill," the Pink Sheet began. That idea, to start with God, was Hobbs's own. Most of the rest of the pamphlet she adapted from Schlafly's essays against the ERA.

The ERA is "THE MOST DRASTIC MEASURE," ever passed by the U.S. Senate, Hobbs declared, because it "strikes at the very foundation of family life, and the home is the foundation of our nation." She asked rhetorically, "Do you want to lose your right not to work?" Because the ERA would force you to support your husband and "put your children in a federal day care center." Wives and children would not be "required to wear the name of husband and father." In all caps, Hobbs asked the wives of soldiers and firemen, "DO YOU WANT YOUR HUSBAND TO SLEEP IN THE BARRACKS WITH WOMEN?" Point for point, the Pink Sheet rejected the very idea of women's equality, not to mention every single measure the majority of American women believed was necessary to make equality a reality.

"The pink sheet is something that I never would have been able to write," Ann Patterson of STOP ERA said later. "I wouldn't have done it, and Phyllis would not have done it." Many of the claims were untrue, but that wasn't why Patterson balked. The pamphlet was simply too emotional and incendiary for these veteran Republican ladies from the suburban upper-middle class. Yet they were pleased to reap what the Pink Sheet sowed.

Although all the ERA said was that "equality of rights under the law shall not be denied or abridged by the United States or by any State on account of sex," Hobbs's claims that the ERA would destroy the God-given natural order of husbands over wives, of parents over children, of the trinity of Family-Church-Nation, echoed throughout the Antis' literature. (Anti-ERA activists became known as Antis, pro-ERA activists as Pros.) Many Antis included a copy of the Pink Sheet with their letters to state legislators asking them to oppose the ERA. Although the Pink Sheet reflected the particular theology of Hobbs's Church of Christ, an exceedingly conservative outpost of the fundamentalist world, the fears resonated across religious divides. Feminists were "a well-financed and vocal minority wishing to reconstruct the American family," the Alabama chapter of STOP ERA wrote to state legislators. "I want [my three daughters] to have the same freedoms I have," Gerry Lowe, a Mormon housewife active in the Illinois anti-ERA campaign, explained. "Freedom to be a homemaker, and the freedom not to join the military if there was a draft." In Ohio, where conservative Catholic women were active, Antis urged, "We, the wives and working women, need you, dear Senators and Representatives to protect us. We think this is the man's responsibility, and we are dearly hoping you will vote NO on ERA." A pamphlet circulating in Illinois titled "A Christian View of the ERA" warned, "Jesus cautioned us about wolves in sheep's clothing . . . of Satan coming as an angel of light so even the elect will be deceived." Its author, Rosemary Thomson, was a fundamentalist who was close to Schlafly.

Wild claims that the ERA would unleash a bacchanalia of sexual depravity kept the Antis in a heightened state of agitation. At meetings of Women Who Want to Be Women, they would pass around copies of *Our Bodies, Ourselves,* a popular women's health guide, to show how pro-ERA feminists were pornographers. One petition, in the course of reeling off a litany of moral horrors, warned that the ERA would legalize prostitution. Bunny Chambers, who was inspired to join the movement by the Pink Sheet and who became the head of Oklahoma's Women Who Want to be Women chapter, admitted that she deliberately used homophobia to recruit women into the anti-ERA movement.

"You can't get people to listen by talking about states' rights," the one-time John Bircher explained, "so I begin with the emotional issues."

What were those? She was asked.

"Homosexuality. I really do believe the ERA will legalize homosexual marriages, and that upsets people."

■ ■ ■

THE ERA HAD broad bipartisan support. Both political parties included endorsements of the amendment in their official party platforms. Roughly six out of ten Americans favored the ERA. Yet by mid-1975, ratification of the ERA had stalled.

Public opinion surveys showed that, on average, 32 percent of Americans opposed the ERA. How did this small minority triumph over the large pro-ERA majority? By taking advantage of the dirty little secret of American democracy. The minority can rule the majority, if it knows how to work the system. Political scientists call these points of leverage "veto points," and our complicated federalist system of checks and balances is lousy with them. When Patterson met with friendly Oklahoma lawmakers the week the ERA passed the U.S. Senate and asked them to call for hearings instead of taking a vote, she was expertly exploiting one of those veto points. Talking a measure to death in hearings is as good as voting it down—even better, if it's something that the majority wants. In a system purposely designed to make it difficult to pass even simple legislation, amending the U.S. Constitution is a nearly insuperable task. More than 3,000 amendments have been introduced in Congress. Only 33 have made it out of Congress, and of those, six have failed to win ratification by the necessary two-thirds of the states. The minority that opposed the ERA simply had to prevent 13 states from ratifying the ERA to accomplish their goal. To enshrine equal rights for women in the Constitution, ERA supporters needed to secure majorities or super-majorities in 38 states. The Antis had, in addition, won a huge advantage when Congress passed the amendment. Conservative congressman had tacked on a seven-year deadline for ratification when they passed it—a condition very rarely placed on ratifying a constitutional amendment.

The anti-ERA women won their victories through hard-nosed, brass-tacks obstructionism. Yet they had a knack for prettying that up with homespun touches, playing off bipartisan assumptions about how women should act. Every year, on the day the state legislature opened its session, Antis delivered home-baked bread to individual lawmakers, each loaf containing a handwritten card with a poem written by Beverly Findley of Women Who Want to Be Women.

It's an honor to be a homemaker,
And this right we want to remain,
But the ERA would take away our choice
And have laws read: Men, Women, Same.

The closing line archly warned,

So enjoy your bread, appreciate it too,
Cause Unless the ERA is stopped,
The Homemaker May be YOU!

Such feminine wiles charmed at least a few legislators to vote their way, even if that vote went against the values of their constituents. Illinois Representative John Edward Porter, who represented a liberal Republican district in the Chicago suburbs, wrote Schlafly that he had received a lot of mail in favor of ERA, "some being very shrill and even threatening." Your letter "was without question the nicest one that I have received." He voted against the ERA.

As the public face of the national anti-ERA campaign, Schlafly traveled widely to give speeches and participate in televised debates. She churned out pamphlets and offered up her deliciously provocative sound bites to an eager media. She met with ordinary women in their churches and kitchens and caucused behind closed doors with the up-and-coming men of the Republican Right. In the midst of it, she enrolled in law school, graduated near the top of her class, and was admitted to the Bar. She drove feminists into delirious fits of invective. Such a hypocrite, they charged. Here she was traveling the country to say a woman's role was to be a wife and mother, while her own children were home with the help. Betty Friedan, NOW co-founder and author of *The Feminine Mystique*, called her a traitor to her sex and said she should be burned at the stake. Schlafly, with two decades of political combat against the GOP establishment under her belt, relished the fight.

ERA supporters and the national press gave Schlafly outsized credit for what was looking to be the imminent demise of the ERA. Schlafly indeed was a brilliant strategist. She devised the legislative and media strategy for the Antis, funded the campaign by tapping her donors, and mentored wives and mothers new to activism in the dark arts of political combat. Yet the real power of the anti-ERA campaign resided with the ordinary fundamentalist women, and Schlafly knew it. After all, circulation for her monthly report was just 3,000 before she started working against the ERA. It spiked to 35,000 afterward. In August 1975, when she had founded the Eagle Forum, "the alternative to women's lib," she named three women from the Church of Christ to her board of directors, including Lottie Beth Hobbs.

Public opinion surveys confirm the preponderance of religious traditionalists in the anti-ERA movement. One national survey showed that 98 percent of anti-ERA activists were church members, disproportionately from the nation's most conservative denominations. The few available state-level surveys reveal that members of the Churches of Christ made up 60 percent of Antis in Texas, 43 percent in Oklahoma, and 45 percent in North Carolina, while making up at most 5 percent of those states' populations. In Oklahoma, 9 percent of anti-ERA activists were Mormon, even though Mormons were only 0.5 percent of the state's population. (Conservative Catholics like Schlafly were heavily represented in northern chapters of STOP ERA, but all northern states, except Schlafly's native Illinois, ratified the ERA.) In a survey conducted by political scientist Ruth Brown, issues that dominated the national debate, such as that the ERA would require unisex restrooms or allow women to be drafted into the military, were far down the list of priorities for these activists. A large majority of Antis gave as their main reasons for opposing the ERA that "it was against God's plan," it would "weaken families," or it would "encourage an unbiblical relationship between men and women."

The right-wing sexual counterrevolution was born in the movement of these traditionalist women against the feminist vision of winning constitutional recognition of and protection for women's equality. In their campaign against the ERA, they developed the necessary tools to move beyond this single issue to forge a broad social movement: a coherent ideology; a communications network; a mass base of committed activists led by charismatic leaders with political know-how; and a viable political strategy to stop their enemies. It was a grassroots movement initiated, led, and prosecuted by ordinary women, who were compelled to act by their belief that the American Way, true religion, and civilization itself all stood on the foundation of the traditional family and its biblically ordained submission of women. As one anti-ERA activist told a reporter at an anti-ERA protest, "I believe God made us different. My religion strictly says women should submit to their husbands. It says so in the Bible, and you can't believe part of the Bible but not all." And they were resolved that the U.S. Constitution should reflect their particular view of the Bible.

A HOST OF new cultural issues revolving around sex, family, gender roles, and sexual identity seemed to confirm the connection the anti-ERA activists saw between attacks on the Christian traditional family, feminism, and the sexual revolution. In the mid-1970s, while the national media focused its attention on northern cities, where whites were protesting against busing designed to desegregate public schools, the white South and border South became consumed with battles against sex education, pornography, gay civil rights, and federally funded child care.

With mothers streaming into the labor force, in 1971 Congress passed a bill sponsored by Minnesota Democratic Senator Walter Mondale to make federally subsidized early education programs and after-school care universally available. As Mondale put it, the bill put "real money" into child care. Despite a large bipartisan vote passing the bill, President Richard Nixon vetoed it, declaring it to be the session's most "radical" legislation. Speaking informally, he echoed a talking point by a right-wing columnist and said it would "sovietize" the American family.

Still, government aid to parents to help them pay for child care retained strong bipartisan support. Republican feminists pushed for federally controlled child care at the 1972 convention and won the party's commitment to various child care measures, short of federal control. Child care bills were introduced in Congress in each year after Nixon's veto of Mondale's legislation. (Another again passed the Senate to die in the House in 1973.) In 1975, Mondale's revised child care bill gained momentum and seemed likely to pass. Until, that is, fundamentalists got word of it. An anonymous flyer began circulating through church networks, attacking Congress for undermining the family and parental authority. (Among the false claims in the flyer was that the bill would remove parents' right to make their kids take out the garbage.) Oklahoma's fledgling chapter of Women Who Want to Be Women targeted the bill as their first major campaign. They recruited their STOP ERA allies to help defeat it and persuaded the Oklahoma PTA council to oppose the child care bill. Similar local efforts produced an avalanche of angry letters from every state to Congress. The bill again passed the Senate but died in the House. Mondale, who would go on to become Jimmy Carter's vice president and the Democratic Party's 1984 presidential nominee, reflected on the child care battles in his 2010 autobiography, *The Good Fight*. "Because most journalists in Washington did not cover children's issues at that time, and because Americans were still just coming to understand the changes in the American family," Mondale wrote, "I think the importance of that episode has widely been overlooked."

When a related bill was floated in 1976, Schlafly pounced, with her characteristic blend of mockery and delirium. The "anti-family women's lib movement" demanded "state nurseries for all children," she wrote, because they believe "it is so unfair for society to expect mothers to care for their babies, and mothers must be relieved of this unequal burden in order to achieve their full equality (by working in more fulfilling paid employment, such as coal mines, construction work, etc.)" Three out of five mothers were in the workforce already, but according to Schlafly, child care for working mothers was a feminist plot to destroy the family.

Child care had passed under the radar of the national press and the majority of the American public, which had no idea that their representatives were being deluged by those who opposed women working. The issue that next galvanized the women fundamentalists into action, by contrast, gained wall-to-wall coverage in the media and remains a central feature of our national political delirium: the right of gay Americans to be free from discrimination.

In early 1977, the Miami City Council passed an ordinance prohibiting discrimination against gays and lesbians in employment, public facilities, and housing. The singer, former beauty queen, and Florida orange juice spokeswoman Anita Bryant emerged as the spokeswoman for a campaign to repeal the law. Bryant, a born-again Southern Baptist, claimed divine mandate for her effort to reinstate lawful discrimination by majority rule. "When the law requires you to let an admitted homosexual teach your children and serve as a model for them, it's time to stop being so tolerant," she explained. "The Bible clearly says homosexuality is an abomination." When pressed, Bryant insisted she was not intolerant, since God hated gays because "The male homosexual eats another man's sperm. Sperm is the most concentrated form of blood. The homosexual is eating life."

A couple weeks before the Dade County referendum, Bryant took time out from the so-called Save Our Children campaign to testify in the Florida Legislature against the ERA. Florida came up one vote short of ratification. In June, Dade County citizens voted by a two-to-one margin to repeal their anti-discrimination law. On election night, Bryant kissed her husband for the television cameras. "This is what heterosexuals do, fellows," he told reporters. She proclaimed, "The 'normal majority' have said, 'Enough! Enough! Enough!'" The leaders of Save Our Children took their campaign on the road to California, where they introduced the Briggs Initiative, an ultimately unsuccessful attempt to ban gays and lesbians from teaching in public schools.

Sexual fundamentalism was the common denominator of these early women's crusades: to defeat the ERA and federal child care legislation; to banish offending textbooks, sex education, and gay teachers from the public schools; to deny gay individuals and nontraditional families legal rights and cultural approval; not only to oppose women's equality but to denigrate working mothers. Members of religious denominations that were most invested in women's traditional subordinate role in the family were those who were most devoted to the sexual counterrevolution. The Mormon Church, for example, discouraged the use of birth control, counseled women to forgo careers and devote themselves to motherhood, and tirelessly condemned homosexuality. It was the only formal religious body in the nation to officially oppose the ERA. The church went so far as to excommunicate members who supported the ERA. Protestant fundamentalists, orthodox Catholics, and Mormons might disagree vehemently about prayer in schools, evolution, and the fine points of theology, such as how literally to read the Bible. Often enough their prejudice against each other caused them to keep their organizations separate. Yet their shared beliefs in women's subordinate role in the traditional family and the horrors of sexual liberation allowed them to look beyond their past hostilities to unite in sexual counterrevolution.

DESPITE THE AGITATION among the newly aroused sexual fundamentalists, feminism and women's rights continued to enjoy broad bipartisan support. Republican President Gerald Ford, who had risen to the presidency following Nixon's resignation in 1974, shared in the national consensus. He was a moderate Republican who supported the ERA; his wife, Betty, was a straight-talking Republican feminist, who once said in an interview that it would be fine with her if their daughter had an abortion and didn't find pot terrible. The Watergate scandal had severely damaged the Republican Party—liberal Democrats had swept the 1974 midterm elections. Ford hoped to restore the reputation of the GOP, as well as shore up the moderate wing of the party in order to win back centrist voters. Supporting women's rights was a key element of that strategy.

In 1976, the year Ford would face the voters for the first time in a presidential contest, Congress passed a bill creating the National Women's Conference. The United Nations had declared the seventies the Women's Decade and 1975 International Women's Year (IWY), and many countries were commemorating the event with conferences on women's status. A bipartisan group of feminist congresswomen, Republican Margaret Heckler and Democrats Patsy Mink and Bella Abzug, sponsored the bill to hold such a conference in the United States. It passed on a bipartisan vote with Ford's strong support. Congress appropriated $5 million for the National Women's Conference and mandated democratic participation. At preliminary state and territorial conferences in the summer of 1977, delegates were to be elected by their peers and to be representative of all races, ethnicities, and income groups. Congress even subsidized the cost of attendance for low-income women. The commission started work under Ford in 1976, but Ford narrowly lost the election to Jimmy Carter. Carter and First Lady Rosalynn Carter were also both strong supporters of the ERA. When President Carter inherited the project, he appointed Bella Abzug, who had just lost her House seat, to head the IWY Commission.

Schlafly snapped into action as soon as the bipartisan group of congresswomen introduced the women's conference bill. Feminists were about to receive the government seal of approval if they didn't act quickly. "We must take over the conferences," Schlafly wrote. "It is your job to make sure that (1) our Federal money is NOT spent to project radical lib, anti-family, anti-homemaker, pro-ERA propaganda, and (2) that the libs do NOT use [the conferences] to make the taxpayers provide them with a free babysitting service so they can go out agitating to destroy homemakers' rights." Schlafly formed a watchdog group, the Citizens' Review Committee, its very name insinuating that something nefarious would transpire when a group of democratically elected women met to discuss the status of American women. She put Rosemary Thomson, a fundamentalist author who likened the ERA to a satanic plot, in charge. Audiotapes mailed out by the Citizens' Review Committee helpfully informed listeners that their children would be corrupted by sex education and homosexual teachers if the IWY went on as planned. The fact that IWY Chairwoman Abzug had introduced the first gay civil rights bill in the U.S. Congress was grist for their mill and the subject of one of the tapes.

On November 18, 1977, 2,000 delegates representing every state, along with about 18,000 alternate delegates, observers, and members of the press gathered in the Houston Coliseum for the National Women's Conference. The conference was opened by three pro-ERA First Ladies: Betty Ford, Rosalynn Carter, and Lady Bird Johnson. The delegates were a remarkably diverse group. A third were non-white, and a fifth were low income. Democrats and Republicans were both well represented, as were Protestants, Catholics, and Jews. Some feminist leaders had been elected to the state delegations, but

the majority of delegates were ordinary women who were not movement activists. Men were not eligible to serve as elected participants.

After debating what measures were required to end the remaining
gender inequities in American society, the delegates voted in favor
of a 25-point National Plan of Action. It called for federal support
for child care, equal pay, equal access to credit, the end to sexism
in school curricula and the media, aid to displaced homemakers
and battered women, and many other measures to support women's
political, economic, and social equality. The plank in favor of ERA
ratification won handily by a large margin. Planks supporting the
right to abortion and lesbian civil rights won too, but by smaller
margins. Coretta Scott King, the widow of Martin Luther King, Jr.,
captured the dominant spirit of the gathering when she said, "Let
the message go forth from Houston and spread all over this land.
There is a new force, a new understanding, a new sisterhood against
all injustice that has been born here. We will not be divided and
defeated again."

As King spoke, members of the minority who voted against the
National Plan sat among the delegates in the Coliseum with "Majority"
streamers pinned to their blouses and suit jackets, printed in letters
legible on even the smallest TV screen. Antifeminists had organized
to try to win control of the state delegations. They had succeeded in a
few states: Mormon women controlled the Utah delegation, and conservative fundamentalists also had a majority in the Bible Belt states
of Indiana and Mississippi. Yet, in total, in the open process chartered
by Congress, only 20 percent of the delegates elected to attend the
Houston conference were antifeminist conservatives.

ACROSS TOWN ON that Saturday morning, about 15,000 mostly
middle-aged women, with children and grandchildren in tow, filled
Houston's Astro Arena. More than 200 buses from nearly every
state in the nation waited in the parking lot, ready to drive through
the night to get the women back home in time for church the next
morning.

The National Pro-Family Rally was Lottie Beth Hobbs's brain-
child. By 1977, Hobbs had changed the name of her Texas chapter

of Women Who Want to Be Women to the Pro-Family Forum, and she was participating in a Pro-Family Coalition, which included Schlafly's Eagle Forum. Hobbs had tried to win control of the Texas IWY delegation, but her slate was voted down. She then decided they should hold a counter-demonstration and convinced Schlafly to help publicize it across the nation. (People close to Schlafly cautioned her not to, worried the demonstration would be a flop.) Hobbs invited the speakers, wrote the petition, and organized through her church and the Pro-Family Coalition to make sure they would fill the venue. Schlafly reprinted Hobbs's petition in her *Report* in September and tasked Thomson with producing an audiotape urging supporters to attend. Thomson's tape drummed up support for Hobbs's protest by claiming there had been "a workshop on witches, conducted by witches" at the Virginia IWY conference. At Hawaii's, it went on, there had been "a dance showing how lesbians make love in a pay toilet."

Hobbs opened the rally by pointing to boxes she asserted contained 300,000 signatures for their pro-family resolutions against the "ERA, Abortion, Federally-controlled Early Child Development Programs, and the Teaching or Glorification of Homosexuality, Lesbianism, or Prostitution." First-term Republican Congressman Robert Dornan called the delegates at the formal National Women's Conference "sick, anti-God, pro-lesbian, and unpatriotic." To wild applause from the throngs of women gathered, Schlafly opened her speech by saying, "I want to thank my husband Fred, for letting me come—I always like to say that, because it makes the libs so mad!" Anita Bryant delivered a supportive message by videotape. One formerly gay man testified that Jesus Christ "can deliver you from homosexuality." Hobbs and her allies were sensitive to perceptions they were an all-white group, and they gave black speakers and church choirs prominent billing on the program. African American Texas state legislator Clay Smothers, who had introduced a bill to bar gays and lesbians from attending Texas colleges, was one of the day's speakers. "I have enough civil rights to choke a hungry goat," he declared. "I ask for public rights Mr. Carter . . . I want the right to segregate my family from these misfits and perverts."

■ ■ ■

THREE YEARS AFTER Hobbs's Pro-Family Rally, the Reverend Jerry Falwell and other male evangelicals would be given credit for awakening fundamentalists from their long political slumber, severing their historic ties to the Democratic Party, forging them into a potent force within the Republican Party, and electing the conservative Ronald Reagan president of the United States. In truth, it was ordinary fundamentalist women, acting to reverse the sexual revolution, feminism, and the gay liberation movement, who deserve that credit. Lottie Beth Hobbs's Pink Sheet, with its delirious warnings to the innocent victims of feminism, turned out to be one of the founding charters of the Christian Right, her Pro-Family Rally the first mass demonstration of the sexual counterrevolution.

Before the sexual revolution of the 1960s, most American institutions, by one means or another, had enforced the sectarian moral code of Christian traditionalists and long-dead Victorians. By the late seventies, Congress, state governments, and the Supreme Court had put a stop to the special favor once accorded to the most culturally reactionary segment of America's Christians. Pornography and obscenity laws were found to violate the right to free speech. Laws criminalizing birth control and abortion were ruled to violate the individual's constitutional right to privacy. In just a few short years, scores of laws based on the conviction that women were inferior and naturally dependent on men were overturned on the principle that those notions were no more than rank prejudice. Abortion became legal, twenty-five states changed their laws to allow no-fault divorce, and public schools started teaching scientifically accurate sex education. In 1970, sodomy was illegal in every state; by the end of the decade, nearly half the states had stricken sodomy laws from the books, thus decriminalizing homosexuality. The U.S. Civil Service Commission had ended its ban on hiring gays and lesbians, and at the federal level, employment discrimination against gays and lesbians remained legal only in the U.S. military. Dozens of cities had passed laws prohibiting discrimination against gay citizens in employment, public facilities, and housing.

Religious traditionalists, orthodox Catholics, Mormons, and, most important, Protestant fundamentalists were incensed by these changes. For four decades, fundamentalists had largely abstained from voting, in an effort to separate themselves from what they perceived to be the morally polluted secular world. Although evangelical entrepreneurs had tried to lead their fold back into politics in the 1960s over the Supreme Court's ruling against prayer in public school, the people would not be moved. In 1972, the last national election to take place before the birth of the sexual counterrevolution, only 61 percent of white evangelicals voted, a turnout 28 percent less than that of whites overall.

Only when the ERA came before them, triggering as it did anxieties about women's sexual freedom and the threat posed to the family and the nation by working women, did fundamentalists return to the political arena. Political separation was a luxury fundamentalists could no longer indulge. In 1976, sixty-six percent of evangelicals voted, cutting their turnout gap in half. Before the sexual revolution, their strict and repressive values had been the law of the land. After it, other traditional American values—privacy, individual liberty, freedom of conscience, and pluralism—set the standard for laws concerning sex, family, and relations between men and women.

The sexual fundamentalists of the Christian Right got political, not to level the playing field but to restore the power they had lost to impose their values on the rest of America. Soon global geopolitics, the business cycle, and the disarray of the Democratic Party would converge to give the sexual counterrevolutionaries an accidental victory and their first taste of real political power.

4

AN ACCIDENTAL
REVOLUTION

O N NOVEMBER 4, 1979, radical Islamists stormed the
U.S. embassy in Tehran and took 66 Americans hostage.
Over the Christmas holidays, the Soviet Union invaded
Afghanistan. As winter turned to spring, inflation in the United States
rose to 18 percent and the prime interest rate reached 20 percent.
Unemployment was up; personal income and business profits were
down. In April, a mission to rescue the hostages failed, literally, to
get off the ground. That month tens of thousands of Cuban refugees
began landing on the shores of Florida; many of them were criminals
released from Fidel Castro's jails. And the president of the United
States swore he had been attacked by a giant rabbit.

In 1976, a Baptist peanut farmer and nuclear engineer, Jimmy
Carter, had won the presidency from the improbable stepping-stone
of the Georgia governorship. With political cynicism and disaffection at an all-time high in the wake of the Watergate scandal and
President Nixon's resignation, with the economy stagnant in the
wake of the budget-busting Vietnam War and the Arab oil embargo,
the born-again Carter had narrowly won election against President

Gerald Ford by casting himself as an outsider with the moral fiber and common sense needed to clean up Washington.

Carter himself was a product of the Democratic Party's inner civil war, a triangulator *avant la lettre*, whose first step onto the national stage in 1972 had been to plug for the dead-enders among the Stop McGovernites. He won the presidency by just 2 points with a ticking time bomb of a coalition—liberals and conservatives, African Americans and southern whites, feminists and sexual fundamentalists. Faced immediately with stunning challenges not of his own making and not very adept at tackling them, Carter also had a knack for alienating the Democratic base—unions and economic populists who wanted to pass universal health care, antiwar liberal internationalists, and even Jews, who rank just below African Africans in their stubborn loyalty to the Democratic Party.

On top of it all, Carter had a woman problem. His first year in office was roiled by the showdown in Houston between feminists and the sexual fundamentalists at the National Women's Conference and the National Pro-Family Rally. Carter blamed feminists, not their opponents, for this. Personally conservative on social issues, the president and First Lady Rosalynn Carter were annoyed that the conference had unequivocally endorsed lesbian rights and legal abortion. After Houston, they began to walk back their unequivocal support for the ERA; the president essentially ignored the IWY National Plan of Action. Carter tried to straddle the fence on abortion, to no one's satisfaction. He accepted *Roe v. Wade* as the law of the land but seemed unable to talk about abortion without calling attention to his personal religious objections to it. When Bella Abzug publicly criticized the president for failing to act forcefully to advance women's rights, Carter fired her from her position on the National Advisory Committee for Women. Most of the remaining committee members resigned in protest. Overreacting feminists dubbed the episode "The Friday Night Massacre."

As the 1980 presidential election approached, the odds were good that Carter would not even have the chance to run for reelection. Carter's approval rating had fallen as low as 28 percent; in polls of Democratic primary voters, Carter trailed his main Democratic opponent, Massachusetts Senator Edward M. Kennedy, by 22 points. Ironically, the hostage crisis initially saved Carter's candidacy. As Americans rallied 'round the flag and the president, Carter was able to amass a commanding lead in the delegate race in early primaries. However, as national economic conditions deteriorated and the hostages remained in captivity, Kennedy surged. He won five of the last eight primaries, including the electorally rich states of California and New Jersey. When polls showed Democratic voters exactly split on their preferred nominee, Kennedy decided to take his fight to the convention. Unlike 1972, when the vanquished Democratic establishment had schemed to defeat McGovern and overturn the will of the voters, Kennedy's challenge reflected dissatisfaction broadly shared at the base and at the heights of the Democratic Party. After all, Carter's approval rating was at the lowest level Gallup had ever recorded for a sitting president.

When the Democratic Party gathered in New York City in August, 1980, for their convention, the fault lines were once again on public display, just as they had been eight years earlier in Miami. Procedural votes on the convention's first day foreclosed the chance of a Kennedy upset, but Kennedy's supporters, not Carter's, controlled the platform committee. With feminists well represented among Kennedy delegates, the full convention passed pro-feminist planks that Carter opposed. One denied party campaign funds to any candidate who opposed the ERA. Rather than lose face and lose in a convention floor vote, Carter consented. (Other progressive planks introduced by Kennedy on economic issues and comprehensive health care had mixed success.) When Kennedy spoke the night of the platform vote, his rousing and now classic ode to liberalism was greeted by forty minutes of roaring, passionate cheers from the delegates. As the convention wrapped up later in the week with Carter's speech, followed by an awkward and too brief handshake between Kennedy and Carter, the delegates erupted with the chant, "We want Ted." A feeling of doom suffused the hall.

Exactly one year after the Americans in the U.S. embassy in Iran were taken hostage, Republican Ronald Reagan won the presidency in an Electoral College landslide. Since that time, popular wisdom has held that Reagan, an unabashed conservative, won a crushing mandate because the American people saw their own heartfelt conservatism reflected in him. But the 1980 election was not a mandate for conservative rule or an expression of popular conservatism. After all, Reagan only won 50.7 percent of the popular vote in the lowest turnout in a presidential election in decades; Carter and the Independent candidate, moderate Republican John Anderson, together won just shy of 50 percent of all votes. Reagan was elected president because American voters rejected Jimmy Carter in a classic throw-the-bum-out election. This was hardly a revolution.

Much of what Americans think we know today about current politics rests on certain myths going back to the 1980 election. Like many myths, the one about the so-called Reagan revolution includes an origin tale: Reagan won because the American people had turned right, especially on cultural issues. Like many myths, it serves to distort, rather than reveal, the actual facts of history. Like some of Western civilization's core myths—Cain and Abel, Romulus and Remus—its symbolic purpose is to forge a sense of common identity, while veiling the original fratricidal conflict through which one party dispatched the other.

Reagan's 1980 election was indeed a victory of the Right, but not in the way conventional wisdom has handed the story down to us. Rather it was a triumph of the minority faction of sexual counterrevolutionaries within an ideologically divided Republican Party. Twice already, in 1968 and 1976, Reagan had lost a bid for the Republican nomination because Republican voters found him too extreme. He finally won with the aid of the sexual fundamentalists, who mobilized evangelical voters and tipped the nomination to him in the hotly contested Republican primary. The story of how Reagan finally won the Republican nomination in 1980 is a story of the victory of the sexual counterrevolutionaries over the rest of the Republican Party.

AFTER REAGAN CAME up 117 delegate votes short of winning the Republican presidential nomination in 1976 from incumbent President Ford, Reagan's advisers assessed his future prospects. There were not enough voters among the old Right of anti-communists and far-right John Birchers to ever carry him to victory over GOP moderates and mainstream conservatives, much less to a popular majority in a national election. So they decided to take a page from Richard Nixon's playbook. A majority could be forged with southern whites, unmoored by the civil rights movement from their historic loyalty to the Democratic Party. When southern evangelicals turned out in record numbers in 1976 to put the born-again Carter in the White House, Reagan's team realized their courtship would have to be as much about religion as Nixon's had been about race.

Reagan's post-1976 come-to-Jesus moment coincided with a similar epiphany among the leading strategists on the ideological Right about how to attract actual voters to their program of cutting taxes, slashing regulations that protected workers, consumers, and the environment, and ending Democratic social welfare programs such as Medicare and Social Security. In the early 1970s, a handful of far-right billionaires, such as Richard Mellon Scaife, Charles and David H. Koch, and Joseph Coors, had started to invest millions of dollars in the creation of right-wing think tanks, lobbies, publications, advocacy groups, and political action committees (PACs), such as the Heritage Foundation, the Cato Institute, the American Enterprise Institute, and *The American Spectator* magazine. Within a few years, a coterie of ultraconservatives, many of whom had worked on the Goldwater campaign, in the College Republicans, or in the Nixon administration, had coalesced as the New Right—a title they gave themselves. Despite their talent, access to limitless funds from the wealthy and corporate leaders, and experience in partisan political warfare, the New Right remained a small circle of like-minded intellectuals and operatives in search of voters willing to sweep them into government.

The New Right found the potential voters they were looking for among the women sexual fundamentalists at the 1977 Pro-Family Rally, which proved to be a milestone for the right-wing sexual counterrevolution. Phyllis Schlafly observed that that was "when 'pro-family' came into common usage as a term to describe our movement." That was certainly a more appealing label than the one she and her allies were typically known by—antifeminist. The rally lit a beacon to like-minded souls across the nation. Soon after it, James Dobson, the evangelical psychologist and best-selling author of *Dare to Discipline*, the authoritarian retort to Dr. Benjamin Spock's liberal child-rearing books, created Focus on the Family, a global Christian ministry, dedicated to teaching "scriptural principles of marriage and parenthood." Beverly LaHaye began meeting with fellow Baptist women in San Diego, directing the spiritual energy of their prayer circles toward killing the ERA. Two years later, LaHaye converted her informal meetings into Concerned Women for America.

Most important, the rally alerted Republican operatives and New Right strategists in Washington, D.C., that the sleeping electoral giant in the Bible Belt had awakened and turned against President Jimmy Carter and the Democratic Party. The women's campaigns against the ERA, child care, and gay civil rights had galvanized fundamentalists to return to the political arena, and Carter, a man who appeared to be one of them, had been an accidental beneficiary of this upsurge. But Carter's positions on matters of women and sex quickly alienated evangelicals. Tim LaHaye, a Baptist preacher who wrote sex manuals for married Christian couples with his wife, Beverly, before he became the mega-selling author of the apocalyptic *Left Behind* series, expressed a typical sentiment. Carter had misrepresented himself "as a Christian and pro-family" candidate, as evidenced by his support for the ERA, which "would be so harmful to the family."

The New Right and the sexual fundamentalists began to tentatively work together after Houston, yet they needed a campaign on which to focus their delirium and cement their relationship. A few months after the IWY conference, Carter unwittingly gave it to them. Carter thought he could defuse the brewing culture war with a big-tent family policy, and he announced that his administration would convene a major conference on the family. Instead, the White House Conference on the Family (WHCF) became Carter's Waterloo. Women Who Want to Be Women, Schlafly's Eagle Forum, and LaHaye's women's circles joined with New Right leader Paul Weyrich in a Pro-Family Coalition. They charged that Carter was out to destroy the traditional family and worked to torpedo the WHCF. When Schlafly, the LaHayes, Hobbs, Dobson, and others met in 1980 for their counter-conference, Weyrich's tone was typical. The idea that a "couple of fornicators" or a "couple of lesbians . . . bringing up a child" counted as a family was "garbage."

Out of the Pro-Family Rally and Carter's WHCF a right-wing coalition made up of the sexual fundamentalists and New Right anti-tax, anti-government market fundamentalists coalesced within the Republican Party. Although the women fundamentalists had been politically mobilized since at least 1975, only when New Right men and male televangelists hooked up, did the American press become interested in the rumblings of the fundamentalist malcontents.

In May 1979, three leaders of the New Right, Paul Weyrich, Richard Viguerie, and Howard Phillips, met with three conservative religious leaders, Ed McAteer, Robert Billings, and Reverend Jerry Falwell and founded the Moral Majority. Its express purpose was to use preachers and televangelists to persuade fundamentalists to vote for right-wing Republicans. A distinguishing characteristic of the New Right leaders, as opposed to some of their more libertarian-minded donors, was their own religious traditionalism. Weyrich, the founder of the Heritage Foundation, founder of the PAC Committee for the Survival of a Free Congress (CSFC), and one-time Republican Party operative, was an orthodox Catholic. So was Viguerie, who was the editor of an ultraconservative magazine and had pioneered the use of direct-mail political fundraising. Howard Phillips, a former Nixon aide, was the head of the Conservative Caucus and an Orthodox Jew. Falwell, whose television show, *The Old Time Gospel Hour*, reached 18 million fundamentalist viewers every week and who ran a sprawling religious enterprise out of Lynchburg, Virginia, became the public face of the Moral Majority. Tim and Beverly LaHaye were named honorary co-chairs of the group. Another important Christian Right group, the Religious Roundtable, was also founded in 1979 by McAteer, with help from Weyrich and Phillips. James Robison, a 31-year-old Texas televangelist, became the group's main spokesman, having impressed McAteer with the devotion he commanded from ordinary fundamentalists. When the ABC affiliate in Fort Worth canceled Robison's show after he contended on air that homosexuals recruited children to homosexuality so they could use them for sex, hundreds of women from the First Baptist Church surrounded the station to demand Robison be put back on the air. The station swiftly gave the televangelist back his show.

Before the master strategists of the New Right could reap the bounty offered by the rising of the sexual fundamentalists, however, they would have to do battle within the Republican Party.

THE STRUGGLE FOR control of the Grand Old Party played out in two acts. By 1979, Reagan was the unrivaled favorite of the Republican Right. He was an outspoken conservative, adored by many of the right-wing activists who had secured Barry Goldwater's nomination in 1964. As GE's spokesman in the 1960s, he had denounced Medicare as socialism. He had won the California governorship in 1966 by crusading against the sixties counterculture, the antiwar movement, and ungrateful college students. The film clips from those years did not present Reagan in the manner that Americans would come to know him, as a genial, confident, optimistic elder statesman. They made him look, from the eyes of an American in 1980, a bit delirious.

"I have here a copy of a report," he ominously intoned in one of those clips from the mid-1960s, from the Alameda County district attorney concerning a dance held at the University of California, Berkeley. "The incidents are so bad, so contrary to our standards of human behavior that I couldn't possibly recite them to you from this platform in detail." And then he proceeded to recount in detail what had taken place.

"Three rock and roll bands were in the center of the gymnasium, playing simultaneously . . . All during the dance movies were shown on two screens at the opposite ends of the gymnasium. These movies were the only lights in the gym proper. They consisted of color sequences that gave the impression of different colored liquids spreading across the screen, followed by shots of men and women, on occasion, shots of the men and women's nude torsos on occasion, and persons twisted and gyrated in provocative and sensual fashion."

The moderate and mainstream conservative wing of the Republican Party remained quite large, but lacked strong leadership after Ford's defeat in 1976, and the Republican primaries opened with Reagan the frontrunner. But Reagan proved to be a lackluster candidate and he unexpectedly lost the first contest, the Iowa caucus, to the leading moderate candidate, George H. W. Bush. Five weeks later, Reagan made a comeback against Bush in New Hampshire, thanks to an infusion of cash from Christian businessmen, a reorganized campaign, and canvassing by the National Rifle Association, anti-ERA activists, and Phyllis Schlafly herself.

The day after the New Hampshire primary, Ford pronounced in a *New York Times* interview that Reagan was too extreme to be electable. After Iowa, Bush had failed to establish himself as the one clear alternative to Reagan. Liberal Republican Illinois Representative John Anderson was doing surprisingly well, and another moderate, Howard Baker, was siphoning off about 10 percent of the vote in many states. Moderate Republicans consistently split their votes between Bush, Anderson, and Baker, leaving Reagan the winner even in states in which moderates were the majority. In desperation, some establishment Republicans formed a Draft Ford committee, but they did not act early enough to give Ford a viable path to the nomination.

As the March 18 Illinois primary loomed, after a string of southern primary wins by Reagan, Anderson was well positioned to win in his home state. A frontrunner and presumptive nominee can rarely survive losing a populous swing state to a long-shot opponent. To meet the challenge from Anderson, Reagan personally enlisted Schlafly, and Schlafly mobilized Eagle Forum and STOP ERA members to canvass for Reagan in her home state. Reagan won Illinois, Anderson came in second, and Bush third. Following Illinois, Reagan decisively won every contest in the South and border South, while the combined Bush and Anderson vote surpassed Reagan's in most states in the North and Midwest. In late April, Anderson withdrew, soon declaring that he would run as an independent for the express purpose of rescuing his party from the radical Right. Bush continued to win some primaries, but Reagan secured enough delegates to win the nomination on May 20. Bush conceded and released his delegates. Overall, Bush and Anderson won 42 percent of the total primary vote. In eight of the nineteen primaries in which the three candidates competed, their combined vote exceeded Reagan's.

The primary thus revealed that Republican voters were split between the Right, establishment moderates, and even outright liberals such as Anderson. The sexual counterrevolutionaries, however, were convinced that they had saved Reagan, and they exacted a steep price for their support. Securing control over the platform committee—and with Schlafly serving on the committee—the sexual fundamentalists scrapped the Republican Party's historic support for the ERA. In its stead, the platform included some vague language supporting women's rights and stated explicitly, "We reaffirm our belief in the traditional role and values of the family in our society." The platform included a new plank that called for a constitutional amendment banning abortion, and the appointment of judges "who respect traditional family values and the sanctity of innocent human life." It called for the end of affirmative action, a policy that women across party lines believed necessary to make up for decades of sex discrimination.

To many Republican women, the platform appeared to be a near total repudiation of the party's historic commitment to women's rights and traditions of respect for individual liberty. These Republicans could credibly argue that for most of the twentieth century, the Republican Party, not the Democratic Party, had been the champion of women's equality. They did not submit to the sexual counterrevolution without a fight.

"We are about to bury the rights of over 100 million American women under a heap of platitudes," warned Republican National Committee Co-Chair Mary Dent Crisp, the highest ranking woman in the Republican Party. A conservative and a former Goldwaterite, Crisp had become a feminist, when, in her words, her consciousness was raised at the 1972 Republican convention. An unexpected divorce soon after deepened her feminist identity, when she found herself pushing 50 with no paid work experience and no savings of her own. To Crisp, Republican values of individual liberty and small government were perfectly aligned with women's rights, and she valiantly tried to preserve a place for the many feminists who still called the Republican Party home. Crisp not only failed to stop the sexual counterrevolution in the GOP, she too became one of its casualties. Right-wing delegates voted to strip her of her RNC co-chairmanship. Reagan himself denounced her for not falling into line with the new traditionalist program: "Mary Dent Crisp should look to herself and see how loyal she's been to the Republican Party for quite some time."

Yet by the time the television cameras started to roll at the GOP Convention in July 1980, the Republican war of the women was contained. Crisp was gone. After being ousted from her official position, she walked out of the convention. (Soon after she went to work on John Anderson's independent campaign.) Maureen Reagan, Reagan's feminist daughter, brokered a compromise between her father and the feminists who did not walk out. Reagan purportedly promised he would enforce federal anti-discrimination laws and consider appointing the first female Supreme Court justice in exchange for their support. Reagan won the endorsement of some prominent Republican feminists, giving him cover on women's rights. With the ERA still favored by a majority of Americans, this was no small achievement.

Having satisfied the sexual counterrevolutionaries on their central demands and having neutralized the party's feminists, Reagan pivoted to the center with aplomb in his convention speech, with little more than a dog whistle to the fundamentalists about "family, work, neighborhood." Speaking to a national audience watching on TV, Reagan eloquently evoked American exceptionalism, contrasted Carter's pessimism and weakness with his own optimism and pride in asserting American power, and effectively pinned the blame for the three "grave threats to our very existence" on the Democrats. "The major issue of this campaign is the direct political, personal, and moral responsibility of Democratic Party leadership in the White House and in the Congress for this unprecedented calamity which has befallen us."

Few Americans in the summer of 1980 would have disputed Reagan's claim that the nation was in a calamitous state. His challenge was to convince them that he was the solution. The Reagan campaign well knew that their man could not win should Democrats, independents, and Republican moderates perceive him to be an extremist in the Goldwater mold. Yet neither could Reagan take the voters on the Right for granted. It wasn't preordained that ordinary fundamentalists would vote for the divorced Hollywood actor who rarely went to church, just because their pastors and televangelists told them to. So when the sexual counterrevolutionaries objected that Reagan had put only feminists on the campaign's pro-ERA Women's

Policy Board, they quickly won a spot on the board for Elaine Donnelly, a grassroots leader in Illinois STOP ERA and a close associate of Schlafly. They also forced the campaign to establish an alternative women's board, the purpose of which was to coordinate with local grassroots antifeminist groups to turn out the vote. Hobbs, Beverly LaHaye, and others had the run of Reagan's Family Policy Advisory Committee to themselves, with no feminists around to interfere.

The most important moment in Reagan's pilgrimage to the sexual counterrevolutionaries was a late August speech to some 15,000 fundamentalists at a nationally televised rally in Dallas's Reunion Arena. "I know you can't endorse me. But I want you to know that I endorse you," Reagan famously said, in a speech laden with attacks on the ungodly policies of Democrats and plaudits for the sexual fundamentalists. Reagan's speech was the capstone of a two-day event convened by the Religious Roundtable to train pastors in the fine art of getting sympathetic voters to the polls without forfeiting their tax exemption for engaging in partisan activity. Reagan's endorsement seemed to extend to televangelist James Robison. "I'm sick and tired of hearing about all of the radicals and the perverts and the liberals and the leftists and the Communists coming out of the closet," the young, intense, dark-haired Robison bellowed from the stage, as Reagan sat there nodding, smiling, and applauding. "It's time for God's people to come out of the closet . . . . We'll either have a Hitler-type takeover, or Soviet domination or God is going to take over this country." Reagan's aides Michael Deaver and Ed Meese cringed backstage.

The press sat rapt at the feet of the colorful televangelists who vowed they were going to take back America. Meanwhile, many of the local campaigns targeted to the rank-and-file sexual fundamentalists passed by without their noticing. Schlafly's Eagle Forum and Weyrich's CSFC teamed up to sponsor training for campaign volunteers in four states in which they had targeted liberal Democratic senators for defeat. Veterans of Women Who Want to Be Women shifted from lobbying on issues like child care and the ERA to voter canvassing. Sandra Grogan Jeter and her mother, Betty, members of the Church of Christ, figured they knocked on 3,107 doors to get out the vote in Oklahoma. Not only did Reagan win the state handily, but an obscure state legislator, Don Nickles, beat several establishment candidates in the Republican primary and went on to serve in the U.S. Senate. Sixteen years later, Nickles would co-sponsor the Defense of Marriage Act, a federal law to ban same-sex marriage and deny federal recognition of legal same-sex marriages. The Sunday before Election Day, Christian Voice, whose mission was "a Christian majority in a Christian democracy," deluged church lobbies and parking lots with 5 x 7 index cards called "moral report cards," rating the opposing candidates. Christian Voice's PAC was the eighth largest of the 1980 election.

ON NOVEMBER 4, Reagan won 489 electoral votes, but only 50.7 percent of the popular vote. Turnout, at 52.6 percent, hit a record low for a presidential election; in effect, only one-quarter of eligible voters had chosen Reagan. In 19 states, Carter and Anderson's combined vote surpassed Reagan's. Forty percent of voters told the pollsters in the nation's first-ever exit poll, "It's time for a change."

But what kind of change? The popular vote and exit polls revealed neither a sharp turn right by the American public nor any clear mandate for conservatism. Exit polls revealed that dissatisfaction with Carter was the overriding issue influencing voters. Two-thirds of voters cited economic problems, such as inflation, unemployment, and taxes, as the most important reason for their vote. Reagan won three-quarters of voters who thought they were worse off financially. Only 10 percent of Reagan's supporters cited his conservatism as a reason for voting for him. Asked if they considered themselves liberal, conservative, or moderate, 36 percent of voters answered that they didn't know or hadn't thought about it—the highest proportion choosing that answer in the thirty-six years of polling on the question.

Political scientists and historians long ago reached a consensus that the election was a referendum on Carter, not a mandate for conservatism. Myths that would congeal later, such as the notion that Democrats voted for Reagan because of their cultural conservatism, have also been refuted. Rather, dissatisfaction with Carter's performance, particularly on the economy, was the major reason Democrats defected from their party. To the extent that the 1980 election marked a conservative shift in the electorate, it was on foreign policy and the role of government. Voters preferred Reagan's militaristic stance on foreign affairs, even if it might make war more likely. The percentage of Americans answering yes to the question, "Do you think the government is getting too powerful," was at a record high of 49 percent. Anti-tax measures modeled on California's Proposition 13 passed in twelve of the sixteen states in which they were on the ballot.

There was no good evidence that the election was a mandate for the antifeminism and cultural traditionalism of the sexual counterrevolution. Nothing in the exit polls indicated that voters had turned right on key tenets of women's rights. Indeed, the National Election Studies showed support for women having an equal role in society up 25 percent since the last presidential election. Gallup showed that a majority of Americans still favored the ERA. There was little polling yet on attitudes toward gays and lesbians, but Gallup polls around that time showed that Americans were becoming more, not less, supportive of gay civil rights. In 1982, a majority of 52 percent supported allowing gays and lesbians to serve in the military, and 59 percent thought that gays should have equal employment rights.

Nonetheless, the polarization on cultural issues that would become a defining feature of American life was already evident among three large groups of voters: women, professionals, and conservative Protestant fundamentalists. Reagan barely won a plurality of the women's vote. He only bested Carter by 2 points with women, even though his margin of victory among male voters was substantial. The 7-point spread between the male and female vote appeared to never have been so large, and led the president of the National Organization for Women to coin the term "gender gap." Observers speculated that Reagan's poor performance among women was due to the Republican Party's retreat on women's rights and Reagan's saber rattling. There is also evidence that Anderson supporters were primarily registering disapproval of the two culturally conservative major-party candidates. Anderson voters, who were disproportionately young, educated, economically well-off professionals, identified him to the left of Carter.

On the other end of the political spectrum, fundamentalists and evangelicals swung sharply away from Carter to Reagan. In 1976, evangelicals had turned out in higher numbers than ever before to give Carter a two-to-one margin over Ford; in 1980, they turned out at that same level, but voted by a two-to-one margin for Reagan. It wasn't that they had become more conservative. Rather, they had returned to politics to reverse the changes ushered in by the sexual revolution, and they had realized that Carter and the Democratic Party weren't conservative enough for them. Evangelicals also played a critical role in the defeat of all four senators targeted by the combined operations of the New Right and the sexual counterrevolution: Birch Bayh (Indiana), John Culver (Iowa), Frank Church (Idaho), and George McGovern (South Dakota). Bayh had been a Senate sponsor of the ERA. The ERA was on the ballot in Iowa. McGovern, of course, was McGovern.

"People were reluctant to come right out and admit they wanted to put women in their place," McGovern speculated after his defeat, "but there was a strong current of that running through much of what happened."

"THE RISING TIDES of the Pro-Family Movement and the Conservative Movement" lifted Reagan to victory, Schlafly triumphantly wrote in her December newsletter. Such a notion that Reagan's election had been a mandate for sexual counterrevolution was widely accepted among voters and leaders of the new Christian Right. Thus feeling emboldened, they moved immediately on their agenda when the new Congress convened in January. In the first weeks of the new session, Senator Jesse Helms and Representative Henry Hyde introduced an antiabortion constitutional amendment, defining life as beginning at conception, just as the GOP platform had promised. Only 10 percent of Americans shared that view. Representative Robert Dornan introduced an even more restrictive antiabortion amendment, one that could have been interpreted to outlaw the intrauterine device (IUD) and the Pill.

It is important to emphasize that abortion had *not* been on the original agenda of the Protestant sexual fundamentalists. Abortion only became a top-line issue for them after 1980. In 1973, when *Roe v. Wade* was decided, Protestant fundamentalists by and large were pro-choice, mainly because they had a healthy skepticism about government interference in matters of individual conscience. Indeed, the fundamentalist Southern Baptist Convention had voted in 1971 to support legal abortion in cases in which a pregnant woman was physically or emotionally endangered by her pregnancy. A small anti-abortion movement had been in existence since before *Roe*, yet it was almost entirely a top-down, official Catholic affair that was spearheaded by the National Conference of Catholic Bishops. (Despite Vatican dictates against abortion and birth control, a majority of Catholic Americans supported the right to abortion and ignored the Church on contraceptive use.) The Catholic Church scored an early victory in 1976, not by mass mobilization, but rather by tried-and-true insider politics. That year Hyde, who was Catholic, attached a rider to an appropriations bill prohibiting the use of federal funds for elective abortions. Most representatives were unwilling to vote against an important funding bill over a distraction, and the measure went into effect, albeit in a way that required renewal every year.

Abortion had first been introduced into the repertoire of the Protestant sexual fundamentalists by the 1977 Pro-Family Rally. The Catholic antiabortion group March for Life was a member of Hobbs's Pro-Family Forum, as were several antiabortion Catholics, most importantly Schlafly. Around the same time, yet separate from the burgeoning women's movement, three eminent evangelicals, Dr. C. Everett Koop, theologian Harold O. J. Brown, and philosopher Francis Schaeffer, began to work together on an antiabortion campaign. They hit the road in 1978 with an antiabortion film, *Whatever Happened to the Human Race*, to disabuse fundamentalists of their pro-choice views. One young evangelical woman who had volunteered for Carter would later credit that film with her conversion to right-wing activism. The 2012 GOP presidential candidate Michele Bachmann left the Democratic Party over Carter's support for legal abortion and, in 1980, signed up with Reagan. After volunteering on Reagan's campaign, she became a regular antiabortion protester, a so-called sidewalk counselor. That same year, 1978, Falwell preached his first sermon ever against abortion. Political calculation also seems to have figured in the emergence of abortion as a central concern in the sexual counterrevolution. Weyrich, himself a devout traditionalist Catholic, thought that abortion could be an effective wedge issue to move Catholic Democrats toward the Republican Party, and for that reason he favored adding the antiabortion plank to the Republican platform. At his first meeting with Falwell to form the Moral Majority, he encouraged Falwell to try to do the same with fundamentalist Southern Democrats.

Later, analysts of the Christian Right would trace its rise to a reaction about abortion. The sexual counterrevolution's grand design, however, was more far-reaching and ambitious than merely making abortion once again a criminal offense. In January, 1981, Christian Right Iowa Senator Roger Jepsen and Reagan's campaign chairman, Nevada Senator Paul Laxalt, introduced the Family Protection Act. It contained dozens of provisions restricting abortion, denying civil rights to gays and lesbians, undermining sex discrimination laws, requiring parental consent for teens to be provided sex education, birth control, or abortion, and turning the public schools over to religious fundamentalists. The proposed bill lavished tax breaks on Christian home-schoolers and families with stay-at-home mothers; it denied federal funds to any school that included any instruction which "would tend to denigrate, diminish or deny the role differences between the sexes as they have been historically understood in the United States." Taking a step onto even shakier constitutional ground, it denied federal benefits, including Social Security, to anyone who *advocated* that homosexuality was "an acceptable life style."

The bill was written largely by Connie Marshner, a top deputy to New Right mastermind Weyrich. Marshner, a young mother of four and orthodox Catholic, had worked for Weyrich at both the Heritage Foundation and the CSFC, and she had first discovered the fundamentalist women activists during the 1975 campaign to defeat federal child care legislation. Marshner worked closely with Hobbs on the 1977 rally and proved to be the key link between the male leaders of the New Right and the female leaders of the fundamentalist base. Marshner was not blind to the seeming contradiction of her job writing legislation and her defense of traditional womanhood.

Women's roles might change, Marshner thought, but not the "traditional value" that "the husband is the head of the family." In a speech to a gathering of sexual counterrevolutionaries, Marshner reasoned, even if the wife earned more than the husband, "the husband is still the head of the family. For that kind of woman, accepting her husband's authority might be more of a challenge, but if traditional values are to be preserved, it must be accepted." Marshner, who had joined the Republican Party Right in college, described the bill as a "strategic tool." The Family Protection Act nicely linked the economic priorities of the Washington elite with the cultural concerns of the base. Cutting government programs would keep the liberals from interfering in the traditional family and using taxpayer funds for abortion and to defend gay rights; tax cuts would go to traditional families with stay-at-home wives and children in private Christian schools.

ONLY EIGHTEEN MONTHS remained on the clock for ERA ratification when Reagan took office in January 1981. Four years earlier, in 1977, the National Organization for Women had intensified its campaign to win ratification. Although a majority of Americans favored the ERA, the amendment remained three states short of ratification as the original 1979 deadline loomed. The bipartisan Congressional Women's Caucus introduced a bill to extend the deadline, which Congress passed. In the years between the Houston conference and the 1980 election, NOW mobilized on the national level, putting on the largest feminist march in history, mounting boycotts of non-ratifying states, and keeping the Democratic Party on board. During this final sprint to win ERA ratification, membership in NOW quadrupled.

The anti-ERA movement, nonetheless, benefited from the division, disarray, and poor strategy of the pro-ERA side. The contest between Kennedy and Carter at the 1980 Democratic convention had shown that the Democratic Party was ambivalent about its commitment to women's rights; it remained a subject of intraparty factional conflict. Feminists also had themselves to blame. They had been slow to respond to the opposition to the ERA. Although they were adept at lobbying Congress and at national protest politics, they were lead-footed at the local and state level, where the votes of individual legislators were susceptible to lobbying from small numbers of their constituents.

On the state level, where the votes for ratification took place, the Antis had the organizing advantage. In 1978, the year feminists won an extension from Congress, three deep South states voted down the ERA, while several other states moved to rescind their previous ratification. Florida, where sexual fundamentalists had early on shown their political élan in Anita Bryant's antigay Save Our Children campaign, became a test of the strength of the two sides. During the legislature's 1978 debate, one Florida senator explained that he was recently born-again, hated "homosexuality, and anyway I want to see women on a pedestal." With several Democrats joining anti-ERA Republicans, the Florida Legislature voted down ERA ratification by a vote of 21 to 19.

Ultimately, after fundamentalists joined the anti-ERA, only two states ratified the amendment, the last in 1977. In 1982 the deadline expired with only 35 of the 38 required states having ratified the Equal Rights Amendment. Of the fifteen states that did not ratify the ERA, all had large fundamentalist or Mormon populations. Only Illinois did not exactly fit the mold. But many fundamentalists lived in the southern part of the state, it was Schlafly's home state, and the state constitution required a 60 percent supermajority for ratification of a federal constitutional amendment. Ironically, Illinois passed a state level ERA by majority vote during the time it rejected the federal ERA.

Paradoxically, legal advances during these years had undermined the most important rationale for the ERA, which had been that gender discrimination permeated federal, state, and local law. By the late 1970s, most of the practices the ERA was designed to make illegal had already been ruled illegal, and government programs were in force to rectify past discrimination and enforce the new laws designed to advance gender equity. There was only one form of gender discrimination that looked like it would survive a Supreme Court review: the exclusion of women from combat and from the military draft. Yet the overwhelming majority of American men and women wholeheartedly agreed with that view. It remained unthinkable circa 1980, except to staunch feminists, that women would be fully integrated into the armed services and deployed in combat zones.

In July, 1982, Schlafly threw a party to celebrate the demise of the ERA. As one fundamentalist woman from Arkansas told a sociologist at Schlafly's party, "I can't believe it didn't pass . . . They had all the votes for it but it was a miracle! God didn't want it to pass so He stopped it in various ways."

After the sexual counterrevolutionaries' victory on the ERA, Schlafly reoriented the Eagle Forum to focus on communism and abortion, while remaining the most prominent antifeminist in the nation. She periodically inveighed against policies to close the gender wage gap—an "elaborate scheme to devalue the blue collar man," she claimed. Lottie Beth Hobbs disbanded her Pro-Family Forum and quit Weyrich's new and secretive right-wing coordinating body, the Council for National Policy (CNP), because she found it to be a waste of time. She returned to her career as a Christian author, and started a newsletter to fight so-called secular humanism, a term popularized by Tim LaHaye as a shorthand for the evils perpetrated by liberals and Democrats in government. One of her pamphlets, "X-Rated Children's Books," inspired mothers in Fort Worth, Texas, to try to ban Judy Blume's coming-of-age novels. Another one, "Is Humanism Molesting Your Child?" made waves too. Beverly LaHaye's Concerned Women for America moved on from the fight to defeat the ERA to concentrate on criminalizing abortion, preserving discrimination against gays and lesbians, and providing legal defense for home-schooling Christians who objected to the teaching of evolution and sex education in the public schools.

RONALD REAGAN, A bona fide yet pragmatic conservative, was first and foremost committed to destroying the "evil empire" and making America safe for capitalism. In August 1981, inspired by supply-side economics, President Reagan won from Congress a major package of tax cuts. The legislation included a 23 percent reduction in marginal tax rates, slashing income tax rates on the wealthiest from 70 percent to 50 percent. To make up for the reduction in government revenue, deep cuts were imposed on domestic programs, especially those serving the poor. But the budget cuts did not make up for the loss of tax revenues, and the federal budget deficit began to grow at an unprecedented rate for peacetime. Compounding the deficit problem, the administration embarked on a five-year, $1.2 trillion program of building new weapons systems, including the so-called Star Wars missile defense system. By the end of Reagan's presidency, the federal debt would be three times greater than it had been when he took office.

With the economy in recession, unemployment rising, and revolutions and civil wars raging in Central America, the president had scant interest in fighting culture wars about sex, women, and gays. He essentially ignored the congressional doings of the elected sexual counterrevolutionaries. The Family Protection Act failed to make it out of committee, and the antiabortion measures fell far short of the votes needed for constitutional amendments. Morton Blackwell, Reagan's liaison to the religious right, later speculated that an administration that included more evangelicals would have won the vote on the antiabortion amendments.

Reagan, furthermore, understood that the GOP's repudiation of the ERA had been damaging with women voters, and he looked for ways to make amends. At the beginning of his presidency, the administration floated the idea of introducing a modified Equal Rights Amendment, one which would exempt women from the military draft. Schlafly quickly quashed that idea, correctly perceiving it would legitimize the idea of gender equality underpinning the ERA. Instead, the Reagan administration undertook two projects to review state laws and federal regulations and strike gender discrimination from the books. Schlafly opposed that too, but without success. The work went on.

Reagan's pragmatic cast of mind was in evidence in the summer of 1981, when he gained his first opportunity to nominate a Supreme Court justice. Reagan instructed his staff to find a woman jurist, just as he had promised Republican feminists he would, and Sandra Day O'Connor emerged as the administration's first choice. But O'Connor, a career lawyer, politician, and judge, had been a strong proponent of the ERA. As an Arizona state senator, she had also voted to liberalize the state's family planning and abortion laws (a stance supported by Arizona's native son Barry Goldwater).

So far, Reagan had been fobbing the fundamentalists off with empty promises, but the O'Connor nomination struck directly at a core goal to change the composition of the Supreme Court so as to overturn *Roe v. Wade*. Many Christian Right leaders saw O'Connor's nomination as a betrayal. Falwell thought it politically inexpedient to oppose the president, but the Moral Majority president, Cal Thomas, issued a statement claiming his members had been waiting patiently while the president focused on the economy, but this was "not a good signal." Connie Marshner took it as a message: "Goodbye, we don't need you." The Religious Roundtable sponsored an antiabortion and anti-O'Connor rally in Dallas. Robison, who had shared the stage with Reagan during the 1980 campaign, turned on the president with especial venom.

Reagan simply ignored the sexual fundamentalists. He liked O'Connor personally, and many mainstream conservatives held her in high regard. O'Connor won Senate confirmation by a vote of 99 to 0. For the first time in 200 years, a woman was on the Supreme Court, and Reagan could claim credit for it.

Reagan nevertheless realized that the sexual counterrevolutionaries who had helped him rise to the head of a divided Republican Party needed to be mollified. And so, through presidential executive orders, appointments to second-tier executive branch posts, and the creation of official but powerless commissions, Reagan ceded authority over women's issues, family planning, education, and civil rights to the sexual fundamentalists.

As the 1984 election approached and the Christian Right threatened they would bolt the GOP, Reagan accelerated his effort to keep them in the Republican column by taking action to limit abortion. In 1984, Alan Keyes, the administration's representative at the United Nations International Conference on Population, announced a new global antiabortion policy by executive order. (It became known as the Mexico City Policy, after the city where the conference was held.) The order denied funding to any group that provided advice, counseling, or information about abortions to its clients in developing countries. A 1961 law already prohibited U.S. funds from being used by international aid organizations to provide abortion. Reagan's executive order denied all U.S. aid to organizations that used nongovernmental funds to pay for abortion-related services anywhere in the world the organization had an office. Because it prevented doctors, nurses, and aid workers from even mentioning that abortion might be a legal option available elsewhere, the order became known among critics as the "global gag rule." The targets of Reagan's order were International Planned Parenthood and similar international groups that provided a wide range of women's health services including abortion or even simply told patients about abortion. Planned Parenthood and some others refused the governmental funds, rather than comply with the gag rule. Other groups accepted the funds and the conditions that went with them. The effect of the policy was not only to limit access to abortion but also to reduce funding for family planning, women's health, and the prevention of sexually transmitted diseases just as the international AIDS epidemic was gathering deadly force.

Reagan's cynical relationship to the sexual counterrevolutionaries was most disturbingly revealed in the president's response to the AIDS crisis. AIDS was first identified in 1982. At the time, the disease was concentrated among gay men, and hence it drove the sexual fundamentalists into a delirium of self-righteousness. "A man reaps what he sows," Falwell piously intoned. "If he sows in the field of his lower nature, he will reap from it a harvest of corruption." AIDS was just God's way of punishing gays for their depravity. Quarantine HIV-infected gays, Republican operatives in the New Right advised. Congress passed a law requiring immigrants to be tested for AIDS. Patrick Buchanan wrote that "nature is exacting an awful retribution," as the sexual revolution began to "devour its children."

Within the administration, senior cabinet officials issued warring policies while Reagan dithered. Secretary of Health and Human Services Margaret Heckler, formerly a founder of the Congressional Women's Caucus, moved funding around to support AIDS research and for that was lacerated by the Right. "A little less research and a little more quarantine might discourage homosexuals from . . . polluting millions of innocent victims," Howard Phillips recommended. William Bennett, Reagan's secretary of education, used the crisis as an opportunity to propagandize for chastity. His pamphlet *Sex Respect* suggested abstinence would make the problem go away. The Justice Department issued a ruling allowing businesses to discriminate against HIV-positive employees. In defiance of his own fundamentalist allies, C. Everett Koop, Reagan's surgeon general, recommended early sex education and the use of condoms to prevent the spread of AIDS. Schlafly and others viciously attacked him.

Reagan said nothing in public about the disease until September 1985, three years into the epidemic. When he did finally speak, he was asked if he would send his child to school with children who had AIDS. He answered, "I'm glad I'm not faced with that problem today and I can well understand the plight of the parents and how they feel about it . . . And yet medicine has not come forth unequivocally and said 'This we know for a fact, that it is safe.' And until they do I think we have to do the best we can with this problem. I can understand both sides of it." The Centers for Disease Control corrected him the next day. Reagan was acting on the advice of a young White House lawyer, John Roberts, who deleted the president's initial talking point that "as far as our best scientists have been able to determine, the AIDS virus is not transmitted through casual or routine contact." (Roberts would be named chief justice of the Supreme Court twenty years later by George W. Bush.) Reagan did not deliver a major speech on AIDS until April 1987, and even then, his position remained ambivalent. Six years had passed since AIDS had been identified. The delay in federal action, caused largely by Reagan's deference to the sexual fundamentalists, had powerfully affected the course of AIDS in America. In Britain, where the government had acted quickly to implement a public health campaign, the rate of infection was one-tenth of what it was in the United States. By the end of Reagan's presidency, nearly 50,000 Americans had died of AIDS. When faced with a choice, Reagan had hesitated to cross the sexual counter-revolutionaries. Tens of thousands of American men and women were sacrificed on his altar of political expediency.

With the exception of AIDS and the Mexico City Policy, most of Reagan's concessions to the sexual fundamentalists were little more than rhetorical gestures with no real-world impact. He called for passage of a school prayer amendment to the Constitution in a pre-election State of the Union Address. It failed to win two-thirds approval. The president invited Falwell and Robison to bless the Republican Party's 1984 convention, while also seeing to it that Tim LaHaye received a $1 million grant to encourage voter turnout. The administration impaneled a pornography commission to address the sexual counterrevolutionaries' contention that obscenity in popular culture was the cause of the American family's breakdown. Another powerless commission, the White House Working Group on the Family, concluded that big government undermined the family and that child care was bad for children. Gary Bauer, the so-called family policy czar, started the report with a word of archaic warning from President Theodore Roosevelt: "If the mother does not do her duty, there will either be no next generation, or a next generation that is worse than none at all."

It is true, of course, that the Reagan administration reduced government programs that were designed to advance gender equality, but not necessarily because he was himself antifeminist or seeking to appease the sexual fundamentalists. Some programs benefiting women were merely roadkill on Reagan's path to reverse fifty years of liberal Democratic governance. Other programs fell victim to the administration's racial calculations. In a not so subtle play to the white backlash, Clarence Thomas, at the Equal Employment Opportunity Commission, and Edwin Meese and William Bradford Reynolds, at the Justice Department, did not pursue cases of sex discrimination. Affirmative action, now cast as "reverse discrimination" in order to woo white men to the Republican Party, was abandoned. On the other hand, some programs for women were subject to all these right-wing currents at once. It is hardly surprising that welfare, which served poor, unmarried women with children born out of wedlock, who were disproportionately black, was under constant attack during the Reagan years.

Only on judicial appointments did the Reagan administration make a significant long-term investment in the sexual counter-revolution, albeit with mixed success. The administration adopted an ideological test for judicial nominees, something no president before had done, in pursuit of Meese's goal to institutionalize "the

Reagan revolution so it can't be set aside no matter what happens in future presidential elections." Intent on overturning *Roe v. Wade* and reversing other liberal court rulings, the Justice Department questioned potential nominees about their views on abortion, affirmative action, and other issues of interest to the Right. By the end of his two terms, Reagan had appointed nearly 400 conservatives to the federal bench, appointed Antonin Scalia to the Supreme Court, and elevated Supreme Court Justice William Rehnquist to chief justice. Reagan tried, but failed, to appoint Robert Bork to the Supreme Court. Bork had distinguished himself by crusading against *Griswold v. Connecticut*, the case that decriminalized birth control and articulated the right to privacy, the constitutional basis for *Roe v. Wade*. Bork made the mistake of talking freely about his reactionary views in his confirmation hearing.

THE MYTH THAT a conservative awakening swept Reagan into office, a myth with which his presidency began, was matched after he left office by the equally false myth of Reagan's overwhelming popularity. Reagan retired from the presidency with Americans viewing him favorably as an individual. But they were not too positive about his presidency. Over the eight years, on average, only 44 percent of Americans thought the country was on the right track. On the question of how he handled the economy, Reagan's approval rating topped 50 percent only once. (During his administration, there was a deficit every year and the national debt tripled.) On areas of governance at the heart of the so-called Reagan revolution, such as black civil rights, judicial nominations, and welfare, a majority of Americans disapproved of Reagan. Americans rated Reagan in the middle ranks of their presidents, alongside Lyndon B. Johnson and Bill Clinton, but below greats such as John F. Kennedy, Franklin D. Roosevelt, and Dwight D. Eisenhower. Democrats and Republicans held sharply divergent views of Reagan. Not until Barack Obama would Americans have such contrasting opinions about a president. Even Clinton provoked less polarized feelings.

Nor was the Reagan era a time when Americans turned right. Reagan won approval on foreign affairs, largely because his early

Cold War militarism evolved into sophisticated diplomacy, after Mikhail Gorbachev, the reformist leader of the Soviet Union, came to power. Together Reagan and Gorbachev negotiated an end to the Cold War and a significant reduction in the world's nuclear arsenal. On the issues of government's role in providing social services and regulating business, it is more accurate to say that Americans grew more self-interestedly ambivalent than that they turned right. They still wanted government to do a lot, but they didn't want to pay for it. Americans did not become more conservative on civil liberties or black civil rights. Likewise, there was a noticeable shift toward cultural progressivism. Even with the pervasive cultural backlash against feminism and feminists, Americans became far more supportive of gender equality. In 1983, six out of ten Americans reported that women's rights were important to them, a sharp increase from the decade before. The percentage of Americans stating unequivocally that "women should have an equal role with men in running business, industry and government" increased 25 percent over Reagan's years in office. On the right to abortion, Americans became more progressive, not more conservative. On the hottest hot button of them all, the place and rights of gays, the evidence mounted that Americans were becoming more supportive of equal civil rights every year.

The sexual counterrevolutionaries who helped lift Reagan to the head of the Republican Party made the mistake of believing Reagan's power and popularity depended on their favor. For eight years, the sexual counterrevolutionaries pressured Reagan to overreach, and he skillfully resisted. His successor would not be so adroit.

5

LOST

THE GOOD MEN and women of suburban Macomb County, Michigan, were the sort of people who were supposed to be Democrats. White men who had a high school education and worked blue-collar jobs in America's auto industry, they had risen into the middle class thanks to strong unions, postwar American prosperity, and generous social welfare programs enacted by Democratic politicians. The federal government had subsidized their suburban homes, built the highways on which they commuted and the public colleges their children attended, and paid out the Social Security and Medicare benefits on which they retired. Macomb was the most Catholic county in the nation, and since World War II the Catholics of Macomb had reliably voted the Democratic ticket.

Americans reelected Ronald Reagan by a landslide in 1984, with Democratic Macomb going for the Republican by a two-to-one margin. The question on every Democrat's' mind was why lifelong Democrats, like those in Macomb, had abandoned the Democratic Party. In March, 1985, the United Auto Workers (UAW) and the Michigan Democratic Party joined forces and sent a pollster to

Macomb to investigate what had gone wrong and to report back on what might be done to win the voters back.

The roughly 30 men and 10 housewives who participated in pollster Stanley B. Greenberg's Macomb County focus groups complained that the middle class had been squeezed, overtaxed to pay for welfare, and passed over for jobs they deserved in order to make room for unqualified minorities. They liked Reagan and his tough anti-government talk because, unlike Democrats, Reagan wouldn't "stomp on the average American white guy." When Robert F. Kennedy's support for "equal opportunity" was mentioned, one man exploded, "That's bullshit. No wonder they killed him." Common racist contentions that blacks were more prone to crime and whites were the real victims of the nation's racial conflict could be heard coming out of the mouths of former Democrats in the nation's most Catholic county—minus the studied coding of "law and order" or "welfare queens" that had given Presidents Nixon and Reagan cover. Greenberg set off a firestorm within the Democratic Party when he submitted his report containing transcripts of the uncensored racial resentment flowing off the tongues of these deserting Democrats.

Greenberg, a short, dark-haired, Ivy League professor, who had been influenced by the Italian Marxist theorist Antonio Gramsci, was like a walking advertisement for Republican claims that elitist, out-of-the-mainstream, not-quite-real Americans controlled the Democratic Party. When he walked into those focus groups in the Detroit suburbs as a paid consultant for the UAW, the participants might have looked at him and thought, "Man never did a day of real work in his life." (Greenberg had in fact worked a minimum-wage factory job to pay his way through college.) He was an unlikely messenger for racist Catholic working men. Born to Orthodox Jewish parents three days after the Nazis surrendered to U.S. forces in 1945, Greenberg had grown up outside Washington, D.C., where he attended one of the capital's first integrated high schools and was active in interracial campus politics. During graduate school at Harvard, he was drawn to electoral politics by Robert Kennedy, inspired by RFK's vision of black, brown, and white workers united. After teaching political science at Yale, Greenberg began to do polling for Democratic politicians in Connecticut. (He met his second wife, Rose DeLauro, on one of these campaigns. She would go on to represent Connecticut's 3rd congressional district and co-found the Congressional Progressive Caucus.) His Macomb report temporarily made him persona non grata at the Democratic National Committee. But in 1988, when he helped the Democratic candidate for the U.S. Senate, Connecticut Attorney General Joseph Lieberman, defeat a moderate Republican by running to his right, Greenberg started his ascent into the big leagues of Democratic Party politics.

Out of the encounter between Greenberg and the Macomb voters came a widely accepted idea about which voters Democrats had lost, why they had lost them, and what they must do to win them back. According to Greenberg, white ethnic working-class men, the backbone of the Democratic Party since Roosevelt's time, felt "betrayed" by the party's cultural extremism and elitism. So-called Reagan Democrats had gravitated to Ronald Reagan because the Republican Party embodied a truer expression of their cultural values. Greenberg's analysis, derived from the relatively new technique of focus groups, was an updated version of the commonly accepted postmortem on the 1972 landslide defeat. In short, death-by-McGoverniks, with a statistical gloss.

When Democrats failed to take back the presidency following Reagan's retirement in 1988, the McGovernik death-by-cultural-extremism theory was revived, the party's inner civil war rejoined, and the Democratic sexual counterrevolution renewed. From then on, the Democratic Party would be led astray by the distorted perceptions, evasions, and ambivalence seared into the consciousness of its leaders during the twelve years of Republican control of the White House that left Democrats lost in the political wilderness.

On the other side of the partisan divide, establishment Republicans were riding high. Their patience during the Reagan years had paid off, and they were back in power with George H. W. Bush. And, according to reliable experts and the wisdom of the political elite, the Christian Right was done and dead. Little did Republicans anticipate a resurgence of their own battles between the Right and mainstream conservatism. In fact, the sexual counterrevolutionaries weren't dead. They were instead organizing in the shadows, quietly taking up positions for a hostile takeover of the Grand Old Party.

THE DEMOCRATS' SEXUAL counterrevolution had changed significantly between 1972 and the end of the 1980s, in large part because many Democratic sexual counterrevolutionaries were either dead or gone. Fundamentalist white southern Democrats, and pockets of fundamentalists and orthodox Catholics in other regions, had marched off with the right wing into the GOP and the army of the Christian Right. Many older Democrats, who tended to be the most resistant to change, had passed away. There were few remaining leaders in the mold of George Meany, Richard Daley, and George Wallace—diehard counterrevolutionaries who would have been happy to return to an America before the sexual revolution and feminism had changed everything.

But the fact that Michael Dukakis could lose to Bush, who was not particularly popular among Republicans or the general public, set Democrats on a frantic search for the cause of their woes. The results of the 1988 election seemed to many Democrats and liberal political observers to confirm Greenberg's interpretation of the electoral perils of cultural progressivism. Two best-selling books by journalists, Thomas Edsall and E.J. Dionne, popularized the idea outside the Beltway. In *Chain Reaction*, Edsall and his wife and co-author Mary Edsall blamed the McGoverniks and their elitist heirs for the destruction of the Democratic majority. When blacks, the poor, and cultural progressives hijacked the party, their extremism had sparked a backlash and driven away the "mainstream" voter. The Edsalls were pretty convinced the Republican majority was permanent. Dionne, temperamentally hopeful and less prone to political delirium than many other anxious Democrats, had a somewhat different take in *Why Americans Hate Politics*. The voters of the "great American middle" were still economic populists (something the Edsalls disputed), but they were social moderates. They had come to hate politics because of partisan extremism: "In liberalism [the middle] saw a creed that demeaned its values; in conservatism it saw a doctrine that shortchanged its interests. To reengage members of this broad middle, liberals must show more respect for their values, and conservatives must pay more heed to their interests." By offering little to alleviate their material distress, in other words, the post-McGovern Democratic Party had left voters susceptible to the traditionalist baubles the GOP dangled before their eyes. The fault lay not with the ordinary voters who had deserted the party but with the McGovernik Democrats who had abandoned their own constituents and lost touch with the values of Middle America.

There was one problem, however, with this death-by-cultural-extremism consensus. Anecdotes abounded, but the statistical and historical research found little evidence that a reaction against a new kind of post-McGovern Democratic cultural elitism was the driving cause of the Democratic Party's losses. In 1984, political scientists Jerome Himmelstein and James A. McRae ran the results of the 1980 election through a sophisticated statistical analysis and concluded that the claim that Reagan voters were economic populists and social conservatives was false. Certainly, the GOP had issued appeals to a "supposedly disaffected group of lower to middle strata Democrats and nonvoters on the basis of social conservatism and anger at government," they wrote. However, "the actual New Republican constituency was not especially socially conservative, angry at government, or from the lower to middle strata." Republicans might have tried to peel voters away from Democrats by going right on values and populist on economics, but such "efforts were irrelevant to Reagan's success." Neither could Reagan's landslide reelection in 1984 be laid at the feet of disaffected union members, such as those in Macomb, according to a landmark study by three political scientists led by Robert Erikson of Columbia University, published the same year as Dionne and the Edsalls' popularization of the Reagan Democrat thesis. Union members, in fact, voted 21 percentage points more Democratic than their counterparts who were like them in every other way but who weren't union members. The award-winning historian Thomas Sugrue went to the source, the Detroit suburbs themselves, to excavate the history of these quintessential Reagan Democrats. It turned out the supposed "backlash" wasn't a backlash at all. Rather, these white voters had been cool to Democratic liberalism since the 1940s. Their defection

to Republican candidates wasn't provoked by the imagined excesses
of the sixties radicals and the McGoverniks but was "the culmina-
tion of more than two decades of simmering white discontent and
extensive antiliberal political organization."

No one questioned that Republicans were picking up former
Democratic voters; the fundamental question was why. Greenberg,
the Edsalls, Dionne, and many lesser-known Democratic sympa-
thizers believed they had found the cause of the Democrats' troubles
in the reaction of ordinary Democrats against the excesses of McGovernik liberalism. In fact, the reaction or, more aptly, the overreaction
was theirs. It was one that Democrats of every variety would repeat
again and again and again.

Meanwhile, the new rising force in the party, the centrist Democratic Leadership Council (DLC), came to the same conclusion that
the cultural progressives had alienated normal Americans and taken
the party down the road to ruin. "Liberal fundamentalism" and an
"adversarial stance toward mainstream moral and cultural values"
had caused Democrats to "lose touch with the American people,"
Elaine Kamarck and William Galston wrote from the DLC's Washington think tank shortly after Dukakis's defeat. "Mainstream"
voters had deserted the party, so they claimed, because Democrats
overtaxed the hard-working middle class, overindulged criminals
and the poor, overregulated business, and apologized too much for
American power.

Kamarck and Galston derided liberalism as "the politics of evasion," yet they indulged in some neat evasions of their own. Along
with the DLC's market-friendly program of business tax incentives,
middle-class tax cuts, and global free trade went a politically calculated intervention in the newly named Culture Wars. Endorsing a
favorite theory of the right-wing sexual counterrevolution, Galston
and Kamarck traced most of America's social ills to "family disintegration." They insisted that New Democrats, as proponents of the
DLC's centrist turn were calling themselves, believed in "the moral
and cultural values that most Americans share" and the "centrality
of the family"—by which they meant the still-married, two-parent,
heterosexual family. They assured everyone that the Democratic
Party could "recapture the middle . . . without losing its soul,"

simply by abandoning the "litmus tests of moral purity" on abortion and affirmative action for women and racial minorities.

At a moment when the sexual fundamentalists were denouncing child care as a socialist plot to destroy the traditional family, the DLC criticized a Democratic bill for comprehensive child care and offered instead only an increase in the child tax credit and increased funding for Head Start. It was a woefully inadequate measure, but exactly the one that the "pro-family" sexual fundamentalists who opposed wives working outside the home were pushing. The DLC's think tank also affirmed that it would be sound government policy to make it more difficult for couples with children to divorce.

At a moment when the Supreme Court seemed poised to overturn *Roe v. Wade*, the DLC promised to clamp down on child abductions before getting around to admitting it supported "rational family planning as an integral part of strengthening the American family." (Americans were in a panic about a supposed epidemic of kidnapping; the stories turned out to be mostly false and everyone gradually settled down.) In the midst of the AIDS crisis and within months of San Francisco adopting the nation's first domestic partnership law, the DLC said absolutely nothing about AIDS or the civil rights of its predominantly gay victims.

One would be hard pressed to discover in all this that most DLC'ers were themselves culturally progressive. They supported women's rights and believed in gender equality, took it for granted that mothers were permanently in the workforce, and favored reproductive rights. They were, however, loath to talk about their own fundamental values. Instead, they seemed always to be looking over their shoulder, afraid the GOP would steal a march on their exposed right flank.

The evasion was commonplace among the anxiety-ridden Democratic partisans during the presidency of George H. W. Bush. Liberals too were reluctant to broadcast their own cultural progressivism because they were convinced that the party's cultural agenda had driven the Democratic base away. In a scathing attack on the DLC, Robert Kuttner, a leader of the party's liberal faction and coeditor of *The American Prospect*, insisted that Democrats were not losing because the party was too "liberal" or "left-wing," as conventional wisdom and the DLC had it. Low voter turnout, not ideology, was killing them. By jettisoning their old New Deal populist economics, Democrats had failed to give low-income and working-class voters an incentive to vote. "The time is overdue to reclaim liberalism, without prefixes, qualifiers, or apologies," he declared in 1990, as the warring factions took up positions for the '92 presidential race. Well, maybe he was rash in promising no apologies. Just two years earlier, Kuttner had called for bowing to the prejudices of the so-called Reagan Democrats. "To the extent that liberal positions on social issues have any effect, they push white working-class voters to the Republican column," so best to say nothing about controversial cultural matters.

What was to be done? Simply put, get right with the white working man by going to the right on culture. The self-styled rescuers of the Democratic Party were understandably reluctant to confront the subterranean racial emotions of deserting Democratic voters, which were so painfully exposed by the Macomb reports. Principle and personal beliefs, for most Democratic leaders, argued against accommodating racism. It is only fair to acknowledge that, as in any social change of the magnitude brought on by the black freedom struggle, they faced a truly difficult dilemma. Yet we also have to acknowledge that their prescriptions for wooing the middle and the mainstream were shot through with racial code of the sort Democrats had excoriated when it came from the mouths of their Republican opponents. Responsibility. The moral superiority of the two-parent family. Rewards for working hard and playing by the rules. Punishment, not rehabilitation, for criminals. Democrats had welfare, crime, and affirmative action—and their specious cultural association with black Americans—on the brain.

The racial passions ignited during the sixties would ultimately be tamed by a combination of chance events and deeper trends. Redistricting after the 1990 Census completed the long-term shift of white Southerners into the Republican Party, thus unburdening Democrats of the albatross of southern white racism. Conversely, white migration from other parts of the nation into the South made the white south more Republican and more conservative but less obsessed with race. The new southern citizens voted Republican because of their views on national security, the economy, and the like, not because they resented the changes wrought by the Civil War or the civil rights movement. President Bill Clinton would prove adept at forging a multiracial Democratic Party no longer riven by racial tensions. On the GOP side, the Right had more critical battles to wage, even though the party would sometimes revert in moments of crisis to Nixon's southern strategy—as in the post-Obama Tea Party–GOP alliance of convenience.

As the Democrats' conflicts about race ebbed, those about sex, the sexes, and culture surged. With little more than anecdotal evidence to go on, Democrats across the political spectrum concluded that cultural progressivism was a losing proposition. Over at the DLC, they conceded family policy to the Right, while soft-pedaling their true beliefs in gender equality and sexual tolerance. New Deal liberals and economic populists faced a more difficult balancing act. More ambivalent about cultural, sexual, and gender issues to begin with, they took a more defensive posture and ended up in a less defensible place.

Stan Greenberg penned emblematic expressions of this liberal ambivalence. He longed for the return of simpler days, when politics was all about the economy, when working Americans voted for the party of the worker. Everything had gone wrong when the reformists, the McGoverniks, took over, he wrote in an article published in Kuttner's *The American Prospect*. Their "momentary ascendancy in the party," best captured, he thought, when they unseated Mayor Richard Daley's Chicago delegates to the 1972 Democratic convention, illustrated the declining power of the party's white, working-class base. "By opening up the new realm of cultural politics," the reformists "gave Republicans and conservatives new ways of winning votes from those with modest incomes and traditionalist values." With their skepticism of military interventions, support for "a welfare system that seemed to many an enemy of the family and of work, to promote dependency, illegitimacy, permissiveness," their support for "the court-led effort to expand rights to abortion and the rights of homosexuals, atheists, and others in a rights revolution," made it so that liberalism itself came "to be seen as a set of abstract, even exotic commitments of the well-educated, upper middle-class." The

McGoverniks and their heirs thus handed the Reaganite GOP a ready recruitment tool. Democrats lost because elitist Democrats ignored the material interests of the middle class to focus on the "exotic commitments" of culture, sex, and identity. Reagan Democrats, Greenberg surmised, "want to 'go home,' if only the party would prove hospitable." Greenberg was so insistent about his idea about a campaign centered on a "populist compact" for the "forgotten middle class" that his employer, Arkansas Governor Bill Clinton, begged him to leave him alone: "I've read this now three times. Enough."

The irony is that neither Greenberg nor any of the other hesitant liberal Democrats had any zeal for returning to traditional ways, as the GOP sexual counterrevolutionaries would have preferred. Many of these Democrats were culturally progressive themselves. Greenberg acknowledged that Democrats had "good reason to remain a secular party associated with the broad voter commitment to modernity and individual rights" and that running on abortion rights could be a winning issue. Greenberg's wife, Rose DeLauro, had been the executive director of EMILY's List, the political action committee devoted to electing pro-choice Democratic women. Kuttner approvingly reviewed a book on working women's unrelenting domestic duties, offering his own opinion that men would have to change to achieve true gender equity. These liberal and populist Democrats were however none too eager to broadcast their sexual liberalism and feminism in the political retail market. In fact, their solution to the Democrats' woes ran in the exact opposite direction.

DLC centrists and populist liberals joined battle in the Democrats' ongoing inner civil war over economic and foreign policy. Their battle on these issues would extend through the present, until early 2011 when the DLC closed shop and many of its veteran operatives took up new positions in Barack Obama's post-shellacking White House. Still, the centrists and the liberals agreed on one essential point. To woo back the estranged ordinary voter, Democrats would have to repent the McGovernik dalliances with feminism, gay civil rights, multiculturalism, and cultural progressivism. Middle America, so the theory went, had deserted the party, repelled by the Democrats' radical cultural agenda. The elitist McGoverniks and their successors had led the party down a yellow brick road, but now the soothsayers had arrived to pull aside the curtain and discover the practical path home. Lost in a delirium induced by political impotence, the Democratic sages failed to notice the GOP's own inner civil war, and its bearing on their own dubious plan for party revival.

TEN DAYS BEFORE the United States invaded Iraq in January 1991, *Time* magazine issued its Man of the Year award to "The Two George Bushes." It took moxie to insinuate that a sitting president with an 86 percent approval rating was either schizophrenic or two-faced. One of the George Bushes "finds a vision on the global stage; the other still displays none at home." Portraying Bush as a man who seemed remote from the cares of ordinary Americans, George J. Church wrote that the "strategy of deliberate drift burdens the nation with a host of problems that have become worse over the past decade."

Deliberate drift must have seemed the better part of valor for the unlikely executor of the Reagan legacy. Bush had never been adept at navigating the fractious assembly that had collected in the GOP: corporate executives, Main Street businessmen, hawkish internationalist realists and neoconservative crusaders, anti-immigrant isolationists, anti–civil rights white Southerners, libertarians, free market fundamentalists, and the sexual counterrevolutionaries. Anti-communism and the force of Reagan's personality had once kept these procrustean fellows obediently in line. Bush lacked the conservative credentials, as well as the political aptitude, to keep them from erupting.

By birth and temperament, the Texas transplant George Herbert Walker Bush was your typical old-school country club Republican: socially moderate, fiscally conservative, and hawkish on foreign affairs. After dutifully serving Reagan for eight years, Bush reconnected with the mainline Republican within, at least on issues that mattered to him. For all the rabble-rousing talk of a New World Order, and despite the hovering presence of his defense secretary, Dick Cheney, Bush worked honestly with the United Nations to assemble an international coalition to expel Iraq from its illegal occupation of Kuwait. (He even got the whole excellent adventure paid for by other countries.)

Yet Bush had learned the hard way that the sexual counterrevolutionaries and other right-wing interest groups must be appeased. He had been schooled by Reverend Pat Robertson, also a son of a U.S. senator and a man of privilege, who ran the Christian Broadcasting Network, one of the most influential Christian media enterprises in the nation. Robertson had initially held back when his fellow televangelists moved into politics with the Moral Majority, skeptical that there was anything to gain by giving up the well-established separation between church and state. The success of the Moral Majority made Robertson a convert to politics and ignited his ambition to be president himself, and he began political organizing through his popular show, *The 700 Club*. Through it, he built a grassroots operation at the precinct level and challenged Bush for the 1988 Republican nomination. When Robertson beat Bush in the Iowa caucus, Bush turned sharply right in New Hampshire and South Carolina to survive within the Republican primaries. Robertson never did particularly well after that and withdrew from the race a month after the March 8 Super Tuesday primaries. But he kept his supporters active, focusing them on the takeover of local and state Republican Party committees.

The equipoise Bush sought between doing right, from a modern Republican point of view, and serving the Right, was a chimera. Bush opposed restrictions on assault weapons, legislation spearheaded by the Reagan aide, James S. Brady, who had survived a shot to the head during the 1981 assassination attempt on Reagan. He supported a constitutional amendment banning flag burning. He changed his position on abortion. He opposed the Democrats' comprehensive child care bill, supported by the majority of Americans, in deference to the sexual fundamentalists. As today's governor of Virginia, Bob McDonnell, wrote at the time while studying for his master's degree at Pat Robertson's Regent University, federal funding of child care was wrong because it "would be used to subsidize a dynamic new trend of working women and feminists that is ultimately detrimental to the family." But enough was never enough. When Bush invited a few gays and lesbians to attend the White House signing ceremony for the 1990 Hate Crimes Statistics Act, the fundamentalist-controlled Southern Baptist Convention canceled the president's speech to their annual meeting.

The true rupture between Bush and the Right came after Bush raised taxes, breaking his famous promise "Read my lips, no new taxes." With Reagan's supply-side economics having produced a record budget-busting deficit of $221 billion, Bush followed traditional Republican verities of fiscal discipline and brokered a bipartisan deficit reduction deal. The package included tax increases as well as spending cuts. House Minority Whip Newt Gingrich and his confidant, market fundamentalist Grover Norquist, blasted the president. Norquist headed Americans for Tax Reform, a corporate-funded lobby created during the Reagan administration to push for tax cuts. (His antipathy to government had been bred in his bones. Grover's father would take the first lick of his young son's ice cream cones and say "That's the income tax." Then he would take a second lick and say, "That's the sales tax.") A founder of the Moral Majority, Richard Viguerie, published a scathing attack as the 1992 election drew near. It was titled *Lip Service: George Bush's Thirty-Year Battle with Conservatives*.

THE SEXUAL FUNDAMENTALISTS were particularly restive, having gained so little under Reagan's rule. And they had a new platform from which to challenge establishment Republicanism. At Bush's inauguration, Robertson met a 27-year-old PhD student with a baby face and the practiced smile of a Bible salesman, whose cool blue eyes hinted at the ruthless Machiavellian within. Ralph Reed had come up through the College Republicans in Georgia, and in 1983, he had been appointed by Jack Abramoff to succeed Grover Norquist as the group's D.C.-based executive director. That same year Reed had a religious awakening while out drinking one night and became a born-again Christian. When Robertson met him, Reed was a doctoral student at an elite university (Emory), finishing up a dissertation on social movements. Robertson pitched Reed on his idea for a new organization for the Christian Right. The Moral Majority had never been able to attract religious conservatives outside Falwell's Baptist network and had operated as a top down do-as-you're-told affair. Christians remained under siege, in Robertson's eyes, by a liberal conspiracy of feminists, gays, Democrats, and teachers' unions.

Robertson wanted to create something different—a grassroots, ecumenical movement of traditionalist Christians, who were willing to take over the Republican Party through collective political action from the ground up. In early 1989, Robertson put Reed in charge of the new Christian Coalition, in the process converting his personal campaign operations, with its supporters, into Christian Coalition chapters. "We decided the days of kowtowing to Republican presidents had come to an end," Reed explained.

Likewise, the antiabortion movement had adopted the new grassroots tactics of mass collective protest and militancy. In 1986, a used-car salesman from upstate New York, Randall Terry, founded Operation Rescue to stop the "business" of abortion. Operation Rescue demonstrators shut down abortion clinics during the 1988 Democratic convention in Atlanta and again in Los Angeles two years later. Guided by the motto "Abortion is murder, act like it's murder," Operation Rescue activists blocked clinic entrances and taunted the women trying to enter. They picketed the homes of abortion clinic staff and hounded their spouses and children at work and school. Terry even boasted that he hired private investigators to pry into the private lives of abortion providers. Terry claimed to be following in the footsteps of Martin Luther King, Jr., but his rhetoric belied King's religious commitment to nonviolent passive resistance. At one point, Terry was captured on videotape telling an audience of pro-lifers, "Pray that this doctor either be converted to God, or that calamity will strike him." Over the years, lone terrorists would be drawn like moths to Operation Rescue, with more than a little encouragement from Terry.

The grassroots women sexual fundamentalists, having defeated the ERA early in Reagan's presidency, had moved on to other threats to the Christian family and were impatient to criminalize abortion. Many participated in the clinic blockades, without necessarily signing on to the more incendiary comments made by Terry. Still, the most likely path for restricting abortion looked to run through the Supreme Court. A closely divided Court ruled in a 5–4 landmark decision in 1989, in *Webster v. Reproductive Health Services*, that restrictions placed on abortion by the state of Missouri were constitutional. The majority opinion opened the door to a challenge to *Roe* itself.

All that was required was for one antiabortion conservative to replace one liberal justice, a couple of whom were due to retire. In 1990, their first opportunity arose with Justice William Brennan's retirement. Bush appointed David Souter to the fill the seat. The Right had doubts about Souter, but Bush assured them Souter would be a safe conservative vote. (He turned out not to be.)

When the legendary liberal justice Thurgood Marshall announced his retirement in the spring of 1991, Bush had zero room left to maneuver. A few weeks before, Reagan appointee Sandra Day O'Connor had voted with the Court's liberal bloc in another abortion case, *Rust v. Sullivan*. O'Connor's vote confirmed the worst fears of the sexual counterrevolutionaries who had opposed her elevation to the court. Although the justices did not take up *Roe* in the case, it seemed likely O'Connor would uphold the right to legal abortion in the future. Indeed, the next year she wrote in an opinion upholding *Roe*, it is "our obligation to define the liberty of all, not to mandate our own moral code."

For Bush, it had been bad enough to alienate anti-tax zealots and the small number of votes they commanded by raising taxes. It would be quite another matter to flout the wishes of the millions of fundamentalist and Catholic sexual counterrevolutionaries praying for delivery from *Roe v. Wade*. Bush immediately signaled he was listening to the sexual fundamentalists when he passed over his preferred choice for the post, Solicitor General Kenneth Starr, and instead nominated Clarence Thomas. Although Starr had been raised in rural Texas, not far from the hub of Women Who Want to Be Women, and was himself the son of a strict Church of Christ lay minister, he had risen into the Republican Beltway elite. Starr's appointment was blocked by the Right, who doubted he could be counted on to be a reliable conservative vote.

Like Marshall, Thomas was African American, but that was about all they had in common. Marshall had been the liberal luminary of the Court; Thomas was a loyal foot soldier in conservative legal circles with a thin record of legal writing. Marshall had argued *Brown v. Board of Education* for the NAACP; Thomas had presided over the Reagan administration's rollback of civil rights enforcement when he served as head of the Equal Employment Opportunity Commission

(EEOC). The NAACP, other civil rights organizations, women's organizations, and abortion rights groups announced they would vigorously oppose his confirmation.

While Bush's advisers were preparing his Supreme Court appointee for confirmation hearings, the abortion wars heated up. Terry announced Operation Rescue was headed to Wichita, Kansas for a "Summer of Mercy," and he called on the residents of the city to join him. Wichita seemed an ideal target. Kansas had always had a large fundamentalist population with an enthusiasm for mixing religion and politics, and Wichita was where Dr. George Tiller operated a clinic, one of the few in the nation where late-term abortions were performed. (Tiller was the victim of many attacks and two assassination attempts; in 2009, an antiabortion zealot killed him while he was serving as an usher in his church.)

Wichita city officials alerted Operation Rescue that they and their disruptive tactics were not welcome. Actually, when Operation Rescue arrived, thousands of Wichita citizens joined in the delirium in the streets. Protesters threw themselves in front of cars to block traffic, charged clinics en masse trying to break down their doors, and surrounded cars and threatened the passengers trapped inside. Operation Rescue packed a local stadium for a rally with 25,000 abortion opponents. Pat Robertson preached to the crowd, while Kansans for Life circulated, not only signing up new members but also registering them to vote. The protests finally ended after 46 days and over 2,000 arrests, with Operation Rescue and the antiabortion movement emboldened. Although a poll showed 77 percent of Americans disapproved of the protests and support for legal abortion stable, it would be a month before abortion rights supporters mounted any counter-protest.

BUSH KEENLY WANTED to avoid a public airing of Thomas's views, which would invite investigation into the president's capitulation to his party's sexual counterrevolutionaries. As a solution, his advisers lighted on a stealth approach: say as little as possible about controversial issues, change the subject, and hope the audience took the bait. The White House knew that the hearings in the

Democratically controlled Senate would focus on Thomas's views on abortion and black civil rights. (Voting Rights Act enforcement, school desegregation, and affirmative action were particularly hot topics at the time.) They coached Thomas to rebuff questions about how he might vote, by saying it would be inappropriate to prejudge a case. If pressed about his advocacy against civil rights and reproductive rights, Thomas should say he was just an employee of the Reagan administration at the time doing what he was told. That of course would leave little to talk about, so to counter these lines of questioning, Thomas should redirect the debate to issues of character and encourage the Senate judiciary committee to explore his life story. Thomas, who had grown up in segregated Georgia under extreme poverty, had a compelling Horatio Alger story to tell. The Senate lapped it up. Judiciary committee chair Joseph Biden pronounced, "I am not so sure but that your roots are not more important in trying to predict what you will do if confirmed, than your writings."

It all went according to plan—until Anita Hill. On October 6, *Newsday* and National Public Radio reported that the judiciary committee had in its hands an affidavit from a former EEOC employee alleging that Thomas had sexually harassed her. On hearing the news, seven Congresswomen and a group of leaders of women's rights organizations literally marched on the Senate to demand a public hearing on the matter.

On October 11, 1991, nationally televised hearings in front of the all-male and all-white Senate judiciary committee began. Anita Hill, a University of Oklahoma law professor, testified about events that had taken place nearly a decade earlier. Hill had worked under Thomas at the EEOC during Reagan's first term. Sitting demurely at the microphone wearing a teal double-breasted suit buttoned up to her neckline, Hill described under oath how her boss, a man nominated to a lifetime appointment to the Supreme Court, had badgered her for dates, boasted of his sexual prowess and physique, made sexually explicit jokes, and graphically recounted scenes from pornographic films. Hill, like Thomas, was African American and a political conservative. In response, Thomas's Republican defenders insinuated that Hill was either insane, a lesbian, or frigid. Thomas, given the last word, deflected attention from the sexual and gender issues on the table and back to race. He accused the Senate of perpetrating "a high-tech lynching for uppity blacks who in any way deign to think for themselves." The Hill-Thomas hearings closed with no resolution about whether the allegations were true or even relevant to Thomas's qualification to sit on the Court. The Senate voted by a narrow margin of 52–48 to confirm Thomas to the Supreme Court, with 11 Democrats providing Thomas's margin of victory

For men and women of the Right, the Hill-Thomas hearings confirmed their image of feminists: man-hating, dour, hell-bent on taking the fun out of life, prone to see venal motives in the mildest of jokes. For a decade, women had been told all their problems stemmed from feminism. Women, at least those not already lined up with the Right and the sexual counterrevolution, weren't buying that narrative anymore (if they ever had). They took away from the episode a different lesson about the relations between the sexes in contemporary America—more 1991's *Thelma and Louise* than 1987's *Fatal Attraction*. Sexual harassment complaints flooded into the EEOC, participation in women's rights organizations surged, and donations poured in to women's political organizations such as EMILY's List. It might not be wise, a lot of women were coming to realize, to leave all the nation's business up to a nearly all-male Congress and a president so disdainful of women's concerns.

Bush had hoped Thomas's appointment would satisfy the sexual counterrevolutionaries in the GOP base and bring them over to his side in silent appreciation. Instead, Thomas's confirmation, given added piquancy by their defeat of Democratic feminists, emboldened them, just as Operation Rescue's victory in Kansas seemed to confirm that extremism in the face of sin was political virtue. Those takeaway lessons could not have been worse for Bush, as it set the stage for the GOP base to overreach. Nor could it have come at a worse time. One week before the Hill-Thomas hearings began, the most gifted politician to hit America since Reagan announced that he was running for president.

———————

6

IT'S FEMINISM, STUPID

O N OCTOBER 3, 1991, William Jefferson Clinton
announced his candidacy for the presidency of the United
States. Clinton was the governor of a small southern state
and only 45 years old, and that he promised to be a contender was
taken as one more depressing example of the sorry state of the
Democratic Party after twelve years of Republican control of the
White House. Spooked by President George H. W. Bush's record-
shattering approval ratings in the immediate aftermath of the first
Gulf War, not one Democrat of national standing had entered the
presidential race. Dick Gephardt, Mario Cuomo, Al Gore, and other
notables all seemed to prefer to stay in the office they already held,
rather than face the daunting task of running against a popular
incumbent president. Little did they anticipate that by the time of
the 1992 presidential election, that incumbent would have to defend
a record that included two years of recession, 4.5 million American
jobs lost, an unemployment rate of 7.5 percent, and the first-ever
case of a jobless economic recovery.

Fortunately for Democrats, Clinton was a Whitmanesque figure,
able to contain multitudes in his burning impatience to be president

of the United States. Clinton had just that year stepped down as the head of the Democratic Leadership Council, and as the DLC advised, he listed to the center on crime, free trade, and welfare. He then blithely ignored the DLC's advice about a similar bolt to the middle on social and cultural issues. With his wife and lifelong political partner, Hillary Rodham Clinton, at his side, Clinton avidly courted working women and feminists, became the first candidate to uncon- ditionally welcome gays and lesbians into the Democratic family, and devoted his nominating convention in New York City to a cel- ebration of the party's unequivocal commitment to women's political power and reproductive rights.

Clinton, by positioning himself as a cultural progressive, put the death-by-cultural-extremism theory of Democratic collapse to a real- world test. After Clinton won election with the largest gender gap ever recorded and an unprecedented number of women won election to Congress, the press dubbed 1992 "The Year of the Woman." It was one of the few occasions when the snap judgment of headline writers would later be confirmed by methodical statistical analysis—even though the truth of it would be lost in historical memory to exagger- ated claims that voters cared only about "the economy, stupid." The Reagan revolution ended by a feminist, pro-choice, pro-gay, white male Southern Democrat? This was hardly the path out of the wil- derness veteran Democratic strategists had mapped.

To his detractors, Clinton was a creature and creation of the DLC, perhaps more ambitious than talented. In the months leading up to the Democratic primary campaign, public feuds between Clinton and the titular leaders of the liberal wing of the party, Rev- erend Jesse Jackson and New York Governor Mario Cuomo, seemed to give credence to the image of Clinton as a DLC company man. Anyone watching carefully, however, could discern that Clinton could not be reduced to such a facile caricature. Clinton's campaign team included not only DLC'ers but also representatives from all the other factions, including former Jackson supporters and bona fide lib- erals. Stan Greenberg, who straddled the division between the DLC and liberals, was part of Clinton's inner circle, and his catchphrase about the "forgotten middle class" would become the touchstone of the campaign. Nor was Clinton's relationship with the DLC quite what it seemed. Al From, the DLC's political mastermind, who had swooned that Clinton "was the most attractive political animal he had seen in his life," complained bitterly that Clinton wouldn't answer his phone calls.

By January, having spent just three months on the campaign trail, Clinton was favored to win the nomination, the most liberal labor union in the country had endorsed him, and everybody was scrambling to claim Clinton as their own. Clinton's speeches in Iowa to rank-and-file Democrats had revealed his enormous talent as a politician, his mastery of the issues, and his crowd-pleasing charisma.

Clinton, born in the segregated town of Hope, Arkansas, to a recently widowed mother, thought of himself as a child of the idealistic New Frontier and the great black freedom struggle. He always claimed that a high school handshake with President John F. Kennedy had inspired him to public service. But to the Right and his many enemies in Arkansas, Clinton was an evil spawn from the other end of the sixties: "a queer-mongering, whore-hopping adulterer, a baby-killing, draft-dodging, dope-tolerating, lying, two-faced, treasonist activist," in the inimitable words of Arkansas judge, unreconstructed segregationist, and professional Clinton-hunter Jim Johnson.

"When you listen to the Clinton haters . . . you notice the same not-very-subliminal resentment of someone who seems to be getting a lot," Texas journalist Molly Ivins observed. "Clinton is not a manly man—he's no John Wayne—and is clearly in touch with his feminine side, as they say in pop psychology. That too touches off some kind of rage with at least a portion of the populace. I have no expertise in American sexual hang-ups, I don't know what it means, I just know it's there."

Bill Clinton and sex. The subject, as the world would learn, just wouldn't go away.

One month before the critical New Hampshire primary, Clinton's candidacy nearly ran off the rails after a tabloid, the *National Enquirer*, reported Clinton's alleged long-running affair with Gennifer Flowers, in a story sold to them (literally) by Arkansans seeking profit and nursing a grudge against their governor.

Flowers's charges put Clinton up against his most unpredictable opponent: himself. In that distant and quaint world of 1992, one year after the World Wide Web was opened for commercial use and four years before Fox News went on the air, professional journalists had qualms about circulating tabloid rumors regarding the private lives of public figures. Cokie Roberts of NPR, who helped break the Anita Hill story, was one of many who found an angle to transubstantiate the lurid rumors into hard news. While moderating a debate between the Democratic candidates, she asked Clinton if he wasn't worried that his womanizing would drive away women voters.

It was a pointed question, because Clinton had been actively seeking the women's vote, the feminist vote, and the pro-choice vote. He had promised that he would defend reproductive rights, fund child care programs, and force "deadbeat dads" to pay child support. His remarkably detailed policy platform included a host of other measures attractive to working women, working mothers, and working dual-earner families struggling to find adequate child care even as their wages stagnated. Bill's advantage with woman voters also depended on Hillary, a public figure in her own right, a leading national advocate for families and children, and a standard-bearer of her generation's politics—and its feminism. (Her commencement speech to the Wellesley Class of 1969 had earned Hillary, at age 21, a feature photo in *Life* magazine.) From the start of the campaign, Clinton had famously promised the American people a two-for-one deal. If he were elected, he promised, Americans would get the brilliant and dedicated Hillary in the bargain.

Rumors of infidelity threatened to nullify everything Bill had been working toward his entire life. Hillary rescued him, as she had before and would do again. On the most respected news show in the nation, *60 Minutes*, immediately following the most watched television show of the year, Super Bowl XXVI, the Clintons submitted to an interview about the Flowers accusations.

Nothing remotely like this had ever happened in an American political campaign. For decades the press had observed an unwritten rule that a politician's extramarital affairs and sexual proclivities were private matters and not subject to reporting. Things had begun to break down in the 1988 election, when Democratic candidate and former McGovern campaign manager Gary Hart, now a senator from Colorado, dared the press to follow him. They did, and found him in Bimini on a yacht called *Monkey Business* with his mistress sitting on his lap. The Hill-Thomas hearings, on one end, and the emergence of new media such as talk radio and cable TV, also eroded the old journalistic customs of discretion.

"You've said that your marriage has had problems," Steve Croft asked. "What do you mean by that? Does that mean you were separated . . . that you contemplated divorce . . . committed adultery?"

"I think the American people know what that, the whole range of things can mean," Clinton answered. "I'm not prepared tonight to say that any married couple should ever discuss that with anyone but themselves."

Pressed again, Clinton remained calm. "Look, Steve . . . I have acknowledged wrongdoing. I have acknowledged causing pain in my marriage. I have said things to you tonight and to the American people from the beginning that no American politician ever has. I think most Americans that are watching this tonight they'll know what we're saying, they'll get it, and they'll feel that we've been more candid . . . and what the press has to decide is are we going to engage in a game of gotcha?"

Next to him on the beige sofa, her shoulder lightly grazing his, Hillary sat wearing a green pantsuit and headband, nodding with a grim yet self-possessed expression. Bill confided in her, she explained, and she herself frequently talked to the women who found themselves named as one of Bill's lovers in the tabloids. She strongly implied, with lawyerly deniability, that Arkansas's female citizens were being pressured by Bill's enemies to invent stories of the governor's sexual predation.

The famous *60 Minutes* interview would go down in popular memory as exemplary of Hillary's cold calculation, in part thanks to a nasty bit of profile journalism published two months later, in which Gail Sheehy portrayed Hillary as the campaign's Svengali. Hillary did form part of the inner circle of advisers and, with pollster Stan Greenberg and consultant Dick Morris, helped manage the campaign's admired quick-response "war room" operation that they created after the first attacks aired. But the idea for the *60 Minutes* interview had been concocted by the Clintons' media advisers as a desperate measure to save their candidate—who they were convinced was going down no matter what they did. Both Bill and Hillary had resisted doing it, and Hillary had feared she could not make it through the televised interview without crying.

The risky *60 Minutes* gambit succeeded. Opinion polls showed that Americans agreed with the Clintons that whatever might have happened, it was not an appropriate subject for political debate. (Voters would be absolutely consistent on this point through the ensuing eight years.) Clinton recovered momentum and the Flowers stories receded. Then another damaging report hit. Two weeks before the New Hampshire primary the *Wall Street Journal* published allegations that Clinton had evaded the draft in the Vietnam War. (Another Arkansan and Clinton nemesis, failed politico Cliff Jackson, was the source for this report.) Like many of the so-called scandals of the Clinton years, there was less to the charge than met the eye. Observers in the know declared the double hit would destroy Clinton. The campaign team agreed. Again they were wrong. Clinton finished second in the New Hampshire primary and declared himself the "Comeback Kid."

Then just before Super Tuesday, Jeff Gerth of the *New York Times* broke a story raising questions about a possible conflict of interest in an investment the Clintons' had made in a real estate venture called Whitewater. (Eight years later, after several -'gates, the expenditure of $100 million in taxpayer funds, countless congressional hearings, and impeachment, the third independent counsel on the case concluded that there was no evidence to prosecute the Clintons in any of the cases and shut down the investigation.) Voters were nonplussed. Clinton won a slew of southern primaries and emerged as the likely nominee. Over the next few weeks, the Democratic candidates who were considered credible general election contenders dropped out of the race, leaving only the protest candidate Jerry Brown to thwart Clinton's nomination.

The New Hampshire comeback, and the subsequent allegations of corruption, confirmed that the Democratic primary had been winnowed down to Clinton v. Clinton.

. . .

THEN THE CAMPAIGN took on a new twist. The candidate was no longer his own worst enemy. His wife was.

In a televised debate in mid-March two days before the Illinois primary, Brown misrepresented a *Washington Post* examination of Hillary's legal work to insinuate that Governor Clinton had funneled state business to her law firm. Clinton erupted, angrily denouncing Brown, who "with his family wealth and $1500 suit, makes a lying accusation about my wife."

At a campaign stop the next morning in a Chicago coffee shop, ace reporter Andrea Mitchell asked Hillary about her law firm's work for state agencies while her husband was governor. Was it ethical? Fair question.

"I suppose I could have stayed home, baked cookies, and had teas. But what I decided to do was to fulfill my profession." Hillary went on, "The work that I've done as a professional . . . as a public advocate, has been aimed in part to assure that women can make the choices that they could make—whether it's a full-time career, full-time motherhood, some combination, depending on what stage of life they are at—and I think that is still difficult for people to understand right now, that it is a generational change."

Hillary's rumination on the difficult choices faced by American women was clipped to its most damaging sound bite, her cookies-and-tea phrase recycled in almost every major news outlet. No comment was necessary—Hillary obviously disdained stay-at-home mothers. Richard Nixon advised Bill to be wary: "If the wife comes on looking too strong and intelligent, it makes the husband look like a wimp." (*Schadenfreude* is sweet. Hillary had served as a staff attorney on the House Judiciary Committee that prepared impeachment charges against Nixon.)

On his path to frontrunner status, Clinton had boasted, "Buy one, get one free." Now his aides were telling him to rein her in. An internal campaign memo warned that Hillary was perceived as power-hungry, and they had to soften her image before it destroyed him. Stage events, they suggested "where Bill and Hillary can go on dates with the American people."

Things were about to get much worse for Hillary. In early April, a few days before the New York primary, *Vanity Fair* released Gail

Sheehy's long profile article, titled menacingly, "What Hillary Wants." The juiciest scoop of the piece had Hillary complaining about the press's double standard. Why didn't they report rumors about President Bush's affair with a certain Jennifer, even though it was an open secret in the capital?

Yet the heart of the article wasn't this gotcha, but rather its enduring portrait of the unlikable Hillary Rodham Clinton.

"One can detect the calculation" in her eyes, wrote Sheehy.

"The public smile is practiced; the small frown establishes an air of superiority; her hair looks lifelessly doll-like," she continued with a clichéd flourish, character-assassination-by-hairstyle.

In Sheehy's hands, Hillary was part Lady Macbeth, part dominatrix; she was at once pathologically dependent on and passively aggressive against her long-cheating husband. The American people should know that Bill depended on her financially and surrounded himself with "exceptionally, strong-willed, capable women." Bill and Hillary have been "a political team for twenty years." Voter beware. "Now they are, despite protestations to the contrary, *co-candidates* for president of the United States."

Indeed, a co-presidency was potentially troubling. A marital partnership was one thing, but how could the unelected spouse be held accountable? Bill and Hillary's professional closeness, combined with their predilection for secrecy and skill with the counterattack, worried their supporters as well as their detractors. The issue would bedevil Hillary in her own bid for the presidency sixteen years later: would she be able to control Bill? Who would be in charge? It was a perfectly reasonable concern, about which rational people across the political spectrum could reasonably disagree.

To Sheehy, however, a co-presidency was something far more sinister. A sapping of the nation's vital powers, with the nation led by an emasculated president whose strings would be pulled by a cabal of harridans. Respectable antifeminism and Hillary-hating had entered mainstream popular culture, introduced in the collaboration of a best-selling female author and a cosmopolitan, liberal magazine.

Vanity Fair and Sheehy might claim they were only reporting on public opinion. Instead, it looked like they were trying to shape it. "Legitimate questions have been raised about Mrs. Clinton that deserve closer scrutiny," wrote the editors of the *Christian Science Monitor*. "But something deeper than customary political scandal mongering is swirling around Hillary Clinton, something that may have elements of an ugly antifeminist backlash"

Glowing press reports of the favorable impression Hillary made on the campaign trail suggests that voters considered Hillary, and the role she had taken on, an advance for American women. One Republican woman in conservative San Diego told a reporter, "She was great. Informative. Articulate." Hillary had her vote. Bill, not so sure. At a cookout in Beaver, Pennsylvania, another woman told a reporter her admiration for Hillary stemmed from her appreciation of her daughters, who were both working mothers. "I'm proud of them," she said. "I think we need more women like Mrs. Clinton, a lot more women, and we'd have this country in great shape." One male opinion writer observed, "Political wives traditionally play the role of 'supporter,' something quite different from 'partner.' It is time we saw our perception of that role change toward a much healthier perspective." Lisa Caputo, Hillary's press secretary, was interviewed after the election. Hadn't it been hard, she was asked, to work for a woman who provoked so much hostility? Caputo, who traveled with Hillary and witnessed her at almost every campaign event, replied that in her estimation, the press manufactured a sentiment that didn't exist for the average voter.

"Hillary represents many of my generation . . . She represents the juggling act . . . of being a mother and having a career that so many women across the country are now doing, either by choice or not by choice, but forced to do so economically," she said. The press corps "wants to make a mountain out of a molehill strictly because there's never been a woman who's had a career in the White House and been a mother." The media "hasn't been able to accept the generational change." But voters had.

"I DOUBT SHE'LL be the new Willie Horton, but I imagine some Republicans will give it their best shot," a University of Texas historian of First Ladies predicted.

Many voters listened to Bill and Hillary on the stump and came to the conclusion that Democrats understood the real American family. Republicans wagered they could make electoral hay by portraying Hillary as a radical feminist out to destroy the American family as they defined it. Hillary would provide a convenient foil for Republican sexual counterrevolutionaries in their ongoing war against Republican moderates and infidel Democrats alike.

"There is little doubt that Hillary Clinton, the cookie monster who mocks stay-at-home, cookie-baking mothers, might conduct some other crucifixions if she became a de facto president," conservative evangelical columnist and former head of the Moral Majority Cal Thomas wrote: "As she said, 'If you elect Bill, you get me.' Given her agenda, we can do without both." Randall Terry of Operation Rescue denounced Hillary as "a Jezebel" for her "hard-core pro-abortion stand." The stakes, he contended, were enormous. "The United States is locked in a war for allegiance, between God's laws and the laws of hedonism and paganism, made by man."

The brewing family-values holy war received the official stamp of approval when Bush's flailing reelection campaign grabbed hold of the lifeline offered by the sexual counterrevolution. The first inkling came when Bush consultant and future Fox News CEO Roger Ailes twisted Hillary's legal writings about children's rights to assert that she thought children should be able to sue their parents. In May 1992, Vice President Dan Quayle, acting on advice of his chief of staff, William Kristol, then doubled-down and blamed the devastating Los Angeles riots of the previous month on a TV sitcom character. That season, the story line of the popular show *Murphy Brown* had the title character, played by Candice Bergen, accidentally getting pregnant by her ex-husband, deciding against either abortion or marriage, and choosing to raise her baby on her own. Quayle declaimed against Hollywood elitists and Murphy Brown for peddling the immoral idea that single motherhood was "just another lifestyle choice." According to Quayle, working off Kristol's advice, the riots were caused not by endemic poverty or police brutality but by a "poverty of values," exemplified by a fictional television character. Bush's approval rating, which had been 65 percent the week Clinton announced his candidacy in October 1991, plunged to 39 percent.

THE ANTIFEMINIST BACKLASH of the Reagan years was boomeranging on its makers. On no subject was the reaction against the sexual counterrevolutionaries' overreach clearer than on abortion, but the GOP seemed oblivious to the sentiments of a sizable portion of the electorate.

On April 5, two days before the critical New York primary, in which Jerry Brown was making a surprisingly strong showing against Clinton, upwards of 1 million women, men, and children marched in Washington, D.C., in the largest ever demonstration in favor of reproductive freedom. "We're not talking to the Court," Kate Michelman, head of the National Abortion Rights Action League, announced from the stage. "We don't trust the Court. We're talking to George Bush and every officeholder and every office seeker." Democratic candidates were already on the same page, familiar with the opinions of American women after the Hill-Thomas hearings and the Supreme Court ruling in the 1989 *Webster* case, which had put *Roe v. Wade* at risk. Both candidates interrupted their New York campaign to attend the rally in D.C. The march was timed to coincide with oral arguments in *Planned Parenthood v. Casey*, a case in which the Supreme Court would likely reconsider *Roe v. Wade* in the course of reviewing the constitutionality of Pennsylvania's restrictions on abortion. One of the provisions of that bill required women to obtain their husband's consent before getting an abortion. The next day, Bush's solicitor general, Kenneth W. Starr, urged the Supreme Court to uphold the Pennsylvania law and to overturn *Roe v. Wade*. On April 7, Clinton won the New York primary, for all intents and purposes wrapping up the Democratic nomination.

Clinton, with Hillary's able assistance, had ignored everyone's advice to retreat to the center on cultural issues. He had not stayed quiet about women's concerns, women's rights, and the hot-button topic of abortion. Clinton forged ahead boldly on an even more controversial subject. On May 17, Clinton spoke at a fundraiser in Los Angeles held by gays and lesbians. The attendees expected the usual Democratic pabulum of faint praise and requests for patience. They were stunned by what they got. Clinton said he would happily give up his presidential ambition if by doing so he could end the AIDS plague. By all accounts of eyewitnesses, he was utterly sincere. Gay activists to this day remember that night as a political tipping point in the relationship between gays and the Democratic Party.

OPPONENTS OF LEGAL abortion had also ramped up for the campaign season, no doubt to keep Bush and the Republican Party dedicated to their cause. Operation Rescue announced it would hold its "Spring of Mercy" in Buffalo, New York, Randall Terry's home turf in conservative upstate New York. It was Operation Rescue's most highly anticipated campaign after their victory in Wichita the previous year. Again most city leaders told Operation Rescue that they were not welcome, but this time so did the League of Women Voters and many local religious groups. (Only the Democratic mayor disagreed and willfully invited Operation Rescue to town, against everyone else's expressed desire.) A judge issued an injunction prohibiting the blocking of clinic entrances, while abortion rights supporters prepared counter-demonstrations and clinic escorts to be ready to go on day one.

The press, anticipating another Wichita, swarmed into Buffalo, expecting another dramatic showdown about babies and when life began. And there they uncovered the antifeminist roots of the antiabortion movement.

Randall Terry was confronted by an NBC *Today* show reporter, who had spoken with some of Terry's relatives who were among the pro-choice counter-demonstrators. "Your aunts say that they are appalled that you are antifeminist because you were raised at the knee of feminists."

On camera, Terry answered, "Radical feminism and all that that includes, child killing, lesbianism, rebellion against authority, is evil."

The interview left the impression that Terry was driven as much by a delirious hatred of feminists and feminism as he was by any concern for human life.

Operation Rescue failed in Buffalo to shut down any clinics, prevent any abortions, or win substantial local support. After ten days of protests, the media moved on, itself a testament to Terry's defeat.

Local Operation Rescue leaders said they were dispirited by their failure. National leaders denied it. The local leaders called a halt to the protests.

As one sign greeting Operation Rescue in Buffalo put it, "You're not in Kansas anymore." Operation Rescue's mistake, and the media's as well, had been to view Kansas as a microcosm of America. Kansas was just one slice of America, and a not very representative one at that. Like the southern states of the old Confederacy it bordered, its population was disproportionately evangelical. Like the so-called heartland states to its west, it was disproportionately white and rural. Operation Rescue's 1991 Wichita protests had been instrumental in flipping the Kansas GOP from moderate to conservative control. But the national consensus was crystal clear even then. A few weeks after those protests ended, a Gallup poll found 77 percent disapproving of Operation Rescue's actions and 57 percent opposed to the reversal of *Roe*. Wichita had been the apogee of Operation Rescue, its success a product of a hospitable local environment and a complacent national abortion rights movement. Buffalo and D.C. were the new normal in the abortion wars: the two sides politically mobilized, advantage pro-choice.

"FRANKLY, I AM fed up with politicians in Washington lecturing the rest of us about family values," Clinton said a few minutes into his acceptance speech on the last night of the Democratic Convention in July.

"I want an America where family values live in our actions, not just in our speeches. An America that includes every family. Every traditional family and every extended family. Every two-parent family. Every single-parent family. And every foster family. Every family."

Clinton's campaign staff would soon be under orders that the main issue was the economy. The now legendary slogan, "It's the economy, stupid," was posted in campaign headquarters to remind them. Yet Clinton was a master orator as well as a sophisticated thinker, and he crafted a compelling narrative of why progressive family values, "putting people first," and progress for "the forgotten middle class" went hand in hand.

Indeed, the Democratic convention played like a four-day advertisement for progressive family values and Democratic women's emerging political power. The first night of the convention, the six Democratic women running for the U.S. Senate spoke. (Five of the six would win their contests.) Day two, Clinton spoke to the women's caucus, in his single public appearance prior to his closing night acceptance speech. The television cameras were at the meeting to broadcast Clinton describing himself as "the son of a single mother, the husband of a working wife," and "the father of a daughter who wants to build space stations in the sky." He reiterated his support for reproductive freedom and women's advancement, and noted, "building up women does not diminish men." That night, when the platform was officially approved, six pro-choice *Republican* women took the podium to endorse Clinton, with the explanation, "We have not abandoned our party. George Bush has abandoned us." Also speaking that night was Bob Hattoy, a gay man who had been diagnosed a few weeks before the convention with AIDS. He and the mother of an HIV-infected child denounced the Reagan-Bush administrations for neglecting AIDS research because of its hostility toward its mostly gay victims. Meanwhile antiabortion Pennsylvania Governor Robert P. Casey groused that Texas Governor Ann Richards, the chair of the convention, wouldn't allow him to denounce abortion from the podium.

The party's embrace of progressive cultural values was amply demonstrated in the platform written under Clinton's leadership. The section titled "strengthening the family" was chock-full of programs benefiting women and dual-earner families. It pledged to crack down on those who did not pay child support and to fund programs preventing child and spousal abuse. Democrats promised to enact laws for family leave and equal pay; to fund improved child care; and to focus resources on health care for pregnant women and newborns in health care reform. The platform unequivocally endorsed abortion rights and called for passage of the pro-choice movement's number-one priority, the Freedom of Choice Act. The platform also declared war on AIDS and promised to extend civil rights protection to gays and lesbians and end the exclusion of gays from the armed forces. In other venues and campaign literature, Clinton and his running mate, Al Gore, promised to end the Mexico City Policy on abortion, sign the Violence against Women Act, fund contraceptive research, provide comprehensive family planning and birth control to low-income women, and create a child care network "as complete as the public school network." Granted, platforms are wish lists, but they are revealing of the aspirations of a political party and the balance of power within it. On many other subjects the platform was DLC boilerplate, yet Clinton brooked no evasions on women's issues and progressive family matters. The DLC's crusade against divorce was nowhere to be found, while Hillary's stump speeches about helping struggling working women to care for their children and improve their wages permeated campaign rhetoric.

Good principles were also good politics, Democrats were starting to discover. The chairman of the Democratic National Committee, Ron Brown, believed Democrats had failed in the past to "take advantage of the gender gap. We are not going to fail this time." Recalling the past struggles of women for recognition within the party and the battles of '72, a former officer of the National Women's Political Caucus and DNC official pronounced that, now, "the Democratic Party is a feminist organization."

ON THE OTHER side of the political divide, Phyllis Schlafly gleefully agreed. Democrats were trapped "in the death drip of the radical feminists," she said, and would be trounced.

Little could most Americans anticipate that the GOP would adopt "family values" as its *cause d'être*, especially with the country mired in a recession. But that is exactly what they did, as the American people discovered when they tuned into the GOP's Houston convention.

The convention opened on August 17 with Bush at a severe disadvantage. Independent candidate Ross Perot had led both Clinton and Bush in the polls through most of the spring and summer. On the eve of the Republican convention, Perot suspended his campaign with praise for Clinton. Clinton had also won the typical post-convention bump in the matchup polls. Fifty-seven percent of Americans disapproved of Bush.

One might have expected the incumbent president to remind

Republicans of the halcyon days. Instead former president Ronald Reagan was bumped from the prime-time opening night spot by the right-wing isolationist Pat Buchanan, who had made a surprisingly strong run against Bush in the early primaries and had won Iowa.

"There is a religious war going on in this country for the soul of America," Buchanan declared.

"It is a cultural war, as critical to the kind of nation we shall be as the Cold War itself, for this war is for the soul of America. And in that struggle for the soul of America, Clinton & Clinton are on the other side, and George Bush is on our side."

"Radical feminism [is] the agenda Clinton & Clinton would impose on America," Buchanan continued, "abortion on demand, a litmus test for the Supreme Court, homosexual rights, discrimination against religious schools, women in combat.

"It is not the kind of change we can tolerate in a nation we still call God's country."

Only 78 delegates were pledged to Buchanan. By contrast, 300 members of Christian Coalition were delegates to the convention, with twenty of them on the platform committee. On Tuesday night, it was Reverend Pat Robertson's turn to inspire the sexual counter-revolutionaries on the convention floor. That summer, he had sent a fundraising letter to drum up support for an anti-ERA campaign in Iowa. "The feminist agenda is not about equal rights for women," wrote the founder of the Christian Coalition. "It is about a socialist, anti-family political movement that encourages women to leave their husbands, kill their children, practice witchcraft, destroy capitalism and become lesbians."

In case anyone still didn't get the message, Wednesday night was billed as "family values" night. During the day many had gone off site to the "God and Country" rally to hear the two Pats a second time. That night, Marilyn Quayle, Dan's wife, a Yale-trained lawyer and born-again Christian, hoped to turn the election into a referendum on the evils of sex, drugs, and working mothers.

"Remember, not everyone joined the counterculture. Not everyone demonstrated, dropped out, took drugs, joined the sexual revolution or dodged the draft," she defiantly declared. "Not everyone believed that the family was so oppressive that women could only thrive apart from it," she continued. "Most women do not wish to be liberated from their essential natures as women." Technically, since Marilyn did not earn money for her work, she could claim solidarity with traditional mothers. She was, however, her husband's campaign manager, a book author, and—to the dismay of Dan's aides—a fixture in his office. Advancing Dan's career sent her around the nation and around the world. (Her travels prompted *Time* writers to quip, "Almost any paying job, short of flight attendant, would give her more time at home with her kids.") Dan, in his speech later that evening, spelled out how Marilyn's family values and Buchanan's holy war were connected. "They don't like our values . . . [W]hen someone confronts them and challenges them, they will stop at nothing to destroy him."

Where did President Bush stand on all of this? One senior aide could claim that the "social issues really aren't at the top of the President's agenda," while another helpfully volunteered that Clinton had "adopted the gay agenda" by speaking to gay and lesbian Angelenos. Bush's speech did little to clarify whether the values crusade would be a priority should he be reelected, nor much to persuade voters to revise their low opinion of the job he was doing.

A glance at the GOP platform would have cleared up any uncertainty about the Republican Party's intentions. The passion play staged at the Houston Astrodome faithfully enacted the script written by the sexual counterrevolutionaries, who wildly cheered from the delegates' floor and had themselves drafted the party's platform. After the preamble, the opening few dozen pages of the 123-page platform explored the existential threat faced by the traditional family, should Republicans lose their bid to rid the country of its moral rot and its rotten liberals. "For more than three decades, the liberal philosophy has assaulted the family on every side," was followed by a claim that Democrats would give 12-year-olds the right to sue their parents if they said no to cosmetic surgery. (Another misleading distortion of Hillary's legal theories.) The phrase "religious pluralism" was stricken from the document, so as not to offend the Christian Right. Democrats were the party of "moral relativism."

On abortion, Bush personally supported exceptions in cases of rape, incest, or danger to the life of the mother. But he was only the candidate. Schlafly had come to the convention with STOP ERA, rebranded as the Republican National Coalition for Life. Always alert to the spectacle of politics in a broadcast age, Schlafly had her followers wear red cowboy hats and oversized stickers saying "Keep Our Winning Platform." She held a press conference standing next to 50 boxes supposedly containing pledges from 100,000 people in support of the existing antiabortion plank. The platform committee, going with Schlafly, not Bush, stated that "the unborn child has a fundamental right to life which cannot be infringed." Fifty-five percent of GOP delegates opposed the antiabortion plank adopted by the platform committee. Republican pro-choice women made their last stand in Houston. Their leader, Mary Louise Smith, the first chairwoman ever of the Republican National Committee, was barred from the convention.

The antiabortion plank was only one sign the sexual counter-revolutionaries had taken over Bush's bid for reelection. The GOP platform accused Democrats of "waging a guerrilla war against American values" and "promoting hostility toward the family's way of life." The party of small government and states rights urged states "to explore ways to promote marital stability," while also opposing "same-sex marriage" and the right of gays to adopt children. It was the first GOP platform to include any mention of gays. In another first for the party, the GOP called for eliminating sex education and replacing it with abstinence-only education. (George H. W. Bush's father, an investment banker and Republican senator, had been an active member of Planned Parenthood.) Along the way, the platform insinuated that Democrats were pornographers. Finally around page 40, the Republican platform mentioned the economy. At about page 100 national security appeared, an issue on which the GOP has a historic partisan advantage, and arguably Bush's strongest suit. The Republicans could hardly have been more explicit that their mission was to reverse the changes in American society that had been unleashed by the sexual revolution.

"None of the big tent garbage," exulted Buchanan's campaign manager, his sister Bay Buchanan.

"Total victory," Schlafly said.

Victory was in the eye of the beholder. Only 5 percent of likely voters said that family values was the most important issue determining their vote, according to a *Time*/CNN poll taken after the convention. Hillary's favorability ratings shot up after the GOP convention; Marilyn Quayle's sank into last place in the rankings of the candidates' wives.

Still, Schlafly had a point. She and hers had chalked up a total victory—over the Republican Party, that is. They had commandeered one of America's two major political parties for their counterrevolution against feminism, working women, gay civil rights, cultural tolerance, and sexual freedom. Such overreach by the sexual fundamentalists proved lethal to Bush.

AFTER THE REPUBLICAN convention, the outcome of the election was never really in doubt. Only Perot's capricious reentry into the race in October created any suspense. Clinton won a landslide in the electoral college but, thanks to Perot's self-funded and surprisingly strong showing, only 43 percent of the popular vote (to Bush's 37.5 and Perot's 18.9). Although the myth persists that Bush would have been reelected if Perot had not run, political scientists reached a consensus years ago that Clinton would have won under every conceivable scenario. Perot did not steal the election from Bush. He robbed Clinton of his mandate.

Clinton won on the economy, just as his campaign thought he would. Exit polls and subsequent statistical analysis both confirmed the importance of the poor economy to Clinton's victory. The number one issue for the majority of voters was the economy; Clinton decisively won those who voted primarily on the issue; a voter who was dissatisfied with the economy was 25 percent more likely to vote for Clinton than for Bush or Perot.

But the economy was not the only issue that mattered to voters, and the 1992 election proved to be a hinge point in the sexual counterrevolution. In signs of a reaction against the Republican attack on working women and reproductive freedom, more women than ever before won election to the U.S. Congress. Senator Barbara Mikulski won reelection, while four first-time women candidates, Dianne Feinstein, Barbara Boxer, Patty Murray, and Carol Moseley-Braun, won their Senate races. Twenty-four Democratic women also joined the freshman class in the House. (The Congress elected in 1992 also included a record number of Hispanics and African Americans, almost all of them Democrats.) Pro-choice Democrat Mel Carnahan defeated the man whose name was attached to the case that had catalyzed the abortion rights movement, Missouri's former attorney general, William Webster.

The issue of abortion likewise proved to be an important factor in the Democratic recapture of the White House. Abortion was the number one issue for fully one-quarter of voters. Abortion had the second strongest effect on vote choice, after the economy, and stronger than welfare, affirmative action, or national defense. Support for legal abortion in all circumstances reached its highest level of all time, 61 percent. The consensus was a bipartisan one. More than two-thirds of all Democrats and a majority of Republicans and independents favored the right to legal abortion. Only 10 percent of Republicans agreed with the party's platform outlawing abortion in all cases.

Bush paid dearly for the position foisted on him by the sexual fundamentalists of the Christian Right. One out of every six Republicans defected from Bush over the party's opposition to abortion. More striking, given Bush's pro-choice past and reputation as a moderate, roughly seven out of ten pro-choice independents voted against Bush. Finally, Bush failed to pick up much support from the minority of Democrats who opposed abortion. Only one out of seventeen Democrats defected from Clinton over the party's position on abortion. In fact, the most antiabortion Democrats happened to be the most pro-Clinton voters in the entire national electorate.

The Republicans' denigration of working women and exaltation of traditional motherhood likewise played poorly with voters, especially women. Clinton garnered 61 percent of the women's vote. The gender gap, which had vanished in 1988, reemerged at a record level of 10 points. (That is, women voted for Clinton by a margin 10 points greater than men voted for Clinton.) The cause of the gender gap, according to a statistical analysis by sociologists Jeff Manza and Clem Brooks, was women's more positive view, relative to men, of the women's movement. Manza and Brooks concluded that Clinton performed better among women because of women's greater "feminist consciousness." Analyses of races involving women candidates also support the conclusion that identification with women's rights redounded to the electoral benefit of Democrats. Women candidates who were perceived as feminist performed better among women voters than did women candidates who were not perceived as advocates of women's rights, according to a study conducted by two political scientists. Although Clinton's support for reproductive freedom contributed to his success with women voters, it did not account for the gender gap. Men supported abortion rights at the same level women did, just as they still do today. Issues, not identity politics, mattered to women voters.

With Clinton's claim to be a "different kind of Democrat," some were tempted to chalk up his win to brilliant DLC centrism. With his appeal to the "forgotten middle class" and Greenberg at his side, hadn't he reassured those elusive Reagan Democrats that he had taken back control of the party from the McGoverniks? The demographic breakdown of the vote, statistical analyses of the election, and Clinton's own rhetoric all suggest exactly the opposite.

Throughout the campaign, Clinton had disregarded the near universal advice to downplay women's issues, abortion, gay rights, and black civil rights. Voters were far more likely to have heard one of Hillary's feminist riffs on the plight of forgotten middle-class women than to have read obscure DLC policy briefs on the devastating culture of divorce and the imperative to make it more difficult to obtain. Culturally progressive voters—Republicans and independents, as well as Democrats—voted for Clinton because of his positions on social issues and his support for women's rights. And it was these voters, not the wayward Reagan Democrat or elusive white man, who pushed Clinton over the top. Indeed, Clinton won the same proportion of white men as Michael Dukakis before him and Al Gore and John Kerry would win after him.

Clinton, unlike many of his advisers, saw no contradiction between economic help to the forgotten middle class and a full-throated endorsement of cultural progressivism and women's rights. Certainly candidates say many things they don't mean on the campaign trail and platforms merely express a politicians' aspirations, rather than their realistic expectations. To Clinton's chagrin, the budget deficit left to him by the Reagan-Bush administrations and pressure from Wall Street and Federal Reserve chairman Alan Greenspan forced him to abandon most of his progressive economic plans to address the recession.

Clinton did however act immediately to fulfill his campaign promises to cultural progressives. On his second day in office, the twentieth anniversary of *Roe v. Wade*, Clinton issued an executive order saying he was "acting to separate our national health and medical policy from the divisive conflict over abortion" and "free science and medicine from the grasp of politics." In it he reversed almost every executive order enacted for the sexual counterrevolutionaries by Presidents Reagan and Bush. The order ended the ban on embryonic stem cell research; lifted the abortion gag order on family planning organizations that received federal funds; ended the ban on military medical facilities performing abortions; repealed the Mexico City Policy, which prohibited international aid agencies from discussing abortion; and ordered a new review of the drug RU-486, a prescription drug widely used in Europe for early first-term abortions, which had been rejected by Bush's FDA. Clinton quickly secured passage and signed the twice-vetoed Family and Medical Leave Act, the first and as yet only federal support for maternity and paternity leave.

A week into his presidency, Clinton instructed his defense secretary to draft an executive order "ending discrimination on the basis of sexual orientation" in the armed forces by July. Although Clinton did not choose the timing, the attempt to end the ban on gays and lesbians serving in the military became the first major controversy of Clinton's presidency. (Things might have gone quite differently if a still unidentified administration staffer had not leaked the information to the *New York Times* while the policy was still in development.) The compromise devised in the wake of an outcry from powerful conservative senators and General Colin Powell, the notorious Don't Ask, Don't Tell policy, was desired by neither Clinton nor gay activists.

Three days after President Bill Clinton wiped Republican anti-abortion policy off the books, he appointed Hillary Rodham Clinton to head his administration's health care task force, and charged it with formulating a plan to provide universal health care for all

Americans. Clinton was acting swiftly to fulfill a signature campaign promise, and just like the next Democratic president, Barack Obama, the political wise men surrounding him told him not to do it. Clinton ignored them. With Hillary's appointment, he signaled once again that he had no intention of bartering away women's interests for the support of the moderate middle. Only a week old, the new administration had already taken on the GOP sexual counterrevolutionaries on abortion, gays in the military, and stem cell research. Now Clinton also had the GOP's market fundamentalism in his sights.

The question however remained. If the going got tough, who would Democrats blame?

7

JUST SAY NO

"I DIDN'T HEAR the whole convention," explained Republican Texas Senator Phil Gramm, after President Bush lost the 1992 election with 37.5 percent of the popular vote—the lowest gained by a major party candidate since Herbert Hoover lost to Franklin D. Roosevelt in 1932 during the Great Depression. Gramm was responding to a reporter who asked if the senator wasn't concerned that the party's televised convention gave the appearance of intolerance and might have contributed to Bush's loss.

The entire leadership of the GOP wished it could say the same, but their claims of ignorance would have been about as believable as Gramm's, who had been the convention's keynote speaker.

The attempt by Republican leaders to distance themselves from the overreaching sexual counterrevolutionaries in the Republican base was commonplace in the wake of the electoral debacle. At the meeting of Republican governors held a couple weeks after the election, the cry went up for "diversity," "inclusion," and the "big tent," while a resolution condemning Clinton for promising to lift the ban on gays in the military got nowhere. Retiring Republican National

Committee chairman Rich Bond condemned "zealotry masquer-
ading as principle" and predicted the party would continue to shrink
if it held to its unpopular antiabortion dogmatism. Republican
moderates such as Arlen Specter and Lincoln Chafee announced they
had formed a moderate group within the GOP. "Our purpose is to
exclude issues of morality and conscience as litmus tests of being a
Republican," said the group's head, Tom Campbell, the pro-choice
Republican candidate who had been defeated by a right-wing rival
in California's Senate primary. Mary Dent Crisp, giving up on the
GOP after a twelve-year-long struggle to preserve a place in the
party for pro-choice Republicans, warned that the fundamentalists'
"moral imperialism . . . threatens the very foundation of this nation."

Leaders of the sexual fundamentalists and their allies on the Right
were having none of it. Pat Robertson claimed it was the economy,
stupid. Ralph Reed, executive director of Robertson's Christian Coalition, warned Specter, Campbell, and their ilk that "pro-family"
voters would abandon Republicans if they abandoned "traditional
values." According to the head of the American Enterprise Institute,
Bush lost because he betrayed Reagan conservatism. The executive
director of the National Life Committee seconded him: "Rich Bond
is advocating political suicide for the Republican Party." Columnist
Paul Gigot mocked the centrists on the *Wall Street Journal*'s archcon-
servative editorial page. There were so few moderates they would
"barely fill the average country club."

By January 1993, the Republican bubble had popped and the
party leadership found itself in a rough spot: underemployed, under-
water on their debts, and desperate to get out of the hole before the
foreclosure notice dropped. Looking ahead, the most relevant fact for
Republicans to contemplate was that their candidate, an incumbent
president, had received the lowest percentage of the popular vote in
sixty years.

There was another equally salient fact to consider. The votes
George H. W. Bush had won came overwhelmingly from a narrow
slice of the party and the electorate: the sexual fundamentalists of the
Christian Right. Those voters interpreted Clinton's election not as the
normal give-and-take of democracy, nor as a wake-up call to temper
their radicalism, but rather as a goad to no-holds-barred partisan

warfare. "It's going to be hand-to-hand combat for at least four years," Reed promised on the morning after Bill Clinton's election.

The GOP leadership's predictable attempt to recover standing by blocking Clinton's legislative agenda and this resurgent sexual counterrevolution would converge in the battle over Clinton's signature initiative, health care reform. And, just as in the '92 election, the fevered delirium of Clinton's opponents would zero in on the existential threat posed to the American Republic by sex and by Hillary, a new kind of First Lady.

"THAT CLINTON, WHO was always the very model of an ambitious young pol," the journalist Molly Ivins observed, "should have come to stand in many minds for the largely mythical generation of long-haired, dope-smoking, draft-dodging, sex-crazed hippies is just one more example of the excess of irony in our time."

It is difficult to imagine that the image of Clinton as a countercultural radical would have stuck had Hillary not been his wife. Hillary was no radical either; personal and cultural conservatism ran deep in her personality. But she was a feminist, and more that that, one immortalized in *Life* magazine as the representative of her generation's new womanhood. Since the Ivy League–educated lawyer set foot in Arkansas as their youngest governor's intended, the locals had been hostile. She was the first female partner in the state's oldest and most prestigious law firm. She had been named by the *National Law Journal* as one of the nation's 100 most influential lawyers—twice. She kept her maiden name. She showed no regard, by Arkansas standards, for her appearance. She was a working mother who dared to tell other parents about their children's inalienable rights.

Hillary, the first career woman to become First Lady, famously remarked that she was a Rorschach test for Americans' views about women. "As the icon of American womanhood," Margaret Carlson wrote in an admiring profile in *Time*, Hillary "is the medium through which the remaining anxieties over feminism are being played out. She is on a cultural seesaw held to a schizophrenic standard." Hillary was a role model: breaking glass ceilings, forever redefining the role of the First Lady. "To millions of women, Hillary Clinton's career-and-family balancing act is a symbolic struggle," Carlson wrote. Carlson, and presumably millions of other working women, were rooting for her success.

Still, Hillary provoked cultural and sexual anxiety among others, who saw her as an all-powerful, cunning, subversive. *Spy* magazine satirized and advanced this trope at the same time, when it put Hillary on the cover inauguration week in dominatrix dress—leather, chains, whip, and all. Floyd Brown, the producer of the infamous Willie Horton commercial from 1988, charged that the president was "a captive of the radical left, of which his boss, Hillary, is a member in good standing." *National Review* columnist Florence King lampooned Hillary's admiration for the activist First Lady Eleanor Roosevelt, whom King said she also despised. Although Eleanor had given White House access to "disgusting" "radicals and "lesbians," at least her consorts "did not rend the social fabric with single motherhood and paranoid harassment charges as modern feminists have done."

The first nine months of the Clinton presidency offered little confirmation for either the hero or the demon caricature of Hillary. Instead, as Bill fumbled one issue after another and Hillary's health care task force missed one deadline after another, the less than flattering impression took hold that the Clintons were engaged in a co-presidency, and a not very competent one at that. It didn't help matters that a large majority thought that President Clinton "has good ideas but can't seem to get them passed." How would Americans take it when an idea they strongly favored—health care reform—couldn't get passed, and Hillary appeared to be the one to blame?

For many Americans, the problem was pillow talk between husband and wife, not that Hillary was a working woman and a feminist. Shortly after Bill announced her role leading health care reform, 57 percent of Americans viewed her favorably. But when asked if she should be involved in developing policy, 47 percent said yes, while 45 percent said no. Americans were evenly divided over the question of the appropriate role for the president's spouse. She was the president's wife, not a confirmed cabinet member or an elected official; there existed no mechanism to check and balance the power she held by virtue of her personal relationship to Bill.

When the long-awaited health care plan was finally unveiled on September 22 in a presidential address, the tide turned in a more positive direction for both Clintons. The following week, Hillary spent three days on Capitol Hill explaining the plan for reform. *The New York Times* said she "dazzled" five congressional committees. The *Washington Post* deemed her a "superstar." Maureen Dowd declared it "the official end of the era in which presidential wives pretended to know less than they did and to be advising less than they were." That week, 57 percent of those polled by *Time*/CNN favored the Clinton health care plan and, for the first time in four months, President Clinton's favorability rating exceeded his unfavorability rating. Hillary's stock rose too. "Perhaps the most startling thing about Hillary Clinton's performance last week on Capitol Hill was the silent but devastating rebuke it sent to her cartoonists. This was not the Hillary as overbearing wife, the Hillary as left-wing ideologue," *Time* wrote. "This was Hillary the polite but passionate American citizen—strangely mesmerizing because of how she matched the poise and politics of her delivery with the power of her position. No wonder some of Washington's most acid tongues and pens took the week off."

As the Christmas holidays approached, the administration believed they had secured some Republican support and a filibuster-proof Senate majority in place for quick passage of health care reform early in the new year. Hillary's approval rating topped 65 percent. One adviser, however, cautioned, "You are too strong . . . They are going to come after you. It's politically imperative for them to take a pound of flesh out of you.

A FEW DAYS before Christmas, a right-wing magazine, *The American Spectator,* published David Brock's "His Cheatin' Heart," the story that would eventually precipitate Clinton's impeachment. It detailed Clinton's alleged sexual escapades while he was governor of Arkansas, as purportedly witnessed by two state troopers on his security detail. Hillary, according to these troopers, was a sexually demanding shrew who hurled lamps around the governor's mansion because she wasn't getting enough. (The troopers' view of Hillary, journalist Joe Klein observed, was "a neanderthal fantasy of what feminists are really like.") Brock's article contained another ticking time bomb. Six weeks later, a former Arkansas state employee named Paula Jones called a press conference at the Conservative Political Action Conference (CPAC) and alleged that the president, while governor, had lured her to a hotel room, exposed himself, and told her to "kiss it."

The American Spectator had been hounding Clinton all year to little effect. Brock, a rising star on the Right for his 1992 book, *The Real Anita Hill*, understood "that right-wing journalism had to be injected into the bloodstream of the liberal media for maximum effect," and leaked his own article to the major news outlets. His leak gave CNN the opportunity to interview the two Arkansas troopers, Roger Perry and Larry Patterson, the night before publication. The national media, given license by CNN's imprimatur, went wild on the story. Brock later wrote, "I was astonished to see how easy it was to suck in CNN." Veteran Beltway journalist and author Elizabeth Drew deemed it "the most bizarre day thus far in this and perhaps any other administration."

The Arkansas press corps quickly rebutted every one of the troopers' claims, and the national press generally concluded there was little credible in the tale—of course, not before they profited from circulating it. No matter. Although Troopergate quickly faded into a non-issue for most of the nation and the mainstream media, Brock was on target when he later wrote that, thanks to his portrayal of Bill as "a sexually voracious sociopathic cipher" and Hillary as "a castrating, power-mad harpy," it would be possible "to say and write and broadcast any crazy thing about the first couple and get away with it." Shortly before Troopergate, two new allegations related to Whitewater had prompted the *New York Times* and the *Washington Post* to resurrect that story. Coming on the heels of new Whitewater charges and three other phony scandals manufactured by old Republican operatives, Clinton had little political choice but to accede to demands from congressional Republicans for the appointment of a special prosecutor. On January 12, 1994, Clinton's attorney general, Janet Reno, named Robert Fiske, a well-respected Republican and experienced prosecutor, to the post.

It was in this atmosphere, the Clintons under investigation by a special prosecutor for political corruption, the president marked as a sexual sociopath, and the First Lady portrayed as a cold, cunning, raging Lady Macbeth, that the health care reform debate in Congress unfolded in the new year.

Just as in the presidential campaign, Hillary had gone from being Bill's greatest asset to his most serious liability. Not only was she the point person on health care reform, but Fiske's investigation was revealing that she, not Bill, had managed the couple's Whitewater investment. She was also the one who devised their legal strategy—essentially to refuse to hand over documents until forced to do so. That might have been legally sound and constitutionally wise, but politically, it was foolhardy. When Hillary finally realized her error, and made herself available for a long press conference, she fell victim to terrible timing. That week, another story broke about the fabulous profit she had earned trading commodities futures. As in every other case, there was a valid explanation for what had happened and nothing illegal or unethical had transpired. But it made people wonder what else the Clintons might be hiding.

In the wake of the cascade of scandals, as well as an anti–health care reform advertising campaign paid for by the insurance industry, support for health care reform plummeted 14 points from the fall high point, to a plurality of just 43 percent of Americans supporting it. In March, a *Time*/CNN poll found a majority of those surveyed believing that the Clintons were hiding something about Whitewater; one-third believed they had broken the law, and only 35 percent said they trusted Bill Clinton. Hillary's favorability rating had dropped more than 10 points from its peak. It was still at 52 percent, but those who had an unfavorable opinion of her had risen 15 points to 42 percent. Mounting a defense against the independent prosecutor investigation distracted the administration from the legislative battle, while media coverage of the scandals turned the public's attention away from the issue of health care reform. In the first three months of 1994, 42 stories aired on network television about health care reform; in just one week in March, those networks aired 92 Whitewater stories.

The pile-on of corruption charges had led most Americans to

suspect that the seemingly unrelated allegations must be connected by the challenged ethics of the first couple. In fact, what tied them together was a coordinated effort to take down the duly elected president of the United States. The conservative credo in the 1950s had been to "stand athwart history, yelling Stop." The Right's operative game plan in the Clinton years was to stand athwart the popular will, scheme, agitate, and obstruct.

"I FIND IT not an accident," Hillary answered in response to an Associated Press question about the troopers' allegations, "that every time [the president] is on the verge of fulfilling his commitment to the American people and they are responding, out comes yet a new round of these outrageous, terrible stories that people plant for political and financial reasons."

Through the years Bill and Hillary Clinton had lived with a barrage of personal attacks. That was the nature of Arkansas politics. Among Clinton's Arkansas enemies were some who sought nothing more than to get rich by selling the tales that bloomed in the state's fecund political swamps. One such was the former Arkansas state employee, Larry Nichols, the man who sold Gennifer Flowers's story to a tabloid, who had been forced to resign from his state job for spending his work hours illegally providing aid to the Nicaraguan Contras. There were some who were driven to exact revenge, such as the party-switching Sheffield Nelson, defeated by Clinton in the nasty 1990 gubernatorial election, who first put Jeff Gerth of *The New York Times* on the Whitewater trail. There were some who were driven by religious zeal and aroused by envy of Bill, such as Cliff Jackson, a fundamentalist and old Oxford rival of Clinton's who failed in politics. Jackson circulated the election-year draft-dodging claim and the troopers' sex stories and encouraged Paula Jones to consider a sexual harassment civil suit against the president. There were some who were fighting the battles of the slaveholders' Confederacy, such as Jim Johnson, a racist Democrat turned Republican, whom a young Clinton had helped oust from office. Johnson turned his provocatively named White Haven estate into central command for the freelancing Clinton hunters, while keeping a low profile himself.

Clinton's Arkansas enemies, however, would have found little traction once Clinton left for the nation's capital, had their tales not been so useful to those seeking to end Clinton's presidency by any means necessary. Little more would have been heard about the many Clinton-gates—Whitewater, Fostergate, Troopergate, Travelgate, and, of course, Monica Lewinsky—without the substantial investments of two national right-wing Republican rainmakers.

There would have been no Troopergate, and thus no Paula Jones case, and thus no Lewinsky scandal, but for the money and efforts of Peter W. Smith, a Chicago investment banker. Smith was one of the top twenty contributors to House Minority Leader Newt Gingrich's political action committee GOPAC, as well as a major Republican Party donor. During the 1992 campaign, Smith had tried to convince the press to write that Clinton had fathered a child with a black prostitute. Smith invested at least $80,000 to get dirt on Clinton's sex life. David Brock was one of the writers who begged off the prostitute story; even he found it lacked all credibility. In 1993, Smith was tipped off that some Arkansas troopers were interested in selling Clinton sex tales, and he persuaded Brock to investigate, offering him $5,000 for his efforts. (Although he promised Brock he wouldn't pay the troopers to talk, he did. Paying sources is a practice forbidden by all reputable news outfits.) Smith's lawyer and political confidant, Richard W. Porter, a former aide to Vice President Dan Quayle, was the person who secured lawyers for Paula Jones, just in time before the statute of limitations on her case against Clinton was due to expire. Smith and Porter would later be instrumental in connecting Linda Tripp, the friend who tape-recorded Monica Lewinsky's confessions, with Kenneth W. Starr's Office of the Independent Counsel. Starr and Porter were partners at the same law firm.

At the same time Brock was being sponsored by Smith to write "His Cheatin' Heart," unbeknownst to him, his employer had signed on to a more ambitious project to take down the president. On December 2, the American Spectator Educational Foundation began receiving checks drawn on Richard Mellon Scaife's tax-exempt nonprofit foundations. Over the next four years, Scaife would invest $2.3 million in the so-called Arkansas Project in order to, as Scaife put it many times, "get that goddamn guy out of the White House."

Among other ventures, those funds paid for Paula Jones's lawyers; funded the work of Ann Coulter, a self-admitted member of the anti-Clinton conspiracy, at the Independent Women's Forum; and paid the living expenses for Starr's prize witness on the Whitewater cases. (That witness was a liar and brilliant con artist, and his story against the Clintons completely fell apart.) The existence of the Arkansas Project remained secret until February 1998, when investigative journalists Joe Conason and Murray Waas broke the story in the *New York Observer*.

Scaife, a beefy, white-haired, ruddy-faced recluse, was the billionaire heir to the Mellon banking and oil dynasty and publisher of the *Pittsburgh Tribune-Review*. He had gotten his start in right-wing politics as a Goldwaterite, and then been a major donor to Nixon. Scaife soured on electoral politics after Nixon's fall, but he remained a Nixonista at heart, enamored of covert operations and prone to conspiratorial thinking. He turned his focus toward funding, in the words of *Washington Post* reporters Robert Kaiser and Ira Chinoy, "the creation of the modern conservative movement in America." Their investigation showed that Scaife donated more than $620 million over the years, targeting large grants to fledgling organizations. Scaife was instrumental in building the Heritage Foundation, the Cato Institute, the Manhattan Institute, *The American Spectator*, Judicial Watch, Accuracy in Media, and the Independent Women's Forum, among others.

"When he gets a hate on for somebody, he tends to pursue it to substantial length," a Pittsburgh lawyer who knew Scaife told Chinoy and Kaiser. A former employee thought Scaife was driven by "a sort of steady thread of hurting people who don't like him or who he gets at cross [purposes] with." And Scaife hated Clinton, and not just in a personal way. Scaife's hatred for Clinton was fueled by ideology. Scaife believed, according to one of his friends, that "Clinton was the embodiment of the sixties antiwar leftist movement that is amoral through and through."

When Scaife told a Democrat seated next to him at a luncheon in Nantucket, "We're going to get Clinton," he seemed to have believed his privately funded Clinton hunt would yield damning truths. It never did. Instead, as time would tell, the value of Scaife's Arkansas

Project lay more in providing fodder to keep the GOP sexual counterrevolutionaries in a heightened state of raging delirium.

AMERICANS AS A whole quickly lost interest in Troopergate, but the sex story and its author, David Brock, became a sensation among the sexual counterrevolutionaries. "While the more secular wings of the conservative movement weren't sure what to make of Troopergate, for the Christian Right, the political war against Clinton had theological underpinnings," Brock wrote. The day the story broke he was interviewed by Republican Representative Bob Dornan on Rush Limbaugh's talk radio show. Citizens United's David Bossie and Floyd Brown started issuing special "Fornigate" reports in their *ClintonWatch* newsletter. Weeks and months after the troopers' stories were refuted, Brock was still recounting their claims in interviews with James Dobson of Focus on the Family, Pat Robertson of the Christian Coalition, and other Christian Right radio talk show hosts across the nation. In February, he was invited to be a headlined guest speaker at CPAC, the event where Paula Jones stood next to the troopers and their lawyer, Cliff Jackson, and tearfully insisted she was filing a civil lawsuit against the president just because she wanted to clear her name. (A name, by the way, which wasn't used in the story—only a "Paula" was mentioned, with no last name.) Brock was a headliner again at the Christian Coalition's annual Road to Victory conference. The secretive Council for National Policy (CNP), created by Paul Weyrich and now a 500-member Who's Who of the Christian Right, gave Brock their Winston Churchill Award for "Courageous and Committed Service to the Conservative Cause." At the ceremony, he dined with Phyllis Schlafly and Ralph Reed.

It was hardly surprising that the leaders of the sexual counterrevolution would latch onto Brock's tale. They were already peddling even more ludicrous ones, in the interest of keeping the base inflamed. In 1994, Reverend Jerry Falwell gave wide play to CNP board member Pat Matrisciana's video *The Clinton Chronicles.* Matrisciana's body of work included a so-called documentary claiming that laws barring discrimination against homosexuals were promulgated to allow gays to recruit children and "procreate" in public school classrooms.

Another exposed Halloween as a plot to initiate children into "Pagan Occultism." *The Clinton Chronicles* purported to document the crimes Clinton committed as governor, including murder and international drug-running. Matrisciana sent copies of the video to every member of Congress, and the CNP sent free copies to every one of its members. Falwell aired excerpts of *The Clinton Chronicles* on his show every week in May, 1994, while evangelical churches played the video during Sunday services.

In the spring of 1994, polls confirmed that anti-Clintonism was all with the sexual counterrevolutionaries. Nina Burleigh of *Time* reported that Clinton's approval rating was 59 percent, but that 25–30 percent of Americans had strong negative feelings toward him. The feelings expressed by a housewife she interviewed at an anti-Hillary protest were typical of that Clinton-hating minority. Pointing to the problem of teen sex, the woman said, "The country has no morals, and they are in charge . . . I fear for the lost." Burleigh concluded, "To the religious right, Clinton is practically the Anti-Christ."

It is impossible to know how much Christian Right voters believed of the Troopergate story or from *The Clinton Chronicles*. The stories, however, were sown in a fertile environment.

With Clinton's election and quick reversal of Reagan-Bush anti-abortion measures, certain lawless elements of the antiabortion movement had taken to violence and terrorism. Six weeks after Clinton took office, Dr. David Gunn, an abortion provider, was murdered by a fundamentalist, claiming to be acting on God's orders. Gunn's clinic in Pensacola, Florida was being picketed by Operation Rescue when the assassination occurred.

Randall Terry responded to Gunn's assassination with the comment, "While we grieve for him and his widow and for his children, we must also grieve for the thousands of children that he has murdered." Later that summer, Dr. George Tiller was shot and wounded in Wichita, Kansas, by a woman who pleaded that her act was a case of justifiable homicide. A rash of firebombings and acid attacks on clinic facilities and several cases of attempted murder of abortion providers prompted Congress to act on legislation designed to protect women's access to abortion and the lives of clinic workers. In November 1993, with bipartisan support, the Senate voted 69–30 to pass the Freedom of Access to Clinic Entrances (FACE) Act. Delayed in the House by the calendar and other legislation, it became law, with Clinton's strong support, in May 1994. FACE outlawed many common tactics used by Operation Rescue, such as vandalism, trespassing, physically blocking people and cars from entering clinics, and stalking a provider or clinic worker. Antiabortion and Christian Right leaders strongly condemned the legislation, saying it was wrong to hold them responsible for the acts of deranged, lone individuals.

THE MANUFACTURED CLINTON scandals were useful, not just for the sexual counterrevolutionaries, but to the Republican Party. The election of 1992 was a change election, and notwithstanding Republican president-in-waiting Bob Dole's claim to the contrary, Clinton had entered the White House with a strong popular mandate. The GOP's electoral future, its leaders believed, hinged on depriving Clinton of victories to take to voters in the 1994 midterm elections. Newt Gingrich, on the eve of becoming House minority leader in October, 1993, promised that his position would be to "slow everything down." Republican obstructionism was nearly indiscriminate. The GOP Senate minority, led by Dole and Senator John McCain, chalked up a record number of filibusters.

The GOP establishment, from center to right, uttered nary a word of protest against the lies of the Clinton hunters or the hijacking of the legislative process by scandal-mongering. The baseless charges against the Clintons bought Republicans time, a valuable commodity for a minority party trying to kill popular legislation. Once the scandals were given credence by a credulous media and the appointment of a special prosecutor, distracted voters wondered if they could trust the Clintons to do right when they had apparently done so much wrong. Gingrich, Dole, maverick McCain, and the rest were not about to look such a champion gift horse in the mouth. It all fit Gingrich's dictum that politics was "war without blood."

Health care reform proved to be their line in the sand. When it looked like some Republican members would capitulate to public opinion and vote for reform, William Kristol, formerly chief of staff to Dan Quayle, conservative strategist, and American Enterprise Institute fellow, faxed around a justly famous memo. A Democratic victory on health care reform, he warned, "will revive the reputation" of the Democratic Party "as the generous protector of middle-class interests . . . . And it will at the same time strike a punishing blow against Republican claims to defend the middle class by restraining government."

The collusion of the GOP leadership with the anti-Clinton conspirators and the sexual fundamentalists in the base came to fruition in fevered summer protests against health care reform. In July 1994, when Hillary and a bus caravan of health care reform supporters went on the road, hoping to evoke positive associations with the civil rights movement's Freedom Rides, right-wing radio talk shows called on listeners to demonstrate against "Hillarycare." Everywhere the pro-reform bus riders traveled, protesters met them. The protests weren't a spontaneous uprising of populist real Americans. They were funded by Richard Mellon Scaife and David H. and Charles Koch through their group Citizens for a Sound Economy, planned by Gingrich's staff, and coordinated by Ralph Reed's Christian Coalition.

"I had not seen faces like that since the segregations battles of the sixties. They had such hatred on their faces," Hillary remarked after experiencing one of those demonstrations in Seattle on the second day of the ride. The Secret Service had to confiscate concealed guns carried by the protesters. In a church parking lot in Louisville, Kentucky, as wheelchair-bound riders of the pro-reform bus were lifted down the steps, antiabortion activists surrounded them shouting, "Go back to Russia." The biggest pro–health care rally, scheduled to celebrate the anniversary of Medicare's passage, was knocked off the headline news by the assassination of a doctor and a security guard who worked at an abortion clinic. The doctor was Gunn's successor in Pensacola. In North Platte, Nebraska, a protester told a reporter she opposed health care reform because "Bill and Hillary are immoral homosexual communists."

On September 26, 1994, Democratic Senate Majority Leader George Mitchell withdrew health care reform legislation. He thought that Democrats would fare better in the upcoming November elections if the bill was tabled, rather than defeated in a vote.

Hillary and congressional Democrats, it must be said, shared part of the blame for the collapse of health care reform. Hillary's proposed bill seemed excessively complicated, and, given the delicate sensibilities of America's legislators, she made countless political blunders. Petty jockeying among congressional Democrats to preserve their prerogatives gave Republicans time and opportunity to kill the bill. Substantive ideological differences further paralyzed the congressional Democratic caucus, as centrist deficit hawks and populist economic progressives argued over the cost of covering the uninsured and the balance between public and private in a reformed health care system.

When in his first week in office President Clinton had taken on health care reform, the entrenched corporate health care interests, and the Republican market fundamentalists, the prospects for passage had looked fairly good. The American public supported reform, the Democratic Party held solid majorities in both houses of Congress, and many Republicans feared it would be political suicide to *oppose* health care reform. Ten months later, after a rough start for the administration, success again seemed to be in sight. Although there was still a long way to go for a bill to be written and passed, with many potential traps along the way, things could well have turned out differently if the Right had not ginned up specious charges against Bill and Hillary.

What can be said without question is that the actual defeat of Clinton's effort to reform health care was inextricable from the phony Clinton scandals. The Clinton administration might have been able to manage Democratic infighting, as well as steamroll Republican congressional opposition, had it had not been for the paralyzing distraction of the scandals. That was in fact how it looked like it was going to play out. During the weeks before Americans started their 1993 Christmas holidays, knowledgeable observers thought health care reform was likely to pass. It is certainly conceivable, given Clinton's centrist tendencies on many economic issues, the substantial number of moderate Republicans who held office in 1994, the comparatively less gridlocked nature of that Congress, and broad public support for reform, that Clinton could have won a compromise along the lines of the compromise health care reform legislation that passed under the next Democratic president, Barack Obama. After all, the historic 2010 health care reform bill, with its reliance on private insurance and its imposition of a mandate to buy insurance, was quite similar to the one proposed by Republicans in 1993. But as Kristol observed, no matter how good health care reform might or might not be for the nation, it would be bad for the Republican Party.

Republican politicians and right-wing billionaires must have been pleased with how well it turned out for them when they stoked the delirium of the sexual counterrevolutionaries.

8

OUT OF THE SHADOWS

I N A STUNNING upset in the 1994 midterm elections, Republicans picked up 60 Senate and House seats to win control of the U.S. Congress for the first time in forty years. Not since 1954, during Eisenhower's presidency, had the Democratic Party been in the minority in the House of Representatives. In the six decades from the New Deal to Clinton's presidency, Republicans had controlled both the Senate and the House for a total of only four years. The 1994 Republican sweep extended to the states. Fifteen state assemblies flipped from Democratic to Republican control, and eleven Democratic governors were thrown out of office. When the 104th Congress convened in January, Republicans would hold a 230-to-204 majority in the House of Representatives, and a 52-to-48 edge in the Senate.

House Minority Whip and speaker-in-waiting Newt Gingrich, the putative architect of the rout, boasted, "We have a clear mandate, and we intend to be revolutionaries." William Kristol, the strategist who helped kill health care reform, declared, "It's the Russian Revolution in reverse." Bill Clinton was reduced to muttering that the president was still relevant in the American constitutional order.

The press and the pundits took their cue from the deliriously ecstatic revolutionary Gingrich and his close confidant and political partner, Americans for Tax Reform leader Grover Norquist, who deemed the midterm victory "The New American Revolution." Six weeks before the election, Gingrich and Texas Representative Dick Armey, the leaders of the Republican minority in the U.S. Congress, had stood with 300 Republican candidates on the steps of the Capitol and unveiled the Contract with America. The Contract promised that Republicans would end "government that is too big," impose "fiscal responsibility," pass a balanced budget amendment, and cut the capital gains tax to spur "job creation." Low-tax, small-government conservatism was back in vogue in the Republican party and had won the hearts and minds of American voters.

Yet in a poll conducted the week before the election by the *New York Times* and CBS News, 71 percent of voters said they had not even heard of the Contract with America. Subsequent analysis of the election results found that the Contract had almost no impact on the vote, and political scientists later reached a consensus that it was hardly a factor in the election.

If the unexpected Republican victory was not due to the allure of the Contract with America and the triumph of small government Republicanism, what then did happen? The resurgence of the sexual counterrevolution through stealth.

"THE MOST IMPORTANT strategy for evangelicals is secrecy," Ralph Reed had told Montana Christian Coalition activists in 1991. "We're involved in a war."

"You must paint your face and travel at night. You must move underground and don't stick your head out of the foxhole until the sun is beyond the horizon." As if to his opponents, Reed warned, "You don't know it's over until you're in a body bag. You don't know until election night."

Stealth, as the political genius at the helm of the Christian Coalition readily acknowledged, was the secret weapon of the sexual counterrevolution. Founded in 1989, the Christian Coalition had its first big local victory in 1990. In San Diego County, the Christian

Coalition ran a slate of candidates for local offices on a platform of "strong, traditional family values" and against "the senseless killing of innocent unborn children." They won 60 of the 88 races they contested. Most San Diego voters, however, were unaware of the candidates' provenance in the Christian Right. That was because the candidates refused to answer the standard questionnaires from interest groups, rarely campaigned in public, and kept their affiliation with the Christian Coalition secret until the morning after the election. Some incumbents who were defeated said they had never even laid eyes on their opponents. As a Christian Coalition manual for taking over a local Republican Party committee used in Pennsylvania instructed, "You should never mention the name Christian Coalition in Republican circles."

In 1992, while the national media was chronicling the immolation of the hapless George H. W. Bush by the family values crusaders, Reed's San Diego model was helping the sexual fundamentalists wrest control of the Republican Party apparatus from mainstream Republicans. In its first few years targeting local Republican parties, the Christian Right gained significant influence in two dozen state Republican parties, and Christian Coalition members controlled the Republican parties of the two most populous states in the nation, California and Texas. In Washington State, sexual fundamentalists adopted a platform that called for banning all abortions; abolishing the National Endowment for the Arts; putting creationism, Bible study, and corporal punishment back in public schools; returning to the gold standard; and banning gays and lesbians from teaching and health care jobs. In Colorado, a campaign led by Focus on the Family's Christian ministry James Dobson convinced Coloradans to pass a referendum writing discrimination against gays and lesbians into the state constitution. (In 1996, the U.S. Supreme Court ruled 6-to-3 that Colorado's Amendment Two violated the equal protection clause and was thus unconstitutional.) In Iowa, a campaign by the Eagle Forum, the National Right to Life Committee, and the Christian Coalition defeated a state Equal Rights Amendment referendum. The Republicans lost the 1992 presidential election in a spectacular fashion, but under the radar, the grassroots sexual counterrevolutionaries vaulted hundreds of their brethren into local political offices.

Their long-term investment in local politics and grassroots organizing paid national dividends in the 1994 midterm election, as Republicans swept to victory on a coordinated but unheralded mobilization of the sexual fundamentalist voter. The Christian Coalition, Dobson's Focus on the Family, Beverly LaHaye's Concerned Women for America, and Phyllis Schlafly's Eagle Forum spent more than $25 million and mobilized roughly 200,000 volunteers out of their combined 4 million members to elect Republicans in 1994. Exit polls showed that 75 percent of evangelical voters went for the GOP and evangelicals made up a larger share of the electorate than they ever had before—fully one-third of all voters. Of all the House seats picked up by the GOP, 87 percent occurred in states in which members of the Christian Right had significant influence within the state Republican Party. By comparison, in states in which the Christian Right had no influence within the state Republican Party, only three Democratic incumbents lost—and one of those was under a 17-count federal indictment. Republican gains were also heavily concentrated in the South, where conservative white evangelicals make up a disproportionate share of the population. For much of the twentieth century, fundamentalists had abstained from voting. In 1994, some 74 percent of white evangelicals voted, closing the historic participation gap with other whites.

"They were dancing upon what they thought was the grave of a pro-family religious conservative movement," Reed had remarked shortly before the 1994 midterm election. "They overlooked one thing: Central to our theology is the belief in resurrection."

STEALTH, HOWEVER, SEEMED to be a one-off. There were signs that the sneak attack wouldn't work a second time. Even as the Christian Coalition picked up hundreds of seats in 1992 in virgin territory by replicating the San Diego model, their incumbents lost in San Diego County itself. A counter-mobilization against the Christian Right defeated almost every one of the right-wing incumbents—including a spokeswoman for Operation Rescue, a Christian Coalition grassroots trainer, and a child care provider who had campaigned to ban a book about witches. In 1993, in founder Pat Robertson's home state of Virginia, Michael Farris, the national leader of the Christian home-schooling movement and former legal counsel for Beverly LaHaye's Concerned Women for America, ran for lieutenant governor with a campaign against the "feminist agenda." His female opponent explicitly called him a "stealth candidate" who hoped to "fly under the radar" by mobilizing fundamentalists. Farris lost.

That's where the Contract with America came in. Emphasizing traditional mainstream Republican ideas of low taxes, free enterprise, and limited government, the Contract made no mention of the cultural issues that had helped Clinton win the presidency, divided Republicans from one other, and alienated independent voters. No imminent destruction of the family, no abortion, no prayer in schools, no flag-burning, not even a single allusion to gays. Just a few dog whistles audible only to the sexual fundamentalists: welfare reform to "discourage teen pregnancy and illegitimacy"; the "family reinforcement act" to strengthen "rights of parents in their children's education." The strategists behind the Contract—Gingrich, Armey, and Norquist—had worked with pollster Frank Luntz to conduct focus groups on the Contract with independent Perot voters. The silence on cultural issues was deliberate—Perot's supporters and many of the Republicans who had deserted the party two years earlier were pro-choice and believed government should stay out of private matters. The word "Republican" hadn't played well with the target group, so the original title, "Republican Contract," had been dropped before the Contract's public debut.

The Contract with America swayed few voters but was eminently helpful for public relations. It allowed the national Republican Party to rebrand, while giving the press a handy meme for writing about Republicans in a way that distracted attention from the Christian Right and the issues of gays, abortion, and feminism, which had galvanized the sexual fundamentalists to vote in greater numbers than ever before. The Contract provided novice candidates with a unifying, if deceptive national message, while their campaigns relied on the mobilization of sexual fundamentalists. Its value was to disguise and distract, a variation of Reed's face-painting.

. . .

In 1994, the silver-haired and silver-tongued Texas governor Ann Richards was one of the most admired Democratic politicians in the nation. Running for reelection, she was having an unexpectedly rough go of it, even though her approval rating was 60 percent and the state economy was booming, with hundreds of thousands of jobs created while the rest of the nation suffered through a jobless recovery. Flying over the state one day on her way to a campaign event, Richards tried to work a reporter in order to undo the damage her opponent had inflicted on her. "You have been hearing a very skillfully crafted Republican message."

The reporter was confused, but Richards remained cryptic. "I know what it is, but I don't want to say."

It was that Richards was secretly a lesbian (she wasn't) and her ulterior motive as governor was to advance "the gay agenda." The proof? She had appointed women, Hispanics, African Americans, and yes, some gays, to state office.

"There was clearly an organized Republican movement to keep out there a couple of issues, gays and guns, in the forefront," said Richards's press secretary, Chuck MacDonald. "And I don't think it's any secret that the person who really set the Republican agenda was Karl Rove. He drove it."

Rove denied his candidate's campaign had anything to do with the rumors. The Republican gubernatorial candidate, George W. Bush, had promised he would run a positive campaign and would not engage in personal attacks and that's what he was doing. What others did? Well, that was their business. In East Texas, where the rumors had first come to Richards's attention, Bush's local campaign chairman said, "Homosexuality is not something we encourage, reward, or acknowledge as an acceptable situation." A push-poll from an unidentified source asked voters if they would be more or less likely to vote for Richards if they "knew her staff is dominated by lesbians."

On November 8, 1994, the day Republicans won control of the U.S. Congress, Richards carried 56 percent of all Texas voters who were not white evangelicals. Bush, however, won 62 percent of the white evangelical vote to win the governorship of the nation's second most populous state, with 53 percent of the vote to Richards's 46.

Political handicappers were surprised, not just that the popular Richards had lost, but that the undistinguished Bush had won. At the time, most people who followed politics saw George's younger brother Jeb Bush as Herbert Walker's heir apparent. George W. was a bon vivant with a somewhat checkered past, who had tried his hand at the oil business and the baseball business. He had lost his one attempt at election sixteen years earlier. They openly doubted that George W. was destined for greatness. But Jeb had run a bit too far to the right and had narrowly lost his bid to become Florida's governor. To everyone's surprise, even it seemed, Barbara and Poppy Bush, the face of the third generation of the Bush dynasty was to be George W. Bush.

Casual observers of the campaign would have been surprised by the strong evangelical turnout for Bush, given how much had been made of the Christian Right's dissatisfaction with the Republican candidates for statewide office in Texas. Bush and Republican senatorial candidate Kay Bailey Hutchison opposed abortion, yet they both favored exceptions in the case of rape, incest, or danger to the life of the mother, compromises that were anathema to antiabortion activists. Common wisdom held that the Texas Christian Right was making the best of a bad situation and had just gone along with the candidates they were powerless to depose. After all, George had the most recognizable family name in the Republican Party.

Despite the success of the sexual counterrevolutionaries in the 1994 midterm elections, many candidates whom voters perceived to be too close to the Christian Right lost. The Christian Right fared poorly in several large, diverse states, such as Florida, Oregon, California, and Minnesota. Oregon and Idaho even voted down antigay initiatives put on the ballot by the sexual fundamentalists. One of the most notorious casualties of the season's overzealous sexual fundamentalists had been Jeb.

In Texas, the birthplace of the sexual counterrevolution and the home of Lottie Beth Hobbs and the Reverend James Robison, the leaders of the sexual counterrevolution had figured out how to mollify the demanding grassroots activists while keeping them safely hidden in the shadows. When Dick Weinhold, the head of fundraising for Reverend Pat Robertson's 1988 presidential campaign, first arrived in Texas to lead the state's Christian Coalition, he hired Alice Patterson, one of Phyllis Schlafly's veteran organizers, to organize the state. Weinhold instituted an invitation-only weekly meeting of right-wing interest groups and Republican Party factions, where leaders could hash out their differences in private. Patterson, the former president of a Texas Eagle Forum chapter, took responsibility for recruiting members. She organized 134 local Christian Coalition chapters.

Patterson's organizing of the grassroots sexual fundamentalists paid off. Among the delegates to the 1994 state Republican Party convention, half had never before served as a delegate. Two-thirds were active in the Christian Coalition, the Christian home-schooling movement, Operation Rescue, the Eagle Forum, or another group of the Christian Right. A survey of state GOP delegates showed that abortion was the most important issue to them, with education—that is, sex education, creationism, and prayer—also at the top of their concerns. Delegates on the district and state level had adopted resolutions calling for the quarantine of people with HIV and declaring that abortion would bring "God's judgment upon our nation." When the pro-choice state party chairman accused the Christian Right of turning the party into a church, she was booed, voted out of office, and replaced with a sexual fundamentalist. Only 8 percent of delegates thought of themselves as opponents of the Christian Right. The convention voted down a resolution introduced by moderates to affirm that Republicans could have different views.

On the campaign trail, the newly mobilized GOP activists acted quite differently. The Texan Christian Right stayed on message denouncing Hillarycare and touting items from the Contract with America. Meanwhile, out of view of journalists, the Christian Coalition distributed 3 million voter guides rating candidates on the issues of abortion, sex education, and prayer in schools.

In public, candidate Bush demonstrated total message control and a talent for retail politics. Over and over, he stated his top issues were education and juvenile crime. As far as the average Texas voter had been told, the Christian Right was weak and without influence. Little was made of the fact that Bush had been his father's liaison to the Christian Right in the 1992 presidential campaign, or that he was

born-again himself. Nor did the GOP's rank-and-file zealotry raise
questions about the man who would soon be lauded nationally as a
pragmatist with bipartisan inclinations. Even Molly Ivins, a sharp-
witted, progressive, nationally recognized, Texas journalist, wasn't
too worried. "As Bush brothers go, Shrub—George the younger—is
not bad. He's less mean and less right-wing than his brother Jeb and
smarter than his brother Neil."

THE VOTING SURGE in the 1994 election by the sexual fundamentalists was met by no counterforce from the Democratic base. The
paralysis at the federal level, caused by Republican obstructionism
and Democratic infighting, had demoralized ordinary Democratic
voters. President Clinton had failed to deliver on the promised change
and the economy remained in the tank, at least as far as job growth
was concerned. Voters who were registered but did not vote in the
midterm elections of 1994 were more likely to be Democrats; those
who did vote were more conservative than the registered voters who
stayed home. Democratic turnout in 1994 was neither better nor
worse than it had been in previous midterm elections. But as Reed
and other leaders of the sexual counterrevolution observed, midterms
are typically low turnout elections, which provide an opportunity for
a craftily organized minority to dominate far beyond its numbers.

Although the resurrection of the Christian Right was duly noted
by the political classes, vanquished Democrats interpreted the results
in far more apocalyptic terms. It had been ludicrous for Clinton to
lead with abortion rights and gays in the military, and Clinton's missteps had alienated the moderate middle. The DLC's Al From crowed
that Clinton had gotten his comeuppance for ignoring their advice.
"For President Clinton there is a pretty blunt message," he said. "Get
with the program, or you'll have to pay the consequences." It was the
second coming of the conservative revolution, brought to you by that
old stalwart, the elusive Reagan Democrat. Democrats, overreacting
once again, conceded far more ground to the sexual counterrevolution than circumstances warranted.

Stan Greenberg insisted Clinton had failed because he had not followed Greenberg's advice. The pollster had told Clinton to lead with

welfare reform and hold off on health care reform; he had disagreed with the executive orders rescinding the Mexico City Policy limiting international family planning and vehemently opposed the one on gays in the military.

Greenberg's settled conviction drew sustenance from the personal slight he had experienced at Clinton's hands. Immediately after the election, Greenberg was eased out of the administration proper with not so much as a personal good-bye from Clinton. "Clinton and I had been joined at the hip," Greenberg wrote, "I simply presumed I was too central to our political project." In his 1995 book, *Middle Class Dreams*, Greenberg dusted off his ten-year-old reports on the Reagan Democrats from his Macomb, Michigan, focus groups to heap condemnation on Clinton, the Democratic Congress, and Democratic cultural progressives alike. He left no doubt that he blamed the McGoverniks and their heirs for abandoning and alienating working and middle-class white men. "The racial and cultural polarization" of the sixties and seventies "changed the imagery of the parties, giving the Republicans access to working- and middle-class voters and making many of them inaccessible to the Democrats." Greenberg would gain the opportunity to retest his theory in 2000, when Al Gore elevated him to a top position in his presidential campaign during the convention. It was always all about the Reagan Democrats.

E. J. Dionne also revisited the subject of the Democrats' collapse, middle-class voter flight, and the unfortunate polarization of American politics. In *They Only Look Dead*, Dionne cast himself as the tribune of the so-called Anxious Middle, "the group that holds the future of American politics in its hands." The Anxious Middle, Dionne wrote, "feels pressed by economic change and worries that the country is experiencing a moral and social breakdown." It "was torn between acceptance of many recent social changes and a strong streak of traditionalism." Its members recoiled when Clinton appeared to be more committed to lifting the ban on gays serving in the military than he was to delivering a tax credit to middle-class parents. "On questions of culture and morality," Dionne concluded, "the Anxious Middle is neither repressive nor permissive." Like Greenberg, Dionne believed Clinton had it right on the campaign trail but had failed to deliver. He viewed "Clintonism" as a brilliant synthesis of the social moderation and economic liberalism craved by the Anxious Middle. But Clintonism had gone off track, derailed by Clinton's misplaced priorities, tawdry character, and the self-defeating infighting within the Democratic congressional caucus.

Dionne, a practicing Catholic whose own political odyssey began in Catholic social justice circles, shared the values he perceived to be held by the Anxious Middle. He was also refreshingly even-tempered, unlike some of his secular Democratic counterparts, who were liberally dispensing blame—to everyone but themselves.

When the going got tough, the economic progressives got going—back to the Reagan days when the cultural progressives were to blame. Clinton's presidential campaign had "signaled cultural moderation and articulated the pocketbook frustrations of ordinary people," Robert Kuttner, editor of *The American Prospect*, ventured. "But in office he seemed a cultural liberal who failed to produce on economics." Making matters worse, according to Kuttner, "Organized minorities and single-cause liberals" are "ungrateful for what [they perceive] as half-hearted support from the president," even though they were unable to produce an electoral majority for the party. "If Democrats fail to restore allegiances based on pocketbook affiliation, they will be swamped by social issues." Jeff Faux, founder of the Economic Policy Institute, a labor-affiliated think tank that did cutting-edge research on the decline of the middle class and the growing economic divide, took aim at the cultural progressives and the DLC alike. "Democrats have always been out of sync with the white working class on social issues . . . When Democrats sound like Republicans on economic issues, they lose because they are not as credible as social conservatives."

Further left in the Democratic Party, some men interpreted the midterm election as a mandate to reassert control over the wayward party and their comrades alike. While conservative Republicans had been waging class war on ordinary Americans for the benefit of corporations, they insisted, the Left had rendered itself impotent by wasting its scarce political capital on so-called identity politics. Todd Gitlin, one-time leader of the sixties' Students for a Democratic Society and an important figure in the antiwar movement, and now a professional sociologist, elaborated this left Zeitgeist in his 1995 book, *The Twilight of Common Dreams*, a screed against identity politics and multiculturalism, which received lavish praise in left circles. The road to progressive victory, Gitlin and others reasoned with reference to American history, was paved with the votes of white working-class men. (They seemed to have overlooked the fact that women and African Americans who lived in the South couldn't vote during the heyday of many of those progressive victories.) "A Left that was serious about winning political power and reducing the inequality of wealth and income would stop lambasting all white men, and would take it as elementary to reduce frictions among white men, blacks, white women, and Hispanics," he asserted with little evidence that anyone was in fact lambasting all white men. But "in the current climate, there are no impediments to the demonization of white left-liberals, males in particular." Feminists, gays, and multiculturalists, in short, were slowing the march of leftist triumph. They should step aside and allow those who understood the real America to lead the charge.

We can only speculate about why so many Democrats who otherwise disagreed with each other settled on the notion that women, gays, and cultural progressives were to blame for the electoral woes of their party. Certainly, without much thought given to the sacrifice they were demanding, many were convinced that the ends, Democratic victory, justified the means. Yet there was more to it than that. Handwringing about the feckless Democratic Party and its betrayal of white men, unsubstantiated claims about the cultural conservatism of the Anxious Middle, and the like all sprung from a common subterranean spring of discontent. Many Democratic men were deeply uneasy about the continuing unfolding of the sexual revolution, feminism, and the gay rights movement and the political changes they entailed. Unlike their GOP counterparts, these Democrats had no interest in turning the clock back to an imaginary Eden of nuclear families, Christian traditionalism, and sexual repression enforced by the state. Still, they had little compunction about essentially demanding that women, gays, and cultural progressives be silent and wait their turn while they courted the elusive conservative white man.

Once again, Democratic leaders misread the mood of the electorate, as well as the motives, machinations, and liabilities of their Republican opponents.

"REGARDLESS OF WHAT any of us tells him," Labor Secretary Robert Reich wrote in his journal after the 1994 midterm election, President Clinton "is gravitating to another spot, a black hole whose pull is overwhelming. The hole doesn't show up at any of our meetings, but its presence can be detected by watching the influence it's exerting on the biggest planet of all. I can't ignore it or rationalize it any longer. The black hole is Dick Morris."

The Democrat-in-chief, by all accounts, was despondent and nearly paralyzed in the wake of the GOP victory. Seeking a way back into the voters' good graces, Bill and Hillary called in an old adviser, the pollster and political consultant Dick Morris, who had engineered Clinton's comeback many years earlier in Arkansas. Morris, widely disliked and described by "everyone" as "mesmerizing, cynical, unscrupulous," in Reich's words, was unusual for a political consultant, as he hired himself out to both parties. By the time he was called in to save the Clintons, he was working almost exclusively for Republicans.

Whereas Democrats were fighting over the soul of the Democratic Party, Morris cared only about winning the 1996 presidential election. To that end, he devised the cynical strategy of triangulation. Triangulation called for Clinton to steer to the right of Congressional Democrats and to the left of Congressional Republicans. As each cried foul, Clinton would appear to stand above the partisan fray, the decisive man who had bucked them all, the champion of the center. As far as Morris was concerned, whatever the polls said was appealing to fickle swing voters, that's what Clinton should do.

The president, of course, wanted to be reelected—too much so, in the eyes of many Democrats appalled by the compromises he was willing to make. But Clinton would also deploy triangulation as a defensive weapon against the Gingrich revolutionaries, in order to protect core Democratic programs—Medicare, Medicaid, Social Security, the environment, and education.

Clinton's task of protecting the legacy of six decades of Democratic liberal rule was made easier when the newly elected Republican Congress, with 73 freshmen put in office mostly by the sexual counterrevolutionaries, quickly overreached. The votes were hardly counted before Gingrich announced his support for a long wish list of the sexual counterrevolutionaries. Even Republican governors balked when Gingrich said a constitutional amendment allowing prayer in schools was on the top of his agenda. Gingrich floated the notion that, rather than reward women who had children out of wedlock with welfare payments, their children should be put in orphanages. He labeled liberals "the enemy of normal Americans" and the Clintons "countercultural McGoverniks"; he circulated talking points to his caucus recommending they describe Democrats as "pathetic, sick, corrupt, traitorous, and criminal." Gingrich's mother told CBS News that her son regularly called Hillary Clinton a "bitch." Tom DeLay, a Texas congressman elected at the same time as Bush with enthusiastic support from the Christian Right, called the Environmental Protection Agency "the Gestapo of government." The House passed bills to cripple the EPA. The budget passed by the Republican House slashed funding for Medicare, and Gingrich predicted the agency running the program "would wither on the vine." House Republicans put forward constitutional amendments banning late-term abortions and flag burning. Republicans repealed several gun control laws and eviscerated funding for National Public Radio and the Department of Education. In the first ninety-three days of the 104th Congress, the House passed all but one item on the Contract with America.

The Republican fulminations about the evils of the federal government fell on more skeptical ears after the April 19, 1995, bombing of the Alfred P. Murrah Federal Building by native-born right-wing terrorists. The Oklahoma City bombing killed 168 people, including 19 children under the age of six attending a preschool in the building. It proved to be a turning point, in part because Clinton recovered his voice and spoke for sanity. Gingrich and the anti-government crowd toned down their rhetoric, but they continued to push a radical anti-government agenda. In November, 1995, Clinton vetoed a Republican budget plan that would have, among other things, raised premiums for Medicare. With no budget in place, the federal government partially shut down. The next budget the Republicans passed slashed programs for the poor and included cuts to Medicare spending of $270 billion, which was almost evenly balanced out by a $245 billion tax break for wealthy Americans. Clinton again vetoed it, and the government shut down for twenty-one days. Americans approved of Clinton's firmness and blamed Republicans for the shutdown. A year after the so-called Gingrich revolution, Clinton's approval rating had risen to 52 percent, support for the Democratic Party had recovered to its pre-midterm levels, and Gingrich was the most disliked politician in the nation.

EVEN AS THE evidence mounted that the public was reacting negatively to the Republican overreach, the sexual fundamentalists forgot that in the previous national election they had triumphed by stealth. As the 1996 presidential campaign season opened in September 1995, Reverend Pat Robertson crowed that the Christian Coalition aimed to take control of every state Republican Party. The Christian Right demanded purity from the GOP presidential contenders. Pro-choice Pennsylvania Senator Arlen Specter, who revived Barry Goldwater's libertarian slogan "out of our pockets, off our backs and out of our bedrooms," was run out of the race months before any Republican had a chance to vote.

In January 1996, at a rally held before the 1996 Iowa presidential caucus, Phyllis Schlafly's Eagle Forum, Beverly LaHaye's Concerned Women for America, James Dobson's Family Research Council, Reed and Robertson's Christian Coalition, and other Christian Right groups introduced the Marriage Protection Resolution. The effort was a textbook case of wedge-issue politics, the purpose of which was to rally the base. With the sexual fundamentalists in control of the Iowa Republican Party, every remaining Republican presidential candidate signed on to the resolution. In May, Georgia Representative Bob Barr, who described himself as a libertarian, introduced a bill called the Defense of Marriage Act (DOMA), defining marriage in federal law as solely between one man and one woman, and denying federal recognition to same-sex marriages performed in the states. Barr argued for the necessity of the law because "the flames of hedonism, the flames of narcissism, the flames of self-centered morality are licking at the very foundation of our society, the family unit."

DOMA dragged President Clinton and Congressional Democrats into a Republican intramural battle between the sexual counter-revolutionaries and mainstream Republicans. Six months away from the presidential election, the economy was once again booming, job creation had picked up, wages were rising, the GOP-controlled Congress was unpopular, and the Republican nominee, Senator Bob Dole, inspired neither the Republican base nor the public at large. Nonetheless, Democrats' outsized fear of the allegedly conservative middle led the vast majority of congressional Democrats to capitulate to right-wing sexual fundamentalists. Only fourteen senators, all Democrats, and 67 representatives voted against DOMA. Granted, gay marriage was a very new issue that garnered little support, even from those who supported all other measures to protect gay civil rights. Still, Clinton and congressional Democrats behaved as though they knew they were in the wrong. To counteract the impression left by their support of DOMA, Democrats called a vote on the Employment Non-Discrimination Act (ENDA). It almost passed. Clinton signed DOMA in the middle of the night, in a futile attempt to bury the news, while his spokesman denounced the bill as gay baiting. A month later, however, the Clinton reelection campaign ran a radio ad targeted to religious voters that touted Clinton's support for DOMA. The ad was designed by Mark Penn, who took over the reelection campaign when Dick Morris was forced out when news broke that he was sharing political gossip with a prostitute whom he employed.

The Republican Right had also conspired to cue up another cultural bombshell they hoped to detonate right before the election. Shortly after the 1994 midterms, David Brock signed a $1 million book contract to write a biography about Hillary Clinton, scheduled for publication during the '96 campaign. Brock's publisher asked him only one question about his plans for the book—"Was Hillary a lesbian?"—and Brock knew he expected *The Real Anita Hill* to be the template for a politically useful campaign tract. Hillary, like Anita Hill, "was a feminist icon," Brock wrote. "Among my audience, she was easily the most reviled figure on the national scene, even more so than her husband."

Troopergate had made Brock a superstar among the sexual fundamentalists. Yet having risen to fame by peddling a salacious story about the president's alleged consensual sexual affairs, Brock's own sex life became fair game. Brock's problem was that he was a closeted gay man.

Soon the contradictions would be more than Brock could bear, as he recounted in his memoir, *Blinded by the Right*, one of the most perceptive and revealing books to date of the Clinton era. Threatened with being outed, Brock came out on his own. Doing so, however, compelled him to take the measure of his gay-loathing comrades on the Right. In the meantime, a definitive book by reporters Jane Mayer and Jill Abramson on the Anita Hill affair convinced Brock that he had been played by Clarence Thomas's friends and, in his ideological delirium, had written a book full of easily discredited lies. For more than a year, Brock drank himself into oblivion while trying to evade his contractual responsibility to write another character assassination. Ultimately, he decided to try to behave like a real journalist and write a balanced portrait of the First Lady. *The Seduction of Hillary Rodham* offered no "red meat" for the election. It was the beginning of the end for Brock in the conservative movement; old friends shunned him and the invitations and accolades vanished. Still, as he wrote in *Blinded by the Right,* "In finding Hillary's humanity, I was beginning to find my own."

Brock's crisis of conscience deprived Republicans of an election-season weapon, but even if he had performed according to plan, it is doubtful it would have had any effect outside the echo chambers of the Right. Clinton's reelection was a foregone conclusion months before Election Day. Only late-breaking reports about potentially illegal fundraising threw the result into doubt.

With most Americans feeling positive about the economic future, Clinton was swept back into office, but deprived once again of a majority of the popular vote by a third-party run by billionaire Ross Perot. Clinton won 61 percent of women voters, Dole 33 percent. At 15 points, the gender gap was even more pronounced than it had been in 1992. Views on the national economy had the greatest impact on voter choice, yet abortion remained an important determinant of the vote, just as it had been in 1992. The bottom line was that economic optimism and support for legal abortion were the deciding issues in Clinton's reelection.

The economy and abortion, however, were not the only factors. Dole had won the Republican nomination by pandering to the Christian Right sexual fundamentalists, which had the effect of driving away other potential supporters. A person who was antagonistic to the Christian Right was much less likely to vote for Dole, even though Dole had after the primary tried to distance himself from the movement. Two years into the Gingrich revolution, the American public had taken the measure of the Republican Party's bedfellows and become disgusted. In the 1996 presidential election, voters who felt negatively toward fundamentalists outnumbered those who felt positively toward them by a 4-to-1 margin. How one felt about the Christian Right was one of the most powerful predictors of how one was likely to vote.

It seemed the GOP couldn't win without the sexual fundamentalists, but it couldn't win with them either. Considered together, the elections of 1992, 1994, and 1996 set in relief the Republican Party's dilemma. Republicans needed the sexual fundamentalists of the Christian Right in order to amass an electoral majority. The nonpartisan Pew Research Center estimated that "moralists" accounted for 40 percent of Republican primary voters. Yet, whenever Republicans won power, the sexual counterrevolutionaries forced Republican elected officials to overreach. The fundamentalist obsession with sex, abortion, and gays was deeply unpopular with the public, liberals, moderates, and swing voters, and once the Republican Party was firmly identified with the Christian Right, voters recoiled. A potential solution to the GOP's problem had a successful trial run in one of 1994's marquee races. It would take Gingrich's self-destructive four-year reign, the impeachment debacle, and another GOP rout before a disciplined Republican Party came to appreciate the beauty of a more sophisticated form of stealth, as practiced by a Texas gubernatorial candidate and his brilliant campaign mastermind, Karl Rove.

9

THE STARR CHAMBER

O N JANUARY 17, 1998, a right-wing website, The Drudge
Report, posted a story about a sexual affair between the
president of the United States and a White House intern.
Within days the story had made the leap from the right-wing Web
to the mainstream press, the latter justifying their tabloid-like
coverage with the disclaimer that they were merely reporting on
reports that were newsworthy. Nine days later, Bill Clinton stood
before the White House press corps, jumpy and red-faced like a
cornered adolescent, and declared categorically, "I did not have
sexual relations with that woman, Miss Lewinsky."

Nine months later, almost five years after Robert Fiske had been
appointed to investigate allegations of corruption in the Whitewater
land deal, Kenneth Starr submitted the report of the Office of the
Independent Counsel (OIC) to the House, outlining eleven possible
grounds for impeachment. Two days later, every Republican and all
but 63 Democratic representatives voted to post on the Internet the
report which neither they nor the president's lawyers had yet had a
chance to read.

Each count concerned Bill Clinton's sexual affair with Monica Lewinsky, an affair discovered through the Paula Jones civil case against Clinton. The recommendation for impeachment alleged that the president had lied about consensual sex under oath, had suborned perjury regarding that sex, and had obstructed justice by proffering a job to Lewinsky in exchange for false testimony about that sex. Starr's 445-page report included helpful subheadings such as "February 4 Sexual Encounter and Subsequent Phone Calls" but failed to mention Lewinsky's closing sworn statement to the grand jury, *"No one ever asked me to lie and I was never promised a job for my silence."* After a diligent journalist found the statement in the supporting documentation some weeks later, it appeared that perhaps Starr had cherry-picked his evidence, given that the only alleged acts that seemed to rise to the "high crimes and misdemeanors" standard involved the question of whether Clinton had tried to manipulate Lewinsky's testimony and buy her off with a job.

Two years later, Starr's successor at the OIC issued a final report and shut down the modern-day Star Chamber for good. Starr's team had come up dry in their investigation of the Whitewater real estate deal, Hillary Clinton's legal work and investments, and the various gates—Filegate, Fostergate, Travelgate, Troopergate, and a host of mini-gates. No wrongdoing, no conflicts of interest, no political favors for personal gain, no abuse of political office for the personal gain of friends, no suborning of perjury. Nothing, that is, on which to prosecute either Bill or Hillary. It had cost American taxpayers $100 million to come to that conclusion.

It is incontrovertible that Bill Clinton did have a sexual affair with Monica Lewinsky, a younger adult woman who was not his wife. In fact, many of America's twentieth-century presidents had engaged in extramarital affairs while they served in elected office. Many of the Republicans seeking to drive Clinton from office because of the Lewinsky affair had also wandered sexually from their wives and husbands. House Speaker Newt Gingrich, who spent $10 million of good Republican money to air attack ads about the Lewinsky affair on the eve of the '98 election, was at that very moment cheating on his second wife with a younger staffer, the current Mrs. Callista

Gingrich. So too had Representative Henry Hyde, who presided over impeachment hearings in the lame-duck 105th Congress. And so had Representative Bob Livingston, elected by his Republican colleagues to succeed Gingrich as speaker in the 106th Congress. And so had Rep. Helen Chenoweth, Rep. John Ensign, Rep. Mark Souder, and Rep. Mark Sanford, all Clinton-hunters and all voted into office in 1994 by the grassroots sexual counterrevolutionaries. Granted, Americans had never been treated to gossip like the Lewinsky affair in real time and in such detail, but until Clinton, the private sex lives of politicians had been largely off-limits in public debate and partisan competition.

How then did this most banal non-news become cause for the impeachment of an American president for the first time since Abraham Lincoln's successor had attempted to reverse the results of the Civil War? How did the nation get to the point where a president could be impeached for lying about sex in a civil case concerning incidents alleged to have occurred before he was president?

Because there was nothing else but sex left, and no one left to care, except the sexual fundamentalists. The problem for Clinton was that the sexual counterrevolution had commandeered not just Kenneth Starr's investigation but the Grand Old Party itself.

BY THE TIME of Clinton's second inauguration in January, 1997, not only had the American people rendered a verdict on the Clinton-hunting that had consumed the years of the Gingrich revolution, but Starr's office had reached a dead end on Whitewater and the other political corruption cases under its jurisdiction. Although they had successfully prosecuted several Clinton associates, none of the cases revealed any credible evidence that the president himself had engaged in any prosecutable offense. As in most federal prosecutions, the OIC hoped the threat of prosecution would persuade the accused to give up a higher official in exchange for immunity. Their problem was that the only ones who wanted to talk were patent liars. The others, who would have been credible witnesses, insisted there was nothing to talk about.

With little prospect of a career-enhancing prosecution of the president, Starr himself tried to exit. On February 17, 1997, he announced he was resigning, effective August 1, to take up two dean-ships at Pepperdine University, a conservative private university in Malibu, California. Starr had been in negotiations with Pepperdine since the fall, but when the news became public, a howl of protest went up from conservative and right-wing pundits. William Safire charged that Starr had "a warped sense of duty." Nor did it help his case when the *Washington Post* reported that the school of which Starr would be dean had been established by a $1.35 million donation from Pepperdine regent and Clinton-hunter Richard Mellon Scaife. (A few months later, for unrelated reasons, Scaife lost patience with his clients in the Arkansas Project and stopped writing checks. He was out of Clinton-hunting before it took its Puritanical turn.)

Called out by his patrons, Starr buckled and decided to stay on. But many of the veteran career prosecutors in the OIC, themselves certain the investigations were not going to yield indictments against the Clintons, did walk away. According to Jeffrey Toobin, the author of one of the best accounts of the legal issues in the Clinton investi-gations, the only ones left in the OIC were the "unemployable and the obsessed."

Leading the obsessed was a full-fledged sexual counterrevolu-tionary, the head of the OIC's Little Rock office, W. Hickman Ewing, Jr. Ewing was a Vietnam veteran, born-again, and the founder of a fundamentalist evangelical church where he served as a lay minister. His wife was an antiabortion activist, and their children attended a Christian school. In the early '90s, Ewing had considered going to work for the Rutherford Institute, a Christian Right legal think tank. (He went into private practice instead.) Most prosecutors in political corruption cases assume the motive of the accused is greed. Ewing and some like-minded colleagues in the OIC convinced themselves that the Clintons and their enablers were compelled to commit illegal acts by a need to cover up their sexual depravity. In the sexual tales they spun in their heads, Hillary's motive for crime was to cover up her sexual affair with Vince Foster, Hillary's friend and law partner, who had served in the administration and com-mitted suicide in July 1993. Whitewater partner Susan MacDou-gal's motive for serving jail time on contempt charges was to avoid admitting to a sexual affair with the president. And so on. Even as leads in the political corruption cases were exhausted and it was clear they would not be able to prosecute the Clintons, Ewing's office instructed FBI agents to interrogate Arkansans in order to dig up sexual dirt about Clinton.

Just as the political corruption cases had, from a legal standpoint, fizzled out, so too had the Paula Jones civil case. And as in the OIC, the more rational professionals who had once worked for Jones had been pushed aside by the sexual counterrevolutionaries.

Shortly after her case became a right-wing cause célèbre, Paula Jones and her husband, Steve, put themselves under the tutelage of Susan Carpenter-McMillan, a self-made right-wing pundit and former antiabortion activist, whose career in the movement had been cut short when she was compelled to admit to having had two abortions herself. As Jones's lawyers negotiated to secure the best settlement possible for Paula from Clinton and advised her that her prospects were dim if the case went to trial, Carpenter-McMillan convinced Steve that his best chance for making money was to sell a tell-all book, capitalizing on Paula's fabricated story of the "distinguishing characteristic" of Clinton's penis. (There was no such distinguishing characteristic, as the evidence in the case proved.) On August 29, 1997, Jones's lawyers resigned. Although they had been paid through Scaife's Arkansas Project, they weren't connected to the political conspiracy and had handled the case professionally. They told her they were pessimistic she could win, given how weak her evidence was. They expressed frustration that the case had been hijacked by right-wing activists more interested in bringing down the president than in getting her the best monetary settlement possible. In their final letter to Jones, they said they could no longer represent her in good faith. "Our opponents may portray your refusal [of a settlement] as a money-grubbing attempt to develop this story for profitable book rights, and portray you as inspired and under the influence of right-wing Clinton-haters."

With the departure of Jones's original lawyers, Carpenter-McMillan took charge and put out a call for new lawyers and additional funding. The man who stepped up was John Whitehead, president of the Rutherford Institute, member of the secretive

Christian Right–dominated Council for National Policy (CNP), and formerly an attorney for the Moral Majority and Pat Robertson's Regent University. Whitehead was the author of a 1982 Christian fundamentalist book, *The Second American Revolution*, which essentially proposed reforming the United States itself into a fundamentalist theocracy. Whitehead volunteered to pay for the costs of the lawsuit and secured a lawyer for Jones, a Rutherford Institute board member named Donovan Campbell, Jr. Campbell too was a sexual fundamentalist. His claim to legal fame was his long-running crusade to preserve Texas's 1973 Homosexual Conduct law, which made sodomy a prosecutable crime. In one of his briefs in the case, he and his colleagues wrote that the law should stand because homosexuality was a "psychopathological condition." (The Supreme Court overturned this Texas law in the landmark case extending the right of privacy to all Americans, including homosexuals, in *Lawrence and Garner v. Texas*. Texas Republicans continue, in 2011, to fight to recriminalize sodomy.) With this new team, Paula and Steve Jones were now even more deeply embedded in the world of the sexual counterrevolution. The prime objective of the Paula Jones case became how to bring down the elected president of the United States through fishing expeditions about his sex life.

It turned out Jones's original team of lawyers had sized up the case accurately. Jones's story fell apart in her deposition in the fall of 1997, in which it was established that she had experienced no damages in her job, the legal issue at stake in her case. (It also seemed questionable that the encounter as she described it had even occurred, as the established facts of the day contradicted her account of an unwelcome sexual advance.) Others who were deposed by Campbell's team about the president's sex life denied the stories or gave contradictory testimony. Considering the weakness of the evidence, Judge Susan Webber Wright issued a summary judgment on April 1, 1998, dismissing *Jones v. Clinton* for lack of merit. In other words, as a matter of law, Jones's charges were baseless and there would be no trial.

Starr's investigation and the Paula Jones case converged at the moment both cases were collapsing, and the only ones with zeal left in the crusade were the sexual fundamentalists. The intricate steps from the Jones case to the Starr report have been detailed by many

other writers. In short, through machinations by right-wing conspirators, including Ann Coulter, Richard Porter (Starr's law partner
in the firm Kirkland & Ellis), Linda Tripp (Lewinsky's friend), the
right-wing literary agent and former Nixon dirty-trickster Lucianne
Goldberg, and many others, news of Clinton's affair with Lewinsky
and the existence of Tripp's illegal tape recordings of her conversa-
tions with Lewinsky were first passed to Jones's team, and then on
to Starr's office. The object of the unethical—and in some instances,
illegal—information exchange was to trick the president into lying
about Lewinsky in his January deposition in the Jones case. That
would then provide the pretext for Starr's office to charge him with
perjury.

Why, after all the conspirators' false starts and phony charges—
about Whitewater and Filegate and Travelgate and Troopergate—was
it the Paula Jones case that ensnared Clinton? The Clinton-hunters
had gotten lost in the funhouse they themselves built. There was
no grand Clintonian corruption scheme with sex at its dark heart.
Rather, the religious fundamentalists' obsession with sex consumed
the OIC prosecutors and the new Jones team. And it found a ready
audience among the rank-and-file sexual counterrevolutionaries who
controlled the Republican Party.

NEWS OF THE Lewinsky affair sent the sexual counterrevolutionaries into a fit of delirium. "Mr. President, if these allegations are true,
you have disgraced yourself, you have disgraced the office, you have
disgraced your country, and you should leave," proclaimed Republican presidential candidate Senator John Ashcroft. He was speaking
before the Conservative Political Action Conference (CPAC), where
four years earlier Paula Jones had accused Clinton of sexual predation.
CPAC's audience gave Ashcroft a standing ovation. Oliver North,
who had been convicted on three felony counts for his role in the
Reagan administration's Iran-Contra scandal, called Clinton "President Caligula." To those who said it was "just sex" and just "lying
about sex," columnist Noemi Emery responded with self-righteous
affront in William Kristol and Rupert Murdoch's conservative magazine, *The Weekly Standard.* "Moral codes have sought to discipline

and regulate—to moralize—sexual conduct, not out of stuffiness, but because unregulated sex can cause havoc . . . The Clinton Project is not really about politics. It is about values. That is, the inversion of values." Herself inverting constitutional standards, Emery's sleight of hand had elevated illicit sex to the highest possible crime in the republic. William Bennett, former secretary of education in the Reagan administration who had since produced a steady stream of portentous and lucrative jeremiads, rushed a book out eight weeks before the 1998 elections. Clinton had "defiled" the presidency; that Americans did not care, according to Bennett, proved that the nation had sunk into a "culture of permissiveness." The theory fit neatly in his long-running refrain that the sexual revolution and feminism had eroded the foundation of American "civilization." (According to Bennett, child care ranked alongside child abuse and poverty as "threats" to child well-being. A few months after the Columbine High School massacre, Bennett sounded the alarm about the rising use of contraceptives, while saying not a word about gun violence.) Bennett, who made a small fortune on his *Book of Virtues* and its companion PBS children's cartoon, was exposed in 2003 to have lost $8 million gambling. He pleaded moral relativism; he had never, after all, said gambling was immoral.

The rank-and-file sexual fundamentalists had always been the most avid consumers of the titillating fare about Clinton's alleged sexual escapades, and the timing of the Lewinsky scandal coincided with a new round of the sexual counterrevolutionaries' disaffection with the Republican Party. That in itself nearly guaranteed that Republican politicians would join in the hysteria in an effort to keep their base mollified.

In February, malcontented leaders of the sexual counterrevolution forced a showdown within the Republican Party. James Dobson, head of Focus on the Family, and Paul Weyrich, father of the Moral Majority and founder of CNP, issued the opening public salvos in the intraparty feud. Weyrich observed that the Republican Party leadership "keeps treating the cultural conservatives as people who belong in the back of the bus, and it has caused great resentment." At the closed-door meeting of the CNP in February, Dobson declared before an audience of 300 right-wing leaders that he would "do everything in my power to tell evangelical and pro-life Christians" of the "moral and philosophical collapse of the Republican leadership." A few weeks later, Weyrich met with fifteen leaders from Concerned Women for America, the Eagle Forum, the Christian Coalition, the Traditional Values Coalition, and Focus on the Family. The Christian Right, they warned, would bolt the party unless its presidential nominee pledged fealty to their orthodoxies.

Newt Gingrich, the leader of the Republican Party after Robert Dole's crushing defeat in 1996, became the first casualty of the Lewinsky affair. Gingrich had ambitions to run for president in 2000, and after Clinton's reelection, he mothballed the Republican revolution and tried to remake himself as a pragmatist. Unbeknownst to the public, Gingrich and Clinton had secretly been negotiating a compromise on Social Security in the fall of 1997. After the Lewinsky story broke, however, Gingrich's pollsters brought him news from Iowa that the Christian Right wanted Clinton taken down and would brook no compromise. To be viable as a presidential candidate, Gingrich had to perform well in the Iowa Republican caucus, in which evangelicals in the antiabortion and home-schooling movements dominated. Gingrich chose to follow the base. He ended negotiations with Clinton and returned with vigor to his old slash-and-burn ways. The week before the 1998 midterm elections, Gingrich would authorize a $10 million ad blitz featuring Lewinsky.

Clinton's denial of the affair to everyone, including his lawyers and Hillary and their daughter, Chelsea, bought him time. In the initial wave of hysteria, Hillary's call-out of a "vast right-wing conspiracy" provided Democrats a compelling and empirically supported counter-narrative for the Lewinsky scandal. As documented in David Brock's "Confessions of a Right-Wing Hit Man," published in *Vanity Fair* six months earlier, and Joe Conason and Murray Waas's groundbreaking investigation of Scaife and the Arkansas Project, published in *The New York Observer* three weeks after the Lewinsky scandal broke, there was indeed a coordinated campaign by right-wing leaders to bring down the Clinton presidency.

But as Starr exerted pressure on Lewinsky, demanding her blue dress as the cost of gaining immunity from prosecution, Clinton realized he would have to admit to the relationship. On August 17,

Clinton told the grand jury that his relations with Lewinsky involved "inappropriate intimate contact." That night he spoke to the nation. His half-hearted admission opened the floodgates for the moralizers in the Democratic Party to join the chorus of those in the GOP.

On September 3, 1998, while the president was on an important diplomatic trip to Russia, Connecticut Democratic Senator Joseph Lieberman stood before the C-SPAN cameras in the Senate chamber and denounced the president. (The room was nearly empty of senators; many of his Democratic colleagues had begged him not to do it.) Lieberman, an observant Orthodox Jew, had always worn his piety on his sleeve, proselytized for more religion in public life, and not infrequently acted as a moral scold.

While other Democrats worried whether the president had in fact committed perjury, suborned perjury, or obstructed justice, Lieberman was in a frenzy about the sex itself. "I must respectfully disagree with the President's contention that his relationship with Monica Lewinsky and the way in which he misled us about it is nobody's business but his family's and that even Presidents have private lives," he began. Clinton's dalliance, Lieberman pronounced, was "immoral" and "harmful, for it sends a message of what is acceptable behavior to the larger American family—particularly to our children." The "stability and integrity of the family" was threatened by the "mind-set" of "today's anything-goes culture, where sexual promiscuity is too often treated as just another life-style choice." Clinton's own promiscuity, he continued, "compromised his moral authority at a time when Americans of every political persuasion agree that the decline of the family is one of the most pressing problems we are facing."

But Lieberman's motives were neither wholly pure nor wholly puritanical, as he later explained to Robert Kaiser of the *Washington Post*. "We had worked so hard," he said, to demonstrate that Democrats had learned "the difference between right and wrong . . . [and to] reestablish the party's connection to mainstream values." And because "Clinton himself was at the center of this transformation, I feared that . . . we were in danger as a party." Invoking the tired trope of the mainstream voter's cultural conservatism and ignoring well-publicized polls showing that the mainstream voter agreed with

Clinton that his sex life was a private matter, Lieberman had made himself the new face of the Democrats' own sexual counterrevolution.

Lieberman's speech emboldened other Democrats to take a swing at their leader, perhaps for reasons having little to do with their own concern for moral rectitude. Senators Bob Kerrey and Daniel Patrick Moynihan, both of whom had sparred with the Clintons on policy and Bill and Hillary's lack of proper deference to the august Senate, entered the empty Senate chamber to echo Lieberman's censure. Moynihan then went on the Sunday news shows to call for impeachment hearings to be hurried up, explicitly saying that "moral issues" are relevant to impeachment. (Lieberman preferred formal censure and thought his speech would help tamp down the impeachment furor.) Throughout the week, reporters trapped Democrats into going on record saying how disappointed they were and that the president should resign or be censured. In this atmosphere, only a handful were willing to call out the Republican conspirators on their games.

All of this transpired before anyone even knew what evidence of "high crimes and misdemeanors" Starr's investigation might contain. On September 11, 1998, Americans finally did learn what Starr and his team of sexual counterrevolutionaries had unearthed. Thanks to the Starr Report, a graphic account of every conversation and intimate encounter between the president of the United States and a young, confused, and love-sick woman is memorialized in America's official historical archives. Thousands of pages have been written about the byzantine 8-year-long "hunting of the president," in the apt phrase of journalists Joe Conason and Gene Lyons. Every American institution involved—the legal system, the media, the political system—has been subjected to well-deserved criticism in these matters. Americans had made it abundantly clear, then and afterward, that they had too much information.

To the dismay of the sexual fundamentalists, the American people responded to the Lewinsky affair by turning against Republicans. Polls showed consistently throughout the year that two out of three Americans did not want Clinton to resign; did not favor impeachment; thought the affair with Monica Lewinsky was a private matter; disapproved of the GOP-controlled Congress's handling of the

Clinton scandal; and thought Starr's investigation was partisan, not impartial. Among Democrats, 68 percent were *strongly* pro-Clinton, most of the rest pro-Clinton, and only 8 percent viewed him unfavorably. Among independents, 79 percent were pro-Clinton. Even among Republicans, 42 percent approved of the job Clinton was doing as president.

The 1998 November midterm elections gave the American people an opportunity to register their disapproval of Republicans. Democrats won five House seats, lost only one incumbent, and defeated two GOP Senate incumbents—Clinton-hunters Al D'Amato and Lauch Faircloth. Not since 1922 had the incumbent president's party picked up House seats in the midterm elections of his second term. Not since 1822 had a political party fared so poorly in a similar point in the electoral cycle. The GOP congressional majority, touted just four years earlier as evidence of a permanent Republican realignment, fell to a precarious 11 seats in the House.

Following the lodestar of the sexual counterrevolution, Starr, Gingrich, and the Republican Party had overreached and found themselves rebuked by the American voter. Neither the economy, nor the president's standing, nor other matters that typically determine voting behavior came into play in the 1998 race. Impeachment was the sole and most important issue influencing the vote. The anti-Clinton crusade depressed Republican turnout, thus undercutting the GOP's historic turnout advantage in midterm elections. As political scientist Alan Abramowitz summed up the results, "It's Monica, Stupid."

Republican politicians were certainly aware of the negative view of their actions, so why did they bulldoze ahead on such a patently self-destructive path? The base demanded it as the price of their support. In solid Republican House districts, pro-impeachment representatives had little difficulty winning reelection. But in swing districts and in statewide Senate races, impeachment was a losing proposition. The sexual counterrevolutionaries' capture of many Republican state parties over the decade had emboldened the Right, while simultaneously undermining the GOP's viability on a national level.

In the end, Gingrich, not Clinton, fell victim to the sexual fundamentalists. Three days after the election, Gingrich resigned the speakership. In January, in the midst of an ethics investigation of his political action committee and revelations that for six years he had been engaged in an extramarital affair with a young staffer, Gingrich resigned his House seat.

If the voters took Gingrich's departure as Speaker to mean Republicans accepted the verdict of the election, they were wrong. On November 19, Starr testified to the House Judiciary Committee that, in the cases for which the Independent Counsel investigation was empowered (Whitewater, Travelgate, and Filegate), he had no grounds on which to charge Bill or Hillary. Nevertheless, he would continue his investigation. Just maybe, he told Congress, something would turn up even after impeachment proceedings were done, and he would be able to slap criminal indictments on the president and First Lady.

Although Starr essentially exonerated the Clintons in that statement, under the direction of Texas Representative Tom "The Hammer" DeLay, Republicans expanded impeachment proceedings. DeLay insisted the Republican base would reward them for impeaching Clinton over a moral issue, but on the day the House began the impeachment debate, a *New York Times* poll reported that public approval of the GOP was at a 14-year low. The same day, the *New York Post* outed Gingrich's designated successor, Representative Robert Livingston, for having extramarital affairs over many years. Not to be deterred, the GOP-controlled lame-duck Congress soldiered on. On December 19, the House voted on a near party-line vote to impeach the president of the United States. Nearly two months later, with 81 percent of Americans approving of Clinton's handling of his presidency, the Senate acquitted the president.

Hillary famously charged during the opening weeks of the Lewinsky scandal that a "vast right-wing conspiracy" was manufacturing phony scandals for the sole purpose of destroying Bill's presidency. No, insisted Ann Coulter, a member of the conspiracy, it was "a small, intricately knit right-wing conspiracy—and I'd like that clarified." The conspirators had been confident they were running the show, for the benefit of Republican politicians, corporate America, neoconservatives, and market fundamentalists. In the first years of the Clinton presidency, the ginned-up scandals had derailed health care reform and put Hillary in her place. But after the Gingrich revolutionaries had ridden to power on the votes of the sexual fundamentalists, things hadn't gone exactly the way Coulter, Scaife, Porter, and the others had planned. The masters had become the puppets of the sexual counterrevolution.

WHAT EXPLAINED THE resurrection of the Democratic Party, so often declared dead since the landslide defeat of George McGovern? The majority of Americans were values voters, and their values had become progressive. The results of the 1998 midterm elections were not simply an eruption of passing voter disgust. Instead they reflected monumental shifts in opinion since 1972 when the bipartisan sexual counterrevolution began.

To appreciate the significance of this sea change in cultural values, consider this. Clinton would have lost the 1992 and 1996 elections had Americans not become more progressive on social and cultural issues. According to an analysis conducted by sociologist Clem Brooks, two-thirds of the increase in Democratic Party support between McGovern's defeat and Clinton's victory was due to the increase in liberal attitudes on women's issues among voters. Almost all of the rest of the increase was due to the electorate's more liberal views on black civil rights. Support for gay civil rights also helped Democrats. But for these shifts in opinion, Republicans would have controlled the White House unbroken for 36 years—longer, by the way, than the New Deal era of Democratic dominance.

Women voters were indispensable to the post-sixties Democratic revival. Women accounted for six out of every ten Democratic votes. Added to that was another developing trend: women voted at higher rates than their male peers. Clinton won women by 20 points against Bush, and 28 points against Dole. Although southern white women were starting to vote more like men and more Republican, northern white women identified with the Democratic Party over the Republican Party by an 11-point margin. These gender gaps, several scholars independently concluded, stemmed from women's support for women's rights, reproductive rights, and gay rights, and the importance of these issues in determining their political behavior.

As the Democrats solidified their advantage with women because of their cultural progressivism, the GOP drove its own voters away with its traditional family values, cultural conservatism, and capitulation to the sexual counterrevolutionaries. Mainline Protestants left the party because of it. Working women were repelled by the party's rejection of programs supporting women's economic advance, often defended by sexual counterrevolutionaries such as Phyllis Schlafly as necessary to protect traditional family-oriented women. Professionals, once the most reliably Republican occupational group, in 1972 switched quickly, sharply, and to this date, permanently, to Democratic identification. Although professionals continued to favor the GOP's more conservative economic policies, their progressive cultural values trumped their material self-interest. Brooks calculated that 107 percent of professionals' vote change over the 20 years from 1972 to 1992 was due to this increasing social liberalism. (In other words, they would have voted even more Democratic had their economic views not inclined them somewhat toward the GOP.) More Americans were worried about the theological takeover of the political system than about the supposed moral breakdown of the American people. Forty-five percent of white voters had a negative view of the Christian Right, compared to only 11 percent who held a positive view. Only 5 percent of the general American public, excluding conservative evangelical Protestants, was at all concerned with the so-called decline of the family. One out of five voters, according to political scientists Louis Bolce and Gerald de Maio, "intensely dislike fundamentalists . . . perceived members of this religious group as militantly intolerant, ideologically extreme, inegalitarian with respect to women's rights, and monolithically Republican." And those anti-fundamentalist views had emerged as one of the strongest predictors of their vote.

By the late 1990s, Democrats approached elections with a built-in advantage. The largest group of voters, women, favored Democrats by solid majorities. So too did those who were members of the fastest growing occupational group, professionals. Already by 1992 professionals and managers were as numerous as blue-collar workers in the Democratic coalition. The fastest growing religious group, the secular or non-affiliated, also favored the Democratic Party. The party's cultural progressivism was the deciding factor for all of these groups.

Nevertheless, the Democrats did seem to have a problem. White men remained cool to Clinton and to the Democratic Party, and the notion lived on that it was because the party ignored their material interests and embraced McGovernik cultural progressivism. Studies by a number of political scientists decisively refuted the common wisdom that lower-income men voted Republican against their class interest. Indeed, class voting among them had become more pronounced since the Age of Nixon. Outside the white South, there was really only one group from the old coalition that stood aloof: male Reagan Democrats. Blue-collar middle-income men, especially those who had not attended college, were true swing voters, quick to punish politicians who failed to deliver. Reagan won six out of ten of them in 1980; he lost six out of ten in 1984. In 1988 Bush won them and then lost them to Clinton in 1992. Then Clinton lost them.

There was a bitter irony here, however, for the tribunes of the betrayed Reagan Democrats. It was old-style populism that drove them away, not the elitism of the cosmopolitan latte drinkers. The social welfare state had fallen out of favor with them, and they tended to perceive their personal economic situation as better under Republicans. Their cultural progressivism, in fact, acted as a brake on these pro-Republican tendencies. Preferring Democratic positions on social and cultural issues, blue-collar middle-class men voted *less* Republican than they would have if their cultural views hadn't counteracted their distaste for Democratic economic policies.

Anyone paying attention to the new American landscape of sex, gender, and family would not have been surprised by these political findings. By the beginning of the third millennium, the demographic and cultural tipping point had been crossed. Divorce was common, leaving just half of all children being raised by two parents in an uninterrupted marriage. Three in ten children lived with only one parent, and one in eleven lived with two unmarried adults. One-third of the nation's babies were born to unmarried women, over 70 percent of whom were *not* teenagers. Two-thirds of mothers were in the workforce. The traditional Christian nuclear family wasn't extinct, but it sure was unusual.

Sexual mores had changed even more radically than had family structures. Just about all Americans settled into a biological groove driven by age, only marginally connected to marital status, and not at all affected by the usual demographic divides of income, race, ethnicity, and region. The average American became sexually active between the ages of 15 and 19, but didn't marry until 25 or older. While Americans disapproved of teenagers under the age of 16 having sex, they were uninterested in preaching and more concerned that the kids know what they were doing. Eighty-seven percent favored sex education in the schools, and 60 percent favored providing contraceptives to teens, regardless of parental approval. About 1.3 million abortions occurred annually, 88 percent of them in the first twelve weeks of pregnancy. Roughly 60 percent of Americans agreed with the Supreme Court decision *Roe v. Wade* and did not want it overturned. Among unmarried Americans, 60 percent were sexually active. Among married couples born after the sexual revolution, four out of ten lived with their spouse before marriage. About 3 million gays and lesbians, denied the right to legally marry, lived with their partners. Only unmarried religious conservatives, who believed premarital sex was immoral, strayed from the norm and abstained from regular sex. For nearly everyone else, the old stricture that sex belonged only in marriage, and accidental pregnancy was a punishment for loose women, was as dead as dead could be.

Teen sex, abortion, divorce, cohabitation, single motherhood, and homosexuality—the reports from the census and the General Social Survey confirmed the deepest fears of the sexual fundamentalists.

Clinton's presidency had begun with the Year of the Woman, trend stories about the new hands-on fatherhood, and a popular frenzy over the castration of John Wayne Bobbitt by his wife, Lorena. In 1992, the youngish Boomer Bill Clinton had to impress an electorate of his elders, whose values had been formed before the sexual revolution, feminism, and the movement for gay civil rights. A lot had changed by the time he faced them charged with impeachment. Americans were more tolerant, perhaps because their own lives hardly lived up to the old imagined ideal of the traditional nuclear family.

Paradoxically, the impeachment of President Bill Clinton over sex did turn out to be a referendum on values. Clinton, the Democratic

Party, and cultural progressives had won the sex wars, as the election results and public opinion surveys attested. Still, a minority hoped to restore the traditional ways among their backsliding neighbors. As Clinton's second term drew to a close and the 2000 election loomed, this minority had become the immoveable gatekeeper of the Republican Party. The impeachment debacle taught these sexual counterrevolutionaries the futility of a public bid for power. Next time up, stealth would rule.

10

ROPE-A-DOPE

A S THE 2000 election season opened, with the nation at peace and enjoying its longest ever economic boom, everything pointed toward a victory for the incumbent party. Yet when Al Gore's presidential campaign hit the skids, Democrats predictably overreacted. Disregarding the results of the 1998 election, Clinton's high approval ratings, and substantial evidence of the public's disdain for the GOP sexual counterrevolutionaries, some Democrats persuaded Gore to distance himself from the president and his own administration's record of achievement. Thanks to Clinton's "stain" on the Oval Office, if Gore were to win, he would have to prove his devotion to mainstream cultural values. It was the shadow of the McGoverniks, yet again, dictating a run to the Right to court the elusive regular American who held the key to Democratic victory.

The Republican Party did not make the same mistake.

"THE FEAR AMONG many party professionals is that the party has marginalized itself to the point of no return," *The National Journal*, the Beltway's premier political newspaper, wrote the morning after the 1998 midterm elections. Even Newt Gingrich, on taking leave of the House of Representatives, denounced the "perfectionist caucus." One Republican strategist acknowledged, "Right now we're whistling past the graveyard."

No piece of wisdom was more widely accepted among the pundit class than the one that the Right was down and the Culture Wars were played out. In a widely circulated letter written after Clinton's acquittal in February 1999, Paul Weyrich ventured that his side had "lost the culture war" and said that he was getting out of politics. "The marriage" between the Christian Right and the Republican Party "is in deep trouble, because one party has taken advantage of the other. The doormat housewife is starting to realize she is being abused." Politics had "failed" the sexual counterrevolutionaries. "While I'm not suggesting that we all become Amish or move to Idaho," he continued, "we need some sort of quarantine."

While Congressional Republicans had spent the year taking the nation down the rabbit hole of impeachment, some of those worried "party professionals" had been visiting Austin, Texas to court the GOP's reputedly reluctant savior. The venerable Republican Party establishment, including many close allies of former president George H. W. Bush, was looking to repossess the party from the sexual counterrevolutionaries who had deposed them at every level of the party apparatus. The times—peace, prosperity, and public disaffection with the GOP—called for pulling the plug on Starr Chambers, sexual McCarthyism, and rightwing overreach.

Although Bush senior had occupied the heights of the Republican Party for close to two decades before his embarrassing defeat in 1992, the American public generally knew little about his son, George W. Bush. As governor of Texas, Bush had gained a reputation as a roll-up-your-sleeves, pragmatic, post-ideological Republican. He won praise for working across the aisle and winning bipartisan victories on issues on which Democrats held a historic advantage, especially education. Reelected in 1998 with 69 percent of the vote, and sporting strong showings among moderates, women, and Hispanics, Bush effectively announced for the presidency during his victory party. The "compassionate conservative philosophy," by which he governed, he promised, had showed the way to "erase the gender gap and open up the Republican Party to new faces and new voices."

I am not one of them, Bush was heard to mean, when he called himself "a different kind of Republican." Or "a uniter, not a divider." Or "a compassionate conservative." To irritated and disaffected voters, Bush's declaration of independence from Tom "The Hammer" DeLay and Dick Armey, Gingrich's even more partisan successors in the GOP Congressional leadership, was welcome. Bush's invocation of compassionate conservatism suggested he believed in a more positive and helpful role for government. It seemed to promise that he would draw a line in the sand between himself and the ideologues of the Right.

The Bush team, led by Karl Rove, carefully honed Bush's image as a moderate and a pragmatist in moves that now in hindsight look like deliberate diversions. In May 1999, the campaign registered the website domain names BushWhitman.com and BushRidge.com, as if in anticipation of the Republican ticket, pairing Bush with the two most prominent Republicans—the governors of New Jersey and Pennsylvania, Christine Todd Whitman and Tom Ridge—who supported a woman's right to legal abortion. A month later Bush said he would not apply an antiabortion litmus test on his Supreme Court nominees. In the fall, Bush launched a public relations offensive against House Republicans, accusing them of cold-hearted extremism, for which journalists, pundits, and Democrats commended him for his Clintonesque triangulation. Bush followed that with a broadside against Grover Norquist, the head of Americans for Tax Reform, who convened a weekly meeting of conservative interest groups he called the Leave Us Alone Coalition. He touted his own plan for taxpayer-funded, faith-based social services as an alternative to Norquist's brutal vision of a federal government so shrunken and weakened you could "drown it in a bathtub." In a speech to Reverend Pat Robertson's Christian Coalition, Bush said "compassion" sixteen times and abortion not once. At conservative meetings with the press in attendance, the candidate denounced conservative icons. One party strategist insisted that Bush was "not going to pander to the conservative base of the party." Sure, they would bring the Right on board, but the candidate would control the terms of the deal.

While Bush elaborately distanced himself from the Right, the sexual counterrevolutionaries complained of shoddy treatment and warned that their votes could not be taken for granted. Weyrich, on reconsideration, rejoined the political fray and announced that he and his would bolt the GOP if Bush or Senator John McCain became the party's nominee. James Dobson agreed. He was backing his more orthodox lieutenant, Family Research Council head and former Reagan administration "family czar" Gary Bauer. Others claimed to be worn out by the futility of their cause. Robertson acknowledged that the constitutional amendment he favored to ban all abortions couldn't pass, so he wasn't going to push it. The contradictory positions emanating from the leaders of the Christian Right were taken to mean that they were too weak to influence the Republican presidential race. "Dubya's skillful handling of the Christian Right—giving them just enough to keep them in line—is probably his most impressive political credential," wrote Molly Ivins, the populist journalist from Texas. "The Christian Right didn't get a dance—they got taken for a ride."

As the Democratic Party celebrated an unexpected victory after the midterm election and looked ahead to the 2000 election, the prospect of holding the presidency looked favorable. Still, could Democrats win without the protean, deeply flawed, but remarkably popular Clinton at the helm? Could Democrats parlay the Clinton years into a Democratic realignment?

Two Democrats had risen into the first ranks of leadership in the Democratic party. One of them was Hillary Clinton. The Lewinsky affair had paradoxically burnished her reputation. In the depths of that crisis, Hillary's personal inclinations and the public's expectation for her seemed to harmonize for the first time. Showing strength and resolve, she deployed her formidable political skills to defend the presidency, the Democratic Party, and the institutions of constitutional democracy, while at the same time standing by her man. Her approval rating did not drop below 60 percent during the entire period. She campaigned vigorously during the midterms and was accorded much of the credit for Democratic gains in Congress.

Gossips wondered if she would divorce Bill after they moved out of the White House. Older feminists, who had cheered her on in the early years, hoped she would. Instead, she announced she would run for the open seat of New York's retiring senator, Daniel Patrick Moynihan, her erstwhile nemesis in the health care reform battle.

The other undisputed leader of the Democratic Party was Gore. He had emerged from the midterms, after serving as President Clinton's surrogate on the campaign trail, with an aura of invincibility for his presidential run. He had also spent the year locking up endorsements and scaring away potential rivals. Gore, one of the founders of the Democratic Leadership Council, was widely expected to run as the DLC's man. The way "Gore is going to hold the presidency is by campaigning and governing as a New Democrat," said the DLC's head Al From. Not only was the 2000 election an opportunity to cement a Democratic majority, but it seemed to the DLC an opportunity to dispatch the old liberals, progressives, and populists into permanent oblivion.

Gore's chief strategist and pollster, Mark Penn, was closely tied to the DLC. Penn had come into the Clinton White House with Dick Morris, the mastermind of triangulation. After Morris was forced out in a prostitution scandal, Penn proved instrumental in Clinton's 1996 reelection and survival post-Lewinsky. Brilliant, gruff, and antisocial, Penn had won few admirers or friends in the Clinton White House. But Bill and Hillary appreciated his loyalty to them and his strategic acumen, and Penn was also running Hillary's New York Senate race. A pioneer in microtargeting voters, Penn concluded that suburban "wired workers" were the key to Gore's victory. Penn prevailed upon Gore to put to rest the old Democratic populism. Class "warfare" was a turnoff for suburbanites. Gore's big idea, Penn decided, should be that suburban sprawl was a threat to a better "quality of life." It wasn't the most promising frame for a politician already perceived to be wonkish and stiff.

Despite high approval ratings for the Clinton-Gore administration, polling showed Bush trouncing Gore in almost every trial matchup. Initially, Gore's troubles were attributed to the typical difficulty vice presidents face in stepping out from the shadows of the president they served. But it was also widely reported that his campaign team was in disarray, and in May, Gore brought in additional consultants associated with the liberal wing of the party, even as he kept Penn on. This inability to settle on a message, a theme, and an identity would plague Gore's campaign from beginning to end.

By the summer of 1999, still seventeen months out from the presidential election, new theories about why Gore was losing gained currency. Gore lacked charisma—he was "Gore the Bore," in the words of one headline. David Broder of the *Washington Post* complained Gore talked too much about the issues. Another more insidious theory took hold while the press corps was enjoying itself mocking Gore. The vice president was going to lose because of "the incredible stain" Bill Clinton had "put on the nation's highest office." In short, Clinton's survival would be Gore's undoing.

Like so many other instances of Democratic panic, the notion had originated among Republican operatives. "I have always thought that the Lewinsky scandal would have its comeuppance for the Democrats in the presidential election," said Republican pollster Fred Steeper in February 1999. Yet the following month, in March, when NBC News and the *Wall Street Journal* asked Americans whether Gore should have defended or criticized Clinton in the Lewinsky scandal, 63 percent said he should not have said anything. In April, Pew reported that "Clinton fatigue" was hurting Gore. Yet the full poll results showed that although 74 percent of respondents were "tired of all the problems associated with the Clinton administration," 60 percent thought the best way to "avoid things like the Clinton-Lewinsky scandal in the future was by 'making sure a president's private life remains private.'"

By the fall, the subject of Clinton fatigue had mushroomed into one of the major narratives of the campaign. Gallup reviewed the Dow Jones news database and by October, 1999, had found 399 references to the term Clinton fatigue. "It is hard to find solid evidence in the latest CNN/*USA Today* Gallup survey, however, that Clinton fatigue pervades the electorate or, more importantly, that it is having a major impact on voter preferences," Gallup observed. Gore's approval rating stood at a respectable 54 percent, and most of those plagued by Clinton fatigue were Republican or Republican-leaning independents, who wouldn't vote for Gore anyway. Gore's real problem wasn't Clinton but Bush. Even though 60 percent of those surveyed thought Clinton's policies were leading in the "right direction," Bush outscored both Clinton and Gore on that key indicator of voter preference.

The Gore campaign should have been far more alarmed by some news about American opinion that was less provocative than the exaggerated one about Clinton fatigue. A comprehensive, multiyear survey by the nonpartisan Pew Research Center showed Democrats holding the biggest partisan identification advantage in at least a decade; independents more like Democrats than Republicans in their views on the issues; and young voters trending sharply Democratic. But Bush still won in matchups, and more than half of Democratic identifiers were not registered to vote.

ON THE EVE of the 2000 Republican primaries, Bush seemed poised to sideline the Right, rebrand the party, and win a general election, all in a single stroke. The saunter to the presidential nomination depended on two unknowns: that the primaries would go as smoothly as anticipated; and that the media would not probe too deeply into Bush's actual relationship with the right-wing sexual counterrevolutionaries. All seemed to be going according to plan when Bush won the Iowa caucus on January 24, 2000. Republican pollster Frank Luntz, of the Gingrich wing of the party, ventured that if Republican Iowans had voted for the man they believed in, not for the candidate who could win, antiabortion purist Steve Forbes would have won by double digits.

But Arizona Senator John McCain had skipped the Iowa caucus, and eight days after Iowa, he beat Bush by 19 points in the New Hampshire primary. The New Hampshire upset suddenly triggered questions about Bush's electability. The candidate who had been anointed to save the GOP from itself needed rescuing himself.

In South Carolina the morning after the New Hampshire upset, Bush debuted a new persona at Bob Jones University, an evangelical Baptist college that forbade interracial dating and whose president had once described the pope as "Satanic" and called Mormonism and

Catholicism cults. (Among the school's illustrious graduates was Tim LaHaye, former head of the Moral Majority, husband of Beverly LaHaye, and best-selling author of the *Left Behind* series of Christian apocalyptic novels.) Bush, the "different kind of Republican," said the word conservative twelve times in two minutes. Campaigning in South Carolina, Bush pledged a massive tax cut. He explained that he did in fact support the absolutist antiabortion plank in the GOP platform first inserted there by Phyllis Schlafly in 1980, even though he had always said he favored exceptions for cases of rape, incest, and to save the life of the mother.

The leaders of the sexual counterrevolution, who a few months earlier had derided Bush as insufficiently conservative, churned into gear to resuscitate his candidacy. Dobson issued a press release calling McCain a hot-tempered adulterer—insisting, however, that as the head of a tax-exempt nonprofit, he was not endorsing any candidate. Reverend Jerry Falwell announced that "McCain had sold out to the liberal element" of the party and that he personally supported Bush "based on his commitment to uphold the conservative agenda." Pat Robertson dispatched Roberta Combs, executive vice president of the Christian Coalition, to visit every county in her home state. Norquist's groups ran TV ads against McCain—ads that would have been prohibited if McCain's campaign finance bill had not been fili-bustered to death by Senate Republicans. South Carolinian voters were deluged with anti-McCain letters, fliers, phone messages, emails, faxes, leaflets, and push polls. Nefarious (and needless to say, false) charges were leveled by anonymous sources. The conservative war hero was magically recast as a sex-addled spawn of the counter-culture. They said that his adopted daughter, a Bangladeshi orphan, was the love-child of McCain and a black prostitute; they said his wife was a drug addict. No one could prove definitively that the attacks originated within the Bush campaign, just as no one had been able to prove eight years earlier when suddenly Texas was awash in rumors that Governor Ann Richards was a lesbian. On February 19, Bush won South Carolina by 11 points.

The power of the Christian Right in the Republican Party, and Bush's relationship to it, suddenly became a topic of interest. In the wake of South Carolina, speculation was rife that the Right had overreached, and that Bush would pay the price. "Will moderates still buy his compassion pitch?" *Time* magazine asked in its wrap-up on the South Carolina primary. McCain looked ahead to the big, diverse states of New York and California, thought he could burnish his maverick brand, and took a stunning, ill-considered risk. Campaigning in the Virginia primary, on their home ground, McCain denounced Robertson and Falwell, the founders of the Christian Coalition and the Moral Majority, as "agents of intolerance." The next day, McCain repeated the attack, condemning the reverends for "the evil influence that they exercise over the Republican Party." McCain was trying to provoke an uprising of moderate Republicans, but he showed little comprehension of his own political party. Bush swept Virginia, with 83 percent of Christian conservatives voting for him. The day before McCain's "agents of intolerance" speech, the Republican nomination had still appeared up for grabs. Seven days after the Virginia primary, Bush wrapped up the nomination. On March 9, McCain formally withdrew from the race. He went on to endorse Bush, although it was an open secret the two loathed each other.

With the nomination in hand, Bush immediately tacked back to the center, returning to the campaign's original message that he was a different kind of Republican. He unveiled ostensibly centrist plans on education, health care, and housing, at the cost of $60 billion in new spending. Considering the tax cut he promised, the figures didn't quite add up. "We don't have to win the education debate to win the election," a Bush adviser acknowledged. It was only necessary "to win the perception that we're a different kind of Republican." Smiling Hispanic and African American children were positioned in the front rows of the pre-screened crowds at Bush's highly theatrical campaign events. The nation's most recognizable pro-choice moderate Republican woman, New Jersey Governor Christine Todd Whitman, toured the country to reassure moderates that Bush was safe.

The sexual fundamentalists publicly indulged Bush as he systematically thumbed his nose at them. "Republicans are hungry to win the presidency," Kansas Republican Senator Sam Brownback explained, "and that makes people more willing to be understanding." On abortion, gays, and school prayer, the Right seemed to be abandoning Holy War for conservatism-lite, because, as Norquist explained, the "culture war rhetoric" had "failed" them in 1996. Phyllis Schlafly acknowledged she would "probably stick with the ticket," even if Bush chose a pro-choice running mate. "There really isn't any option." *New York Times* reporter Richard L. Berke found it "striking" that "not one leading conservative organization has aggressively spoken out against Mr. Bush."

Perhaps that was because, all along, Bush had been dogwhistling to the sexual counterrevolutionaries. The punditry shared a collective guffaw when Bush named Jesus Christ as the philosopher by whom he had been most influenced. Fundamentalists and evangelicals appreciated exactly what he meant. He declared June 10 "Jesus Day" in Texas. Bush averred that, to be fair, schools should teach the supposedly competing theories of the origins of life, that is, creationism along with evolution. He frequently used the phrase "culture of life"—a code word in the sexual counterrevolution to signify one's opposition to abortion in all circumstances.

Bush's choice of conservative Dick Cheney as his vice president and the Republican Party platform briefly rekindled the debate from South Carolina about who Bush was and where the Republican Party stood in the new millennium, only to have the conventional wisdom of Bush's centrism confirmed. The platform was a mash-up of compassionate platitudes and traditionalist dicta. Republicans who supported legal abortion rights were once again turned away at the door. On paper, the Republicans repudiated affirmative action, gay marriage, gun control, and abortion in all cases. On television, the convention podium looked like the silver anniversary reunion of the Reverend Jesse Jackson's Rainbow Coalition, the members mellowed, wiser, and in bankers' suits. General Colin Powell told the mostly white delegates that many blacks did not feel welcome in the Republican Party, but he believed that Bush could "bridge our racial divides." Polls taken immediately after the August convention showed independents swinging toward Bush.

GORE EASILY DISPATCHED his one significant opponent, former Senator Bill Bradley, in the Democratic primaries. As Gore pivoted to take on Bush, however, his blows were parried at every turn. Reports of Clinton fatigue resurfaced. Gore's campaign chairman was forced out over ethics questions. Polls showed Gore was having trouble with the Democratic base. Union members didn't appreciate his free trade stand and were lukewarm to the DLC candidate. Ralph Nader, who had filed to run as a candidate of the Green Party, was picking off voters on the left, putting safe states like Oregon and Wisconsin into play. More ominously, many voters were still not paying any attention to the presidential race. In March of 2000, three weeks after Gore and Bush had won their parties' nomination, one in five voters could not name either nominee.

"We thought at the end of the primaries that Bush was all the way to the right and Gore was well-positioned and I had hoped we would see a change in the polls," one New York Democratic representative told a reporter, "but we're seeing slippage and that's disappointing." Gore had indeed shined a spotlight on Bush's embrace of the sexual fundamentalists and the Right. In Gore's words, the South Carolina primary battle had "pulled the mask off" Bush, revealing the self-avowed compassionate conservative to be a hard-hearted extremist. Pointing out that Bush had shared a stage with anti-Catholic fundamentalists at Bob Jones University, spoken under the Confederate flag, promised to cut funding from public education, and adopted the most extreme position of the antiabortion movement, Gore promised that when he was through, no one would be fooled by the different kind of Republican branding. For the first time in the race, the Gallup tracking poll showed Gore tied with Bush.

To Gore's misfortune, some Democratic leaders were aiding and abetting Bush's stealth strategy. Although the Bush-McCain dust-up in South Carolina had provided a strategic opening for the Gore campaign, the effort was sabotaged by his fellow Democrats, playing out internal party battles at the expense of their electoral prospects. Some, including those presumed to be Gore's ideological partners, had been early adopters of the Bush party line. "Bush is trying to emulate what we did," the DLC's Al From claimed. "Maybe the Republican right will roll over dead and he'll have a free ride. Then it will be up to Gore to show who's the imposter." There was the whiff of challenge about From's remark, as if he admired Bush more than his erstwhile ally, who, like Clinton before him, was putting too much distance between himself and his DLC launching pad. While Gore labored through the spring to portray Bush's ideas as risky and deceptive, centrist Democrats damned Gore with faint praise. Bush's new ideas, they chortled, were cribbed directly from their New Democrat manifestoes. Disappointed in their prodigal son, too many DLC Democrats succumbed to Bush's flattery of imitation. Although they continued to support Gore, and saw through Bush's centrist ruse, they were loquacious with reporters about their domestic frustrations.

As Americans began their summer vacations in June, Bush was firmly back in the lead, the primary turn to the Right a dim memory, and Gore's troubles were the main story. "The prevailing view at this point in the presidential campaign—still with many months to go before Election Day—seems to be that Vice President Al Gore may be too cold and calculating, too aggressive, even too mean about his opponent to be electable," wrote the *National Journal*. Voters were confused about the candidates' stance on the issues, and the evidence was mounting that Bush's poaching on Democratic territory had worked. Only a third of voters knew Gore opposed Bush's plan to partially privatize social security. Fewer than half of the voters knew that Gore opposed Bush's tax cut and instead favored using the budget surplus to pay down the debt.

What had gone wrong? Gore and his advisers decided it must be Clinton's fault.

Gore was floundering because of the spillover effect of the Lewinsky scandal, Stan Greenberg reasoned in an article in *The American Prospect* in the summer of 2000. Peace and prosperity should have vaulted Gore into the White House, according to Greenberg, but the affair had reminded voters of their discomfort with the Democrats' cultural permissiveness. "At a time when the electorate is increasingly open to the Democrats as a party of sensible investment, the party has lost ground in the battle over values." Hadn't the 1998 election put that notion to rest? Not if you saw it as a Pyrrhic victory, as Greenberg did. "Democrats saved Clinton's presidency and even made gains in the 1998 midterm elections, but at a price. The Democrats again were identified with 1960s-style irresponsibility." To recover standing with the voters and win the upcoming election, the progressive wing of the Democratic Party needed to rediscover religion and family values, to "give itself permission to recognize the benefit of two-parent families to children."

In the time-honored tradition of the Democratic sexual counter-revolution, Greenberg advised that Gore had to turn right on cultural issues if he were to secure the votes of alienated conservative Democrats. This became the official campaign strategy when Gore hired Greenberg as a key adviser, overhauling his campaign staff yet again just four months before the general election. Greenberg gave Gore a makeover as a "fighting" populist, a message targeted to Greenberg's Reagan Democrats, conservative blue-collar white men. Economic populism was necessary, but not sufficient. Gore's values deficit, created by Clinton's stain on the office of the presidency, required a bolder response.

How Gore, under Greenberg's direction, would prove his fidelity to his mainstream moral values became clear on August 7, when he announced that Senator Joseph Lieberman would be his running mate. Lieberman, who was close to Greenberg and Gore alike, beautifully solved Gore's Clinton problem. Appended to Lieberman's name was not so much Connecticut senator as some variation of first-Democrat-to-rebuke-Clinton for soiling the presidency. "Inoculation" was a word much in vogue among reporters and commentators, as if Clinton's sexual sins were a contagious disease that Gore was in danger of contracting. Beltway pundits and campaign reporters deemed Lieberman an inspired choice for this unpleasant task.

Lieberman played his part to the hilt. He opened his acceptance speech with a prayer and a reading from the Book of Chronicles and invoked the name of God thirteen times. On the campaign trail, he would lace his stump speeches with sermons. The week Gallup released a poll showing Americans reluctant to mix faith and politics, Lieberman spoke at an interfaith prayer breakfast, and said, "This is the most religious country in the world, and sometimes we try to stifle that fact or hide it. But the profound and ultimately most important reality is that we are not only citizens of this blessed country, we are citizens of the same awesome God." In many ways Lieberman perfectly embodied the moderate middle of the Democratic punditry's imagination. He

was for unions and against Hollywood. He was pro-military and anti–
affirmative action. He tended to vote with progressives on cultural issues
but in a manner that hardly inspired love. He opposed immediately
before "Don't Ask, Don't Tell" because it weakened the American military; he supported antidiscrimination legislation to protect gays but
opposed gay marriage. He supported the right to legal abortion but
was one of only a handful of Democrats who voted for the Republican
version of the ban on partial birth abortion.

Still, inoculation didn't seem to be quite enough protection
against the threat Clinton posed to Gore's ambitions. So the Gore
campaign instituted a quarantine as well. Gore implored Clinton *not*
to campaign for him or any other Democratic candidates. The Gore
campaign rejected requests from Democratic congressional candidates that Clinton campaign with them, even when the state was
safe for Gore. Gore even kept silent about the booming economy and
the role of the Clinton-Gore administration in creating prosperity,
afraid that any mention of their record might conjure images of an
intern in a blue dress. "Pretty much everyone in the White House
thinks this is so nutty it must be personal, not tactical," reported the
National Journal.

AS THE CAMPAIGN entered the final eight weeks, Bush was again
the compassionate conservative, the Republican triangulator, having
adeptly maneuvered during the post-primary season and convention
to reestablish his preferred brand. Pollster Andrew Kohut, the head
of the Pew Research Center, warned that after the primaries the differences between the two candidates had "blurred," not sharpened.
A third of voters said either could do a good job. Another third said
that it didn't matter who got elected. Although voters believed Gore
and the Democratic Party were far better able to handle the issues
that mattered to them, 53 percent said Bush shared their views. The
task for Gore, Kohut offered, was to "sharpen the differences." By
late October, voters still trusted Democrats more on the issues, but
Bush had cut the Democratic margin significantly. "Militant Moderates" was the ironic headline of a *National Journal* analysis, and with
few exceptions the nation's journalists and pundits agreed.

Three weeks before the election, reporters Jules Witcover and Jack Germond filed a story about a Democratic-leaning swing state, making it clear how much Bush's prospects depended on the survival of his image as a moderate. To win Pennsylvania and its 23 electoral votes, Bush had to win over Republican women who had voted twice for Clinton. Bush "must convince them that he is more acceptable on social and cultural issues than the party leaders who have held sway for most of the past decade." Moderate women felt estranged from their party, not only on abortion, Witcover and Germond noted, but also on other issues important to them, such as child care, education, and gun control. The reporters thought Bush's only real chance in the state was that Democrats, especially youth and African Americans, appeared so apathetic they might stay home.

On Tuesday, November 7, 2000, Americans went to the polls to vote in what had for a year been billed as the dullest presidential election in memory. Gallup's final pre-election national poll had said that the race was too close to call. At 7:50 in the evening on the East Coast, the networks called Florida for Gore, based on projections from the exit polls. Florida was a swing state where Gore had made a late surge in the polls and Bush's brother Jeb was governor. At 9 PM, Gore was ahead in the electoral college count, but at 9:54 PM, the networks took back Florida from Gore, returning the state into the too-close-to call column. For the next three hours, Bush and Gore traded places in the lead in the electoral vote, while Gore's popular vote lead steadily grew. At midnight, the candidates were a few electoral votes apart with several states, and the electoral college, undecided.

At 2:16 AM on Wednesday morning, Fox News announced that Bush had won Florida to become president-elect. (Florida put Bush at 271 electoral votes, one more than is needed to win the electoral college.) Fox News based its call on Bush's lead in the still unfinished count of the Florida vote. Within a few minutes every other network had followed their lead. Gore called Bush to concede, but in the car at 3:15 AM on his way to deliver a speech to his supporters, his advisers called him to say that Bush's lead in the Florida vote count had narrowed to just about 1,000 votes, and the exit polls and their people on the ground indicated Gore would ultimately win Florida.

Gore headed back to his hotel, and called Bush to inform him he would not concede. The networks reached the same conclusion that Florida was too close to call, and at 4 AM they retracted their call that Bush had won Florida and the presidential election.

As day dawned on the East Coast, Americans woke to learn that Gore had a 13-vote lead in the electoral college and had won the national popular vote. But Florida remained undecided, and its 25 electoral votes would determine who would be the 43rd president. Later that morning, Florida released its count, showing both Bush and Gore with more than 2.9 million votes each, Ralph Nader with 97,000 statewide, and Pat Buchanan with 17,000 votes. Bush's lead of just 1,784 votes over Gore was within the margin to trigger an automatic machine recount. Florida Governor Jeb Bush recused himself from the recount.

Thus began the unprecedented contested election of 2000, the memory of which continues to rankle politically engaged Americans on both sides of the political divide. Complaints from Palm Beach County surfaced that morning that the "butterfly ballot" design had confused elderly, mostly Jewish, mostly Democratic voters into accidentally voting for both Gore *and* Buchanan, thus spoiling their ballot with an "overvote." (Conservative icon William Buckley had made a strong case during the lead-up to the 1991 Gulf War that Buchanan was anti-Semitic, and most American Jews agreed, making it highly unlikely that Buchanan could draw votes in the county.) Even Buchanan acknowledged the votes were surely in error. A study by political scientists in 2001 confirmed through statistical tests that the design of the ballot led to more than 2,000 unintentional votes for Buchanan. Later it came to light that 20 percent of ballots in predominantly African American areas of Duval County were spoiled by overvotes, as voters followed the ballot instruction to mark every page. Gore lost up to 3,000 votes from this confusing ballot.

Short of a re-do election in selected counties, there was no way to impartially determine for whom an individual intended to vote when a ballot had two candidates marked. But quickly, another issue surfaced. There were thousands of ballots where a hanging or dimpled chad could not be read by the machine. With this discovery, the discrepancy between the exit polls showing Gore the victor and the first count by machine was explained. On Thursday, while the machine recount proceeded, Gore requested a hand recount in four counties, all of them Democratic-leaning, but all where reports of a possible miscount were credible.

Bush, the candidate who had crafted an image of himself as a "uniter, not a divider," quickly showed the partisan general concealed under that façade. The same day Gore requested a hand recount, Bush's advisers announced they were meeting to choose his cabinet. That audacity continued unabated for the next thirty-three days. Despite Gore's half-a-million vote advantage in the popular vote, the practical evidence that thousands more Floridians intended to vote for Gore, and the continuing recount, Bush's team demanded that Gore concede the election. On the Saturday after the election, the GOP (usually the champion of states' rights) filed an injunction in federal court to stop the state's hand recount. Bush and Cheney put a crack team of lawyers and spin doctors into the Florida fight, while the Republican secretary of state, Katherine Harris, consistently interpreted Florida election law in ways favorable to Bush and adverse to Gore. Republican congressmen such as Jim DeMint and Tom DeLay sent their congressional staffers to Florida, where they masqueraded as Florida citizens outraged by the recount in staged and coordinated protests. Four days before the state Supreme Court's mandated deadline for the hand recount, the Republican D.C. staffers broke through the doors of the Miami-Dade canvassing board, shouting "Shut it down" and chasing the election officials, who feared for their safety, into another room. The officials stopped their recount with more than 10,000 votes left uncounted and never resumed it again.

As the delirium of the recount mounted, the results of the national vote were never in doubt and remained essentially unchanged from November 8 on. By the standard of every other presidential election in U.S. history but one, Gore had won. Gore's national popular vote margin over Bush was 547,079 votes, giving Gore 48.4 percent of the popular vote to Bush's 47.9 percent. Ralph Nader had picked up 2.9 million votes, or 2.7 percent, while Buchanan, running to Bush's right, had won just under half a million votes, for 0.4 percent of the national vote. As the historian James Patterson observed, the combined vote for Gore and Nader, at 51.1 percent, was the highest for the center-left since Johnson beat Goldwater in 1964.

But Gore of course did not become president. From the moment Fox and then the other networks called the election for Bush, Gore was operating at a disadvantage in the court of public opinion. The 2000 election presents an endless series of what-ifs. What if the networks had been more cautious and not named Bush the winner in Florida, and the recount had started with the two candidates essentially equal in Florida? Would it have been possible for the Bush team to claim the mantle of presidential legitimacy and accuse the popular vote winner of being a sore loser and stealing the election? What if just a few hundred Nader voters had realized Florida was more in play than they thought? What if a few hundred retirees in Palm Beach had remembered to take their reading glasses into the voting booth? I suspect that there is not a single Republican or Democrat who has left a chad hanging since 2000, but frankly, who then knew the machine wouldn't read a vote if the chad was askew?

Ultimately, the 2000 election was decided by the U.S. Supreme Court. On December 12, five conservative justices ruled in *Bush v. Gore* that the recount as ordered by the Florida Supreme Court violated the Equal Protection Clause of the Fourteenth Amendment and was unconstitutional. Any recount must be statewide, they said, but since there was no time for a recount to be completed by the deadline of December 12, the recount must stop. Incidentally, the justices said the decision applied to this case alone and was not to be seen as a precedent. Two other justices, including Bush senior's appointee David Souter, agreed that the standards for the recount underway were unconstitutional but joined the dissent arguing that it was fully possible to design a constitutionally valid recount. In such fundamental matters as the right to vote, they wrote, protecting the right was far more important than meeting a deadline. That five Republican appointees had not only decided the election in favor of the Republican who had lost the popular vote, but had gone on to state that *Bush v. Gore* only applied to that case and no case in the future, left many Gore supporters with the feeling that the election had been stolen by partisan operatives and partisan justices. It was left to two liberal justices, Ruth Bader Ginsburg and John Paul Stevens, to stand up for the principle of states' rights: the U.S. Supreme Court should not intervene to overturn a decision of a state court. Moreover, they concluded, the Florida decision had been right on the merits, as it was designed to insure that every vote would be counted.

Every vote that could be counted eventually was counted by a professional body of statisticians convened by a consortium of eight news organizations. The results gave no comfort to the extreme partisans on either side. The consortium acknowledged that more Florida voters intended to vote for Gore but left the overvotes uncounted. A later statistical analysis of the butterfly ballot showed that Gore would have netted roughly 2,000 votes from the butterfly ballots alone, but there are election rules for a reason and under no scenario in a democracy is it possible to legitimately count overvoted ballots. The consortium concluded that a Florida recount conducted by the rules Gore's lawyers requested would have resulted in a Bush win by 225 votes. Gore's team had been too clever by half. Had they requested a statewide recount of undervotes too and if those had been tallied according to the standard required by the U.S. Supreme Court, Gore would have won Florida by 200 votes. No matter how one looks at it, however, Florida was a tie and either candidate could legitimately be deemed the winner of that state and its electors.

Gore decided it was time to end the uncertainty and what many pundits were calling a constitutional crisis. On December 13, he went before a national television audience and said, "I call on all Americans—I particularly urge all who stood with us—to unite behind our next president . . . This is America and we put country before party; we will stand together behind our new president."

After Gore's speech ended, Bush addressed the nation and echoed Gore's plea for unity and promise of bipartisanship. "Tonight I chose to speak from the chamber of the Texas House of Representatives because it has been a home to bipartisan cooperation," Bush explained.

"The spirit of cooperation I have seen in this hall is what is needed in Washington, D.C. It is the challenge of our moment. After a difficult election, we must put politics behind us and work together to make the promise of America available for every one of our citizens.

"I am optimistic that we can change the tone in Washington,

D.C.," the president-elect continued. "I believe things happen for a reason, and I hope the long wait of the last five weeks will heighten a desire to move beyond the bitterness and partisanship of the recent past.

"I was not elected to serve one party, but to serve one nation. The president of the United States is the president of every single American, of every race and every background."

THERE WERE SEVERAL ways Democrats could have interpreted the election and spun it to the public. They could have chalked Bush's victory up to a perfect storm of unfortunate, unique, and politically mishandled events. They could have claimed the popular mandate the party had indeed won. Republicans, after all, had claimed Clinton had no mandate both times he won the presidency, on the thin claim that he hadn't won a full majority of the nation. Instead, Democratic leaders went hurtling into delirium.

The old death-by-McGovernik notion, that Democrats lose when regular Americans perceive cultural progressives to be in charge, was rendered anew as a morality play, the countercultural villain personified in Clinton, the valiant Lieberman and the southerner Gore standing up for the morally upright, economically anxious white man. (Never mind that Clinton's sexual escapades were of *Mad Men*, not Summer of Love, vintage. Men and women born after the sexual revolution had fewer extramarital affairs than their boomer elders.) Gore's general election campaign had provided the group of Democratic leaders most attached to this theory, populist liberals such as Greenberg, a laboratory to put their ideas to a practical test. They had rebranded Gore as a populist who would "fight for you." On his advisers' advice, Gore soft-pedaled his progressivism on hot-button issues such as abortion and gay rights in order to win over economically insecure and culturally conservative white working men, The result? Gore lost white men overall, by almost the exact same margin as Clinton, Dukakis, and Mondale had before him. Instead of taking responsibility and reevaluating their prescription for Democratic preeminence, the populist liberals doubled down.

Greenberg asserted that Gore lost because these downscale

conservative white men deserted the party over morals. Ruy Teixeira, an up-and-coming Democratic Party think-tanker, largely took
Greenberg's side on the question of the impact of the Lewinsky affair
and voters' conservatism. "The idea that the Clinton record should
undoubtedly have been a strong suit ignores the undeniable legacy
of the Clinton scandals. Being associated with these scandals—either
indirectly, in the case of the Lewinsky incident, or directly, in the case
of the campaign finance difficulties—made it harder for Gore simply
to run on the Clinton record." Teixeira then reviewed the findings
of a recent poll to conclude, "Social issues—gun control, gay rights,
abortion—are a problem for the Democrats." That poll, however,
had been done by Greenberg's firm for another populist think tank.
Teixeira was already starting to articulate a more nuanced position
about the relationship between cultural and economic issues, but,
nonetheless, he agreed that Clinton's morals had damaged Gore.
Even four years later Greenberg's convictions held firm. Democrats
had failed to parlay Clinton-era success into a permanent majority
because "the issues of gays in the military, Monica Lewinsky, and
impeachment broke the Democrats' link to the value of responsibility and with it, their link to many mainstream families." Clinton's
affair, in other words, had recapitulated the McGovernik betrayal of
real Democrats, yet again, compelling the Reagan Democrats to run
away from home.

Clinton could not have disagreed more vehemently. "The whole
world thinks Gore ran a poor campaign from a strong hand. Yet
Gore thinks he had a weak hand because of Clinton, and ran a valiant campaign against impossible odds," wrote the journalist Taylor
Branch, recounting a conversation with Clinton. Clinton had a point
about the strong hand the administration's record had dealt the vice
president. On every measure that has historically been predictive of
presidential victory, Gore should have won. The nation was at peace,
and although it is hard to fathom now, hardly anyone foresaw any
major conflict ahead. The United States was in its longest running
period of economic expansion, at 73 months and counting. Clinton's
second term, indeed, was the only period in the last three decades
that average Americans have seen their real income increase. Both the
unemployment rate and the poverty rate were at historic lows, and

Americans' confidence in their own situation and the nation's future were staggeringly high. Clinton had presided over a three years and running federal budget surplus. Academic experts had unanimously predicted a Gore victory, with margins ranging from a narrow 51 percent to landslide margins of 60 percent.

Clinton's job approval rating was unusually high for a two-term president—averaging roughly 60 percent for the year preceding the election. By contrast, Reagan's approval rating hit 60 percent in only three discrete polls in his entire last two years as president. Clinton begged in the last days before the election to be allowed to campaign in Arkansas, Tennessee, New Hampshire, and Missouri, when polls showed the states in play. Gore refused. Arkansas certainly could have succumbed one last time to Clinton's charm, especially since its citizens had a front-row seat to the scandalous Clinton hunters. Bush won the other three states by less than 5 percentage points, with a big assist from Nader in New Hampshire, a state Gore would have tied if Nader had not been in the race. The electoral votes of either New Hampshire or Arkansas would have made Gore president, regardless of the outcome in Florida.

Clinton and the experts' view of the favorable circumstances of the election were borne out by Gore's strong performance among groups that tended to favor Democrats. Gore won women by 12 points, chalked up a 9-point gender gap, and won 70 percent of women who rated the economy their top priority. Gore won two-thirds of Latinos, just as Clinton had, and additionally picked up Asian Americans, who before had trended Republican. He won African Americans, youth, and low-income voters, secular voters and progressive evangelicals, the coasts and the cities, the unmarried and unarmed. He won a majority of low-income men, baby boomer men, and unmarried men.

The many proponents of the stain theory, who claimed Gore would have won but for the Lewinsky affair, pointed to the exit polls for proof. One piece of evidence was that white men, the prototypical representative of the forgotten, socially conservative majority, broke strongly for Bush, giving the Republicans their best performance among white men in years. The reason for that, however, was Ross Perot, not Lewinsky. Gore won the same percentage of white men that Clinton had, but with Perot out of the running, the Republican tendencies of white men again became apparent. The exit polls showed that a group of voters who voted for Clinton in 1996, currently approved of his job performance, but disapproved of him personally, and did not vote for Gore. All told, these so-called disaffected Clintonites accounted for 2 percent of the electorate. Although many commentators speculated that the sex scandal caused the defection, no statistically sound investigation has ever proved that concerns about Clinton's morals, rather than some other reason, was why these voters favored Bush over Gore voters.

There is substantial evidence that Gore lost more than 2 percent of his potential support by letting his obsession with Clinton's moral failings dictate his campaign strategy. Running away from Clinton and his sex scandal, also meant running from the achievements of the Clinton presidency. "Gore neglected to put the election into a broader context of the administration's record, of party, or of the Republican record in Congress," wrote Gerald Pomper, a political scientist and veteran analyst of elections. "In editing his own message so severely, Gore made it less persuasive."

Gore underperformed with several key groups that were historically inclined to vote for Democrats. There is wide agreement that Gore's single greatest mistake was to squander the opportunity provided by the roaring economy. Gore rarely talked about the Clinton administration's role in the boom, apparently because Greenberg convinced him that any mention of his role in the administration evoked hostility toward Clinton among swing voters polled in focus groups. Among the one-quarter of the electorate that credited Clinton with the good economy, Gore won a commanding majority. But those voters who did not automatically attribute the good times to wise governing by Democrats split their votes between Gore and Bush. Certainly the then current New Economy fantasy that the business cycle had given way to permanent prosperity made Gore's task more challenging. (One pre-election survey by *Time* reported that nearly 40 percent of Americans thought they were or were soon to be in the richest 1 percent of the nation.) But more reminders from Gore about the Clinton-Gore administration's economic achievements, as well as more effort to clarify the clear differences between Democrats and Republicans on the economy, could have helped. The income gap—in which low-income voters favor Democrats and high-income voters favor Republicans—was narrower than typical, according to a leading expert, Jeffrey Stonecash, as "most voters did not recognize just how conservative George W. Bush would be." It is conceivable that a more vigorous campaign on the Clinton economic record could have moved enough of these voters to choose Gore instead and offset any supposedly lost to the Clinton sex scandal.

The Gore-Lieberman ticket likewise failed to capitalize on the greater popularity of the Democratic Party and Democratic positions on most of the issues, especially cultural and social issues. The Democratic Party held a 7-point advantage in party identification, at the same time the GOP's support had plunged to near all-time lows. Gore, however, rarely mentioned the Democratic Party or its more popular positions, for example, on gun control and abortion. He rarely criticized the GOP-controlled congress. Considering that polls throughout the year had shown that Gore was less popular than his party and the president, his campaign should have made extra efforts to shore up Gore's image with Democrats. Gore also had an advantage with independents, whose views were very close to Democrats on environmental and cultural issues—women's and gay rights, abortion, religion. Most seriously, Gore lost a small but critical margin of progressive Democrats to Nader. Nader's vote was drawn two-to-one from Democrats, the vast majority of them on the party's left. Nader's 2.7 percent of the national vote alone would have given Gore an undisputed popular and electoral college victory; even a few hundred of his votes from Florida would have made Gore president. Gore also underperformed Clinton among liberal and moderate Republicans, such as those women in suburban Pennsylvania, quintessential swing voters who trended strongly Democratic when they perceived the sexual counterrevolutionaries to be in control in the Republican Party.

Just as Gore unnecessarily ceded potentially hundreds of thousands of voters to Bush by default, he failed to inspire other potential supporters to bother voting. The dramatic and history-altering contested 2000 election witnessed the lowest turnout ever in a competitive presidential election. Polls comparing the preferences of voters and nonvoters demonstrated that Gore would have won the electoral vote, as well as the popular vote, if everyone had voted. Nonvoters had less information about the election, had less faith in the system, and saw little difference between the parties. In a CBS poll before the election, Gore had a 14-point lead with people who said they would not vote; during the recount, Gore had a 20-point advantage among those who regretted not voting.

Many potential Democratic voters just stayed home. Turnout by low-income voters, a group that had benefited from Clinton policies, was lower than usual. Gore won the youth vote by a hair, but young voter turnout, which had surged for Clinton in 1992 and 1996, plunged in the 2000 election. The implicit message Gore sent by placing Lieberman on the ticket, the explicit emphasis on Social Security and Medicare prescription drug plans, and Gore's relative silence on the Democrats' cultural progressivism left younger voters cold. If every eligible American under the age of 30 had voted, they would have outnumbered eligible elderly voters by almost 9 million. As it turned out, voters 65 and older cast roughly 7 million more votes than young people did.

In a close election, it is impossible to say with certitude that any one factor determined the outcome. Yes, the Lewinsky scandal may have cost Gore votes he otherwise would have won. Yet Gore's other shortfalls arguably cost him more than 2 percent of his potential vote, and each one can be traced in whole or in part to the strategic decision to prove himself morally credible by running away from Clinton. Gore and the Gore campaign suffered from other problems, most notably a press corps irrationally hostile toward him and credulously indulgent toward George W. Bush. Perhaps, in a fair media environment, Gore could have won by casting Bush as the candidate of the sexual fundamentalists and far right that he was. But Gore took his sights off his quarry. He misread the views of the Democratic base and the public at large, not only about Clinton but about the culture wars in general. By allowing his campaign to become obsessed with a courtship of the elusive conservative white man of Democratic lore, Gore sprung a trap of his own making.

. . .

IN THE TWO years leading up to the 2000 presidential election, Bush had marketed himself as a pragmatic moderate and publicly flaunted his independence from the Right. The Republican establishment had boasted that candidate Bush was their man to defang the party's right wing. The leaders of the sexual counterrevolution had bewailed their impotence, flamboyantly denounced Bush, bemoaned the GOP's betrayal of cultural conservatism, and yet confided that they were beat and had nowhere else to go.

On Election Day, the sexual counterrevolutionaries provided Bush with 40 percent of his total vote, an indispensable bloc in a tied election. Among all who identified themselves as conservative Christians, 89 percent voted for Bush. Bush won 75 percent of all evangelicals, and the evangelicals who voted for Bush were overwhelmingly fundamentalists, highly observant, and traditionalists on sex and family matters. In every one of the twelve states lost by Gore and won by Clinton-Gore in 1992 or 1996, the Christian Right held significant influence in the state Republican parties. In all but one of the six states outside the South that switched, Bush's popular vote margin was under 5 percent. The one exception, Colorado, was home to Dobson's Focus on the Family and its affiliated megachurches.

Given the very public two-year-long feud between the Christian Right and Bush, what accounted for such ardor? Fourteen days into the recount, *Newsweek* revealed the Bush campaign's well-kept secret. Grover Norquist, who during the New Hampshire primary had denied that he supported Bush, told the reporters, "Bush went to every piece of [my] coalition and said, 'I know you want to be left alone on guns. Deal.' 'I know you want to be left alone on taxes. Deal.' 'Property rights? Deal.' 'Home schooling? Deal.'" Norquist himself began parsing voter lists with Rove in early 1999. "Went to everyone and got 'em signed up or neutralized, including me, two years before the election."

The public message broadcast by the charming Texas governor had been moderation, but as Norquist revealed, the Bush campaign was also engaged in a parallel campaign, a narrowcast courtship of the sexual counterrevolutionaries, in language sufficiently encoded so as to escape detection by most observers. Four out of five evangelicals who voted for Bush received political communication from their pastor, the Christian Coalition, or another religious source. Three out of four evangelicals who voted for Bush identified closely with the Christian Right. Stealth had worked nicely for Bush and Rove in 1994, as well as for other candidates of the sexual counterrevolution over the years. No one should have been surprised they would once again pull out the winning playbook.

The American press bears significant responsibility for the voters' failure to recognize Bush's conservatism. When journalists and commentators did specifically investigate Bush's extensive ties to the Christian Right, they frequently misread the terms of the relationship. Shortly before Bush selected Cheney as his running mate, for example, Harold Meyerson of *The American Prospect* said a Bush campaign staffer had told him that Bush would pick Tom Ridge, a pro-choice Republican, as his running mate, and the Christian Right was going along with it. "From the moment Ralph Reed clambered aboard the Bush express," Meyerson confidently quipped, "the right has made clear that Bush could call for collective farms without forfeiting conservative support." A joint study by Pew's Project for Excellence in Journalism and the Committee of Concerned Journalists reported that 40 percent of stories about Bush reinforced his claim that he was a different kind of Republican.

A few journalists, notably columnist E. J. Dionne, and reporters Richard L. Berke, Terry Neal, Dan Balz, and Steve Benen did deftly expose the workings of Bush's shell game. In June, Dionne wrote, "Bush is far more conservative than his sunny and compassionate speeches would suggest. That has largely been lost, even though Bush isn't hiding anything. But it has not been lost on shrewd conservatives." Berke reported in October that right-wing organizations were "pouring millions of dollars into phone banks, commercials, and voter drives to help elect Mr. Bush. And they are hammering away on issues that Mr. Bush is not addressing in his campaign speeches, from abortion to guns to Vice President Al Gore's character." Their alarms, however, were drowned out by the din of conventional wisdom.

Just as the Bush campaign had advanced the notion that Bush was not beholden to the sexual fundamentalists, the movement's leaders had also labored to cover up their support for Bush. Instead of demanding public statements of orthodoxy from Bush, antiabortion groups allowed him to campaign as he wished. They simply attacked Gore and privately informed their members that Bush was fully on board with the absolutist doctrine. In 1992, the sexual counterrevolution had commandeered Bush's father's convention. In 2000, Falwell said to reporter Steve Benen, then writing for a magazine with a tiny circulation, "Our crowd needs to get into the battle, keep their mouths shut, and help this man win."

Bush was liberated to campaign as a "different kind of Republican" and a "uniter not a divider" by the deals he had sealed, in private, with the sexual counterrevolution and other right-wing special interest groups. The ruse paid off. Moderates and independents swung more toward Bush than they had to any Republican since 1988, when W.'s father's reputation as an establishment moderate was still intact. In 2000, Bush received 28 percent of his total vote from people who rated education, Medicare, Social Security, and health care their highest priority—issues on which Democrats historically have an advantage.

Feign weakness and hold your secret punch. It was brilliant political rope-a-dope.

STILL, BUSH'S ROPE-A-DOPE would have all been for naught if Democrats had not fallen for it. Overreacting to polling indicating ambivalence about President Clinton, key Democratic strategists and opinion leaders misinterpreted public opinion and helped deliver the presidency to George W. Bush. Remarkably, their claim that Gore lost primarily because of moral revulsion over the Lewinsky scandal remains part of the conventional wisdom about the contested 2000 election, even though the voting statistics do not bear them out.

The GOP took due note of how the sexual counterrevolution's Clinton-hunting had driven voters away in '98. In practice, however, the GOP establishment could not cut loose from the sexual counterrevolution; the bloc of Christian Right sexual fundamentalists was the largest single group of voters to support the Republican Party. How to square that circle? Moderation for the masses, confidential promises to the base.

Little noticed within Bush's December 13 victory speech was a discreet message to the shadow movement that had won him the election. "I believe things happen for a reason," suggesting in a code familiar to fundamentalist Americans that the hand of God could be seen in his election, before quickly pivoting back to the central theme of unity: "I hope the long wait of the last five weeks will heighten a desire to move beyond the bitterness and partisanship of the recent past."

The sexual counterrevolutionaries had been waiting eight years for deliverance from government by gays, feminists, progressives, and the anti-family, pro-sex, civilization-destroying Clintons. They could plausibly claim Bush owed his presidency to them. Whatever Bush's presidency might bring, they were in no mood for national reconciliation and unity.

11

THE PANIC SEASON

ON JANUARY 20, 2001, for the first time in 125 years, the candidate who had lost the popular vote was inaugurated as president of the United States. The 107th Congress was one of the most evenly divided in all of American history. Republicans held just nine more seats in the House than Democrats, while each party held 50 seats in the Senate, thus giving Vice President Dick Cheney the tie-breaking vote. Given George W. Bush's lack of a popular mandate, and the nation's even partisan split, everyone expected the new president to govern from the center. Bush flattered those expectations in his inaugural address, elaborating on his earlier call for unity and bipartisanship with a call for "civility." Presumably that meant Bush would not condone Gingrich-style partisan warfare among his Republican colleagues.

Once Bush started work, however, his turn to the Right was dramatic and immediate. Bush had billed himself as a compassionate conservative. He governed as a pseudo-conservative, to use the phrase coined by the great historian Richard Hofstadter during an earlier upwelling of right-wing radicalism. Within his first 100 days, Bush reversed widely recognized centrist accomplishments of

his predecessors—including his father George Herbert Walker—
and reneged on many of his campaign promises. In March, he pulled
out of multilateral talks designed to end North Korea's nuclear
program, directly contradicting his secretary of state, Colin Powell.
On the campaign trail he had promised to reduce America's carbon
emissions to deal with climate change. In March, he ignored advice
from Christine Todd Whitman, his appointed head of the Environmental Protection Agency, and Paul O'Neill, his treasury secretary,
and announced the United States would neither regulate carbon
emissions nor join the Kyoto Protocol for reducing greenhouse gas
emissions. Instead, the president adopted the recommendations of
an undisclosed group of oil and gas executives convened by Cheney
to proceed full speed ahead with expanded oil and coal production.
All this was done in plain sight. What the American people did not
know was that the neoconservatives in the Bush administration were
already gaming out the strategic benefits of unilateral U.S. military
action to remove Iraq's Saddam Hussein from power.

The sheer political audacity and pseudo-conservative radicalism
of the Bush administration was most publicly apparent on the issue
of tax cuts. Fiscal prudence was one of the bedrocks of mainstream
Republicanism. Both Ronald Reagan and the first Bush had raised
taxes when they were faced with mounting budget deficits. On the
campaign trail, Bush had promised a tax cut, contending that it
was the best use of the large budget surplus accumulated during
the Clinton administration. By the time he took office, however, the
dot.com boom had busted, the nation was headed into recession, and
the Bush campaign's already inflated projection of the amount of the
surplus now bore no relation to the reality of plunging tax revenues.
Yet administration spokesmen insisted that the surplus would be
even larger than they initially thought. "There are very large opportunities and contingencies that could expand the surpluses over ten
years," Mitch Daniels, a key White House economic adviser and
future Indiana Republican governor, wrote in an internal White
House memo. In March, even as the Dow dropped below 10,000 for
the first time in a year, the administration and GOP Congressional
leaders Tom DeLay, Dick Armey, and Trent Lott called for even
more cuts on top of those already on the table. When O'Neill and

a bipartisan centrist coalition in Congress countered by proposing a trigger to automatically end the tax cuts should the surplus turn to deficit, the political team in the White House rebuffed them. On May 26, 2001, Congress passed Bush's tax bill. A third of the $1.35 trillion, ten-year tax cut benefited the richest 1 percent of American taxpayers, who each received about $38,500 per year. The average taxpayer in the bottom 80 percent received just $600.

Bush's embrace of the sexual counterrevolutionaries, likewise, was instantaneous and dramatic. "When George W. Bush nominated John Ashcroft for attorney general," observed a reporter for *The American Prospect*, "commentators portrayed it as the one bone that George W. Bush would throw to the religious right—a way of shutting up the Jerry Falwells and Pat Robertsons so he could ignore them henceforth. Oops."

President Bush's second full day in office coincided with the anniversary of the annual antiabortion rally on the Capitol Mall to mark the anniversary of *Roe v. Wade*. Bush sent a warm personal message to the protesters, implying he did indeed look favorably on their constitutional amendment to ban abortion in all cases. Until that amendment was passed and ratified, or new Supreme Court justices overturned *Roe*, the president's power to restrict abortion was limited. Bush, as the first Republican to assume the presidency since Bill Clinton had reversed the Reagan administration's antiabortion executive orders, made a dramatic point of reinstating the Mexico City Policy barring monies to family planning organizations that provided abortion services with their own funds. An administration spokesman announced they would send RU-486, a safe and effective pharmaceutical alternative to surgical abortion widely available in Europe, back for study. The Food and Drug Administration had already approved the drug a few months earlier, after several years of study.

A week later, Bush issued an executive order creating the White House Office of Faith-Based and Community Initiatives. Although the federal government already provided funds to religious groups to deliver social services, it barred them on constitutional grounds from proselytizing to those they served. According to Marvin Olasky, the originator of the concept of compassionate conservatism, the new office would allow faith-based groups to evangelize their clients on the federal dime. Bush then issued an education plan that included taxpayer-funded vouchers, a long-standing wish of fundamentalist Christians who home-schooled their children to shield them from secular humanism, sex education, and evolution in the public schools. The Family Research Council enthused that Bush, the "first evangelical president," was receptive to "all our faith-based abstinence" programs, and commended him for denying funds for the "abortion providers." Soon all federal money for sex education was earmarked exclusively for abstinence-until-marriage education. Since the sexual fundamentalists had never been able to end sex education, they had shifted tactics and sought to guarantee that no education about sex would actually take place in sex ed class. The regulations prohibited teachers from talking about birth control or safe sex, while requiring them to teach that sex outside marriage "is likely to have harmful psychological and physical effects."

Many savvy commentators were surprised by the administration's rightward tilt and sharp-elbowed politicking, as were some Republicans who wound up in the administration. In late May, one of the few remaining Republican moderates, Senator James Jeffords, left the GOP in protest against Bush right turn and the pressure the administration and GOP leaders were exerting on everyone to fall in for the party line. Jeffords went into the Democratic caucus as an Independent, thus giving Democrats control of the Senate. By the end of the year, O'Neill was out of the administration. "What became clear to me," O'Neill told reporter Ron Suskind, "is that the presence of me and Colin and Christie [Todd Whitman] helped convince people that this would, actually, be an administration that would look hard for best solutions, without regard for which party had claimed an idea or some passing political calculation . . . [I]t now seems like we inadvertently may have been there, in large part, as cover."

On August 1, while the president vacationed at his new ranch in Crawford, Texas, the Treasury Department announced it would have to borrow $51 billion to cover the cost of the tax rebate checks that had just gone in the mail. The next week Bush announced that he would impose a ban on federal funding for embryonic stem cell research. In doing so, he flouted broad bipartisan support for stem cell research so as to appease the antiabortion sexual fundamentalists, whose slogan was now "pro-life from conception to natural death." Bush was planning to spend the month on vacation. Three days before his announcement on stem cell research, the CIA had briefed the president on a report titled, "Bin Laden Determined to Strike Inside U.S." Bush told his briefer afterward, "All right. You've covered your ass now."

THE NATION'S POLITICAL balance of power was instantaneously revolutionized by the terrorist attacks of September 11, 2001. Before, it did not look like Bush would have a very successful presidency. The GOP had lost control of the Senate, and Bush's approval rating was oscillating around the 50 percent mark. After September 11, Americans rallied around their president and their flag, and by late September, approval of Bush stood at 89 percent. The Republican Party, following Karl Rove's advice to campaign on terrorism and security, rode the crisis to a historic midterm victory in November 2002. The Bush administration forced a vote on authorizing the use of force against Iraq less than a month before the 2002 midterm election. Only twenty-one Democratic senators and fourteen Democratic representatives, two independents, and seven Republicans voted against the resolution. Democrats tried to campaign on the economy, especially against endemic corporate corruption revealed in the Enron case and similar scandals, but it didn't work. Republicans picked up seats in the House and Senate, an exceedingly rare feat for the incumbent president's party.

Although some commentators speculated that the serious business of war would put an end to the unserious politics of sex scandals and culture wars, that proved naïve. How Bush might square what he called the Global War on Terror with the sexual counterrevolution was previewed forty-eight hours after the attacks of September 11. Pat Robertson, Bush's earliest backer in the Christian Right, interviewed Reverend Jerry Falwell on his show, the *700 Club*.

"I really believe that the pagans, and the abortionists, and the feminists, and the gays and the lesbians who are actively trying to make that an alternative lifestyle . . . All those that are trying to secularize America. I point the finger in their face and say you helped this happen," Falwell said.

"Well I totally concur," Robertson responded.

Televangelist James Robison, who had stumped for Ronald Reagan in 1980 by warning that the alternative was a "Hitler-style takeover," said about Bush, "I think God gave us the man we need right now."

Even though the Bush administration's focus shifted toward war and terrorism, the sexual counterrevolution was far from over and the sexual fundamentalists were far from neglected. The Bush administration was, so to speak, able to walk and chew gum at the same time.

Campaign promises to the Christian Right had not been empty ones. In the give-and-take of right-wing coalition politics, Bush gave to the sexual counterrevolutionaries, even if that meant taking from the rest. Diplomatic service in the neoconservative laboratory of post-Hussein Iraq? Sure, as long as you passed the antiabortion litmus test in your interview. A Supreme Court appointment? The sexual counterrevolutionaries exploded at Bush's nomination of Harriet Miers. The support for the right to privacy she expressed to Republican Senator Arlen Specter was suspicious; Bush cut her loose and instead nominated Samuel Alito, a safely orthodox antiabortion judge. A believer in Grover Norquist's dictum that government should be so small you could "drown it in a bathtub"? Perhaps, but many federal department, even the Department of Agriculture, must have its own new Center for Faith-Based and Community Initiatives. A White House internship? One out of every fourteen Bush administration interns were graduates of Michael Farris's Patrick Henry College, a private college created to turn home-schooled evangelicals into crusaders against secular humanism. The sexual counterrevolution set the terms even on the one initiative for which Bush would win bipartisan accolades: his global leadership on AIDS funding. The President's Emergency Plan for AIDS required that a third of all U.S. funding for AIDS prevention worldwide be spent on programs advocating sexual abstinence until marriage, even though millions of women worldwide were most at risk of HIV infection from their husbands.

The rest of the GOP was none too happy about the preeminence of the sexual fundamentalists in the Bush-led GOP. Cabinet member

Christine Todd Whitman, the pro-choice head of the Environmental Protection Agency, left the administration in June 2003 and then wrote a book denouncing the "social fundamentalists" who had hijacked her party and the Bush presidency. As Franklin Foer of *The New Republic* reported on the eve of the 2004 presidential election, "The breadth of the unhappiness with Bush is . . . striking. Although it began on conservatism's isolationist fringe, it has moved to the movement's mainstream and now emanates from every segment of the right's coalition, from neoconservatives to libertarians, with the exception of social conservatives."

AN EPIDEMIC OF political apathy had been one of the fruits of the peace and prosperity of the Clinton Era. That political disengagement had been crucial to the election of George W. Bush. The radicalism of Bush's actual governance, combined with the Democrats' paralysis after September 11, jolted millions of Americans out of their apolitical torpor.

The political reawakening had its roots in the Democrats' 1994 debacle, when the party had lost control of Congress in the first midterm election of Clinton's presidency. In 1995, within organized labor, a reform ticket defeated Lane Kirkland, George Meany's hand-picked successor, in the AFL-CIO's executive board election. Together Meany and Kirkland had exerted control over the AFL-CIO since its founding in 1955. This was "not your father's union movement," as one supporter put it. Linda Chavez-Thompson, elected on the reform slate to the executive board, became the first woman and first person of color to ever hold one of the federation's top positions. The powerhouse unions were the ethnically diverse and progressive service and public employee unions. John Sweeney, the new AFL-CIO executive secretary, had been president of the Service Employees International Union (SEIU), Chavez-Thompson had been an officer in the San Antonio Texas AFSCME, and Richard Trumka, today the current leader of the AFL-CIO, headed the United Mine Workers and was known as a militant populist. The new leadership made a commitment to rejuvenating labor's political influence and organizing new union members. Focusing resources on getting its members out to vote, the AFL-CIO increased union Democratic turnout in 1996 and 1998 and contributed significantly to Democratic victories. Between 1992 and 2000, the share of the electorate that was a member of a union increased 37 percent.

But only 15 million Americans, one out of every eight American workers, belonged to a union. Few young people, pink-collar working women, or professionals, all groups that by the late 1990s leaned strongly Democratic, belonged to unions. For that matter, they tended not to be members of any of the civic groups or old political clubs with experience in educating and mobilizing voters.

Some of the first people to fill this void in progressive political organizing fell into electoral politics entirely by accident. Joan Blades and Wes Boyd, a married couple who ran a Silicon Valley software company, were having dinner at a Chinese restaurant when the subject turned to Bill Clinton and the Lewinsky scandal. It was 1998 and Kenneth Starr had just released his report to Congress. Blades and Boyd went home, wrote a one-sentence petition, and emailed it to about 100 friends and relatives—including lots of Republicans. Within a week, their email had gone viral, with roughly 100,000 people having signed their petition calling on Congress to "censure President Clinton and move on to pressing issues facing the nation." Soon up to 300,000 people were connected online and organizing for the midterm election less than eight weeks away.

Even though voters repudiated the GOP in that election, the GOP-controlled House voted to impeach Clinton a few weeks later. "We just got hundreds of thousands of people to engage in electoral politics for the first time in their lives and leadership essentially thumbed their noses at them," Joan Blades told me. "We're not feeling really good about that." They had thought that that election would be a one-time effort. "It just didn't feel right when your elected leadership is basically disrespecting you, your job as a citizen is to find people that better represent your views." So they launched a new campaign geared toward the 2000 elections, aptly titled "We Will Remember." MoveOn created a political action committee (PAC) and raised over $1 million in small donations, averaging under $50. "We still expected to go away," Blades explained, but after the contested election, "Our members wouldn't let us."

The Bush administration's response to the attacks of September 11 and the lead-up to the Iraq War proved to be another milestone for MoveOn. Blades and Boyd joined forces with Eli Pariser, a young antiwar activist from Maine, whose own petition calling for restraint after 9-11 had gone viral. By late 2001, MoveOn's membership had reached 500,000. With the Democratic congressional leadership terrorized by Rove's cynical use of the terror card in the 2002 election campaign, MoveOn again stepped into what Blades calls the "vacuum of leadership."

MoveOn provided a forum for people outside the established political networks, such as those provided by the political parties, unions, or politicized churches, to get involved in politics. While MoveOn was growing and becoming a recognized force mobilizing progressive voters to influence the Democratic Party, progressive blogs were offering an alternative source for news, commentary, and messaging. Throughout the Clinton years, the Right had dominated political debate on the Internet. After the 2000 election, a progressive alternative emerged. Blogs such as Daily Kos, MyDD, and Talking Points Memo gave technologically savvy political junkies a means to shake up the stale and cautious debate within the Democratic Party. The dot.com revolution provided the tools for this novel type of political communication; the actions of the Bush administration provided the impetus.

The question was, would all this new energy amount to anything?

ON MARCH 15, 2003, two days before President Bush warned Saddam Hussein he had 48 hours to leave Iraq or face war, the California Democratic Party hosted the party's candidates for the 2004 presidential race. Senator Joseph Lieberman sent a message via videotape. North Carolina's first-term senator John Edwards, who had voted to give Bush authority to go to war, was greeted by near silence. When he called for removing Hussein by force, if necessary, the crowd of Democratic Party activists booed him. The night before, Massachusetts Senator John Kerry had been greeted by shouts, "No war, John, no war." Kerry too had voted to give Bush authority to go to war.

The nearly 3,000 Democratic Party activists and local politicians weren't warming up to anyone. That is, until Howard Dean stepped up to the podium, and asked, "What I want to know is, what in the world so many Democrats are doing supporting the president's unilateral intervention in Iraq?" The crowd went wild. "What I want to know is what in the world so many Democrats are doing supporting tax cuts which have bankrupted this country and given us the largest deficit in the history of the United States?"

Borrowing a line from the late progressive Democratic Senator Paul Wellstone, he declared, "I'm Howard Dean, and I'm here to represent the Democratic wing of the Democratic Party."

Dean was a former two-term governor of Vermont and a medical doctor. He came out that night unequivocally for universal health care, affirmative action, and gay civil unions, and against off-shoring jobs, tax cuts, and the Iraq War. He proudly boasted that he had signed the nation's first gay civil unions bill, when only a third of Vermonters supported it, because on principle it was the right thing to do even if it wasn't popular. Dean's impassioned defense of progressivism was a rarity in the immediate post–9-11 years of Democratic cowardice, passivity, and capitulation to the GOP.

"I don't think we can win if we vote for the Iraq War and then come to California and say we're against it," he called his opponents out, to loud whoops and cheers. "And I don't think we can win the White House if we skip the most important abortion vote in the last year and then come to California and talk about pro-choice," he continued. "I'm not surprised that only 15 percent of people between the ages of 18 and 25 vote because we haven't given them a reason to vote. And we're going to give them a reason to vote now."

He ended in a rasping shout, his face reddening, his fists clenching and unclenching, arms up like a boxer, reflecting back to the audience its palpable craving for a fighter. "I want my country back! We want our country back! I'm tired of being divided! I don't want to listen to the fundamentalist preachers anymore! I want America that looks like America, where we are all included. We have a dream. We can only reach the dream if we are all together—black and white, gay and straight, man and woman . . . Stand up for America! Stand up for America! Stand up for America!"

When Dean took the stage that night in California, he was polling at about 5 percent. By the fall he was the insurgent frontrunner.

Dean's stand-up-and-stand-for-something fighting spirit had struck a chord throughout the nascent progressive movement. Still, it's unlikely Dean would have been able to rise from the crowded pack of candidates without the institutional support provided him by two progressive, multiracial, national labor unions. SEIU and AFSCME money and volunteers turned Dean's improbable run into a viable campaign for the Democratic presidential nomination.

As far as the Democratic establishment was concerned, Dean's rise was a catastrophe waiting to happen. And a familiar one at that. Dean seemed to be a typical ultra-liberal insurgent, like Edward Kennedy, Walter Mondale, or even George McGovern, and they set to work to marginalize him. "What activists like Dean call the Democratic wing of the Democratic Party is an aberration; the McGovern-Mondale wing, defined principally by weakness abroad and elitist, interest-group liberalism at home," read a memo from the Democratic Leadership Council. Here was the old death-by-McGovernik charge, still potent after thirty years in continual circulation. "Real Democrats are real people, not activist elites." Dean was unelectable. His main opponents, Dick Gephardt and John Kerry, were happy to agree.

Dean did resemble other insurgents. He appealed to the progressive base—college-educated Democrats, working women, the young, and the culturally progressive. He believed in revitalizing democracy with a small "d," something all too many Beltway insiders feared. But they failed to appreciate how he and his campaign were different. With the backing of two progressive unions, Dean had a solid working-class constituency, even if those workers didn't look like the followers of George Meany from thirty years ago. Dean also was a pioneer of using new media to expand the electorate and circumvent the narrow range of political debate shaped by the established Beltway media. (MoveOn had offered all the candidates technological training in new media. Only Dean had accepted.) The electability argument proved compelling to panicked Democrats across the political spectrum. When Dean did worse than expected in Iowa and stumbled in his concession speech, Democratic voters fell in for Kerry, and he quickly wrapped up the nomination.

ALL OF THE historical predictors pointed toward George Bush's reelection. The economy was growing, albeit weakly. No incumbent had ever lost reelection in time of war. Although Bush's approval rating was not high, he polled at least 15 points better than the two other modern incumbents who had been defeated for reelection: Jimmy Carter and his father, George H. W. Bush.

Still, Bush's prospects looked surprisingly shaky. No weapons of mass destruction had been found in Iraq, and claims that there were links between Al Qaeda and Hussein had also been debunked. Opposition to the war was growing. Pre-election polls showed a neck-and-neck race between the incumbent and his Democratic challenger, Massachusetts Senator John Kerry and his running mate, North Carolina Senator John Edwards.

With so much at stake and an apparent path to victory, the new groups that had emerged post-2000, as well as Dean's activists, dedicated themselves to reengaging voters in the general election, even though many felt at best lukewarm toward Kerry. In the 2004 election cycle, MoveOn's membership topped 3.5 million, 230,000 members volunteered, and their PAC raised nearly $32 million—more than two and a half times what the National Rifle Association put into the election. The Sierra Club and SEIU, as well as big donors such as George Soros and Peter Lewis (chairman of Progressive Insurance Companies), poured millions of dollars into Americans Coming Together (ACT), enabling it to fund a skeletal staff to organize thousands of volunteers in seventeen battleground states. Women's Voices, Women's Votes, another new group, focused on registering unmarried women, who made up nearly the majority of all women but had low turnout. A consortium of groups targeting young voters joined forces, adapted a decade's worth of experiments in best practices in youth turnout, and mounted field operations in six states.

The new activism was not enough to carry Kerry to victory, yet it did reveal a strategy for a future Democratic resurgence: get nonvoters to vote. National turnout overall increased by 6 percentage points. In Nevada, a state heavily targeted by ACT, turnout increased 22 percent. Unmarried women cast one-quarter of all votes in 2004; they favored Kerry by a 25-point margin. The youth voter project achieved the largest election-to-election increase in young voter turnout in history.

Other signs of the future prospects of the Democratic Party could be seen in the two young senators who would be joining the Democratic caucus. Democrats picked up a Republican Senate seat in Colorado. Ken Salazar was pro-choice, Roman Catholic, and a rancher. He would be the first Hispanic to serve in the U.S. Senate in a generation. In Illinois, an obscure state senator had triumphed against long odds after not one, but two, of the frontrunners had their divorce papers unsealed. In the Democratic primary, the frontrunner's ex-wife had accused him of threatening to kill her. The Republican candidate, a pro-life compassionate conservative, was accused by his wife of forcing her go to sex clubs and demanding she have sex with him while others watched. He dropped out of the race. An African American sexual counterrevolutionary, Alan Keyes, the former Reagan administration official responsible for the antiabortion Mexico City Policy, stepped into the gap. But when he denounced Vice President Cheney's daughter for being a lesbian, even the Illinois state GOP chairman said that was "idiotic." Keyes ended up with only 27 percent of the vote. But he did contribute something lasting to America's post-Bush political culture. "Christ is over here," Keyes said during a debate. "Senator Obama is over there—the two don't look the same."

Kerry had lifted the Illinois Democratic candidate for U.S. Senate, Barack Obama, out of obscurity by inviting him to give the keynote address at the Democratic convention. Barack Obama's 2004 convention speech turned out to be a high point for Democrats in a depressing year. In a reminder of how much the Democratic Party had changed since it had been the party of the New Deal *and* the white South, Obama became the first African American man ever to be elected as a Democrat to a seat in the U.S. Senate.

As late returns from Ohio showed Bush with the popular vote majority that had eluded him before, the question on everybody's mind was, what had carried Bush over the edge? Bush won, according to the National Election Pool exit poll, because of his appeal to "values voters." When voters were asked "which one issue mattered most in deciding how you voted for president," more chose "moral values" than any other issue, and 80 percent of those answering "moral values" voted for Bush.

The revelation about America's morality-based voting seemed to provide the key to deciphering the striking map of a disunited country broadcast on every channel. The map showed the lands of the amber waves of grain, the purple mountains majestied, and the fruited plains bathed in red. Isolated on the edges of the nation, hugging the oceans and the Great Lakes, Democrats clustered in slivers of land colored blue. The citizens of the Blue states looked on in dismay at the hostile, uncrossable land, as if they had woken one morning in a time-warped alternative universe, in which the Southern Confederacy had won the Civil War.

It was but a short leap of logic from the exit poll reports to the conclusion that more Americans were deeply religious, and more religious Americans preferred the moralistic GOP. "Can the Democrats ever connect with the country's cultural majority?" Chris Matthews asked on his cable TV show. California Senator Dianne Feinstein blamed the defeat on San Francisco Mayor Gavin Newsom, who had briefly made gay marriage legal in his city. A Los Angeles Times editorial bluntly concluded that voters "don't believe that the Democrats share their values." Politicians, pundits, and scholars of all partisan persuasions declared that the GOP would be in power for at least a generation. Americans, so they agreed, were a conservative people, governed by a president and a party which faithfully embodied their heartfelt values. The few voices of reason were ignored in the flight to the old nostrums. E. J. Dionne, who had wised up to Bush's stealthy ways earlier than most, stated bluntly—and presciently—in his first column after the 2004 election, "Ours is not a right-wing country. An alternative majority is out there, waiting to be born."

For anyone who cared to examine the matter objectively, the evidence was clear that Kerry had lost on the issues of war, terrorism, and national security. Why the confusion then, about so-called moral values?

Because the 2004 exit poll was flawed.

The main problem had been poor wording on a key question. Gary Langer, one of the nation's most respected nonpartisan pollsters, characterized the exit poll this way: "The question in effect asked voters: 'What was the most important issue in your vote for president—the economy, terrorism, Iraq, health care, taxes, education—or, rather, are you a conservative, religious person?'" Not only was the exit poll question poorly designed, it had little value as a predictor of the vote. Christian Right voters did favor Bush, but in the same proportion as they had in 2000.

Proponents of the values voter interpretation pointed to two other indicators: votes on gay marriage referendums and Bush's remarkable performance among Latinos. Many commentators believed that state referendums banning gay marriage energized the Christian Right and tipped the election. Not so. The issue of gay marriage had no impact on the presidential vote, concluded political scientist Alan Abramowitz. The election instead was largely a referendum on Bush. Indeed, Rove's ploy to use gay marriage referendums to lure fundamentalists to the polls apparently backfired. Evangelical turnout was "more than offset" by higher turnout of African Americans, college students, and other "anti-Bush voters," Abramowitz wrote. Likewise, the much-ballyhooed jump in Bush's Latino vote reported by the exit poll, treated as evidence that Latinos were voting their conservative cultural values rather than their working-class economic interests, was almost certainly wrong. A rigorous study concluded that Latinos did not swing toward Bush, but voted for Kerry by their typical pro-Democratic 3-to-2 margin.

What worked for Bush was the focus on terrorism and security. Bush's margin over 2000 wasn't provided by values voters, nor by conservative evangelicals, Langer observed, but rather by nonobservant white Protestants and white Catholics, who swung to Bush on security and terrorism, not values. National security issues, terrorism, and the Iraq War were so dominant that they temporarily scrambled historic class divisions in partisanship, according to Jeffrey Stonecash, a leading scholar of class voting. Lower-income supporters of the war only gave Kerry 11 percent of their vote. Upper-income voters who opposed the war gave Kerry 72 percent of their vote. Likewise, women's different views on security issues and Bush's leadership, not values, were behind the narrowing of the national gender gap. Non-southern women voted as strongly Democratic as they had since 1992, when the contemporary gender gap first began. The shift of white southern women toward Bush, because of their support for the Iraq War and their positive assessment of Bush's leadership, accounted for the entire change in the national gender gap.

The election did not signal a partisan shift in favor of the Republican Party, as Rove argued, the media repeated, and the Democratic delirium would have led one to believe. The strongest predictor of how someone voted in 2004 was how that individual had voted in 2000, and party loyalty was as strong as it had ever been. Nor did independents swing toward the Republican Party on values. According to political scientists D. Sunshine Hillygus and Todd Shields, "Put simply, to correctly predict who an Independent voted for in the 2004 presidential election, we need to know their evaluation of the Iraq war, not their opinions about abortion or gay marriage." Independents who opposed the administration on the war, terrorism, and its economic policies were "almost sure bets" to vote for Kerry; those who supported the administration on those issues, "sure bets for Bush."

In short, the experts on American elections reached a consensus that Bush's reelection was largely due to the issues of security and terrorism, and that the nation remained pretty much exactly where it had been in 2000: ideologically polarized and equally divided.

JUST A FEW days after the 2004 election, long before any of these definitive statistical studies of the election had been published, a closer look at the exit polls convinced objective analysts that swing voters had swung toward Bush on terrorism, not "moral values." It was too late, however, to rescue Democrats from the collective panic to which they had already succumbed. Surveying the wreckage, Democratic leaders concluded that Democrats had lost their shirts because they shorted values. Thomas Frank, a talented journalist, historian, and polemicist, who had optioned the values-interpretation before its initial public offering, suddenly became the most sought-after expert on Democratic Party woes.

In his best seller, *What's the Matter With Kansas: How Conservatives Won the Heart of America*, Frank contended that the GOP seduced working-class Americans to vote against their material interests by appealing to heartland America's heartfelt social conservatism. After the votes were counted, the GOP ignored the culturally conservative rank and file and governed according to the dictates of its corporate overlords. It was an elaborate bait and switch: "The trick never ages; the illusion never wears off. *Vote* to stop abortion; *receive* a rollback in capital gains taxes."

"People getting their fundamental interests wrong is what American political life is all about. This species of derangement is the bedrock of our civic order," Frank pronounced. He reserved his sharpest outrage, however, not for Kansans who chose "self-destructive policies," but for cultural progressives in the Democratic Party. Who could blame white working and middle-class men for succumbing to the siren song, when Democrats refused to talk about "class" and their real "material concerns"? Democrats had given blue-collar voters "the big brush-off, ousting their representatives from positions within the party and consigning their issues, with a laugh and a sneer, to the dustbin of history." (Frank cited only one specific piece of evidence of class discrimination in the Democratic Party—an episode from Chicago that took place in 1972.) Seeking votes from "affluent, white-collar professionals who are liberal on social issues," Democrats "have left themselves vulnerable to cultural wedge issues like guns and abortion and the rest whose hallucinatory appeal would ordinarily be far overshadowed by material concerns." Such was "the criminally stupid strategy that has dominated Democratic thinking off and on ever since the 'New Politics' days of the early seventies." In short, the latte-liberal elitist heirs of the McGoverniks had once again hijacked the party, driving the betrayed real Democrats into the arms of a cynical and hypocritical Republican Party. "A more ruinous strategy for Democrats would have been difficult to invent."

The entertaining (and condescending) portrait of Kansan dupes and myopic Democratic elitists perfectly captured the Zeitgeist of Bush-era Democratic delirium. Stan Greenberg, often writing with his daughter, professor and pollster Anna Greenberg, implored Democrats to concede the moral conservatism of the fickle Reagan Democrat and get religion—literally. Two other leading party strategists associated with the Clintons, James Carville and Paul Begala, took Frank's report as gospel. Abortion, gay rights, and gun control "have probably cost more Democrats more elections in the last thirty years than anything else," they wrote in their 2006 book, *Take It Back*. "Anyone who has read Thomas Frank's book has a sense what happened." Thomas Edsall and Todd Gitlin, whose books of the eighties and nineties respectively had helped keep alive the idea that cultural elitists had destroyed the Democratic Party, got to work on new books, reprising their tales of betrayal in anticipation of the 2008 election.

Even interpretations of Democratic problems that directly contradicted Frank's Kansas remake of the McGovernik myth were sucked into the vortex of conventional wisdom. The renowned cognitive linguist George Lakoff, who in his best seller *Don't Think of an Elephant* tried to give some advice to Democrats, was dragooned into the conservative "moral values" frame. Drawing on his pioneering scholarship, Lakoff told progressives to stop repeating GOP talking points in their efforts to debunk Republican ideas. Instead, Democrats needed to frame their message in a way that expressed their values—their compassionate, nurturing, egalitarian family values. Lakoff became a victim of exactly what he had warned against. When he used the term values, progressives and other Democrats seemed unable to imagine that the word could mean something other than the traditionalist values of the Christian Right sexual counterrevolution. "If only the Democrats had read George Lakoff a few years ago," the one-time insurgent candidate Howard Dean wrote in the foreword to the 2006 edition of Lakoff's book, "we might not be in the position we find ourselves in today." At the time, Dean was running a religious voters office out of the Democratic National Committee, trying to woo conservative evangelicals, and warning progressives to get with his program or get lost.

It was high time to get tough with cultural progressives, time to repossess the party for its true owners and real Americans. Carville and Begala provided detailed instructions. If someone baits you about gay marriage, "shift the debate." Just say "you believe marriage is between a man and a woman" and then start talking about the need to pass the federal Employment Non-Discrimination Act (ENDA). Self-professed liberal Eric Alterman laid out a kind of tough love for Democratic cultural progressives. In an author's Q&A

on the progressive blog Talking Points Memo, Alterman explained the "assumptions" in his 2008 book, *Why We're Liberals: A Political Handbook for Post-Bush America*. "Liberals made a series of fundamental mistakes beginning in the mid-sixties. They were arrogant. They were 'elitist.' They did treat white working-people—their primary political constituency—with disdain. They were insufficiently sensitive to the cultural concerns of everyday Americans, particularly with regard to issues relating to religion, and even more particularly with regard to abortion. And they became wrapped up in the divisive politics of identity that made it impossible to communicate with much of the country or cooperate with one another."

Alterman, who was employed by three leading progressive institutions, including the Center for American Progress, Media Matters for America, and *The Nation* magazine, intimated that Democrats could win again if they would just let good Americans put the right to an abortion to a vote. Alterman became so carried away with blaming "elitist" feminists for nearly all of the party's "self-inflicted wounds" that he wrote this eye-popping analysis of the 2004 election: Kerry lost because he "*sported* an outspoken foreign wife with a strange accent" and he "hailed from the most liberal state in America, one in which a *female judge*—the wife of the liberal ex–*New York Times* columnist Anthony Lewis—had just decided to legalize gay marriage."

Frank's spin on Democratic woes had gone viral, despite the fact that by this time substantial evidence had accumulated that proved he was wrong. Political scientists decided it was time to speak directly to *What's the Matter with Kansas*. "Working-class whites have not become more Republican in their presidential voting behavior," Princeton political scientist Larry Bartels wrote in his devastating review of *What's the Matter with Kansas*, citing his own statistical analyses as well as the work of many other scholars (including many cited earlier in this book). "They have become less Democratic in their party identification over the past forty years, but *at a considerably slower rate than middle- and upper-income whites*." Whatever decline there was in low-income whites identifying with the Democratic Party was "entirely confined to the South." Did culture trump class in determining the votes of working-class whites? No. "Traditional economic issues" shaped low-income voters' decisions; they attached little weight to cultural issues. Middle-income and affluent whites tended to factor in their cultural views in their vote, but working-class voters did not. Low-income whites had not even "become more conservative." (Only on abortion had they shifted slightly since the Clinton era, but still they remained "noticeably more pro-choice than they were in the 1970s.") Abramowitz and Ruy Teixeira, in a separate paper for the Brookings Institution and American Enterprise Institute, reached a similar conclusion. Those who spent their lives analyzing election results, votes, and voter opinion agreed: Frank's central claim that working people voted against their pocketbook values because of their cultural conservatism was simply, plainly, demonstrably not true. At the same time, political scientists were amassing persuasive evidence that Democrats had been following the pied piper in their decades-long courtship of the elusive white men. Targeting white men, political scientist and *Baltimore Sun* columnist Thomas Schaller tartly put it, "is a classic sucker's bet."

A dispassionate assessment of the political moment should have made Democrats skeptical of Kerry's prospects for election from the start and less prone to hysteria in the wake of defeat. Given Americans' unbroken record of reelecting incumbents in time of war, the reasonably good economy, and Bush's not terrible approval ratings, it was hardly surprising Kerry lost. As it would turn out, 2004 was not the inauguration of the permanent conservative majority, but another chapter in the perennial overreach of the sexual fundamentalists.

"I EARNED CAPITAL in this campaign, political capital, and now I intend to spend it. It is my style," Bush said gleefully in a press conference a few days after his reelection. He would indeed try to steamroll Congress to pass the priorities of the market fundamentalists and neoconservatives in his inner circle: privatize Social Security, expand the Global War on Terror, and double down in Iraq. (The Democratic minority leaders, Nancy Pelosi and Harry Reid, thwarted Bush on Social Security privatization.)

As Democrats convinced themselves that the culture war was just a bait and switch, Bush marched on with the sexual counterrevolution. Several events in the first year of Bush's second term gave

Americans a bitter taste of the brew of cynicism, zealotry, and corruption in store for the nation under the rule of a Right delirious in
its near-absolute power. "When a people no longer controls its 'appetite,' the public consequences require an external force, most likely
the government to step in," Pennsylvania Senator Rick Santorum
wrote in his 2005 book, *It Takes a Family*. The sexual fundamentalist
and 2012 presidential candidate had won notoriety for comparing
homosexuality to "man on dog" sex. He also, less famously but no
less vehemently, opposed consensual sex between unmarried heterosexuals in one's own home.

What Republicans under the leadership of men like Santorum
meant by stepping in was made clear on Easter weekend of 2005,
when President Bush rushed back from vacation at his Texas ranch
to be present when emergency legislation reached his desk. At 1:11
AM, about 40 minutes after the House suspended its rules to allow a
vote to take place, Bush signed into law the bill titled "For the Relief
of the Parents of Theresa Marie Schiavo." The U.S. Congress, under
the rule of small-government, freedom-loving Republicans, had leg-
islated that a comatose Florida woman's feeding tube be reinserted,
in contravention of any number of judicial rulings. Talking points
circulated by the office of Florida's Republican Senator Mel Martinez
justified the act by its political currency: "This is an important moral
issue and the pro-life base will be excited that the Senate is debating
this important issue." The GOP, which a few years later would insist
that a full year of debate on health care reform was "shoving it down
Americans' throats," passed the Schiavo bill in the Senate by a voice
vote with only three members present. In the House, only 60 percent
of representatives were in attendance. Despite passage and Bush's
signature, the Florida and U.S. Supreme Courts refused to enforce
the patently unconstitutional law. Schiavo's autopsy confirmed the
diagnosis of every doctor who had personally examined her: she was
in a persistent vegetative state.

The public was repelled by this intrusion into private family
matters. According to a CNN/ *USA Today* Gallup poll, 76 percent
disapproved of Congress's involvement in the Terri Schiavo case.
Undaunted, Bush again delivered to the more extreme elements of
the antiabortion movement when he vetoed a popular embryonic

stem cell research bill. The bill was sponsored by two moderate Republicans, Delaware Representative Mike Castle and Pennsylvania Senator Arlen Specter. It was Bush's first veto in more than five years in office.

Five months after the Schiavo case, when Hurricane Katrina made landfall in New Orleans at 7 am on August 29, the president was again on vacation. Half an hour later the Bush administration was notified that a levee had been breached. That morning Bush left his ranch—first to attend Senator John McCain's birthday party in Arizona, later to California to talk to seniors about the Medicare Drug Benefit he had signed. The next day, as the levees protecting the city broke, Bush went to San Diego and played guitar with a country music star. He flew home to Crawford to enjoy the last night of his summer break. Finally, on August 31, Bush flew over New Orleans on Air Force One, gazing down from his helicopter as thousands of the city's citizens went without food and water in the Superdome and Convention Center. Katrina dramatized the fundamental incompetence of Bush's administration of anti-government conservatives. After Katrina, an e-mail circulated, showing an aerial photograph of a flooded New Orleans, its center an oblong pool, only a few trees and freeway ramps visible above the brackish water, with a quote from Grover Norquist superimposed at the top: "My goal is to cut government in half in twenty-five years, to get it down to the size where we can drown it in a bathtub."

Over the next few months, corruption was added to the list of indictments against the Republican leadership. In September, the GOP majority leader and force behind Clinton's impeachment, Representative Tom DeLay, was indicted for violating Texas election law. DeLay resigned in April to prevent his seat from falling to a Democrat in the midterm election. (A Texas jury convicted DeLay of money laundering in November 2010, and DeLay was sentenced to three years in prison. At this writing, he remains free on appeal.) Soon after the initial reports of DeLay's indictment, two of his former top aides pleaded guilty in the massive corruption scandal involving lobbyist Jack Abramoff. Also implicated in the Abramoff scandal were Norquist and Ralph Reed, formerly of the Christian Coalition, and now running in the Republican primary for lieutenant governor of Georgia, a race Reed went on to lose to an obscure state senator. Paul Weyrich, the first New Right leader to perceive the electoral significance of the grassroots movements of women sexual fundamentalists, was sorry to see DeLay go. DeLay "actually cared about" the "social issues," Weyrich said. He "absolutely put the movement ahead of everything else."

IN NOVEMBER 2005 the only openly gay Republican in the U.S. Congress announced he would resign after serving eleven terms. A moderate from a southwestern border state, he had easily won reelection until 2004, after barely fending off a primary challenge from his Right. The district leaned Republican and had twice favored George W. Bush, yet the open seat attracted four Democrats to the race. The victor in the Democratic primary was the youngest woman ever elected to the State Senate. She had grown up in the district and ran her family's tire business. She was pro-choice, pro-business, pro-environment, pro-gun, and pro-military. Labor, business, and environmentalists backed her, as did EMILY's List and MoveOn. The charismatic, gregarious, blond outdoorswoman cut a new figure for a Democratic woman politician. She was, granted, a Fulbright scholar, Jewish, and an urban planner who had once lived in New York City, but she shot guns for sport, rode a motorcycle, and was engaged to a recently divorced astronaut. Democrat Gabrielle Giffords won the 2006 election with 54 percent of the vote in her sprawling 9,000-square-mile Arizona district. That same day, Arizonans rejected a ban on gay marriage, the first and still the only time American voters defeated a measure limiting gay marriage. Shortly after Giffords arrived in Washington, President Clinton's first labor secretary, Robert Reich, remarked, "I wouldn't be surprised if she's the first or second female president of the United States."

In the 2006 midterm elections, Democrats unexpectedly won control of both houses of Congress for the first time since the Gingrich revolution of 1994. With a 233-to-202 majority, Democrats proceeded to elect Nancy Pelosi speaker of the House of Representatives, the first woman ever elected to the post. Just twenty-four months earlier, the media had pronounced the permanent triumph of the GOP upon the unshifting bedrock of American cultural conservatism, so the logical thing to do was to fit the Democratic victory into the Center-Right nation frame of reference. A few days before the election, the *New York Times* explained, "In Key House Races, Democrats Run to the Right." After the election, Bob Schieffer of CBS News agreed, the "Democrats that were elected last night are conservative Democrats." While tracking Democrats racking up victories election night, Fox News's Brit Hume claimed, "from what we could see from all the polling and everything else, it remains a conservative country."

They weren't entirely wrong, but they weren't exactly right.

In the post-2004 slough of despond, the Democratic Party had gone to extraordinary lengths to inoculate itself against the Culture War, with little reflection that there might be an alternative path to resurrection. The old fear of death-by-cultural-extremism overshadowed the Democratic upsurge that culminated in the 2006 midterm victory.

"I didn't care where a seat came from," explained Illinois Representative Rahm Emanuel, Nancy Pelosi's choice to head the Democratic Congressional Campaign Committee (DCCC). Democrats needed fifteen seats to win back control of the House, and it was Emanuel's job to recruit the candidates for what promised in early 2005 to be a thankless task. He persuaded Brad Ellsworth, a tall, handsome sheriff who looked great in a uniform, to challenge one of Congress's fiercest sexual counterrevolutionaries, Indiana Republican Representative John Hotstettler. (Bay Buchanan, Pat Buchanan's sister, loved Hotstettler. After hearing him denounce "the homosexual agenda, which goes beyond gay marriage," she effused, he's "sooooooooo good.") Emanuel convinced Heath Shuler, an antiabortion, born-again, former NFL quarterback to run in a swing North Carolina district. In Indiana, a bastion of the Christian Right, Emanuel supported Baron Hill, an antiabortion former Democratic representative, seeking to win back his old seat. Howard Dean, head of the Democratic National Committee, implemented a 50-state strategy and found similarly culturally conservative Democrats to run, including Ted Strickland, a Methodist minister, whom the DNC encouraged to seek the governorship in Ohio. Senator Charles

Schumer and the Democratic Senatorial Congressional Campaign, likewise, ran every other Democrat out of the field in the Pennsylvania U.S. Senate race to clear a path for Robert Casey, Jr., an antiabortion, anti–stem cell research Catholic, to challenge the antiabortion, anti–stem cell research Catholic Santorum. Pelosi cared not a whit that Baron Hill explicitly distanced himself from her, and Emanuel was impressed when Shuler cut an ad boasting he was further right on immigration than his GOP opponent. To win Republican districts, Emanuel claimed, "There has to be a cultural, a philosophical fit." So what if these neophyte Democrats would hardly ever vote with the party on its signature measures? All that mattered to the Democratic leadership was the first vote to be taken in the 110th Congress: the vote for Speaker of the House. On everything else, the Democratic leadership decided that Democrats would just have to be flexible. Emanuel again: "No sentiments. It was pure winning."

Desperate times called for desperate measures. In time-honored fashion, Democratic leaders had suited up to fight last year's war. Overreacting to the results of the 2000 and 2004 elections, Democrats panicked and concluded that party survival required a right turn to meet the sexual counterrevolutionaries on their own hallowed ground. In the Democratic sweep of 2006, culturally conservative candidates such as Shuler, Hill, Ellsworth, Strickland, and Casey won, seemingly confirming the wisdom of the Democratic Party's conservative turn, as well as giving credence to the media's preferred Center-Right narrative.

But these conservative candidates were the exception in the 2006 Democratic field. On the hot-button issues, only five of the thirty Democrats who picked up Republican seats in the House described themselves as pro-life and only two opposed embryonic stem cell research. The vast majority of Democrats elected that day were cultural progressives in the mainstream of the Democratic Party. "My belief is that the power of government stops at the front door unless there is a compelling reason for it to come inside," said Jim Webb, a Vietnam veteran and secretary of the navy in the Reagan administration, who unseated Virginia's Republican senator. Among the winners were Pennsylvania's Joe Sestak, a Catholic and retired two-star admiral, who supported the right to abortion and gay rights and won a suburban Philadelphia House seat long held by a Republican, and Ohio's Sherrod Brown, who was both an economic populist and a cultural progressive and won a Senate seat previously held for two terms by a Republican. Twelve of the fifty newly elected Democrats were pro-choice women, including rising party stars Kirsten Gillibrand of New York and Giffords of Arizona.

While many eminent party leaders had looked to the socially conservative white man for redemption, a new progressive generation had awakened, dismayed not only by the disastrous radicalism of President Bush, but also by the passivity, impotence, and complicity of their own Democratic Party. A concerted effort by the rising progressives, in groups that had emerged outside the normal party apparatus since the contested 2000 presidential election, had a large hand in the 2006 Democratic midterm victory. MoveOn's members raised $27 million, made 7 million phone calls, and held 6,000 events in Congressional districts. Rock the Vote and fourteen other nonpartisan groups registered 500,000 voters under the age of 30 and then contacted thousands of them to make sure they voted. ACT was out of business, but the unions mounted their own in-house get-out-the-vote (GOTV) campaigns. Women's Voices, Women's Votes registered and turned out unmarried women in eighteen states. All the attention the party had paid to the religious, however, did not pay off. Democrats gained almost no ground among evangelicals.

A look at who voted calls into question the assumption that Democrats won by turning right on cultural issues such as abortion and gay rights. About the same proportion of Americans voted in 2006 as had in the previous midterm election, but progressive groups accounted for a larger share of the electorate than they typically did in a midterm election. People under the age of 30 turned out at their highest level in twenty years, increasing their participation compared to 2002 by 23 percent, and favored Democrats by a 23-point margin. Two-thirds of union members and their families voted Democratic; they accounted for almost a quarter of the electorate. Two-thirds of unmarried women, who now made up the majority of women in America, voted Democratic. The 52 percent of voters who attended church occasionally or rarely voted in supermajority proportions for Democrats.

Ironically, the Democratic Party had offered some of its most conservative candidates in recent history to an America becoming more culturally progressive, especially among the generation newly entering the electorate. The annual survey of college freshmen conducted by the University of California, Los Angeles and the American Council on Education showed college students moving to the left and more engaged in politics than freshmen of recent years past. Three-quarters of college freshmen favored gun control and gay rights, and six out of ten favored same-sex marriage. The views of young college students were shared by the rest of their generation. A Pew Research Center survey revealed that "millennials"—those under the age of 25—were the most liberal and least conservative generation in the nation. Compared to other generations at the same point in their lives, millennials were the least Republican generation in Pew's twenty years of tracking. Nearly six out of ten had voted Democratic in the midterm election, and 48 percent identified themselves as Democrats. Millennials were more pro-government, more pro-immigrant, less militaristic, and less worried about terrorism than all other generations. On questions of race and sexuality, "Gen Next," the Pew report observed, "stands out in its progressive approach." Millennials were strongly pro-choice. Whereas only 44 percent of older Americans supported the right of gay couples to adopt, 61 percent of Millennials did. Almost half of Americans under the age of 25 supported gay marriage.

The events since the contested 2000 election had provided Democrats all too many opportunities to reprise the battles of their long-running inner civil war and to wallow in self-defeating delirium. Unexpectedly, with two years left in Bush's presidency, the tide had turned in the Democratic Party's favor. It wasn't immediately clear which approach had won the day for Democrats. Had it been the awakening and mobilization of culturally progressive voters or the leadership's turn to the right to appeal to conservative voters? As Bush's popularity continued to plummet and both parties looked ahead to the 2008 presidential election, which route would lead to the doors of the White House? One Democrat, who had at different times traveled down each of the alternative paths, was about to find out for herself.

12

RORSCHACH TESTS

H ILLARY RODHAM, at age 22, had been heralded by *Life* magazine as the voice of a new generation. Some friends at the time had envisioned her as the first woman president. But when she finally made her run, she was under the sway of a different sort of visionary. Mark Penn, Hillary's chief strategist, instructed her to look to Britain's Iron Lady, Margaret Thatcher, for a roadmap to victory. "Most voters in essence see the presidents as the 'father' of the country," Penn wrote in an internal campaign memo obtained by Joshua Green of the *Atlantic*. "They do not want someone who would be the first mama, especially in this kind of world. But there is a yearning for a kind of tough single parent . . . They are open to the first father being a woman." Penn continued, "the most liberal, activist, difficult group of voters in America" might seem to be an "obstacle" to their ambition. But Hillary had to "only neutralize" them. "The real base of the party is of working class and middle class Americans who feel left out of the waves of prosperity they see all around them." Penn sought to allay any concerns she might have. "The brie and cheese set drives fundraising and the elite press but not does not drive the vote. Kerry beat Dean. Gore beat Bradley."

Ironically, Hillary, the first woman with a real chance to become president, eventually lost the election by following Penn's advice to court "real" Democrats and downplay her appeal to women and the "brie and cheese set." That advice had been offered by party officialdom since the Democratic Party's sexual counterrevolution began. Barack Obama ignored it. Instead, he put his faith in a larger universe of Americans, expanded the electorate, and won.

ON NOVEMBER 10, 2007, seven Democratic presidential candidates and 10,000 of their supporters gathered for the Iowa Democratic Party's annual Jefferson-Jackson dinner. The first contest of the 2008 primary, the Iowa caucus was less than two months away. Hillary had led the pack by double digits in nearly every poll for the past eleven months.

Well after 11 PM, candidate Barack Obama stepped up to the podium at the Jefferson-Jackson dinner. Just like every Democrat who appeared before Iowans from time immemorial, he cast himself as a populist and promised to "fight for the American worker." Through well-crafted allusion, Obama landed several punches squarely on Hillary's jaw. "Triangulating and poll-driven positions because we're worried about what Mitt or Rudy might say about us just won't do. If we are really serious about winning this election, Democrats, we can't live in fear of losing it." His supporters, most of them young, cheered. Obama then took aim at the soft underbelly of Clintonism. "I am asking you to stop settling for what the cynics say we have to accept. In this election, in this moment, let us reach for what we know is possible." The Democratic Party "has always made the biggest difference in the lives of the American people when we led, not by polls, but by principle; not by calculation, but by conviction; when we summoned the entire nation to a common purpose—a higher purpose. And I run for the Presidency of the United States of America because that's the party America needs us to be right now."

Speeches weren't the only point of the event; it was grand political theater in the old style, the audience the marquee draw. Earlier that day, the Iowa Obama campaign put on a John Legend concert for thousands of its supporters. Afterward, they paraded through the streets of Des Moines, Michelle and Barack in the lead, dancing part of the way. The campaign immediately posted a video of the enthusiastic crowd on its social media hub, mybarackobama.com. That night at the dinner, Obama's supporters outnumbered those of every other candidate, and they didn't look like the typical Democratic caucus-goer. Later that night, Mark Penn said they "look like Facebook," and then said to a reporter, "Only a few of their people look like they could vote in any state."

The J-J dinner was a near perfect execution of the two-pronged strategy David Axelrod and David Plouffe, Obama's lead campaign strategists, had mapped from the inception of Obama's presidential run. Personal history, principle, and ambition neatly dovetailed in that plan: expand the electorate by running a grassroots-driven campaign; transcend the stale partisan divide by offering a vision of change.

Of the two, expanding the electorate was the more critical ingredient. Obama's life-changing experience as a community organizer in Chicago in his twenties taught him the value of grassroots organizing. According to Plouffe, the campaign's manager, Obama's "belief that the American people needed to reengage in their civic life" was one of the essential principles that motivated him to run for the presidency. Of course, there weren't any other clear paths to victory against the Clinton juggernaut. She had, after all, been the presumptive nominee since the morning after George W. Bush's reelection. So the Obama campaign had little choice but to look for staff and voters outside the Clinton orbit. "We would build a ragtag militia to compete against her regular army."

Electoral politics, Axelrod once observed, "is a function of math." Iowa, by necessity, was the proving ground for the Obama campaign's hypothesis that a grassroots effort to expand the electorate could carry the improbable candidate to victory. After all, when Obama entered the presidential race, he was just four years out of the Illinois State Senate and one year out of student debt. He came to the contest burdened with his race, his middle name, and his unusual childhood spent in foreign countries. Plouffe observed, "The great conventional wisdom is that there's a finite universe of old and white caucus goers, give or take 25,000 people. Barack was willing to roll the dice on the strategy of building a new coalition, getting out young people and bringing in every minority community in the state. It was a gutsy move." Long shots typically have to win one of the first two contests to stay in the running. The campaign put organizers in the field early and hired Steve Hildebrand and Paul Tewes, who had experience in grassroots organizing and had run Al Gore's successful Iowa campaign, to run this outside the box campaign. The focus was to be on recruiting volunteers, who would then recruit new caucus participants through their online, school, and personal social networks. Almost all of the staff and thousands of volunteers were younger than 25. Tewes adopted the motto "Respect. Empower. Include."

Obama needed a message, of course, to persuade the uninvolved to volunteer and vote. Axelrod, a Chicago political consultant and Obama's chief strategist, contended that the outgoing president sets the shape and tone of an election. Bush was unpopular because he was perceived as hyperpartisan, stubborn, and in thrall to fundamentalists, right-wing ideologues, and corporate special interests. Independents and Republicans, as well as Democrats, were looking for different qualities.

"You are uniquely suited for these times," Axelrod wrote. "No one among the potential candidates within our party is as well positioned to rekindle our lost idealism as Americans and pick up the mantle of change." Obama's 2004 Democratic convention keynote address, with its rejection of the Red-Blue divide, Axelrod explained, "remains the touchstone for our campaign moving forward . . . No one better represents a new generation of leadership, more focused on practical solutions to today's challenges than old dogmas of the left and right . . . Perhaps by running and winning, you can help change our politics too."

It was as if Obama were the avatar for a new political philosophy: transpartisanship. Hillary, the Democratic frontrunner, was herself conveniently tainted by the partisan bickering of the recent past, and Axelrod appreciated when idealism and expediency aligned. He encouraged his client to exploit the festering uncertainties voters harbored about Hillary, which were of course the legacy of the right-wing wars against the Clintons and antifeminist Hillary-hating. "For all her advantages, she is not a healing figure. As much as she tacks to the right, she will have a hard time escaping the well-formulated perceptions of her among swing voters as a left-wing ideologue."

FOR NINE MONTHS, Hillary coasted along in the lead on the power of the Clinton machine, a message of electability, and her own very considerable talents. To the public, Hillary promised, "let's bring back the good times.' To Democratic insiders, Bill and Hillary warned, 'leave it to us, or welcome to a replay of 2000 and 2004."

Obama opened strong, but he faltered during the summer of 2007, and it seemed he would go the way of every other sparkly Democratic insurgent. At the beginning of October, an ABC News/*Washington Post* poll showed Hillary ahead of Obama by 53 to 20, with 57 percent of voters rating her most likely to win a general election. She even bested Obama by 14 points on the question of who stood for change. As the pundits declared Obama dead, Obama's top fundraisers panicked. Penn's strategy that Hillary project strength and toughness, if you were to believe the polls, seemed to be going swimmingly.

When the seven Democratic candidates met on October 30, 2007, for a debate in Philadelphia, everyone naturally went after the frontrunner. Two of the moderators peppered Hillary with hard questions, while ignoring the others, in a fairly typical stance for journalists at a moment when one candidate seems poised to wrap up the nomination. John Edwards, a one-term former senator from North Carolina and the 2004 vice presidential nominee, aggressively challenged Hillary. Killing two birds with one deftly lobbed stone, transpartisan Obama followed Edwards with a weary lament about the vitriol. What "we don't need," Obama said, "is another eight years of bickering." Was he referring to Bush's eight years in office? Or perhaps to the previous occupants of the White House? Hillary withstood the questioning and the attacks by her fellow Democrats, until NBC's Tim Russert asked her a question about whether illegal immigrants should be able to get driver's licenses. She stumbled and contradicted herself, feeding old concerns that the Clintons were congenitally incapable of telling an inconvenient truth.

It was her first major gaffe in nine months on the campaign trail. Perhaps it wouldn't have been fatal had her campaign staff not immediately made it worse. Without consulting Hillary, they posted a video titled "The Politics of Pile-On," implying that Hillary had been the victim of sexism in Philadelphia. Hillary was furious at her own people. She saw the debate as a classic and predictable attack on the frontrunner, not an instance of sexism. She ordered it down immediately, but it was too late. By chance, the video coincided with a scheduled speech at Wellesley, where Hillary quite reasonably said, "this all-women's college prepared me to compete in the all-boys club of presidential politics." In the context of the video, however, many read it as more crocodile tears about sexism.

Something about this particular episode tripped the safety valve that had kept the delirium of men of a certain age contained. MSNBC host Chris Matthews was, on the Democratic side, the most unhinged. Matthews charged that Hillary was running "an anti-male" campaign; on the subject of Democratic politicians endorsing Hillary, he asked a guest, "Aren't you appalled at the willingness of these people to become *castratos* in the eunuch chorus?" On another occasion he said that "Hillary's loyal lieutenants are ready to scratch the eyes out of the opposition." So the woman who was very likely to be the leader of the free world was a castrating man-hater who didn't fight fair? Outside the Right, such caricatures of strong women had rarely been heard since the bipartisan antifeminist backlash of the 1980s.

The carryings-on by Democratic-leaning pundits helped provide cover for the eruption of misogyny on the Right, the likes of which had not been seen since, well, since Hillary was First Lady. On November 13, a woman asked candidate John McCain, "How do we beat the bitch?" McCain laughed and said, "That's an excellent question." Conservative MSNBC television host Tucker Carlson engaged liberal radio host Bill Press in a discussion about Hillary "pandering" to women's "resentment and anger" against men. Matthews had been speaking figuratively when he called Hillary's supporters castratos. Carlson and Press reached back fifteen years to the infamous Lorena

Bobbitt case, to link Hillary to an actual case of castration. "I think men have a reason to be angry at women based on what Lorena Bobbitt did," Press said. Carlson replied, "Well, I couldn't agree with you more. No man would ever defend the corollary. But women are like, 'Oh, I understand why Lorena did that.' I mean, they're really mad. And she's taking advantage of it."

By the end of November, in the midst of the general eruption of sexism and after Obama's surge following the J-J dinner, Gallup reported that Hillary's approval ratings had flipped from positive to negative. Fully 50 percent of Americans had an unfavorable view of her, one of the highest levels the firm had recorded in Hillary's sixteen years in the national spotlight. Rarely has a frontrunner fallen so far so fast.

On January 3, 2008, more than 238,000 Iowans showed up to participate in Iowa's Democratic caucus, almost twice as many as had participated in the record-breaking 2004 caucus, and twice as many as showed up for that night's Republican contests. Tom Vilsack, the former Democratic governor of Iowa and a strong Hillary supporter, walked into his local caucus and hardly recognized anyone. Most of those new voters had been mobilized by the Obama campaign, and most of them were young. Men and women under 30 made up the same proportion of voters as did those over 65. Typically, seniors outnumbered youth by at least two-to-one. By the end of the night, Obama had won 38 percent of the delegates awarded in the Iowa caucus. Hillary placed third, with 29.47 percent of the vote, just 0.04 percent lower than Edwards. Obama's gamble that he could beat the Clinton machine and neutralize Edwards by expanding the electorate had paid off.

"You know, they said this day would never come. They said our sights were set too high," Obama began his victory speech. Obama had no intention of drawing attention to a great moment in black history, in which an African American won a presidential contest in a heartland state that was 97 percent white. The day that wasn't supposed to come was a day of Red and Blue, not black and white, unity. "They said our country was too divided, too disillusioned to ever come together around a common purpose." You are here at this historic moment of transpartisanship and you will tell your kids about it. "This was the moment when we finally beat back the policies of fear and doubts and cynicism, the politics where we tear each other down instead of lifting this country up."

Directed by Penn's Zeitgeist-defying battle plan, Hillary had aggravated her greatest vulnerability, her 2002 vote to authorize the use of force in Iraq, and downplayed the historic nature of her candidacy as the first woman with a serious chance of winning the presidency. In the fall of 2007, according to Gallup, 36 percent of Americans said the Iraq War was the most important issue in determining their presidential vote, more than those who cited the economy and health care combined. Penn's Margaret Thatcher frame was the reason Hillary could not recant her Iraq War vote, as John Edwards did early in the campaign season. Doing so, Penn insisted, would call into question her strength, her resolve, and invariably raise questions about a woman's fitness to be commander in chief.

That focus on passing the commander-in-chief test had additional unintended consequences. Projecting toughness and strength required that Hillary keep her authentic personality hidden behind the steely façade of the leader-in-waiting of the free world. It entailed that she avoid any explicit appeal to women. For women of a certain age, there was no need to draw attention to the obvious. But it was different for younger Democratic women, who had grown up in a multiracial America and strongly opposed the Iraq War. Forced to make a choice between identity politics and their progressive political beliefs, young women chose the latter. Only 11 percent of Iowans under 30 voted for Hillary. If Hillary had as much as tied Obama among Iowan women overall, she would have significantly narrowed the margin of her loss to Obama and easily topped Edwards. Hillary's campaign failed to recognize the danger of taking her appeal to women for granted. Until, that is, it was too late.

THE NIGHT OF the Iowa caucus, with votes in from 238,000 Americans, the media declared Hillary's presidential ambitions DOA. Like her husband's before her, Hillary's fate was in the hands of the voters of New Hampshire. Personally wresting control of her dysfunctional campaign, she rejected Penn's recommendation to go sharply negative on Obama, the New Hampshire staff's warning not to talk openly and unscripted to voters, and hints from her closest friends to quit. With only five days until the primary, she arrived in New Hampshire the morning after her Iowa loss for an old-fashioned barnstorming of the state. Like Obama, she drew thousands of cheering, excited supporters to her rallies and town hall meetings. She started to let her personality show through the armor. She handled herself with self-deprecating grace at a debate when Obama remarked, while looking at his notes, "You're likable enough, Hillary," a moment that magically lifted the arrogant mantle off her shoulders and placed it on his.

And then, two days after that debate and less than twenty-four hours before all the experts predicted she would be forced to concede the Democratic nomination to Obama, she sat down with sixteen voters at the Café Espresso in Portsmouth. One woman asked how she was able to survive the stress of the campaign trail.

"It's not easy," Hillary began in a soft voice, "and I couldn't do it if I didn't passionately believe it was the right thing to do. You know, I have so many opportunities from this country." She rested her chin in her palm, nodding and shaking off strong emotion.

"I just don't want to see us fall backward. You know this is very personal for me—it's not just political, it's not just public. I see what's happening," her voice quavered.

"And we have to reverse it. And some people think elections are a game, they think it's like who's up or who's down. It's about our country. It's about our kids' futures. It's really about all of us together."

Within seconds, she regained her composure and returned to her talking points. The media said she had "cried." She had not. They called it a "breakdown." She had made some hand gestures. Unseemly glee erupted in many circles. Obama had to rebuke his tittering campaign aides. Give her a break, he told them, it's hard to do this day after day. Edwards, himself now enmeshed in an extramarital affair that, when exposed, would make the Lewinsky affair look mundane, made a statement that commanders in chief had to be tough.

The next day Hillary won the New Hampshire primary by 7,600 votes. Pre-election polls had shown Obama with an edge with women, yet Hillary won women by 12 points, making women the deciding bloc.

By this time, a large part of the media was in Obama's camp, and many male political junkies seemed deliriously infatuated with Obama. Already legendary was Chris Matthews's comment that Obama's speeches sent tingles down his leg. Having projected onto Obama their own fantasies of the progressive utopia, they were shocked, just shocked, that New Hampshire voters did not share their opinion. So they pilloried Democratic women, who with their daft emotion-driven identity politics were destroying the party's chance at the White House by rallying for the unelectable Hillary. The progressive blog Talking Points Memo blamed Matthews for stoking the women's backlash. If it hadn't been for his sexist ranting, they maintained, Obama would be the nominee. Matthews defended himself by doubling down. "Let's not forget," he said the next morning, "and I'll be brutal—the reason she's a U.S. senator, the reason she's a candidate for president, the reason she may be a front-runner is her husband messed around." Venerated *Meet the Press* host Tim Russert tried to corral *New York Times* columnist Gail Collins into the narrative. "Is it ironic that this self-avowed feminist went to New Hampshire, showed some emotion, and that seemed to be a real help to her with women voters?" Collins put Russert in his place with gee-whiz cheeriness. She agreed that showing some authentic humanity helped Hillary against the charismatic man from hope and change. But Collins batted away the rickety premise of Russert's insinuation. "If you look at women voters, women voters are conservative in sort of a nonpolitical way." They test candidates on the issues, she said. "I think even if she was a man, she'd be, in the end, the one that women would gravitate to."

Just as New Hampshire activated ancient feuds in the Democratic sexual counterrevolution, so too did latent racial tensions flare as the contest heated up. In the lead-up to the late January South Carolina primary, Bill Clinton and several Clinton supporters made remarks to the press that appeared to be playing the race card. (One of Bill's remarks was taken out of context, a couple by him and others were almost certainly an effort to stir the racial cauldron, and the rest could be called either way.) The remarks left a reservoir of ill-feeling among African American voters, who felt particularly betrayed by the Clintons, who had a long record of sincere and successful advocacy for black civil rights. (Bill's first political victory in his twenties was to help take down Arkansas's own Bull Connor, Jim Johnson, one of the original anti-Clinton conspirators.)

On January 26, Obama swept the African American vote and picked up a quarter of white voters to win the South Carolina primary with a commanding 55 percent of the vote. Although the racial slights would leave relations between Obama and Bill Clinton strained for quite a long time, they had little to do with why African Americans in South Carolina swung from Clinton to Obama. Again, Obama proved that ignoring Democratic Party conventional wisdom was the path to victory.

In Iowa, expanding the electorate ran through young voters. In South Carolina, it meant directly taking on the historic racial gap in voter participation. In a deliberate and much-opposed end run around the party establishment, the Obama campaign convinced 13,000 ordinary South Carolinians, most of them African American women, to volunteer for the campaign. Michelle Obama, like Hillary in 1992, turned out to be one of her husband's greatest assets in this key primary. While Barack campaigned on inclusive and universal themes and hardly ever mentioned race, Michelle personally went to African American women voters and stiffened their spines. Yes we *can* elect a black president, she insisted. Oprah's first-ever endorsement in a presidential race also played an important role in convincing African American women to take a chance. Of course, inspiring more Democratic participation was perfectly in line with cold-blooded pragmatism. African Americans are a key constituency in Democratic primaries. They had crushed most other insurgents in the past, and they had been critical to Bill's triumph in 1992. With his South Carolina victory, Obama accomplished four critical tasks in Axelrod's electoral math challenge. One, he proved he was electable by winning white voters in the Deep South. Two, he forced Edwards out of the race by winning a solid majority in Edwards's home territory, allowing him to claim the progressive voters who disparaged Clintonian centrism and who could not forgive Hillary's Iraq War vote. Three, he signaled to African American voters in every other state that the Clintons weren't invincible. And, four, he stole a bloc of voters from Hillary that she had taken for granted.

With South Carolina, Obama moved into a slight lead among pledged delegates. Yet Gallup showed Democratic voters still favoring Hillary by more than 10 points. Ten days after the South Carolina primary, on Super Tuesday, February 5, 2008, Hillary and Obama tied the popular vote. Obama, however, won 31 states to Hillary's 8, to end the night netting 100 more delegates than Hillary. Half of all delegates in the Democratic race had been at stake that night.

It appeared to many observers and voters that a surge of enthusiasm among women to elect a woman president had been critical to Hillary's New Hampshire win and her popular vote tie on Super Tuesday. But Hillary was receiving exactly the opposite message from Mark Penn, and four days before the make-or-break primaries in early March in Texas and Ohio, she acceded to Penn's advice and ran an ad titled "It's 3 AM." The ad insinuated that the nation would be imperiled by putting the inexperienced Obama in charge of the nation's military. On March 4, Hillary again rose phoenix-like from the ashes with victories in Ohio and Texas, and Penn was keen to claim credit. "Strength has been the key at any time we have been ahead because it brings men as well as women to our cause, and weakness has been our downfall, isolating us to smaller and smaller constituencies," he wrote in an internal campaign memo of March 5. Penn discounted the importance of women in her New Hampshire win, and referencing only his own internal polls, claimed that going personal had lost her the male vote. "The idea that this can be won all on smiles, emotions, and empathy is wrong."

The 3 AM ad might have resonated with those whom Penn called "beer drinking men"—the evidence is inconclusive—but it cost Hillary dearly among liberal and progressive Democrats. It did as much as anything in the entire campaign to rekindle latent anti-Clintonism among Democrats themselves.

Whatever that ad might have gained her, thanks to other strategic calls by Penn, candidate Hillary was already sojourning in the land of the walking dead. Penn had very early on presumed that no one could dislodge her from her frontrunner status or overwhelm the power of the Clinton machine, and he had simply ignored many states that voted on Super Tuesday or after. Hillary ended Super Tuesday broke, with no staff or volunteers in the remaining primary and caucus states. Between Super Tuesday and the day she won Texas and Ohio, she had lost 12 contests in a row. As Penn himself made explicit in his March 5 memo, Hillary had no path to victory, short of Obama self-destructing on the campaign trail.

ON THE OTHER side of the partisan divide, the Republican Party had its own Iowa surprise. Had anyone bothered to consult Republican voters, however, it would have come as no surprise.

On January 3, as Obama swept the Iowa Democratic caucus, the Southern Baptist pastor and former Arkansas governor Mike Huckabee won the Republican race with 35 percent of the vote. Huckabee had polled in the single digits throughout most of 2007; the highest he had hit in national polls had been 16 percent. Former New York City mayor Rudy Giuliani won only 4 percent of Iowa caucus-goers, even though every major polling outfit had shown him in first place in virtually every single poll for over a year. Mitt Romney had virtually lived in Iowa since declining to run for a second term as Massachusetts governor in order to run for president. After sinking millions of dollars from his own personal fortune into Iowa, he came in an unsatisfying second place with 25 percent of the vote. Senator John McCain, who had been the presumptive nominee for much of George W. Bush's presidency, tied with Fred Thompson, an evangelical former actor and senator, for fourth place. McCain didn't really mount a campaign in Iowa, because he couldn't. The previous summer, right-wing opposition to his immigration reform bill had made it impossible for him to raise money for his campaign. Virtually broke, he cut back to a bare-bones operation, just enough to stay in the debates and shoot for a miracle comeback in New Hampshire.

It wasn't supposed to go this way. 2008 was supposed to be the year of the Republican moderate, according to Beltway wisdom. "For the moment, at least, September 11 has replaced abortion, gay marriage, and other social-sexual matters as *the* issue that binds the GOP together as a party," veteran journalist and commentator Thomas

Edsall wrote in the spring of 2007, expressing the common view. Edsall had placed his bet on Giuliani, the man who "owned" 9-11. So what if Christian conservatives disliked the pro-abortion, pro-homosexual, pro–gun control, thrice-married, cross-dressing, lapsed Catholic New Yorker? "What if the salience of a certain kind of social conservatism is now in decline among GOP voters and a new set of conservative principles are emerging to take its place? What if Giuil-ianism represents the future of the Republican Party?" According to Edsall, the Christian Right had been eclipsed by younger voters no longer in thrall to the preachers and the Culture Warriors. Edsall's 1989 *Chain Reaction* had given the definitive statement of the post-Reagan Democratic sexual counterrevolution, and at each subsequent Democratic setback, Edsall had registered his dismay at the elitist betrayal of the white cultural conservative. Edsall now cautioned Democrats that the law-and-order Italian American would do well with "white, working-class voters: the Reagan Democrats who became the angry white men of the 1990s."

The other top contenders, McCain and Romney, seemed to be cut from the same pragmatic cloth as Giuliani. Romney was the son of a moderate Rockefeller Republican who himself had been governor of Michigan and had run for president in 1968. Romney had assured Massachusetts voters that he supported abortion rights and gay rights when he ran for governor. He had personally taken on the task of pushing through universal health care in Massachusetts. Romney's Massachusetts health care law mandated that everyone in the state buy health insurance or be fined and provided for lower-income residents to have their health care paid for or subsidized by federal funds.

On the eve of the 2008 contest, no Republican had more of a reputation as an unconventional Republican than Senator John McCain. McCain had been so disgusted with President Bush that, according to reliable reports, he had entertained the idea of running on the 2004 Democratic presidential ticket with John Kerry. He believed in cutting taxes, yet had refused to sign Grover Norquist's radical anti-tax pledge and had voted against Bush's 2001 and 2003 tax cuts. He opposed abortion, but favored exceptions for rape, incest, and the life of the mother, and rejected the absolutist platform the antiabortion movement had foisted upon the Republican Party. He opposed gay marriage but had refused to go along with the sexual counterrevolutionaries' attempt to ban it through a federal constitutional amendment.

McCain's independent streak was often misinterpreted as proof that he was a moderate, but it stemmed more from three personality traits: impulsiveness, recklessness, and a conviction that the normal rules, whatever the situation, did not apply to him. McCain, the son of a four-star admiral, was not the type to take orders from the unelected self-appointed leaders of various right-wing special-interest groups. McCain was a survivor, most famously of a North Vietnamese prison camp, but he was less than eager to advertise that he had crashed three Navy fighter planes due to his own recklessness.

As it played out, Giuliani was the only putative moderate who dared to thumb his nose at the Christian Right. Both Romney and McCain spent the early months of their presidential campaigns desperately trying to erase their record of cultural pragmatism, in craven pursuit of the sexual fundamentalists in the Republican base.

Romney had a couple of advantages and one huge disadvantage in the competition to win over the sexual counterrevolutionaries. He was a religious conservative, with five handsome sons, who was still married to his high school sweetheart. (McCain, by contrast, had left his first wife, after she was disfigured in a car accident, for Cindy McCain, a rodeo beauty queen and heiress to a beer fortune.) Romney and his wife, Ann, campaigned as the poster couple of family values, reprising Dan and Marilyn Quayle's 1992 attacks on working mothers. When Romney reversed his position on abortion rights and gay rights, he could credibly claim he was rediscovering the verities of his religion. Romney had served as the highest-ranking Mormon lay leader in Boston for thirteen years. But his Mormonism was also his Achilles' heel. Although Mormons had been foot soldiers in the sexual counterrevolution since the early 1970s campaign against the Equal Rights Amendment, and even though the Mormon Church was one of the major funders of the multimillion-dollar initiative campaigns to outlaw gay marriage, prejudice against Mormons remained powerful, especially among conservative Protestant fundamentalists. Even if the sexual counterrevolutionaries accepted

Romney's conversion story about gays and abortion, many simply would not vote for a member of a religion they considered to be a cult. When Romney made a highly publicized speech on religion, in December 2007, he was dogwhistling to those fundamentalists in his Orwellian formulation that "freedom requires religion."

In anticipation of the open 2008 race, McCain entered into a Faustian bargain with the sexual counterrevolutionaries and other right-wing factions in the GOP. He now called for the Bush tax cuts to be permanently extended, even though his prediction that they would create a huge deficit had been borne out. He told Republican voters he had gotten their message and now denied he supported the comprehensive immigration reform bill he had co-authored with liberal icon Senator Ted Kennedy. In the 2000 GOP primary, McCain had famously denounced Jerry Falwell and Pat Robertson for "the evil influence" they exerted over the Republican Party. In 2006, he went hat in hand to the temple of the agent of intolerance himself to deliver the commencement address at Falwell's Liberty University. That prompted comedian Jon Stewart of *The Daily Show*, hitherto an admirer of McCain's, to ask the senator, "[This] strikes me as something you wouldn't ordinarily do. Are you going into crazy base world?"

"I'm afraid so," McCain answered.

Although Beltway insiders convinced themselves that a moderate would win, the many Republican debates suggested that McCain and Romney were more clear-sighted about the far-right state of the GOP in the waning hours of the Bush administration. A throwaway question about evolution in a May 2007 debate sparked a clamor among three Republican candidates to have the opportunity to testify they too didn't believe in it. In late November, Giuliani was the only one of eight candidates who stated he would not seek to overturn *Roe v. Wade*. After McCain denied he supported his own immigration bill, Tom Tancredo, the anti-immigrant nativist fringe candidate, marveled that everyone was trying to "out-Tancredo Tancredo." When a retired brigadier general who had come out of the closet in retirement stood up in full uniform to ask about repealing Don't Ask, Don't Tell, Californian representative Duncan Hunter said homosexuality was against the "principles" of "conservative" troops and it would be unfair to them to make them serve with gays.

While no one was really paying attention, Huckabee had been working the sexual counterrevolutionaries in Iowa. Huckabee focused particularly on Christian home-schoolers and antiabortion activists. Sexual fundamentalists had often played the role of collective kingmakers in the state. In 1980, Phyllis Schlafly and Paul Weyrich had teamed up to organize fundamentalist voters to elect Charles Grassley to his first term in the U.S. Senate. Iowa fundamentalists had fueled Reverend Pat Robertson's 1988 insurgency against vice president George H. W. Bush. It was in Iowa that the sexual fundamentalists first unveiled the Defense of Marriage Act in the lead-up to the 1996 Republican primary. As the former president of the Arkansas Southern Baptist Convention, who had likened abortion to the Holocaust, condemned gay marriage as well as no-fault divorce, and believed that the role of the president was "to move cultural norms to meet God's standard," Huckabee needed little money or paid media to mobilize religious voters in Iowa. In the 2008 Republican caucus, born-again and evangelical Christians accounted for 60 percent of caucus participants, and more than 8 out of 10 of them voted for Huckabee. Romney did well among voters who cared most about electability, but they made up only 7 percent of the caucus-goers; five times as many Iowan Republican voters said that the most important quality in a candidate was that he "shares my values."

Romney, who had banked on winning Iowa, was the most weakened by Huckabee's surprise win. But the New Hampshire primary five days later, on January 8, was a make-or-break moment for McCain, whose campaign had pretty much shut down in the summer of 2007. In a pattern that would be replicated over the next month, McCain narrowly won the New Hampshire primary after the sexual counterrevolutionaries split their vote. McCain topped Romney by six points, but the combined vote for Romney and Huckabee was greater than McCain's. Romney and McCain tied among Republican voters, while McCain racked up a lead with independents.

By Super Tuesday, just one month after Iowa, the Republican primary was for all intents and purposes over. After New Hampshire, Romney won his native state of Michigan, but that would be the only state he would win outright. McCain won South Carolina four days later by just three points. Romney and Huckabee had

both scaled back their campaigns in that critical state to focus on
Michigan, and Fred Thompson, a southern fundamentalist, pulled
out 16 percent of the vote. Combined, the three religious conservatives, Romney, Huckabee, and Thompson, had won almost twice as
many votes as McCain. Ten days later, religious voters split between
Huckabee and Romney in Florida, Giuliani collapsed, and McCain
emerged the victor. Giuliani, who had been running a risky late-
state strategy that hinged on winning Florida and sweeping the field
on Super Tuesday, withdrew from the race and endorsed his friend
McCain. The moderate savior of the GOP had won a total of less than
3 percent of Republican voters. On February 5, with many states
holding winner-take-all primaries, McCain moved into an overwhelming lead in the delegate count. Two days later, Romney quit
and endorsed McCain.

Although Huckabee would not concede until early March, McCain
was the presumptive nominee. Had the early conventional wisdom
been right after all, that Bush had discredited the Republican Right,
the Christian Right was weak, and a moderate would prevail? One of
the least desirable candidates to the sexual fundamentalists did win,
but not because they were weak. Rather, McCain won the Republican nomination because the sexual counterrevolutionaries split
their vote among the three religious conservatives in the race. In the
Bible Belt of the South and the border South, with disproportionately
large populations of conservative fundamentalists and evangelicals,
Huckabee was the favorite, but Thompson and Romney also drew
votes. Where Mormons, orthodox Catholics, or non-southern evangelicals were numerous, Romney tended to prevail, but his vote was
depressed by the 10 to 15 percent Huckabee siphoned away. Likewise other factions of conservatives preferred Romney or Huckabee,
while independents, moderates, and party-line–crossing Democrats
favored McCain. For example, McCain secured the nomination on
Super Tuesday by winning nine Blue states that were highly unlikely
to go Republican in the general election. Together, Romney and
Huckabee won twelve states that day, ten of them solid Red ones.

McCain was the Republican nominee by default, and the most
committed Republicans in the base were not happy. A Pew poll
the week before Super Tuesday showed that only a third of white

evangelicals favored McCain. At the February Conservative Political Action Conference, where right-wing activists gathered yearly and Paula Jones had first charged President Clinton with sexual harassment, McCain was booed. Ann Coulter, who had been one of the band of conspirators in the Lewinsky scandal, said she was going to vote for Hillary. Right-wing leaders such as James Dobson and Rush Limbaugh continued to denounce McCain as insufficiently conservative. Despite McCain's effort to woo the rank-and-file sexual counterrevolutionaries by pandering to their whims, they remained unmoved. After he won the nomination, he made the mistake of thinking that didn't matter.

DEMOCRATS HAD NOT witnessed such an inspirational, exciting, and close primary contest since 1968, which, of course, few of the most excited voters knew anything about. Every poll showed that either Hillary or Barack would be a likely winner in the November general election. Yet instead of exuberance at the prospect of taking back the White House, Democrats were at war with each other. Hillary's controversial ad, "It's 3 AM," essentially said that someone who had served only four years in the Senate wasn't as ready as she was to be commander in chief. The Obamas said that Hillary had no relevant experience besides that gained through "osmosis," in other words, by virtue of being a wife. Attacks to be sure, but still quite mild. By comparison, remember that it was the Democrat Hubert Humphrey who first called the Democrat George McGovern the candidate of "acid, amnesty, and abortion."

Still, Hillary and Obama supporters found the attacks on their candidate outrageous and despicable and were quick to impugn the motives of the other side. Many interpreted the conflict between Clinton and Obama as an episode in the eternal war of the sexes; others saw in it the depressing persistence of racism. With the involvement of millions of people who had never voted or never paid much attention to the blood sport of electoral politics, perhaps it was understandable they would take offense. With the first real chance to elect a woman or an African American president, emotions were bound to run high. But to say that sexism and racism influenced the contest was a truism, not a revelation. Hillary didn't lose ultimately because of sexism. She was done in by her dysfunctional campaign team and Penn's tone-deaf strategy. And it wasn't Obama's race that nearly derailed him in the Democratic Party but the suspicion that he might be a closet cultural elitist who disdained real Americans.

On March 13, 2008, eleven days after Hillary won the bellwether state of Ohio with a commanding lead among older white voters, ABC News aired a segment on Reverend Jeremiah Wright, the Obama family's pastor and the man from whom Obama had borrowed the term "audacity of hope." The report showed footage of Wright in the pulpit shouting "God *damn* America." His voice could be heard two days after the September 11 attacks using the phrase "U.S. of K.K.K.A." in a chickens-coming-home-to-roost metaphor. So much for Obama's carefully cultivated theme of American unity and transpartisanship. From the earliest moments of Obama's plan for a presidential run, the campaign had consciously downplayed race. "The rule was: no radioactive blacks," Don Rose, a Chicago political strategist who was close to Axelrod, told author David Remnick. "Harold Ford, fine. Jesse Jackson, Jr., fine. But Jesse, Sr., and Al Sharpton, better not." Whenever Obama alluded to his race, Rose said, "He got whacked and the campaign noticed. You don't raise it, that's the axiom, and you let it work. The less said, the better." Now the man who had married the Obamas and baptized their children had become radioactive.

Five days after the Wright video aired, with Obama's poll numbers having fallen to their lowest point, Obama delivered a speech titled "A More Perfect Union." It was the most nuanced and moving speech about race an American public official had made since the civil rights movement. The mainstream media and the progressive blogosphere were enormously impressed. Obama quickly recovered in polls of likely Democratic voters and went back into the lead, a sign that Democratic voters approved of him confronting the subject of race and embracing his own mixed racial heritage. Although Obama was widely predicted to lose the next primary, in Pennsylvania in late April, he was almost certain to be the nominee. The crisis had passed, it seemed.

Then, on April 6, at a private fundraiser in San Francisco, a citizen journalist caught Obama on tape saying, "In a lot of these communities in big industrial states like Ohio and Pennsylvania, people have been beaten down so long . . . So it's not surprising then that they get bitter, they cling to guns or religion or antipathy to people who aren't like them or anti-immigrant sentiment or anti-trade sentiment as a way to explain their frustrations." He was trying to explain why voters distrusted government. "The truth is that our challenge is to get people persuaded that we can make progress when there's not evidence of that in their daily lives . . . The jobs have been gone now for 25 years and nothing has replaced them."

The confluence of countercultural San Francisco, rich liberal donors, and Obama in his cool professorial mode unloosed the latent Democratic sexual counterrevolution. Would the Democratic Party snatch defeat from the jaws of victory by handing the nomination to an unelectable, exotic, biracial Ivy League graduate with a strange name? The old theory that Democrats lose when the cultural progressives, the McGoverniks, control the party, came back to life on cable TV and in the mainstream press. "And let's not forget Barack Obama bowling," a Reuters reporter said on MSNBC, referring to an incident a few weeks earlier when Obama had thrown nothing but gutter balls. "You know, this cuts to 'is this person real? Do they connect with me as a voter?' You know, for someone who's in a bowling league in northeast central Pennsylvania, in Scranton and Wilkes-Barre, they can't identify with someone getting a 37 over seven frames." Ironically, although Hillary had been a victim of this false frame throughout her political career, she was quick to join in the attack. She called Obama elitist and out of touch with mainstream values. She went overboard, however, with her own unscripted gaffe, that was widely taken as suggesting only white people were hard-working. It was a moment tailor-made for Penn, who had just a week earlier in an internal campaign memo unsuccessfully tried to persuade Hillary to exploit the resentments of the Reagan Democrats, those beer-drinking white men. "Won't a single tape of Wright going off on America with Obama sitting there be a game ender?" But Hillary had removed Penn as chief strategist three days earlier, after the *Wall Street Journal* had reported that Penn had lobbied in favor of a free-trade deal for the Colombian government, a deal Hillary expressly opposed.

"Bittergate," as the San Francisco incident was quickly dubbed, could have been Obama's moment of self-destruction, except that 2008 proved to be different than all other seasons of Democratic delirium. Although the chatter in the media was as fevered as it had ever been, the sting had gone out of the claim that following the McGoverniks was the road to the Democratic Party's ruin. Charging a candidate with being weak on defense and culturally elitist simply no longer had the effect of scaring Democratic voters into submission.

Sixteen days after Bittergate, Hillary did win the Pennsylvania primary with a sizable advantage among older, white voters, as she had long been projected to do. Nevertheless, two weeks later, even though Reverend Wright had resurfaced in full-on crazy mode, Obama performed well in two heartland states that had gone for George W. Bush in 2004. He decisively won North Carolina with a respectable showing among white voters. That same night, he held Hillary to a narrow win in Indiana with strong support among new voters, young voters, and independents and a good showing among whites. In both states, more voters said Obama, not Hillary, shared their values. With the delegates won on May 6 in those two states, Obama hit the number needed to win the nomination at the Democratic convention.

Hillary had won 17.7 million votes, more than any other Democratic primary candidate in history—except for Obama. Of Obama's 17.8 million voters, a couple million of them were new to the electoral process. The numbers—of new voters, of people newly registered to vote as Democrats, of volunteers, of individual donors, of doors knocked on and phone calls made—were staggering. Nothing like it had been seen in American politics for at least a century.

Had Obama not expanded the universe of voters, he simply could not have won. Since the sixties, scholars and civic leaders have lamented how Americans turned off and tuned out to politics. The question, then, was how was he able to do it, to inspire people to vote and to volunteer on his campaign? Obama "gave them something to believe in," said Heather Smith, the head of Rock the Vote, who has worked for the last decade on nonpartisan voter education and mobilization of youth. "He provided leadership at a time when people were struggling with jobs and with education . . . Here's a vision, it doesn't have to be like this, and in fact we can make it better. It was exactly what young people wanted to hear, and it gave them something to work towards." It wasn't just the young who responded. More than twice as many people voted in the party's 2008 contests than in those of 2004. Obama inspired these new voters with a message that Americans were good enough and sane enough to transcend the bitter partisanship of the past. He inspired them with a progressive vision of change. State by state, he empowered Americans who had never been involved in politics to help define the campaign's vision for the nation's future. And in so doing, he won the party's presidential nomination.

ON JUNE 7, three days after the primaries ended and long after Obama's supporters had wished, Hillary conceded and endorsed Obama. She struck the populist themes that had won her strong support among older working-class voters in the last months of her tenacious fight.

"We all want an economy that sustains the American Dream . . . . An economy that lifts all of our people and ensures that our prosperity is broadly distributed and shared. We all want a health care system that is universal, high quality, and affordable."

Like Bill in 1992, at least in her concession speech, she linked economic populism seamlessly with cultural progressivism. "We all want an America defined by deep and meaningful equality—from civil rights to labor rights, from women's rights to gay rights, from ending discrimination to promoting unionization to providing help for the most important job there is: caring for our families."

Her most memorable lines spoke, after so many months of near silence on the matter, to the historic nature of her candidacy. No woman had ever won a single presidential primary, much less come so close to the nomination: "We weren't able to shatter that highest, hardest glass ceiling this time, but thanks to you it's got about 18 million cracks in it. And the light is shining through like never before, filling us all with the hope and the sure knowledge that the path will be a little easier next time. That has always been the history of progress in America."

Apparently Hillary did believe it would be historic and significant for a woman to be elected president. Indeed, she had wanted to give a "gender" speech much earlier but had missed the moment when it could have made a difference and not looked too opportunistic. She did believe that the role of the Democratic Party was to be the champion of the middle class and to work for equality and meaningful opportunity for all Americans. Despite the charges from many Obama supporters that she would be a right-leaning triangulator, in defeat she revealed the progressive passion that to all accounts has motivated her through her many decades in public service.

There was wide agreement that her concession speech was one of Hillary's finest moments, as well as broad despair among her supporters that she had kept this part of herself hidden behind the Iron Lady armor forged in Penn's dark workshop. More than fifteen years earlier, when she was First Lady, Hillary Rodham Clinton had observed, "I am a Rorschach test." Oddly, Hillary had campaigned for the last eighteen months as if she weren't quite sure herself of her own identity.

One of the tragic consequences of the sexual counterrevolution has to be counted the political crippling of the progressive woman who was probably best equipped to become the first woman president of the United States. Carrying the psychic scars of the vicious, sexist attacks on her during Bill's presidency, Hillary shied away during her own presidential campaign from presenting herself as the pioneering feminist and progressive that she was, or at least had been. Given all the things that had been said about her over the years, you can see why she might have wanted to downplay the woman angle.

Yet Hillary is nothing if not tough, and her decision to let herself be rebranded by Penn as an American Margaret Thatcher had deeper and more toxic roots in the Democrats' own sexual counterrevolution. As a practical matter, by forfeiting the progressive mantle, she missed an opportunity to secure the votes of young women, or at least hold down Obama's margin of victory with them. By taking Penn's fears of the flight of the Reagan Democrat too seriously, she was rendered speechless in the face of Obamamania, that sense of exultation many Democrats indulged at the thought of electing the first African American president. Hillary could have been the progressive champion in the race. She could have been the historic candidate. At least she could have given Obama a good run on those counts. But in choosing to follow Penn and court the elusive and fickle "beer drinking men," she ceded the progressive territory to Obama without a contest. Given where the nation was in 2008, demographically and ideologically, that was fatal to her presidential ambitions.

For nearly nine months, the nation had been transfixed by the spectacle of open warfare among those Americans who supposedly agreed with each other about every important public matter. That eruption had brought out into the open the subterranean force that for nearly four decades had been fueling Democratic infighting and self-defeating hysteria: the sexual counterrevolution. In 1992, a young Democratic couple had rejected false history and the advice of false counsel. Bill and Hillary had blithely disregarded the death-by-cultural extremism theory of Democratic woe and had unequivocally stood up for gay rights, women's rights, abortion rights, and a tolerant and open embrace of the cultural and ethnic diversity of America. In 2008, Obama, not Hillary, followed the path to victory discovered by the original man from Hope, right into the White House.

13

RAPTURE

T O SOME OF Hillary's 18 million supporters, the famous maxim about history repeating itself, the first time as tragedy, the second time as farce, must have seemed apt. The morning after Barack Obama's lavishly praised speech to the Democratic Convention, John McCain debuted his running mate. "She's exactly who I need, exactly who this country needs to help me fight the same old Washington politics of me first and country second," McCain said as he introduced Alaska Governor Sarah Palin. McCain told the American people that he chose Palin because she was a reformer, an outsider, who had fought corruption and was devoted to the "common good." Here was the maverick brand, with a youthful, attractive upgrade.

The 44-year-old Palin was a career woman with five children, including a five-month-old boy with Down syndrome. She had preternatural charisma and the All-American good looks of a former beauty queen. Standing at McCain's side in Dayton, Ohio on his 72nd birthday, Palin presented herself as nothing less than the executor of Hillary's feminist legacy. "It was rightly noted in Denver this week that Hillary left 18 million cracks in the highest, hardest glass ceiling in America. But it turns out the women of America aren't finished yet. And we can shatter that glass ceiling once and for all."

The media marveled at McCain's brilliant bid to capture women voters, at how he had stolen the change meme and sucked the air out of Obamamania. A fortuitous hurricane the following week kept President George W. Bush and Vice President Dick Cheney from making their scheduled appearance at the Republican National Convention in Minneapolis. The McCain campaign had been at pains to put distance between the ticket and the failed Bush administration and its right-wing base. They looked to Palin to assist in their rebranding of the Republican party. Too bad for McCain that she refused to play along.

FIVE DAYS BEFORE McCain and Palin's Dayton appearance, Karl Rove called John McCain's first choice for the vice presidential nomination and told Senator Joseph Lieberman that his presence on the Republican ticket would destroy his dear friend's chances of winning. Lieberman's problem, from Rove's perspective, wasn't that he had been a Democrat. Lieberman had since left the Democratic Party, become an Independent, and established himself as one of Bush's most ardent defenders on the Iraq War and the war on terror. Lieberman was unacceptable because he supported abortion rights. Having taken the measure of the Republican base, Rove knew that the sexual counterrevolutionaries of the Christian Right would bolt the ticket if McCain chose any pro-choice running mate.

McCain had wanted Lieberman as his vice president to reinvigorate his image as a maverick with the voters whom he would have to attract in a general election: moderates, independents, and Democrats. Instead, the Lieberman gamble led him into a head-on collision with the GOP's sexual counterrevolutionaries.

McCain, of course, had adjusted his positions and courted the Christian Right during the GOP primary. After he won the nomination, he cavalierly assumed that his obligations were done and ignored the warning signs that he was not right with the Right. But the days of flattery and idle promises had long since passed. The sexual counterrevolutionaries could count, after all. They knew they made up at least 40 percent of likely Republican voters and a far larger proportion of party activists and state party officials. Not since Reagan towered over the conservative movement had they allowed their support to be so cheaply bought. And McCain was no Reagan.

In mid-August, after rumors circulated about McCain's intention to nominate a supporter of abortion rights as his vice president, the sexual fundamentalists schooled the GOP nominee about who was in charge. Just a few weeks before the Republican Convention, the McCain campaign learned that they were willing to mount a floor fight against Lieberman or any other pro-choice running mate. Republican Convention rules allowed for a majority of just four state delegations to trigger a roll-call vote on the vice presidential nominee, and the Christian Right controlled the delegations of far more than four states. Some of McCain's aides who held little truck for the fundamentalists thought that would be just fine. But Rove thought these aides were deluded. Even if McCain could win the floor vote, it would entail a bitter public fight played out in front of a national television audience already soured on Bush's subservience to the Christian Right. Even worse, McCain's internal polling indicated that 40 percent of his likely voters might defect over a pro-choice vice presidential nominee. The attempt at mavericky independence slapped down by the sexual fundamentalists, McCain caved and dropped Lieberman.

With the polls showing an almost certain victory for Obama, McCain strategists Steve Schmidt and Rick Davis believed their only chance at the presidency was to shake up the race with an unconventional running mate. A woman might be able to do exactly that. Not only would McCain win plaudits for putting a woman on the GOP ticket, he might also win over Hillary's diehard supporters, who according to the latest media fixation, were too embittered to vote for Obama. But the threatened revolt of the sexual counter-revolutionaries made that play more complicated. Although there were several Republican women with national name recognition and extensive governing experience, such as Senators Kay Bailey Hutchison, Olympia Snowe, and Susan Collins, none of them could pass the extreme antiabortion litmus test imposed by the sexual fundamentalists.

McCain had secured the nomination in March, but the Republican Convention was just a week away, and his short list for the vice presidency included only two reliably antiabortion candidates: Tim Pawlenty and Sarah Palin. Pawlenty, a born-again evangelical, was the governor of Minnesota, a swing state with a good number of electoral votes, and had long been talked up in conservative Republican circles as a rising star who possessed presidential qualities. But Pawlenty, Schmidt and Davis thought, was too bland to spark any game-changing buzz.

Only Palin gave McCain a shot to regain momentum, and thus a chance to win. The McCain campaign had only started to consider Palin seriously in July, when they realized how poorly McCain was doing with women voters. With just a few days to make a decision, Schmidt and Davis made the case for Palin. They anticipated that the press would be so taken by McCain putting a woman on the Republican ticket, and be so impressed at the bold play for Hillary's supporters, that the wind would go out of Obama's change message. They bluntly told McCain that it was a high-risk play. McCain, who is temperamentally disposed to confuse risk with superior virtue, signed off on the greatest Hail Mary of them all.

McCain had his first conversation about the vice presidency with Palin just thirty-six hours before he presented her as the person he believed most qualified to be a heartbeat away from the presidency. His staff had only begun to vet her three days before that. McCain had spent the summer mocking Obama as a puffed-up celebrity with no relevant experience to assume the presidency in a time of war. Palin had at that moment served twenty months as governor of Alaska, population 688,125.

Who was Sarah Palin? No, really, who was she? Obama's campaign manager David Plouffe was so taken by surprise he had to Google her before he could make a statement. A Gallup poll that night showed that 71 percent of registered voters had never heard of Palin or had no opinion about her.

Some politically savvy Americans, on the other hand, knew Palin quite well. "In just 38 hours, disheartened conservatives were transformed into enthusiastic Republicans," wrote Phyllis Schlafly. "Sarah Palin and the 2008 Platform have given Republicans a new lease on life." At her debut, Palin had presented herself as a plucky feminist hockey mom, her nomination as a great leap forward for American women. Had Schlafly, who had long attacked working mothers for neglecting their home duties and who had led the campaign to kill the Equal Rights Amendment, undergone a feminist conversion? No, a week later she condemned Obama for supporting the Lilly Ledbetter Fair Pay Act and the Paycheck Fairness Act, federal bills aimed at ending gender discrimination in the workplace in order to improve women's economic standing. (Palin was against the bills too.) On the night before Palin's speech to the Republican Convention, she was scheduled to receive an award from the antiabortion group founded by Schlafly, the Republican National Coalition for Life. The McCain campaign abruptly canceled the speech, evidently worried that their grab for Hillary's older women voters might fail should they see his running mate feted by the most recognizable and detested antifeminist of their generation.

Jubilation at Palin's nomination coursed through the ranks of the senior echelon of the sexual counterrevolution. At a meeting of the Council for National Policy, an executive with James Dobson's Focus on the Family said, "That speech by Alaska Governor Sarah Palin—people were on their seats applauding, cheering, yelling . . . That room in Minneapolis watching on the television screen was electrified. I have not seen anything like it in a long time." Dobson, who had been hinting that he would bolt the party, was a convert too. The choice of Palin, he said, "should be extremely reassuring to the conservative base." Ralph Reed viewed Palin's nomination as a "shot directly into the heart of the evangelical movement." The director of the Susan B. Anthony List (SBA List), a political action committee that funded antiabortion candidates, said, "Sarah Palin is going to be our poster woman." Indeed, one of Palin's daughters was literally the poster child for Alaska Right to Life.

They had reason to be ecstatic. For twenty-eight years the sexual counterrevolutionaries had been helping to elect Republican presidents, only to find themselves frustrated, disappointed, and jockeying for attention among the competing factions on the Right. George W. Bush, himself a born-again evangelical, had delivered more than any other politician, but he too at times had wavered.

Palin was something entirely new. One of their own was poised to be next in line for the presidency of the United States.

MCCAIN INTRODUCED PALIN to the American people as an independent-minded, corruption-fighting regular American, who wasn't afraid to take on her own party and preferred to work in a bipartisan way. Palin was in fact a sexual fundamentalist who approached politics as a kind of spiritual warfare.

Palin, who is a born-again Pentecostalist, got her first taste of electioneering in the early 1990s when she mobilized her fellow church members in the Assembly of God to take over the school board and a local hospital board. In 1992, Wasilla's mayor, John Stein, determined Palin would be willing to raise taxes and recruited her to run for City Council. Palin won with a few hundred votes. By 1994, the Christian Right had become the dominant power in the Alaska GOP. With their support, Palin challenged the Republican incumbent mayor in 1996—the man, Stein, who had first encouraged her to run for political office. It was the first time the state GOP had ever intervened in Wasilla's local elections. Palin kept mum about her ties to the Christian Right and ran a stealth campaign. She hired a pro-choice Republican woman as her campaign manager; asked about her platform, Palin told her, "Bike trails are my baby." Meanwhile, antiabortion fliers supporting Palin circulated in Wasilla, as did others calling Palin "The Christian Candidate." Palin's supporters spread a rumor that Stein was Jewish. He was in fact a Lutheran. Her supporters contended Stein and his wife weren't married, because she used her maiden name at work. The Steins had to produce their marriage certificate.

Palin crafted a political persona as just a "hockey mom" who stood for free enterprise, small government, and individual freedom. But in her career in Alaska, she labored to advance the mission of the sexual counterrevolution, often to be rebuked for her overreach. The Valley Hospital board, which she had helped put in office, banned all abortions, even medically necessary ones. The Alaska Supreme Court overturned the ban and ordered the hospital to pay legal costs to the groups that had brought the successful lawsuit. While members of Palin's childhood church were lobbying bookstores not to carry *Pastor, I Am Gay*, a 1995 book by a local minister calling for churches to show Christian love and welcome gays and lesbians into their community, Mayor Palin asked Wasilla's librarian to remove the book from the stacks. The librarian refused and found herself out of a job, until public outcry won her reinstatement. During Palin's mayoralty, Wasilla made rape victims pay for their own investigation kit. No other municipality in Alaska did so. The Alaska State Legislature felt compelled to pass a law prohibiting local governments from charging victims for rape kits. Wasilla's police chief, who reported to Palin, lobbied against the bill, claiming the fee had been adopted as a cost-saving measure. It is more likely that Wasilla's sexual fundamentalists objected to the emergency contraception provided in rape kits to prevent a possible pregnancy. Palin, as do many of the more extreme pro-lifers, oppose abortion even in the case of rape and also oppose the use of the morning-after pill, which prevents a fertilized egg from implanting in the uterus. Against the definition of medical science, some orthodox Christians insist that pregnancy begins at fertilization, or in their term, the moment of "conception."

In 2006, while the national Republican Party was suffering an electoral bloodletting, Sarah Palin won the Alaska governor's race by running against the Alaska Republican Party. She was aided by the local chapters of the sexual counterrevolution. The Alaska chapter of Schlafly's Eagle Forum endorsed Palin after she told them that she opposed "explicit sex-ed programs" in favor of abstinence-only education, opposed abortion in cases of rape and incest, and believed that banning gay marriage was a priority. The Alaska affiliate of Dobson's Family Research Council distributed an ostensibly nonpartisan voter guide rating her solid on their issues. Palin focused, in office, on accelerating oil production. She also raised taxes on oil production, which produced a $1,200 bonus payment to every Alaskan, bringing their annual haul from the oil companies to nearly $4,000. Palin won high approval ratings from Alaskans for this generous state redistribution of the oil companies' wealth. Nonetheless, like President Bush, she continued to advance the mission of the sexual counter-revolutionaries. After the Alaska Supreme Court ruled that denying family benefits to the same-sex partners of state employees violated the state's constitutional guarantee of equal rights, Governor Palin lent her support to a ballot initiative denying benefits to same-sex couples.

McCain and his advisers were fully conscious that they were perpetrating a ruse on the American public. They knew what Palin stood for—that she was a creationist, rejected the scientific consensus on climate change, and opposed abortion even in cases of rape and incest, all positions with which McCain disagreed. There were plenty of Republicans that could have checked the antiabortion litmus test box. That wasn't the sole reason Palin had been chosen as McCain's vice-presidential nominee. The men who chose Palin knew that she was not only a believing and practicing fundamentalist Pentecostalist but equally a starlet of the Right and a distinguished member of the rising generation of sexual counterrevolutionaries. Palin was a natural and appealing heir to Phyllis Schlafly, Lottie Beth Hobbs, and the grassroots women sexual fundamentalists who had forged the Christian Right into a political powerhouse. She was on the ticket to fire up the base.

McCain, however, was trying to have it both ways. That Palin was obscure and unknown was essential to the game plan. Palin was to be the blank slate onto which Democratic women would project their frustrations.

WHEN SARAH PALIN stepped up to the podium at the Republican National Convention on September 3, just five days after McCain unveiled her to the nation, what most Americans had learned about her so far didn't bode well for McCain. Palin was under investigation in Alaska; her husband, Todd, had been a member of a far-right party that advocated Alaskan independence from the United States; her teenage daughter was pregnant and unmarried; and Palin had taken federal money for local pork-barrel projects even though she claimed to be against such practices. Journalists had quickly uncovered how superficial the McCain's vetting had been, and CNN's Campbell Brown had left a campaign spokesman speechless with unrelenting questions about why Palin's "command" of the Alaska National

Guard could possibly constitute foreign policy experience. Senior Republicans were liberally offering journalists anonymous comments about how anxious they were that someone so inexperienced was on the ticket. The McCain campaign was frantically trying to spin the reporting as sexist and proof of the media's liberal bias.

Palin quieted much of the second-guessing with her expertly delivered speech. Like Obama's, her life story made for a compelling and marketable personal narrative. She remixed the mythology of the frontier West with an exotic underbeat, showing off Todd, her "part native Alaskan" husband. In a bid for women's votes, she gave off the impression she held no truck for gender conventions. She was a self-admitted beneficiary of the women's rights movement, career woman, and mother of five, and Todd was a snowmobile racer, a union member, and, it seemed, a stay-at-home dad. She spun tales of her great Alaskan adventures and offered up herself as a humble savior from the last frontier of the "real" America. The speech, written by McCain's advisers, was peppered with folksy homilies about small towns and free enterprise. But as the minutes wore on, the rhetoric darkened, and Palin tapped the rich vein of subterranean longing and resentment in the hall. "Terrorists are plotting against us and he worried about their rights," Palin boomed with a smile and a snarl. The choruses of "Boo, Obama," got louder and longer after each count against Obama, palpably energizing Palin. Thirty minutes into her speech, the Republican Convention had morphed into a rave, Palin's scripted nastiness the drug sending the delegates into a delirium of rage and exaltation.

What most impressed the media, however, was Palin's natural ease in front of an audience, and her performance sent the commentariat into a swoon. That week 35 percent of all news featured Palin. Four days after Palin's speech, the federal government placed failed mortgage giants Fannie Mae and Freddie Mac into conservatorship, but only 1 percent of news coverage that week had dealt with the economy. Dazzled by the new and improved Republican brand, the media only really settled down after comedians Tina Fey and Amy Poehler appeared on the September 13 *Saturday Night Live* with a widely viewed parody of the sexist treatment of both Palin and Hillary.

During the weeks of Palinmania, few bothered to probe what

this allegedly historic step for womankind might mean for American women circa 2008. Over the years, McCain had voted against expanding the Family and Medical Leave Act, the law that many women relied on to take pregnancy leave, and to end funding for birth control provided through the Title X federal program. He had even voted against the Violence Against Women Act. The day before McCain announced that Palin was to be his running mate, the finishing touches had been put on the maverick's platform. "I think he would be aborting his own campaign," Tony Perkins of the Family Research Council had said in May, when questioned about McCain's desire to allow for exceptions for rape, incest, or risk to the life of the mother in the party's antiabortion plank. McCain got the message. With Schlafly watching over the platform committee proceedings, absolutism on abortion prevailed—a position consistent with Palin's, but not McCain's, personal beliefs. The platform also endorsed a federal constitutional amendment against gay marriage, something McCain had claimed to oppose on states' rights grounds. It urged states to "review their marriage and divorce laws in order to strengthen marriage." Slipped in was an endorsement of a late-term Bush executive order that grossly expanded the so-called conscience clause in abortion regulations. Pushed by elements of the antiabortion movement that oppose birth control, the GOP platform called for allowing anyone in the health care delivery system—say a clerk at a drugstore—to refuse to accept birth control prescriptions as a matter of "conscience."

Momentarily, when the polls showed Obama lagging behind McCain, Democrats became hysterical. One side effect of empowering voters was the creation of 18 million amateur David Axelrods. Suddenly every ordinary Democrat had the key to winning the presidential election, if only Obama would listen. Overreacting, as was their wont, too many Democrats lamented that all was lost. "Really, we evacuated several hurricane-prone states with more cheer and optimism," *New York Times* columnist Gail Collins quipped. Obama and his campaign strategists knew better than to panic. Their internal polling showed that Palin's nomination had in fact solidified support for Obama among Democrats. David Plouffe, in a pointed and deliberate message to the chorus of doom, told a reporter, "We're familiar with this and I'm sure between now and November fourth there will be another period of hand-wringing and bed-wetting. It comes with the territory."

Ordinary women, other polls showed, never fell for McCain's cynical play for Hillary's voters. Stan Greenberg's firm reported that "Palin's impact isn't the one the press has conveyed. In truth, rather than persuading Hillary Clinton's supporters to vote for McCain, Palin drove Clinton's primary voters further into the Obama camp, with roughly 80 percent of Clinton's primary supporters now voting for Obama." Nor did veteran feminists view Palin's nomination as a feminist victory. Gloria Steinem facetiously wrote, "Here's the good news: Women have become so politically powerful that even the antifeminist right wing—the folks with a headlock on the Republican Party—are trying to appease the gender gap with a first-ever female vice president . . . But here is even better news: It won't work." Women vote the issues, and the GOP platform, McCain, and Palin oppose "pretty much everything Clinton's candidacy stood for." Obama was the one upholding the Clinton legacy. "Palin shares nothing but a chromosome with Clinton."

EXACTLY 50 DAYS before Election Day, the global economy collapsed. That weekend the federal government had opted not to bail out the investment banking firm Lehman Brothers, fearing it would set up expectations that the government would rescue other weak banks and financial firms. On Monday, September 15, 2008, Lehman collapsed and sent the markets into a panic. On September 16, the Federal Reserve, desperately trying to stave off the collapse of insurance giant AIG under the weight of its now worthless collateralized debt obligations (CDOs), lent the company a boatload of cash. Fed chairman Ben Bernanke and Bush's treasury secretary Henry Paulson warned the president that there was a real chance of "a depression greater than the Great Depression" if Congress didn't act immediately to shore up the banking system.

On the day Lehman was shuttered, McCain was campaigning in Tallahassee, Florida and said, "the fundamentals of our economy are strong." It was a patently absurd statement, which highlighted

McCain's self-admitted inexperience and lack of knowledge about economic matters. In an effort to recover, McCain did what he often did when he was down. He threw yet another Hail Mary. On September 24, McCain claimed to be suspending his campaign in order to deal with the national emergency and called on Obama to do the patriotic thing and suspend his campaign too. McCain announced that he would not participate in the first debate scheduled later that week and prevailed upon Bush to convene a White House meeting about the crisis. (He did not actually suspend campaigning.) Bush invited Obama to the meeting—it is unclear if that was McCain's intention. At the Oval Office meeting the next day, Obama forcefully presented the Democrats' position, making it clear that Democrats would support a bailout to save the economy, but demanded greater transparency and better safeguards for the taxpayers forced to bail out the irresponsible financial wizards. McCain sat mutely by as GOP House minority leader John Boehner and other House Republicans derailed a rescue plan that had been agreed to by the president and a bipartisan group of congressional leaders just three hours earlier. The press widely reported McCain's ineptitude in the meeting, and a consensus emerged that the episode had spooked the markets and made the situation worse. On September 29, congressional Republicans voted down the Republican president's plan to rescue the economy, prompting the biggest one-day drop in the Dow Jones index to date. That was followed by the market's worst week ever. On October 3, Congress finally passed the Troubled Asset Relief Program (TARP). Over the weeks of the crisis, Americans had lost $2 trillion of their retirement savings.

JUST AS MCCAIN faltered when faced with a practical test of presidential leadership, so too did Palinmania run aground in Palin's shallows. For several weeks after the convention, the McCain campaign largely prevented the press from talking to or interviewing Palin. One interview had bombed when Palin seemed not to know what the Bush doctrine—the rationale for the Iraq War—was. Palin had also been flummoxed when questioned by a pre-screened audience at her first town hall meeting.

On September 23, Palin sat down for a series of interviews with CBS Evening News anchor Katie Couric, for what the McCain camp saw as a chance to reintroduce Palin to America. Palin wasn't poised, confident, and witty, as she had been on the convention podium. She was ill informed, uncomfortable, and visibly annoyed. She couldn't name a Supreme Court decision other than *Roe v. Wade*. She stammered when asked what newspapers and magazines she regularly read. She was unable to back up her claims about McCain's record with a single example, in part because she had mischaracterized his actual record. Within days of the interviews airing, prominent conservatives were deserting the GOP ticket.

Couric also gave Americans an opportunity to take the measure of Palin's roots in the sexual counterrevolution. When Couric asked her whether she thought it should be illegal for a 15-year-old to get an abortion if she were raped by her father, Palin kept repeating that she would recommend that the girl "choose life." When pressed directly on the morning-after pill, Palin said she was "all for contraception" but "I am one to believe that life starts at the moment of conception." To many viewers, it seemed she was evading the question. But to many of her supporters in the antiabortion movement who wrongly believed that the use of the Pill, the IUD, and Plan B were tantamount to abortion, her position was crystal clear. Most analysts speculated that Palin didn't answer questions about the Supreme Court or what she read because she was ignorant and unlettered. It is more likely, I think, that she realized at that moment that to answer honestly would have unmasked her as a far-right sexual fundamentalist and theocrat. From the two books she has authored, for example, it is clear her reading tilts far right and her view of American history derives from Christian nationalist mythology. Likewise, many of her compatriots in the antiabortion movement want the Supreme Court to reverse *Griswold*, the 1965 decision that overturned all laws limiting the sale of birth control to married couples and established the right to privacy.

McCain had believed he was salvaging his chance to be president when he chose Palin. Instead, in his selfish desperation, he had opened Pandora's box. By elevating Palin, he set the stage for his campaign to become a vehicle for the right-wing sexual counterrevolutionaries.

The remaining weeks of the 2008 presidential campaign were some of the ugliest witnessed in modern elections. The final act of the 72-year-old John McCain's eight-year-long quest for the presidency was overshadowed by an outpouring of delirium such as America had not seen since the upheavals over civil rights and the Vietnam War.

The delirium was given form, legitimacy, and a national platform by Sarah Palin, a sexual fundamentalist, commandeering the campaign of the man who had lifted her out of obscurity. As Obama's victory became more and more certain, Palin went rogue, McCain be damned, in apparent preparation for her own political future. McCain explicitly forbade members of his campaign to raise the issue of Reverend Jeremiah Wright. In an interview with Bill Kristol, Palin's most influential cheerleader, she insisted that Obama's relationship with Wright should be fair game. "I don't know why that association isn't discussed more," she coyly said. Two weeks before the election, in a radio interview with James Dobson, she falsely said that McCain opposed embryonic stem cell research and that he supported a constitutional amendment banning gay marriage.

On October 6, in front of 8,000 supporters in Clearwater, Florida, Palin enthusiastically delivered an attack written for her by the McCain campaign. "I am just so fearful that this is not a man who sees America the way you and I see America, as the greatest force for good in the world. I'm afraid this is someone who sees America as 'imperfect enough' to work with a former domestic terrorist who had targeted his own country." The reference was to William Ayers, a University of Chicago professor who had engaged in violent crimes as a member of the sixties' Weather Underground. Obama had been a child when Ayers had been a revolutionary radical. The *New York Times* had reported that Ayers and Obama had socialized on several occasions and had served on a philanthropic board together. The paper concluded that the two were at most distantly acquainted and, in any case, Ayers had become a respected and prominent figure in Chicago. In a classic right-wing guilt-by-association charge, Palin portrayed Ayers as a "domestic terrorist" in whose living room Obama "launched" his political career. At one mention of Obama's name, a man shouted from the audience, "Kill him." Palin did nothing. In that same speech, Palin attacked Couric for the "kinda mainstream media" attacks on her, to which her supporters responded by threatening and taunting reporters. One of Palin's fans called an African American soundman a racial epithet and told him, "Sit down, boy." Palin's line that Obama "pals around with terrorists" became routine in her stump speech. Palin would stand mute and smiling at her rallies as, at the mention of Obama, her fans shouted "Murderer!" "Treason!" and "Off with his head!" McCain, too, surfed the rage. "Who is the real Barack Obama?" he ominously asked at a New Mexico rally. To which someone in the crowd clearly shouted back "Terrorist," while McCain paused for the audience to finish laughing. At times, McCain would attempt to tamp down the more deranged outbursts, but there is no record of Palin calling for restraint. Her surrogates excused it, asking how she could possibly have heard what people were saying in such large halls. Apparently they hadn't watched the video posted from Bethlehem, Pennsylvania, by Dana Milbank of the *Washington Post*. After a man in the stadium shouted "You're a hottie," Palin laughed, flashed her pearly whites, and quipped, "Now what does that have to do with anything?" Reporters clearly recorded shouts of "liar" and "socialist" issuing from the crowd that same day, but those elicited no comment from Palin.

Two weeks before the election, General Colin Powell, George W. Bush's former secretary of state, appeared on *Meet the Press* to endorse Barack Obama. Powell, the paragon of mainstream Republicanism, had served in two Republican administrations and had himself considered a run for the Republican presidential nomination in 1996. He was visibly pained to be breaking with his party and his friend John McCain. He felt he had no choice, he explained, as McCain had moved so far to the right in pursuit of the presidency, and the selection of "Governor Palin had indicated a further rightward shift." Powell did not think Palin was ready to be president, and he was disturbed by what he witnessed at her rallies, the expression of sometimes racist and often incendiary rhetoric that went unchecked by Palin. He pointedly noted that Obama was not in fact a Muslim but a Christian, but that it should be no insult in the United States to be thought a Muslim. Powell, like many Republican moderates, supported abortion rights, and he voiced his concern that a Supreme

Court under a McCain-Palin administration would undermine women's freedom and other important individual rights.

By the time Powell appeared on *Meet the Press*, all the tracking polls predicted an Obama victory. McCain's Palin gambit had backfired. In the few weeks Americans had known her, Palin's negatives had soared 42 points, independents had shifted decisively against her, and young voters had formed an almost "visceral" dislike for her. By Election Day, 60 percent of Americans would say that Palin was not qualified to be president. What was not yet clear was whether Powell represented the advance guard of the GOP's return to realism, or the last dying gasp of the endangered Republican moderate.

ECSTATIC CELEBRATIONS ERUPTED across America at 11 PM on November 4, 2008, at the moment Obama topped 271 in the electoral college vote and was declared the president-elect of the United States. In Chicago's Grant Park, where several hundred thousand people had gathered to hear Obama's election night speech, the crowd was jubilant. All across the nation, men and women, especially the young, danced and partied in the streets, shouting, squealing, and crying in a kind of mass delirium. The celebrations around the world were only slightly more restrained. Germans gathered and waved American flags in Hamburg, while a few hundred Italians held aloft Obama-Biden campaign signs in a central square in Rome. The residents of Obama, Japan, decked themselves in hula skirts and leis for their victory party, while Obama's relatives wrapped themselves in American flags in Obama's father's ancestral village in Kenya. "America is the last best hope of Earth," pronounced the mayor of London. "For people that love America, it's been a tough few years, the election of Barack Obama restores faith and hope." France's minister of human rights claimed. "This is the fall of the Berlin Wall times ten," and suggested the centuries-old French love affair with America had been rekindled. "We all want to be American so we can take a bite of this dream unfolding before our eyes." Oprah Winfrey, the wealthiest African American woman on earth, resolved, "I am going to try not to fall down and cry." The Reverend Jesse Jackson, who had been at Martin Luther King's side when he was assassinated, was caught by the cameras during Obama's speech wiping away a tear. Colin Powell tried to pull everyone down from the stratosphere. "President-elect Obama is going to be a president for all America. He also happens to be black, which makes it a very, very historic occasion."

Four years earlier, George W. Bush had been reelected and the conventional wise men had pointed to the map of Red America as irrefutable proof that Americans were a conservative people and the Republican Party had triumphed for a generation. Two days before the 2008 election, 70 percent of Americans had said they disapproved of Bush. Democrats now commanded the heights of the Rocky Mountains, the headwaters of the Mississippi, and the capital of the Southern Confederacy. Blue America comfortably controlled not just the edgy coasts, but also the Great Lakes, the Midwest's waterways, and the Florida peninsula. Democrats had penetrated the heartland of the Great Plains, the rust belt of the Reagan Democrats, the sunbelt of the New Right, and ground zero of the Christian Right.

When McCain began his gracious concession speech that night, his supporters booed at the mention of Obama. McCain was barely able to quiet them down. A few weeks earlier, a Pennsylvania Republican Party chairman had opened a McCain-Palin rally by asking, how will you feel if you wake up November 5 and "you see the news that Barack Obama, that Barack Hussein Obama, is the president." Red America went to sleep the night of November 4 with plenty of material for its nightmares. Its landmass was eroded, its borders overrun, its loyal soldiers decimated, outnumbered, and surrounded.

Barack Obama had achieved the largest majority and biggest margin for a Democratic presidential candidate since Lyndon Johnson defeated Barry Goldwater in 1964. Obama won 9.5 million more votes than McCain, for a 53.3 to 45.6 percent majority, a margin of 7.7 points. The Democratic Party picked up 29 congressional seats, giving Democrats a supermajority in the House and a filibuster-proof majority in the Senate. Nine states that had gone for Bush in 2004 went for Obama in 2008: the heartland states of Iowa and Indiana; the big swing states of Ohio and Florida; Nevada and New Mexico with their growing Latino populations; the southern states of Virginia and North Carolina; and Colorado, home to Dobson's many enterprises of the sexual counterrevolution.

Obama's victory was achieved on a surge of unprecedented popular participation. Sixty-two percent of eligible Americans turned out to vote, the highest level in forty years, for a record 131 million voters. Roughly four out of every ten Americans reported that they tried to influence the way another person voted or were very much interested in the presidential campaign, levels matched only once in fifty-six years of polling on the questions. The coalition that elected Obama president was broad. Liberals favored Obama by 80 points, yet moderates also supported him by a healthy 20-point margin. Obama and Biden won union members and lower-middle-class voters, but also the wealthiest voters. The least educated and the moderately educated voted for the Democratic ticket and so too did the most highly educated Americans, those with postgraduate degrees.

Building upon the upsurge of political activism among a generation defined by the contested 2000 election, the Iraq War, Katrina, and radical Culture Wars, the Obama campaign had focused its resources and its message on expanding the pool of voters, and first-time voters were the key to Obama's commanding victory. According to exit polls, approximately 15 million voters were first-time voters, nearly half of them were under the age of 30, and 69 percent of first-time voters favored Obama. These new voters accounted for anywhere from 8.5 million to 12.5 million of Obama's national total. New voters came almost entirely from Democratic-tending groups: the young, African Americans, Latinos, and other minorities. Nearly half of all eligible young Americans voted, whereas only a third had in 2000 when Bush prevailed by stealth in a low-turnout election. They made up a record 18 percent of all voters. Among Americans born since 1978, two-thirds went for Obama. They also favored Democratic congressional candidates by large margins. Enthusiasm among minorities about Obama's candidacy helped significantly increase their share of the electorate, pushing the share of white voters down three percentage points. African American turnout surged 23 percent, for the first time erasing the historic racial gap in voting. Nearly 2 million more Latinos, 2 million more African

Americans, and 600,000 Asian Americans voted than had done so four years earlier.

Women were also indispensable to Obama's victory. Six out of every ten Obama voters were women. Women went for Obama-Biden over McCain-Palin by a 13-point margin. Working women went for the Democratic ticket by a 21-point margin. Women turned out to vote at a higher rate, 66 percent to men's 62 percent, and outnumbered men in the pool of voters by 10 million. African American women voted at a higher rate than any other group in the nation. It bears underscoring: had women voted more like men, the election would have been a toss-up.

Obama attracted voters whom pundits had always insisted would be reluctant to vote for an African American candidate. Despite Republican efforts to cast doubt on Obama's support for Israel, 78 percent of Jewish Americans voted for Obama—a high even for this traditionally Democratic group. Despite a decade of press coverage of the mutual hostility between Latinos and African Americans, two-thirds of Latinos voted for Obama. Sixteen years earlier, open warfare had broken out between African Americans and Asian Americans in the streets of Los Angeles. In 2008, Asian Americans, a historically Republican-leaning group, gave Obama 62 percent of their votes. Even one group of white voters, those under the age of thirty, favored Obama—by a resounding 10 points.

Obama likewise swept the votes of cultural progressives, professionals, the unmarried, and gays, by margins of two, three, and four to one. The 58 percent of voters who attended religious services occasionally or never favored Obama by a large margin, as did evangelicals and other religious activists who considered themselves progressive. A *Time* survey shortly before the election showed that Obama's supporters were significantly more progressive than McCain's on all issues, from the Iraq War, to health care reform, to the role of the government, to abortion and gay marriage.

Middle America sided with the Obama-Biden ticket, the progressive Democratic coalition, and cultural progressivism. Moderates voted for Obama over McCain by a 21-point margin, and independents voted for him by an 8-point margin. Obama won 54 percent of all Catholics, although he lost white Catholics by 5 points. Obama even maintained a narrow edge with two mainstays of the Republican Party, suburban voters and married women with children. The Democratic ticket won 57 percent of Americans born since 1964, and a majority of everyone under the age of 65. In some parts of the West and Northeast, Obama won white voters by up to a 20-point margin. Outside the states of the South and border South, Obama won a landslide-size victory with 57 percent of the popular vote. Progressive referendums allowing medical marijuana, doctor-assisted suicide, and stem cell research all passed. Support for legal abortion reached 58 percent, its second-highest level ever in a presidential election. Obama won more than two-thirds of voters who supported legal abortion, and all three state ballot measures limiting abortion rights were defeated. The most extreme one, Colorado's Personhood Amendment, lost by a vote of 73 percent to 27 percent. By endowing full constitutional rights to a fertilized egg, not only would it have made all abortions illegal, it would also have banned many forms of birth control, fertility treatment, and medical research.

The 2008 elections, however, also reminded progressives that the battle for hearts and minds, as well as the political war, was far from over. Antigay measures passed in Florida, McCain's Arizona, and Bill Clinton's Arkansas. California, the most Democratic state in the nation, voted Yes on Proposition 8 to take marriage rights away from gay couples.

Republicans and the Right pointed to Prop 8 to shore up their claim that the election changed nothing, that Obama won merely on an anti-incumbent tide and Americans remained as conservative as ever. Among those who had experience in California politics, the vote proved rather that campaigns matter and you can't take victory for granted. "This was political malpractice," an unnamed Democratic consultant told *Rolling Stone* reporter Tim Dickinson. "They snatched defeat from the jaws of victory, and now hundreds of thousands of gay couples are going to pay the price."

The No on 8 campaign conducted itself as though California were a province of Bizarro World, where up is down, right is left, and elections are won by insulting the voters, ignoring your friends, and alienating your supporters. For months No on 8 turned away volunteers, saying they had no need for help. On Election Day, they deployed 11,000 volunteers, who stood 100 feet away from polling places holding signs. The Yes on 8 campaign assigned five people to each precinct to monitor and turn out the vote; their volunteers outnumbered the pro-gay marriage side by 9 to 1. In the weeks leading up to the election, black and Latino leaders, including Los Angeles's first-ever Latino mayor and the former heads of the Urban League and the SCLC, all opposed Prop 8 and offered to help. The No on 8 campaign never contacted them. No on 8 told the man who had once been the highest-ranking gay official in the California Democratic Party that there was nothing for him to do, but perhaps he could come by after the election to clean up the office. Yes on 8 aired an ad of a Latino girl coming home from school to tell her mother, "I learned how a prince married a prince and I can marry a princess." The No on 8 campaign refused to run a Spanish-language ad against Prop 8 featuring Dolores Huerta, the revered co-founder of the United Farm Workers. The campaign had to be strong-armed into accepting a call to voters recorded by Bill Clinton. After the election was over, the No on 8 campaign still had $1 million in their account. In the most diverse and bluest state in the nation, they had never communicated to black and Latino voters that Obama opposed Prop 8.

Progressivism was the new center, but nevertheless, Obama won the nomination and the presidential election only by a deliberate effort to inspire and mobilize potential voters. Politics was no longer a spectator sport; Obama, Hillary, and Palin had all proved that. In no state were the new dynamics of American elections more in evidence than in California. Over the course of the 2008 election, 700,000 Californians volunteered for the Obama campaign. They made 10 million phone calls, and 18,000 of them traveled to the swing state of Nevada to go door-to-door. Yet, 2 million Californians who voted for Obama, many of them African American and Latino, voted yes on proposition 8 to overturn gay marriage. Californians lost marriage equality, in large part, because a few political consultants thought that the laws of American political physics circa 2008 did not apply to them.

. . .

PALIN'S INCLUSION ON the ticket enabled McCain to hold onto the Republican base, a feat that had been very much in doubt that summer as rumors of McCain's preference for a pro-choice running mate swirled among the sexual counterrevolutionaries. But that base was an unrepresentative and shrinking portion of the national electorate. McCain-Palin's 45.6 percent of the national vote came overwhelmingly from white, elderly, married, less educated, Southern Christian conservatives. Nine out of ten McCain-Palin voters were white, five out of ten were older than 45, and four out of every ten were white Southerners. Sexual fundamentalists were the largest faction of the Republican minority. Traditionalist white evangelicals made up 42 percent of McCain-Palin's votes. White Catholics were the only swing group that favored the GOP, and that by only a few points.

McCain's attempt to win women voters by offering Palin as a substitute for Hillary was an epic failure. The first Republican presidential ticket in history to include a woman garnered only 43 percent of the women's vote; even Bush and Cheney had done better. The candidates who made so much of being from the real America lost suburbanites, moderates, independents, Catholics, and even, by one point, men. Only a third of voters from the three fastest-growing demographic groups in the nation—the young, Latinos, and the unmarried—favored the Republican ticket.

McCain's capitulation to the sexual counterrevolution had driven away the mainstream American voter, and the Republican Party faced a stark dilemma. The most reliable Republican voters, married, traditionalist white Christians, were a shrinking minority of the population, half as small in 2008 as they had been in the 1950s. Their cultural extremism moreover alienated just about everyone else, making it difficult for Republicans to attract voters beyond the aging and ever-dwindling base. Even with 9 million more voters in the pool, McCain still fell about 3 million votes short of Bush's popular-vote total. There was compelling evidence that the small fraction of white Americans who refused to accept the changes in race relations brought about by the civil rights movement had sought refuge in the GOP. Only in regions with large concentrations of native white southerners and traditionalist fundamentalists did McCain's vote surpass Bush's.

McCain had made a desperate last-ditch attempt, with Palin's nomination, to have his stealth and the indispensable votes of the sexual fundamentalists too. Like so many Republican politicians before him who had tried to harness Christian Right voters to their own ends, McCain turned out the loser. In essentially surrendering to political blackmail over the choice of his running mate, McCain legitimized the demands of the sexual fundamentalists. At their lowest ebb of national approval, McCain endowed them with more leverage over the GOP than they had ever had. Palin's candidacy acted like an aphrodisiac to the dwindling Republican base. Once the sexual fundamentalists tasted the power that went with having one of their own on the presidential ticket, they would be loath to give it up.

The presidential candidate who promised he would put "Country First" was the one who shattered what was left of the mainstream Republican Party. On the cusp of the second decade of the 21st century, a minority making up roughly 15 percent of the nation's population controlled the GOP. Standing with their backs turned resolutely on the future, they took up position to lead the GOP on a forced march backward toward a mythical time, circa 1950, when traditional Christian morality ruled the nation and the sexual revolution had not yet destroyed the true and good America. McCain's self-interested high-stakes gamble virtually guaranteed that the unchecked delirium of the sexual counterrevolution would become a lasting feature of American politics.

JUST AS PALIN'S meteoric ascent revealed that the Republican Party had become a wholly owned subsidiary of the sexual counterrevolution, so too did Obama's commanding victory mark the triumph of the cultural progressives within the Democratic party. The young, women, minorities, the unmarried, the multiculturalists, the irreligious, gays, and professionals—here were the heirs of the McGovernicks in all their resplendent glory. Since 1972, these sorts of men and women had been blamed for the Democratic Party's woes. They had been condemned for hijacking the Democratic Party, betraying its historic mission with their cultural extremism, alienating real

Democrats, and taking it down the road to ruin. It turned out that cultural progressives had expanded the electorate, attracted Middle America, and forged a new majority that carried Democrats to their largest victory since the civil rights movement.

"Goodbye Reagan Democrats," Stan Greenberg wrote one week after the election. The quintessential Reagan Democrats had come home, Greenberg reported. Macomb County, Michigan, went for Obama by 8 points. Even more interesting to Greenberg, the man who had done so much to keep alive the Democratic Party's obsession with the elusive conservative white man, was the vote in Macomb's neighboring county, Oakland. Once a tony, lily-white, country-club Republican enclave, Oakland was now a racially and ethnically diverse suburb of professionals where voters went for Obama by a 15-point margin, giving him a 96,000-vote lead over McCain. According to Greenberg's election night poll, Oakland voters were more supportive than Macomb voters of gay marriage and affirmative action. Greenberg discovered what political scientists had been proving for over a decade: cultural progressivism was a winner. Demographic changes "have produced a more tolerant and culturally liberal population, uncomfortable with today's Republican Party," he wrote. "So, good riddance, my Macomb barometer. Four years from now, I trust we will see the candidates rush from their conventions to Oakland County, to see the new America."

If Greenberg was willing to say good riddance to the Reagan Democrat, would the Democratic Party in the age of Obama be able to transcend its paralyzing conflicts over issues of culture, sex, and gender? Would Democrats embrace the cultural progressivism of their enthusiastic and vastly expanded base? All the signs, from demographic trends to public opinion polling, suggested that time was on their side, even if there would still be a few losses, like Prop 8, along the way. The main danger to the Democrats' ability to cement their victory into an enduring majority lurked from the historic tendency of new voters to take a lackadaisical approach to less exciting off-year, midterm, and local elections. New voters, young voters, and minority voters are infrequent voters. The promise of Obama had produced a voter surge. What would the surge voters do if the promised land proved more distant than they had imagined?

As more than a million Americans lined the streets of Washington, D.C., and gathered on the Mall on a frigid January day to see Barack Obama be inaugurated as the 44th president of the United States, few of those who voted for Obama were thinking about that. They were transfixed by their hopes for change.

Obama was keen to linger in the rapture. "While we breathe, we hope. Where we are met with cynicism and doubt and those who tell us we can't, we will reply: Yes we can."

14

DELIRIUM

"IS THE PARTY OVER?" *Time* magazine asked in their May 2009 issue "Republicans in Distress," published shortly after Republican Senator Arlen Specter defected to the Democratic Party. "GOP Losses Span Nearly All Demographic Groups," Gallup headlined its annual survey on political identification, in which Democrats held a 14-point partisan advantage. Only 29 percent of Americans felt at all positive about the Republican Party. Only after the Watergate scandal, in 1974, had fewer Americans identified as Republicans, the nonpartisan Pew Center reported. Pew's surveys went all the way back to 1929, when the stock market first crashed during Republican Herbert Hoover's first year in the presidency.

Meanwhile, President Barack Obama was basking in the glow of popular approval of his leadership, his character, and his plans for the nation. At the end of his benchmark first one hundred days in office, 64 percent of Americans felt very positive toward him, and 61 percent approved of the job he was doing as president, according to a *Wall Street Journal*/NBC News poll. At similar times in their presidencies, far fewer Americans had felt good about Bill Clinton and George W. Bush. Fifty-nine percent of Americans thought Obama had accomplished a great deal or a fair amount so far. A majority of Americans favored Obama's top domestic policy goals, such as addressing climate change, enacting health care reform, and improving education. Eight out of ten Americans found him likable, easygoing, and admired him for "his personality and the kind of family man" he was, while six to seven out of ten gave him high marks on leadership, compassion, honesty, for improving America's leadership in the world and being an inspirational leader. Fifty-five percent of Americans rated Obama highly on representing "traditional American values." A solid majority gave the president credit for "uniting the country" and "bringing real change to the direction of the country." Almost two-thirds of Americans felt "more hopeful" when they were asked about Obama's leadership and plans for the country.

Circumstances prevented Obama from devoting his first one hundred days to change. Instead, the administration was compelled to attend to the economic crisis that had worsened during the time between the election and his inauguration. In February, unemployment hit 8.2 percent, the credit markets remained frozen, and housing prices continued to plunge. On March 9, the S&P 500 fell to a low of 676, a 57 percent drop from its peak in October of 2007, the largest decline in the stock market since the Great Depression. On February 10, the 111th Congress, with Democrats holding nearly 60 percent of the seats in both chambers, passed the American Recovery and Reinvestment Act. The bill provided $787 billion in public spending and tax cuts in order to "stimulate" the weak economy. Since the Great Depression of the 1930s and the development of Keynesian economic theory, every president, whether Democratic or Republican, had used government spending to counteract the devastating effects of recession on individual Americans while jumpstarting the economy back into a growth cycle. The only thing unusual about the stimulus bill, by historical standards, was the dollar amount, warranted by the scale of the crisis as well as by the size of the U.S. economy. Indeed, many economists thought the stimulus was too small and too heavily weighted toward tax cuts, given the depth of the economic crisis. But the administration insisted it was the best it could do politically. Obama was able to advance some of his long-term goals within the stimulus. As Jonathan Alter wrote in *The Promise: President Obama, Year One*, a measured inside story of the first year of the Obama administration, the stimulus included large investments in alternative energy, education, and health care. In addition, a few days before passing the stimulus bill, the president had signed legislation, vetoed twice by Bush, expanding the children's health insurance program to an additional 4 million low-income children and pregnant women.

After winning the battle over the stimulus bill, the administration pivoted quickly to health care reform, a signature campaign promise made by Obama, and one particularly popular with Democratic activists. Nearly all of his political advisers and cabinet members tried to dissuade Obama from that politically risky path. Democrats had been trying to enact universal health care since Harry Truman was president in the late 1940s. The only major step in that direction had been after Lyndon Johnson's 1964 landslide election, when just six months into the 89th Congress, the legislature passed Medicare, universal government-funded, single-payer health care for Americans over the age of 65. Obama reasoned that if he delayed, his political capital would be too depleted to succeed. Considering the depth of the economic crisis, Obama's determination to reform the health care system was an act of political courage and vision. If winning health care reform made him a one-term president, he told those close to him, so be it.

Once Obama insisted that he would not be deterred from health care reform, the responsibility for making it happen fell to Obama's chief of staff, Rahm Emanuel. Emanuel's political philosophy had been forged in the cauldron of the Clinton administration and the minority House Democratic Caucus during the Bush years. Emanuel's temper, impatience, hardball tactics, and gutter mouth had by now become legendary; Obama once famously joked that Emanuel had been rendered "mute" from a workplace accident in which he had lost half of his right middle finger. From his time in the Clinton administration, Emanuel had deduced two rules that would prove to be enormously consequential for the Obama administration: let Congress take the lead, and no distractions. Under the no-distraction order, the administration consciously fended off pressure to act on all other priorities dear to various Democratic constituencies, regardless of how popular they might have been. Labor law reform, action to address climate change, financial regulation to rein in the banks and Wall Street, the repeal of Don't Ask, Don't Tell (DADT), the Freedom of Choice Act, the repeal of the Hyde amendment—all were put on hold while health care was tackled.

On issues important to cultural progressives, Emanuel's no-distraction order combined with Obama's temperament to produce unpredictable results. The administration moved quickly to pass and sign the Lilly Ledbetter Fair Pay Act of 2009. The purpose of the act was to restore the ability of women to sue employers for wage discrimination, a right eviscerated by a broadly criticized 2007 decision by the Supreme Court, headed by former Reagan aide John Roberts. Where improving women's economic standing touched on matters of sex and culture, however, Obama showed ambivalence. In Obama's first week in office, the stimulus bill passed out of the House Energy and Commerce committee included $200 million to expand birth control coverage under Medicaid. The reasoning behind the measure was that many families who had lost their jobs and health insurance in the recession could no longer afford to pay for birth control. The Congressional Budget Office scored it a money saver; historically couples delay childbearing during economic hard times. Lobbied by Operation Rescue and other Christian Right groups, House minority leader Republican John Boehner pounced: "How can you spend hundreds of millions of dollars on contraceptives—how does that stimulate the economy?" Obama, who hoped for many Republican votes on the bill, instantly ordered House Democrats to remove the provision from their bill. House Republicans proceeded later that week to vote unanimously against the bill anyway. Obama had been in office seven days.

There were also signs that Obama's vaunted transpartisanship might tip over into indulgence of the right-wing sexual counterrevolution. Obama invited Rick Warren, the pastor of the Saddleback megachurch, to deliver the invocation at his inauguration. Warren had likened homosexuality to pedophilia and incest, compared abortion to the Nazi Holocaust, and had been a leading advocate of California's antigay marriage referendum, Prop 8. Gays strongly protested Warren's role in the inauguration. Obama defended his

choice, saying that he had spoken at Warren's church even though
Warren knew he disagreed on issues of gays and abortion. "I had an
opportunity to speak. And that dialogue, I think, is part of what my
campaign's been all about, that we're not going to agree on every
single issue, but what we have to do is to be able to create an atmosphere when we—where we can disagree without being disagreeable."
In his first State of the Union address in 2009, Obama pledged to
work with the military and Congress to repeal DADT. But when
Obama convened a White House celebration marking the fortieth
anniversary of the Stonewall Uprising in June, little progress had
been made. A few weeks earlier, the Justice Department had filed
a brief defending the Defense of Marriage Act (DOMA), a law that
candidate Obama had described as "abhorrent." To the 200 LGBT
activists, Obama said, "I know that many in this room don't believe
that progress has come fast enough, and I understand that. It's not
for me to tell you to be patient, any more than it was for others
to counsel patience to African Americans who were petitioning for
equal rights a half century ago. But I say this: We have made progress and we will make more." In other words, I "will be your champion," but please give me time.

Obama's ambivalence was most pronounced on the issue of abortion. NARAL Pro-Choice America and some individual pro-choice
leaders had endorsed Obama over Hillary, arguing he would be a
more forceful advocate for reproductive freedom. He had in fact
strengthened the pro-choice plank in the party's platform. (It had
been significantly watered down for John Kerry's 2004 pursuit of
conservative Red America.) He had come into office with support
for legal abortion near an all-time high. In his first week in office,
just as President Clinton had done, Obama reversed the antiabortion
Mexico City Policy that had been reinstated by George W. Bush.
The reversal on international abortion policy was by now a well-
established ritual when control of the White House changed parties. But Obama altered the ceremonials. In 1992, Clinton had held
a press conference, spoken about women's rights and birth control,
stated "he was acting to free science and medicine from the grasp of
politics," and overturned six separate antiabortion policies enacted by
the Reagan and Bush administrations. Obama, by contrast, delayed

a day in issuing the memorandum, so as not to offend the protesters in the annual antiabortion march marking the anniversary of *Roe v. Wade*. Instead that day he issued a presidential statement calling for conversation seeking common ground on abortion. Obama too decried the "politicization" of the issue, yet repeated his call to find common ground. He signed the memorandum late Friday afternoon with no media or cameras present. In May, Obama gave the commencement speech at Notre Dame, a Catholic university. His invitation had sparked protests by antiabortion Catholics, so Obama went to Notre Dame with an olive branch in hand. "Maybe we won't agree on abortion, but we can still agree that this heart-wrenching decision for any woman is not made casually, it has both moral and spiritual dimensions." He continued by enumerating five measures of "common ground," each proposed by the antiabortion movement. Only vaguely worded phrases about "science" and "respect for the equality of women" even hinted that there might be a moral argument on the other side rooted in women's health and freedom.

THE DEMOCRATIC PARTY entered the Age of Obama in possession of the largest working majority in decades. As the GOP had moved increasingly to the Right since the 1980s, the Democratic Party had welcomed former Republican moderates and independent-leaning politicians and voters into their own big rickety, overstuffed tent. The Democratic caucus in the 111th Congress was made up of men and women who spanned a wide ideological spectrum. The 2006 and 2008 Congressional elections had brought 65 new members to the party's House and Senate caucuses, many of them through Rahm Emanuel's anyone-goes recruitment plan. The caucus included a couple who were DINOs, that is Democrats in Name Only. It included Joe Lieberman, an Independent who had been Al Gore's running mate and nearly John McCain's. It now included Arlen Specter, an 82-year-old pro-choice Pennsylvanian who had entered the U.S. Senate as a Republican when Ronald Reagan was president. The Blue Dog Caucus of conservative-leaning centrists claimed 52 members, while the Congressional Progressive Caucus claimed 79. The two-party system was indeed alive—inside the Democratic Party.

Within no time at all, congressional Democrats were nearly paralyzed by their internal divisions. The stimulus bill of February gave an early indication that the Democratic Party could easily become a casualty of its own success. Fiscally conservative Blue Dogs had prevailed in their demand for a smaller stimulus, less investment, and more tax cuts in the package, all of which most economists considered unwise. Progressives, inside and outside the government, already were feeling ignored, excluded, and used.

In the House, the rules and customs of the institution accorded enormous power to the majority party and its leader. The Democratic Speaker of the House and leader of the Democratic caucus, Nancy Pelosi, was both a progressive from a safely progressive district, and a brilliant legislative leader, in a league with the legendary Speakers of the past. As Norman Ornstein, a widely respected expert on Congress at the conservative American Enterprise Institute, said, "She ranks with the most consequential speakers, certainly in the last 75 years." She was adept at the persuading, trading, cajoling, arm-twisting, and vote-counting, which the ordinary voter despises but is in fact demanded of any party leader who wants to get anything done in America's lumbering legislative system. Within the first six months of the Obama administration, the House increased the minimum wage, passed the Lilly Ledbetter Fair Pay Act, expanded health insurance to 11 million children, and increased funding for college loans. Pelosi had presided over difficult votes on the stimulus, to cap carbon emissions, and other controversial measures that had met resistance from members of the Democratic caucus.

But the Senate, and the Democratic Party within it, was another matter. The very structure of the Senate, with two senators for every state, is inherently undemocratic—just as the Founding Fathers intended. The 689,000 residents of Alaska, for example, have two votes in the Senate, as do the 40 million residents of California. The archaic institutional rules of the Senate, especially the filibuster, give additional leverage to the minority party and to outliers or grandstanders in the majority party. The musty traditions of the clubby chamber give individual committee heads inordinate power over legislation.

Health care reform nearly expired in the Senate under the force of all of these institutional obstacles to passing major legislation. The

Senate Health, Education, Labor and Pensions Committee passed a strong health care reform bill on July 15, 2009, on strict party lines. The bill included the key progressive demand, a government insurance plan to be offered in competition with private insurance. It was from here that committee chair Senator Edward Kennedy had mounted his long fight for universal health care. Senator Chris Dodd had shepherded the bill through to passage while Kennedy was being treated for brain cancer at his home in Massachusetts. The day before, the House had announced the details of their plan and their intention to begin committee votes that week. But health care reform was also being considered by the Senate Finance Committee. Even though Democrats held a 13-to-10 majority on the committee, committee chair Montana Democratic Senator Max Baucus had convened a group of three Democrats, including himself, and three Republicans to hammer out a so-called bipartisan compromise in secret. The six senators all hailed from small, overwhelmingly rural states, with a combined population less than that of several large counties in other states. Month after month the Gang of Six had been meeting, and month after month they missed deadlines that the Obama administration had set in order to get a vote on health care reform before it had spent down Obama's political capital. On the day the health committee passed its proposed health care reform bill, the committee members informed the press that they were going to take their time with a bill. They didn't consider the president's insistence that a vote be taken before Congress's August recess binding on them.

By midsummer, six out of ten Americans blamed Democrats as well as Republicans for the rancor, partisanship, and lack of compromise in Congress. Support for health care reform had fallen to a dangerously low level and Americans were clearly confused about what it entailed. Only 36 percent supported health care reform when asked, "From what you've heard of Barack Obama's health care plan, do you think it is a good idea of a bad idea?" When the actual legislation was described, however, 56 percent still favored health care reform. Meanwhile, 2 million jobs had been lost since inauguration day. Hope had been frittered away.

. . .

TEN DAYS BEFORE Obama's inauguration, Republican House minority leader John Boehner and House whip Eric Cantor gathered the Republican caucus for a closed-door meeting and unveiled a plan to obstruct Obama's legislative agenda. They would use "guerrilla style tactics to attack Democrats" in their districts and force them to answer for difficult votes. Anyone with reelection ambitions, Boehner and Cantor told their fellow representatives, was to be advised that voting against the party was not an option. The entire mission statement for the GOP in the 111th Congress, according to the head of the National Republican Congressional Committee, was to "retire Nancy Pelosi."

Congressional Republicans' disciplined politics of obstruction succeeded in arresting Obama's post-inauguration momentum, but it wasn't moving voters into the Republican column. Nonpartisan public opinion surveys in the spring of 2009 gave a good indication why: the GOP's out-of-the-mainstream sexual and cultural politics. Cultural progressivism was the nation's new center. A CBS News/ *New York Times* poll showed a majority of Americans under the age of 40 favoring gay marriage and a fifth of young Americans answering "none," when asked about their religious identification. A CNN poll reported that support for *Roe v. Wade* was at an all-time high of 68 percent. Independents, who now made up the plurality of voters, were according to Pew "left-of-center" on gay civil rights, gender roles, religion in public life, and abortion. Pew noted that they were in this way very similar to Democrats. On economic issues, however, independents had "taken a turn to the right."

Time, then, for the biennial Republican rebranding. Republican establishment figures, such as Cantor, John McCain, Mitt Romney, retired Florida Governor Jeb Bush, and others, formed the National Council for a New America. They announced they would conduct a "listening tour" across America; first they censored any talk in their own ranks of gays, abortion, creationism, immigrants, or religion.

The sexual fundamentalists did not receive an invitation to the new party, and they lashed the establishment. "Too many Republican leaders are running scared on the claims of the left and the media that social conservatism is a dead-end for the GOP," the Family Research Council's Tony Perkins said. Hadn't they seen how much enthusiasm Mike Huckabee inspired in the conservative base? Ken Blackwell, a failed Republican gubernatorial candidate in Ohio also employed by James Dobson's Family Research Council, asserted, "It's a losing proposition to try to divide social and economic conservatives." Venerable New Right founder Richard Viguerie contended that the problem with the Republicans was that "we've moved left." Grassroots conservatives disdained the "wet-finger politicians who are going to be looking at how the political winds are blowing," Viguerie contended. They were hungry for the true warriors, those like Representative Paul Ryan, Senator Jim DeMint, Governor Mark Sanford, and Sarah Palin. Cantor clarified that the new group had never had any intention of excluding the base. Soon nary a word was heard from or about the National Council for a New America.

By June, six months into Obama's presidency, with unemployment and home foreclosures up, the economy uncertain, and health care reform stalled, the numbers of Americans feeling very negative about Obama had inched up above 20 percent and the approval rating of the Democratic-controlled Congress started to dive. Still, the dial had hardly moved on the GOP's favorability rating. Forty-four percent of Americans had negative feelings toward the GOP. Only 6 percent felt very positive about the Republican Party.

Then, on June 14, Nevada Senator John Ensign admitted to having had an affair with a married staffer, whose husband was also on his staff. Later it would be revealed that Ensign's parents had given $96,000 to the mistress and her husband and helped him land a lobbying job. (Ensign stayed in the Senate, only resigning in 2011 when a Senate censure and possible indictment looked imminent.) Later that month, South Carolina governor Mark Sanford, the head of the Republican Governors' Association, and a strong conservative contender for the 2012 presidential nomination, went missing for almost a week. His staff first said he had been working hard and was "out of pocket," then that he was hiking the Appalachian Trail and had no cell phone access. The truth came out on June 24, when Sanford confessed he had been out of the country with his Argentinian lover. Both Ensign and Sanford had first been elected to office in 1994 as candidates of the pro-family sexual counterrevolution.

A second Republican rebranding campaign kicked off shortly

after the Republican sex scandals. What good was it to be the star of the reality show of American politics when your team had been voted off the island? Late Friday afternoon, on the Fourth of July weekend, Sarah Palin resigned her governorship, a year and a half short of completing her first term. Flanked by her family and framed by the rugged Alaska landscape, Palin blamed the media for harassing her with unfounded ethics investigations. She then reached back to her high school years for a metaphor to describe her bizarre and unexpected play.

"Let me go back to a comfortable analogy for me—sports . . . basketball. I use it because you're naïve if you don't see the national full-court press picking away right now: A good point guard drives through a full court press, protecting the ball, keeping her eye on the basket . . . and she knows exactly when to pass the ball so that the team can WIN. And I'm doing that—keeping our eye on the ball that represents sound priorities—smaller government, energy independence, national security, freedom! And I know when it's time to pass the ball—for victory."

A brutal exposé by Todd Purdum in *Vanity Fair* released earlier that week had reported what many had suspected during the 2008 presidential campaign: Almost everyone in McCain's camp had believed her unfit to be vice president. Now, most pundits declared her a quitter and forecast the end of her political career, but Gallup reported that 72 percent of Republicans said they would likely vote for her should she run for president in 2012.

An alternative brand, under development by old Republican hands but at a remove from the tainted Republican Party, was simultaneously being test-marketed in the winter and spring of 2009. On February 19, CNBC commentator Rick Santelli stood on the floor of the Chicago Mercantile Exchange shouting at the top of his lungs. He denounced President Obama and blamed the housing crisis on average middle-class Americans. "This is America. How many of you people want to pay for your neighbor's mortgage that has an extra bathroom and can't pay their bills? . . . We're thinking of having a Chicago Tea Party in July. All you capitalists that want to show up to Lake Michigan, I'm going to start organizing." The capitalists on the trading floor cheered. On April 15, 2009, "tax day" protests took place in about 750 places throughout the nation. The protesters, overwhelmingly white and well past middle age, sported revolutionary costumes and sun-protective headgear festooned with tea bags.

Just a few months into the Age of Obama, as far as the press was concerned the really interesting news was the Tea Party, spreading like prairie grass across the real America. Seeking to explain the unusual characteristics of this new protest movement, conventional wisdom took its cue from the Tea Party itself. This, they said, was an authentic grassroots uprising of freedom-loving political neophytes, jolted into action by a populist revulsion at big government and a desire for fiscal conservatism and personal liberty.

But the Tea Party, contrary to initial accounts, was not a grassroots social movement. From the start it was an Astroturf campaign, that is, a coordinated effort directed from on high to give the impression of a spontaneous bubbling up of ordinary, real Americans. Certainly many ordinary Americans showed up at demonstrations of their own volition to express their dissatisfaction. Nonetheless, veteran Republican powerbrokers, the right-wing media, and Republican billionaires played an outsized role in supporting and funding the local uprisings and providing the decentralized groups with a cohesive national agenda.

Two of the most influential Tea Party groups, FreedomWorks and Americans for Prosperity, were new ventures of the old Clinton-hunting Citizens for a Sound Economy, now funded mostly by the Koch brothers. Charles and David Koch were the sons of one of the founders of the far right John Birch society, and heirs to their father's privately held petroleum fortune. (Robert Welch, the founder of the Birchers, had accused World War II hero and Republican President Dwight D. Eisenhower of being a Communist agent. In the fifties and sixties, mainstream conservatives had disavowed the group for its conspiratorial bent and extremist views. The John Birch Society had long been assumed moribund; its resurgence during the Obama administration was a surprise.) FreedomWorks was run by one of Ralph Reed's former business partners and Dick Armey, the Republican majority leader during the Gingrich era. Newt Gingrich himself, who since his resignation from Congress in 1999 had spent his time as a conservative pundit and perennial presidential candidate, pivoted his own corporate-funded organization into Tea Party alignment. Fox News also was instrumental in the rise of the Tea Party. The first "tax-day" demonstration against the stimulus plan in 2009 was orchestrated by Americans for Prosperity, another Koch-funded group, and publicized by Fox News commentator Michelle Malkin. Indeed Malkin had publicized protests against the stimulus package on Fox News before Santelli's rant introduced the Tea Party frame into common use. Likewise, Glenn Beck announced a march on Washington for September 12 in February before any Tea Party movement had arisen. In the lead-up to the tax day protests in April 2009, Fox News essentially ran a month-long infomercial. Distinguished Harvard political scientist Theda Skocpol and two coauthors later concluded in a study of the Tea Party's rise that Fox News "helped to create and sustain the Tea Party mobilization in the first place."

CONGRESSIONAL REPUBLICANS' OBSTRUCTION, Tea Party faux-populist protest, and Palin's reinvention as a freedom-fighting outsider all converged in late July, as Congress went home for the summer recess to speak to constituents about health care reform. In town hall meetings to discuss health care reform, Democratic representatives were met with rancor and rage from constituents identifying themselves with the Tea Party. On the Eastern Shore of Maryland, for example, protesters hung freshman Democratic Representative Frank Kratovil in effigy. Freed from the demands of governing the state of Alaska, Palin took to her Facebook page on August 7 and wrote, "The America I know and love is not one in which my parents or my baby with Down Syndrome will have to stand in front of Obama's 'death panel' so his bureaucrats can decide, based on a subjective judgment of their 'level of productivity in society,' whether they are worthy of health care. Such a system is downright evil." On August 11 outside a New Hampshire town hall where the president appeared, one man openly carried a gun strapped in its holster and a sign reading, "It's time to water the tree of Liberty!" The rest of that famous Thomas Jefferson quote goes, "with the blood of patriots and tyrants." Tea Party spokesmen had made it quite clear who they thought the tyrant was. Earlier that spring on Fox News, former U.S. senator and 2012 Republican presidential candidate Rick Santorum had said Obama was "contemptuous of American values."

The summer 2009 town hall protests against so-called Obamacare bore an uncanny resemblance to the demonstrations against so-called Hillarycare fifteen years earlier, no doubt because they were funded and coordinated by many of the same people who had defeated health care reform that time around. Even Palin's lie that the bill contained "death panels" had originated in the Clinton-era corporate-funded opposition to health care reform. At the end of June, FreedomWorks sent out a "Health Care Action Kit." Armey encouraged recipients to download and share it. "If everyone does their part to make a difference in this campaign, we can throw sand in the gears of the government-run health care scheme." The handouts in the package included mock health care cards. Next to an illustration of an eagle pouncing like a vulture, it said "ObamaCare Card—a collective plan administered by the politicians and bureaucrats of the U.S. government." At the bottom of the card was written "Take a number."

Republican leaders, commending the Tea Party–identified protesters at the town hall meetings, seemed content to surf the delirium to power, just as they had been during the fight over health care reform during the Clinton era. When Gang of Six member Iowa Senator Charles Grassley denounced the "death panels" in the proposed legislation, it became apparent that two of the three Republicans Baucus had been courting to give health care reform bipartisan legitimacy had all along had been running down the buzzer. (The other saboteur was Wyoming senator Michael Enzi.) Indeed, a memo leaked to *The Hill* newspaper that "delay," then "kill," was the heart of the Republicans' strategy.

The summer Tea Party protests culminated on September 12 at a Washington, D.C., demonstration sponsored by FreedomWorks, Fox News's Glenn Beck, the Tea Party Patriots, and a Republican PAC calling itself Our Country Deserves Better. According to a FreedomWorks spokesperson, the rally was destined to be "the largest gathering of fiscal conservatives ever." Nonpartisan reports

put about 70,000 people in attendance. Several Republican politicians, including Mike Pence and Jim DeMint spoke at the rally.
Many in the crowd held up signs about the Constitution, taxes,
freedom, and ObamaCare. But there was also a noticeable under-
current of extremism among some of the participants. Many people
held up signs suggesting Obama was an agent of Osama Bin Laden.
Other signs said that Democratic House majority whip, James Clyburn, a veteran African American civil rights leader, was a "racist."
A middle-aged white woman, wearing gold rings on her impeccably
manicured hands, held aloft a sign saying "we came unarmed . . .
THIS TIME." A white man wore blackface. Posters of the president
done up with a Hitler mustache or as Heath Ledger's Joker in the
Dark Knight were ubiquitous. So was the claim that Obama had not
been born in the United States, a lie first spread by Christian Right
evangelical missionaries that had metastasized into the full-blown
"birther" conspiracy theory. Patriot and armed militia movements
canvassed for new recruits. A few days after the demonstration, Our
Country Deserves Better spokesman Mark Williams wrote on his
blog, Obama is "an Indonesian Muslim turned welfare thug and a
racist in chief." Although Beck was the most prominent culprit in
the escalation of rhetoric—in the weeks leading up to the protest
he had called Obama a "racist" and joked about poisoning Pelosi's
wine—the GOP was essentially silent about the violent rhetoric and
escalating racism that appeared almost every time Tea Partiers held
a demonstration.

ON SEPTEMBER 9, 2009, after many months of allowing Congress
to take the lead on a plan and set the terms of the health care debate,
President Obama delivered a televised speech to Congress and the
nation. Obama finally enumerated what he thought should be in
health care legislation and why reform was a national imperative.

"I am not the first President to take up this cause, but I am deter-
mined to be the last. It has now been nearly a century since Theodore
Roosevelt first called for health care reform," the president asserted.
"We are the only advanced democracy on Earth—the only wealthy

nation—that allows such hardships for millions of its people. There are now more than thirty million American citizens who cannot get coverage."

As he drew to a close, Obama told the nation of a letter by Senator Ted Kennedy he had received after Kennedy's death two weeks earlier. Kennedy had written the letter in May, after he was told his cancer was terminal. He expressed optimism that Obama would succeed in the cause to which Kennedy had devoted three decades. Obama gave to Kennedy the honor of raising the debate to a higher plane. "What we face," Obama read from Kennedy's letter, "is above all a moral issue; at stake are not just the details of policy, but fundamental principles of social justice and the character of our country."

Progressives were delighted the president had finally taken ownership of health care reform, if typically disappointed that he had waffled on their key objective and had equated their letter writing and lobbying with the extremist tactics seen at the summer Town-hall meetings and Tea Party demonstrations. Many Congressional Democrats were themselves frustrated at Baucus's delay and appreciated that Obama had signaled his patience had worn out. After the summer recess, the pundits had thought health care reform was dead. Whether that was true or not, Obama's speech revived it. After all, Democrats held massive majorities in both houses of Congress, and a unified party could carry it through. The story of health care reform will eventually fill several books. What concerns us is how it nearly died at the hands of conservative sexual counterrevolutionaries in the Democratic Party.

In accord with Rahm Emanuel's rule on distractions, Congressional Democrats had originally agreed that the status quo on abortion would be maintained within health care legislation. Even though Obama had pledged during the election that he would do away with the Hyde amendment, which prohibited federal funding of abortion except in cases of rape, incest, or the life of the mother, pro-choice Democrats agreed that health care reform would not be the vehicle for this long-standing goal. It is worth underscoring that this stance was a significant compromise, as well as a sharp turn to the right, compared to that proposed by the Clintons fifteen years earlier. Clinton's health care reform plan had mandated that insurance companies include abortion coverage as part of the minimum essential insurance plan. As health care reform was pushed into the summer, antiabortion Democrats demanded more, insisting that no government subsidy go to any insurance plan that included abortion as a covered service. The House Democratic caucus offered a compromise, which involved segregating private and public funds for health insurance in separate accounts. Pro-choice advocates pointed out that this added accounting burden was likely to reduce private insurance coverage of abortions, thus restricting women's access to abortion. But they believed health care reform was a top priority for women's health. Insurance companies routinely charged women more than men for insurance and often did not cover medical care for pregnancy or breast cancer screenings. The prospect of ending the discriminatory treatment of women in America's private health care system led them to go along, reluctantly, with the restrictive provision on abortion.

Still, antiabortion Democrats weren't satisfied. In early September, Michigan Representative Bart Stupak offered an amendment to the House health care bill. Presented under the guise of prohibiting federal funding of abortion—already prohibited by the Hyde amendment—it was in fact consciously designed by the antiabortion movement as a way to compel private insurance companies to drop abortion coverage in all their private plans. (They assumed the bureaucratic costs and burden of maintaining separate accounts would lead insurers to take a simpler route: eliminate all abortion coverage for everyone.) Stupak's amendment was defeated in committee in September. In late October, as both houses of Congress were moving forward on health care reform and getting close to a vote they now knew would attract no Republicans, Pelosi tacitly instructed the Democratic caucus that they could afford no more delay and therefore no one should offer an amendment to the bill once the floor debate began. Yet at the eleventh hour, Stupak reintroduced his antiabortion amendment and, in a classic act of legislative blackmail, announced that he and a couple dozen Democrats would torpedo health care reform if their demand was not met. The day before the House vote, Pelosi, a pro-choice Catholic, engaged in frenzied negotiations between the pro-choice representatives and the antiabortion forces. Only one of those groups, Stupak's, was content to kill health care reform. Faced with the defeat on health care reform if she didn't allow a vote on the Stupak amendment, Pelosi allowed the amendment to reach the floor. On November 7, the Stupak amendment passed, with every Republican and 64 Democrats voting in favor of it. Many of these Democrats were relatively new to Congress, recruited by Rahm Emanuel when he believed it didn't matter where a Democratic vote came from. Health care reform passed the House later that night, but every Republican and many of the Democrats who had voted for the Stupak amendment voted against it.

Reporters later uncovered that the real legislative mastermind of this feint was not Stupak, but members of the U.S. Conference of Catholic Bishops and their lobbyists. The bishops, Stupak told *Newsweek* reporter Lisa Miller, were "very, very, very engaged" in writing his amendment. Stupak's staff had been working with them since the summer, and Stupak essentially admitted that he and the Bishops were together counting and whipping votes. "I asked them to come by, to make sure we were on the same page. After that first meeting, I said, 'I'm not moving forward until you know what I'm doing.' We had to coordinate forces. They'd ask us about members. I'd say, 'I've talked to this one but not to that one.'" Officials of the U.S. Conference of Catholic Bishops were in the room with Stupak the night of the vote as his contingent negotiated with Pelosi. Throughout the controversy, the Vatican and the U.S. Catholic Church exerted pressure on American Catholics who held political office. Bishops called their representatives directly, sent out notices to local dioceses, and prepared inserts to be distributed during Mass. The bishops even ordered a few Catholic legislators, including Patrick Kennedy, the late Ted Kennedy's son, not to take communion unless they changed their votes on abortion rights. Neither Kennedy nor the other prominent pro-choice Catholics caved to individual pressure. Nevertheless, in the final vote, Catholic representatives were disproportionately represented among those who voted in favor of the Stupak amendment.

The Democratic Party, with huge majorities in Congress and

control of the White House, had passed the most onerous restrictions on reproductive rights since the Hyde amendment. Although Stupak's antiabortion stance did accord with the views of his constituents in his sparsely populated, rural, heavily Catholic district in northern Michigan, it did not represent the view of mainstream American public opinion. Various surveys all put support for legal abortion around 60 percent. Although a majority of Americans opposed using public money to pay for abortions, that was already the law of the land. Stupak's amendment was designed to make abortion, if not illegal, far more difficult to obtain.

After their victory in the House, the U.S. Conference of Catholic Bishops moved on to apply pressure in the Senate, working primarily on conservative Democrat Ben Nelson of Nebraska. Despite Obama's hope to have a completed and signed bill before Congress's 2009 holiday recess, Nelson waited to sign off on a bill until the bishops had time to review the language. Eventually Nelson offered the Bishops' amendment, but pro-choice senators, especially women, were better organized by this time, and the Senate defeated Nelson's amendment. It was already December 8. The compromise eventually included in the Senate bill was far from the original agreement on neutrality, but it did strike the provisions in the Stupak amendment that would have effectively ended abortion coverage in private insurance plans. Needing to overcome united Republican opposition and hold the votes of Senators Nelson and Joe Lieberman to maintain a filibuster-proof majority, the health care reform bill put before the Senate was less robust than progressives and even many centrists wanted. Thwarting repeated Republican filibusters, and that Senate Majority Leader Harry Reid calling in cots on several nights and keeping the body in session, the U.S. Senate passed health care reform by a 60–40 vote at 7 AM on Christmas Eve. And just as in the House, not a single Republican joined in.

All that remained was for the House and Senate to reconcile their bills and pass the result. Many were hopeful that the conference committee would be able to substantially improve the bill. When the House and Senate returned from their winter recess in a few weeks, everyone assumed, Democrats would iron out the differences and the Democrats' dream of universal health care would be a reality.

■ ■ ■

ON JANUARY 19, 2010, Tea Party–backed Republican Scott Brown stunned the political establishment by winning a special election to fill the late Ted Kennedy's Senate seat in Massachusetts, one of the Bluest, most liberal states in the nation. Anyone following the news knew that Brown had won *Cosmopolitan's* "Sexiest Man of the Year" in 1982 and had posed nude in the magazine. He had won his improbable campaign by driving around Massachusetts in his old pickup truck and talking to voters. His Democratic opponent had been so sure of her victory she had gone on a long vacation weeks before the election. Even more absurdly, she had scoffed at the idea of shaking hands outside Fenway Park, where Boston's revered Red Sox played. Brown's down-to-earth persona reinforced the perception of the Tea Party as a movement of populist libertarians awakening to politics for the first time. Only a few media outlets reported that the Tea Party Express, a Republican PAC, donated more than $300,000 to the Brown campaign. Or explored what it meant that Christen Varley, the founder and key organizer of the Greater Boston Tea Party, was the chair of her local Republican committee, blogged under the name GOPmom, and was employed by the Coalition for Marriage and Family, a group working to overturn gay marriage in Massachusetts.

A cry went up for Democrats to surrender on national health care reform and accept the verdict of the 100,000 citizens of Massachusetts that had provided Brown his margin of victory. With Brown's election, the Republican Senate caucus grew to 41, the magic number for mounting successful filibusters. For a few weeks, the fate of health care reform was touch and go. But Obama's legendary coolness proved to be a useful dam against the Democratic propensity to overreact, and Democratic leaders Nancy Pelosi and Harry Reid once again displayed their legislative acumen and devised a strategy with the White House to overcome a Republican filibuster. The complexities of the plan meant that there was no mechanism to strengthen the Senate bill, as progressives had hoped in December when they originally acceded to the measure after much protest.

On Sunday, March 21, the 45th anniversary of the historic civil rights march from Selma to Montgomery, the prelude to the 1965 Voting Rights Act that secured the vote for African Americans,

House Democrats knew they had the votes to pass health care reform. Before heading into the Capitol to take the vote, Georgia Representative John Lewis, who had been clubbed nearly to death by Alabama state troopers in the Selma campaign, steeled the Democratic caucus for the day by comparing the task before them to the historic struggle for black civil rights.

It was the first day of spring and the trees along the Washington Mall were still bare as Pelosi, Lewis, and other Democratic representatives linked arms to walk from the Cannon House Office Building to the Capitol. Pelosi was carrying the oversized gavel used to call the vote for Medicare in 1965. Along their path gathered hundreds of Tea Party protesters, angrily shouting "Drop Dead Pelosi" and "Kill the Bill." When the Congressional Black Caucus made their way through the crowd, protesters dropped the Kill the Bill chant and simply booed, in unison, until the African American legislators had disappeared through the door of the Capitol. The day before, Lewis and other civil rights movement veterans had endured shouts of "Nigger, Nigger, Nigger," while one protester spat on Representative Emanuel Cleaver. (The man was arrested but released when Cleaver declined to press charges.) In the days leading up to and including the vote, Representative Anthony Weiner received an anonymous note signed with a swastika. Tea Party protesters called representatives Ciro Rodriguez a "wetback," José Serrano an "elitist pig with a cutesy haircut," and Barney Frank a "faggot." When asked by reporters about the documented bigoted conduct of some of the protesters, Representative Steve King, a middle-aged white male evangelical from Iowa, said, "I just don't think it's anything. There are a lot of places in this country that I couldn't walk through. I wouldn't live to get to the other end of it." Another said, "When you use totalitarian tactics, people, you know, begin to act crazy," apparently referring to Congress's now twelve-month-long consideration of the health care bill.

Republicans in Congress cheered the protesters on, Dana Milbank of the *Washington Post* reported. While the House debated the bill, "dozens of GOP lawmakers walked from the chamber, crossed the Speaker's Lobby, stepped out onto the members-only House balcony—and proceeded to incite an unruly crowd." The elected members of Congress, Milbank continued, "whipped the masses into a frenzy. There on the House balcony, the GOP lawmakers' legislative dissent and the tea-party protest merged into one. Some lawmakers waved handwritten signs and led the crowd in chants of 'Kill the Bill.' A few waved the yellow 'Don't Tread on Me' flag of the tea-party movement. Still others fired up the demonstrators with campaign-style signs mocking [Pelosi]." Another reporter heard Representative Louie Gohmert bellow to the crowd below, "Remember the Alamo," a well-worn Texan battle cry. "If we lose this battle, millions of Americans are going to die." Representative Michele Bachmann egged on the protesters: "Don't be faint hearted, don't be weary of doing well with all your might today. Knock on those doors and make your case!"

On Sunday night, March 21, the House of Representatives voted to pass the Senate bill and thus pass health care reform. Despite the months devoted to crafting a bipartisan compromise, not one Republican in the House or Senate voted to support the bill, even though it included many of the compromises they had demanded. Half an hour after the vote, the president spoke, "This is what change looks like . . . We proved that this government, a government of the people and by the people, still works for the people."

On Tuesday morning, with 200 lawmakers assembled in the East Room of the White House, Obama took in his hand the pen with which President Lyndon Johnson had signed the Medicare act and signed health care reform, the Patient Protection and Affordable Care Act. Few Democrats thought the bill was perfect. Its main provisions would not go into effect for another four years, and until then most of the uninsured would remain uninsured and in the meantime, costs would not fall significantly. Some progressives were bitterly disappointed at the absence of a robust public insurance plan in the overhaul. Nevertheless, it set in motion the provision of health care to all Americans, an achievement that had eluded the Democratic Party for half a century. "Tonight, after nearly one hundred years of talk and frustration, after decades of trying, and a year of sustained effort and debate, the U.S. Congress finally declared that America workers and America's families and America's small businesses deserve the security of knowing that here in this country neither illness nor accident should endanger the dreams they've worked a lifetime to achieve."

In the days after the vote, Republicans swore their undying opposition to health care reform. Boehner and Senator Jim De Mint said the GOP would repeal the bill. McCain said he had serious doubts about its constitutionality. Representative Paul Ryan called it a "fiscal Frankenstein." On Tuesday, Palin tweeted "Don't Retreat— Reload." On Wednesday, she posted a map on her Facebook page, marking the districts of twenty Democrats who had voted for health care reform that her political action committee, SarahPAC, was targeting in the upcoming midterm elections. On Thursday, Minnesota Governor Tim Pawlenty and Minnesota Representative Michele Bachmann spoke at a closed-press fundraiser for the antiabortion PAC, the Susan B. Anthony List. "We don't honor the Constitution when we elevate a vague idea that is the right to privacy over the right to life," Pawlenty said, and urged the movement on for the fight. "Our values are under attack and under siege." Bachmann remarked, "I said I had very serious concerns that Barack Obama had anti-American views," referring to a call she had made during the 2008 election to investigate members of Congress for disloyalty. "And now I look like Nostradamus."

Outside Congress and the Republican Party, the rage against the bill spilled over into violence. At least ten Democratic representatives had their offices vandalized or received death threats. Bricks were thrown through the windows of the offices of Louise Slaughter. James Clyburn received a fax with a picture of a noose and threatening messages on his home phone. A coffin was placed on Mel Carnahan's front lawn by Tea Party protesters.

On Thursday, one of the targeted Democrats, Gabrielle Giffords, was interviewed by MSNBC and asked if she was fearful. Her Tucson office had been vandalized a few hours after the House vote; it was still unclear if a brick or a gunshot had shattered the glass door in front. Giffords said she wasn't afraid. She was used to the demonstrations, as the Tea Party had been protesting outside her office throughout the health care reform debates. Asked if Republican leaders should be speaking out more forcefully to calm people down, she explained that it was the responsibility of all community leaders, not just politicians, to speak up. "They need to realize that the rhetoric, firing people up, and you know, things for example, we're on Sarah Palin's targeted list, and the way she has it depicted has the cross-hairs of a gun sight over our district. When people do that, they've got to realize there are consequences to that action." MSNBC host Chuck Todd challenged her. Didn't campaigns always use war rhetoric? "Do you really think that's what she intended?" "You know, I can't say, I'm not Sarah Palin," Giffords answered. "What I can say is that in the years that some of my colleagues have served, 20 or 30 years, they've never seen it like this . . . Community leaders not just political leaders need to stand back when things get too fired up and say, whoa, let's take a step back here."

The Democratic National Committee agreed. On Friday, the DNC hand-delivered a proposed joint statement to the offices of the Republican National Committee calling on "elected officials of both parties to set an example of the civility we want to see in our citizenry." The statement went on to call for all Americans "to scale back rhetoric that might reasonably be misinterpreted" by those who were committing the violence. That week the RNC had raised $1 million with a letter that said "Fire Nancy Pelosi" and showed the speaker surrounded by flames. Michael Steele, the head of the RNC, declined to sign the joint civility statement.

15

THE TEA PARTY

A YEAR AFTER the Tea Party had burst on the scene, half of all Americans still hadn't heard enough about it to form an opinion. When detailed surveys of public opinion finally appeared shortly after health care reform passed, they showed that the Tea Party had few adherents. CBS News and the *New York Times* reported in April 2010 that just 4 percent of the general public had donated money or attended a Tea Party meeting or rally. To put this in perspective, during the 2008 presidential election, 40 percent of Americans said they had been active in similar ways. Only 21 percent of Americans viewed the Tea Party favorably, and even fewer, 18 percent, identified themselves as Tea Party supporters. Every nonpartisan survey following this one came to similar conclusions.

Not only was there no mass, grassroots upsurge behind the Tea Party, it was also far more homogeneous than its proponents claimed. Few Tea Party supporters were independents, moderates, Democrats, or hard-pressed working-class populists. Rather, they were whiter, wealthier, older, and more conservative than the population as a whole. At a moment when fewer than three out of ten Americans identified with the Republican Party, eight out of ten Tea Partiers identified themselves as Republicans. Nor were Tea Party supporters political neophytes. Only 10 percent had not voted in 2008, and 96 percent of those who did voted for McCain-Palin. Rather they were experienced political activists. Fully 43 percent had been active previously in a political campaign. They also held atypically positive views about polarizing Republicans such as George W. Bush and Sarah Palin. Two-thirds of Tea Party supporters viewed Palin favorably. Less than a third of the general public did.

No myth about Tea Partiers was more inaccurate than the one that they were overwhelmingly libertarians—that is, people who favor minimal government in all areas and value personal freedom above all else. The surveys showed that the Tea Party was full of sexual fundamentalists. Whereas most libertarians oppose any government intervention in personal life, two-thirds of Tea Party identifiers were conservatives who favored legislating so-called traditional morality. According to the CBS News/*New York Times* survey, four out of ten Tea Party supporters were born-again or evangelical Christians, and Tea Party identifiers were more religiously observant than other Americans. They held more conservative views not only on abortion and gay marriage but also on whether gay couples should be accorded any legal recognition. A later survey by the Public Religion Research Institute reported that only 11 percent of adults said they were "part of the Tea Party movement," and nearly half of those identified with the religious right. Racial resentment and anti-immigrant sentiment were also common within the Tea Party, as well as more prevalent within it than outside it. On every question gauging racial attitudes, Tea Partiers were prone to dismiss the idea that Americans still faced discrimination and quick to charge that Obama favored blacks, an atypical view among non–Tea Partiers. More than half said "too much" had been made of "problems facing black people" in recent years, an opinion not shared by non–Tea Partiers.

BEGUILED BY THE Tea Partiers' period costumes and quaint Revolutionary Era rhetoric of liberty and constitutionalism, the media had overlooked the shadow movement of sexual fundamentalists within it. All over the country there was evidence that the Tea Party and the Christian Right had become one, and their main target in the spring of 2010 was their own Republican Party.

In Texas, the birthplace of Lottie Beth Hobbs and Women Who Want to Be Women, the headquarters of Operation Rescue, and the proving ground for the Karl Rove strategy of stealth, the sexual fundamentalists secured total domination of the state Republican Party. Disguised in Tea Party garb, the Christian Right finally derailed Senator Kay Bailey Hutchison, a mainstream conservative, from her intended political path to the Texas governorship. Hutchison had never, to their lights, been sufficiently orthodox on abortion.

Instead, they endorsed the reelection of Governor Rick Perry, who at a March 2009 Tea Party rally had intimated that secession might be a reasonable response to the federal stimulus bill. "We got a great union. There's absolutely no reason to dissolve it. But if Washington continues to thumb their nose at the American people, who knows what may came of that." Perry's comment was met with chants of "Secede! Secede!"

The sexual counterrevolutionaries gained a majority on the Texas school board and rewrote the standards for teaching American history. They removed Thomas Jefferson, the author of the Declaration of Independence and the Founding Father who coined the phrase "separation of church and state," from the group of writers who influenced the ideas of the American Revolution. They required, however, that students study the contribution of Phyllis Schlafly to the American nation. The state Republican Party platform called not just for defining marriage as only for one man and woman, but for criminalizing gay marriage, gay sex, and even consensual sex between two straight minors. Perry, who assumed the governership after George W. Bush, had ended all sex education in the state and replaced it with a Christian-oriented abstinence-based curriculum. Texas had the highest rate of repeat teen births in the nation.

In Florida, the Tea Party scored a big trophy kill when they forced Florida Governor Charlie Crist out of the Republican Party and into a quixotic independent run for Florida's open U.S. Senate seat. A year earlier, Crist had been talked up among demoralized Republicans as one of the party's bright hopes. But Crist was a cultural moderate, who had vetoed antiabortion legislation and supported some civil rights for gay Americans. Crist also gratefully accepted federal stimulus money to help Florida's economy, one of the states hit hardest by the housing crisis. So had almost every other Republican governor, but Crist had literally embraced Obama in public.

In Maine, two pro-choice, moderate Republican U.S. senators, Olympia Snowe and Susan Collins were not up for reelection. But a Tea Party candidate won the Maine gubernatorial primary, and Republican delegates rewrote the state's moderate party platform. The new platform included typical Tea Party invocations of "respect for the U.S. constitution" and demand for "lower taxes and a responsible fiscal policy." In an original move, Maine Tea Party Republicans called for constitutional amendments to outlaw abortion and ban gay marriage, citing the U.S. Constitution's "domestic tranquility" clause as their inspiration—a novel interpretation of the clause as a mandate for enforced heterosexuality, which seemed to confuse the word "domestic"—as in domestic affairs as opposed to foreign affairs—with the domesticity of the traditional nuclear family.

IN THE MIDST of a political season in which the Tea Party had upended dozens of Republican primary races, *The New Yorker* published reporter Jane Mayer's exposé of the role of the Koch brothers in the Tea Party. The Kochs claimed to be libertarians, even though their businesses profited from government contracts and subsidies. In their past unsuccessful efforts to spark a Libertarian upsurge, they had experimented with the Tea Party concept and studied the Boston Tea Party as an instance of successful social protest. That the Kochs, with their extensive chemical and petroleum holdings, were in repeated violation of environmental laws, certainly gave an urgency to their philosophical fulminations against government regulation of the free enterprise system.

"The problem with the whole libertarian movement is that it's been all chiefs and no Indians," Bruce Bartlett, a conservative economist who has been critical of the Right, told Mayer. "There haven't been any actual people, like voters, who give a crap about it."

The Age of Obama had given the Kochs and other market fundamentalists an opportunity to attract some actual people to their historically unpopular goals of eviscerating middle-class government programs, such as Medicare and Social Security, while cutting taxes on the wealthy and eliminating government regulations of business.

The voters they were able to attract were the same sexual fundamentalists who had powered the rise of the Right within the Republican Party for forty years. Discredited as much as any single group by the Bush administration's overreach, they too were game for a makeover, and their most popular leader was perfectly suited to obscure the sexual counterrevolution under the more appealing new brand of the freedom-loving Tea Party.

In the escalating delirium, as in so much else in American popular culture after the 2008 election, it soon became all about Sarah Palin.

Even before Palin abruptly resigned her governorship in July of 2009, she had taken a stand as an early champion of the "freedom-loving" Tea Party. Soon after her resignation, she had touched off a firestorm with her charge about "death panels" in health care reform. Her full-time return to the public stage came with her national bus tour in November 2009 to promote her memoir, *Going Rogue*. Almost everywhere she went, hundreds if not thousands of fans, most of them women, waited in lines to see her in person. They screamed and hugged and jostled each other to get closer to their heroine. Palin's memoir and her speeches were full of libertarian Tea Party bromides about small government, fiscal conservatism, individual liberty, the U.S. Constitution, the Founding Fathers, and "the real America." "We felt our very normalcy, our status as ordinary Americans," Palin wrote in her memoir, "could be a much-needed fresh breeze blowing into Washington, D.C."

Palin had already proved to be an irresistible character, a kind of one-stop shop for Americans' insatiable appetite for melodrama, spectacle, and sensationalism. Palin, the Alaskan frontier individualist and former athlete, offered spectators the vicarious charge of the no-holds-barred competition of reality TV with her Twitter and Facebook fusillades aimed at her political opponents. In *Sarah Palin's Alaska*, a reality TV show that aired in the fall of 2010, Palin improbably but winningly claimed, "I'd rather be out here being free." In fact, she appeared supercharged by the thrill of the political brawl. Pundits and journalists developed an unhealthy co-dependent relationship with her, one that knew no ideological bounds. "Though it is embarrassing to admit this in public, I can no longer hide the truth. I have a Sarah Palin problem," veteran *Washington Post* commentator Dana Milbank wrote later, as he called on fellow journalists to "join me in [a] pledge of a Palin-free February." A flurry of coverage of the media's coverage of Palin followed. At the end of his Lent, Milbank declared success, although he acknowledged, "Yes, there was some transference of my addiction. I used Michele Bachmann as my methadone." Bachmann, a Minnesota representative who had first run for office to ban gay marriage, was the founder of the House Tea Party caucus.

Still, at the height of Tea Party mania after Scott Brown's victory in Massachusetts, Palin was the one crowned the queen of the Tea Party. In January, Fox News announced that they had hired Palin to be a paid commentator, with a contract rumored to be worth $1 million. In February 2010, Palin was paid $100,000 to give the keynote address at the first national gathering of Tea Party members. When right-wing blogger Andrew Breitbart hailed Palin at the National Tea Party Convention in Nashville as "the first person to tell us about the death panel," the crowd cheered. "I will live, I will die for the people of America," she swore. "This party that we call the Tea Party, this movement, as I say, is the future of politics in America." She left the stage to cries of "Run, Sarah, Run."

On May 14, 2010, Palin made a bid to appropriate feminism to add to her brand appeal and to reframe the upcoming 2010 midterm elections as the Year of the Republican Woman. She debuted her "common-sense conservative feminism" at a fundraiser for the antiabortion PAC, the Susan B. Anthony List, which endorsed both male and female candidates. The PAC had been a key behind-the-scenes player in the battle over abortion in health care reform, and it considered the vote to be a "career-defining" one. (After Stupak voted for the final bill, the group took back an award they had given him.) Ironically, Palin's claim to feminism was couched in terms almost identical to those used by Phyllis Schlafly to rally right-wing women against Republican feminists more than forty years earlier. After her speech, Palin Tweeted that a "cackle of rads" had hijacked feminism from its true founding mothers, "common sense conservatives" whose most cherished cause was ending abortion. On her Facebook page that week, Palin wrote that the upcoming victories of "conservative feminists" would fulfill the dreams of the suffragettes who, she claimed in contradiction to the historical record, cared primarily about ending abortion.

Palin certainly agreed with one basic feminist idea, that individual women were entitled to power as much as any man was, and her SBA List speech also won attention for Palin's new meme, the Mama Grizzly. Two weeks later, female candidates she had taken some political risk to endorse won their Republican primaries. Nikki Haley of South Carolina and Carly Fiorina of California were both successful businesswomen, biographical facts that cast them as common-sense fiscal conservatives, in the mainstream of American public opinion. Palin was cleverly taking a page from John McCain's playbook of cynical identity politics. What better proof that the Tea Party was just a bunch of regular Americans rising up for common sense than that the eminently practical American woman was behind it. At the very moment there was plain evidence of the resurgence of the Christian Right in state Republican politics, the media helpfully broadcast Palin's rebranding of the midterm election as the Year of the Republican Woman.

Hardly anyone bothered to observe that the "Mama Grizzly" candidates and the stampede of "pink elephant" voters were the fundamentalist heirs of the original female sexual counterrevolutionaries. The director of Beverly LaHaye's Concerned Women for America wrote of Palin, "She is beautiful and accomplished, has a hunk of a manly-man as a husband, and lovely children . . . Sarah Palin is the type of woman we want our daughters to emulate; she is a role model for young women in high school and college. She embodies the values of faith and family that young married mothers hold and want to pass along to their children." CWA was still on record claiming careers make women unhappy and child care is bad for children. Speaking at the evangelical Women of Joy conference a few weeks before her SBA List talk, Palin compared herself to Queen Esther, the wise biblical heroine who saved her people from destruction, and thanked the women who protected her with their "prayer shield." (Prayer shields were an old technique of the Southern Baptist–dominated CWA;

LaHaye had started them as a weapon to defeat the Equal Rights Amendment.) Evangelical women identified with Palin's veneration of her family, her evangelical faith, and her Christian patriotism; they thrilled to her uncompromising stand against abortion, sex education, and gay marriage.

The reductio ad absurdum of Palin's conservative feminism became manifest with three high-profile Tea Party endorsements late in the primary season. In the first, Palin's victim was a woman, the beneficiary a man. On August 24, Palin scored a major upset in the Alaska Republican primary, when Joe Miller, the Tea Party candidate she backed and funded, defeated Senator Lisa Murkowski. Murkowski was one of the most powerful women in the U.S. Senate and was in line to head the Energy and Natural Resources Committee should Republicans win control of the chamber. Palin spent enormous political capital to take her out. Although there was a lot of personal animosity between the two, the fundamental reason was that Murkowski is, by today's standards, something of a moderate Republican. She has voted to bar same-sex marriage but also to repeal Don't Ask Don't Tell; she opposes abortion but supports funding family planning programs through Planned Parenthood. Joe Miller ran as a small-government, freedom-loving Tea Partier, but he was endorsed by the Alaska chapters of the Eagle Forum, Right to Life, and Concerned Women for America. His victory in a low-turnout Republican primary was powered by the sexual fundamentalists who had been mobilized to vote by a ballot initiative mandating parental consent for any woman under 18 seeking an abortion. Palin had ensured the measure would be on the ballot shortly before her resignation the previous July.

Palin did lift a female "Mama Grizzly" to victory that same day, but by no stretch of the imagination was she a feminist. Sharron Angle of Nevada had long political experience in the trenches of the sexual counterrevolution. Her roots were at the juncture where the sexual counterrevolution and extreme Christian nationalism and nativism meet. She had been a member of the American Independent Party of Nevada, a branch of the far-right Constitution Party, whose stated goal "is to restore American jurisprudence to its Biblical foundations and to limit the federal government to its Constitutional boundaries." Angle's extremist statements were legion, but none more so than those calling for "second amendment solutions," advising rape victims to "to make a lemon situation into lemonade," and one denigrating working mothers for neglecting their duty to their family. She had also made ambiguous statements indicating a desire to either eliminate or radically transform Social Security. Palin's endorsement was significant in Angle's primary victory. Despite her extremism, Angle was not disavowed by the national Republican Party. When she emerged from the primary victorious but broke, Karl Rove came to her rescue. Rove's American Crossroads, a new fundraising entity created in the wake of the Supreme Court's *Citizens United* decision, which eliminated limits on corporate donations in elections, blitzed Nevada with ads against Angle's opponent, Senate Majority Leader Harry Reid. Once again, just as in the days of Clinton-hunting or John McCain's presidential campaign, leading Republicans pursued power at any cost.

In September, in the third case, Palin gave a game-changing endorsement to a candidate for the U.S. Senate in Delaware. Even though there was a genuine descendant of a Founding Father in the race, Palin and the Tea Party backed his opponent. (Mike Castle, a former governor of the state, and a popular nine-term U.S. representative, is a descendant of Benjamin Franklin." Castle was widely expected to win the seat that had been vacated by Joe Biden when he became vice president. He was a classic Republican moderate. On abortion, he had earned a good rating from Planned Parenthood and a zero from the National Life Committee. He had co-sponsored the embryonic stem cell research bill with former Republican Arlen Specter, a bill vetoed twice by Bush at the behest of the antiabortion movement but finally signed into law by Obama.

Palin endorsed Tea Party candidate Christine O'Donnell, an unmarried and childless evangelical who looked uncannily like Palin. With her Tea Party and Palin endorsements, O'Donnell gave off that female-empowered, freedom-loving, regular-American vibe. She was, so everyone said, as outsider as outsiders get. Soon, however, the clips from O'Donnell's years as a missionary for sexual fundamentalism went viral. In one of them, a segment of a 1990s MTV show, O'Donnell sits in a living room. With a huge smile and wide innocent eyes, she leans into the camera and says, "The Bible says that lust in your heart is committing adultery. You can't masturbate without lust!" O'Donnell's path to that MTV show started at the 1992 Republican Convention. Born-again and politically activated in college in the late 1980s, she had served as an elected delegate to the 1992 Republican Convention, where CNN first discovered the telegenic 23-year-old. Soon after, Beverly LaHaye's Concerned Women for America had hired her to be one of their media spokeswomen. After that job, O'Donnell founded her own organization, which promoted sexual abstinence until marriage. (The 41-year-old candidate, for the record, said she was chaste.) From the moment she won the Delaware primary, most observers doubted such an inexperienced candidate could win a general election. But when the MTV clip resurfaced, O'Donnell became the poster child of the season's anti-establishment delirium. It turned out she had left a long video trail of sensational jaw-dropping remarks. In one of her many guest appearances on Bill Maher's *Politically Incorrect*, O'Donnell had riffed about dabbling in witchcraft. To put that worry to rest, she cut an ad for her campaign for the United States Senate that began, "I am Not a Witch. I'm nothing you've heard. I'm you."

By the end of the primary season, the common denominator of Palin's Tea Party arithmetic had become manifest, and it was neither minimal government, nor fiscal conservatism, nor women's empowerment. Overwhelmingly, Palin's choices were zealous and experienced sexual counterrevolutionaries. And although her endorsees were not feminists, her targets overwhelmingly were. She singled out pro-choice Democratic women in swing or Republican-leaning districts, such as Colorado's Betsy Markey, Florida's Suzanne Kosmas, and Arizona's Gabrielle Giffords, and she weighed in strongly in governor's races, such as in Iowa and Wisconsin, where gay marriage, abortion, and birth control were in contention.

RUNNING ON A national message of job creation, minimal government, and fiscal discipline, the Republican Party picked up 63 seats in the 2010 midterm election to win control of the House of Representatives. The GOP also picked up six seats in the Senate—not enough to win control of the chamber—and six governorships. The

House Democratic caucus was reduced to a minority of fewer than 200 members, a nadir it had not seen since the 1920s. Republicans declared they had a mandate to repeal President Barack Obama's policies, above all, health care reform. Obama called the election a "shellacking" and began negotiating with himself in front of the television cameras.

According to conventional wisdom, the Age of Obama was at an end and the reign of the Tea Party had begun. It seemed that every news outlet had gone to their morgue, disinterred a headline from Bush's 2004 reelection or the 1994 Republican revolution, and merely added a splash of Tea Party color. The *New York Times* chose the Bush-era heartland trope in one headline: "Away from Coasts Democrats Seen As Declining Breed." The media largely ignored the Pew Center's finding, a few days after the election, that fewer than half of all Americans were happy with the Republican win.

Republicans in fact owed their sweep to a surge by the sexual fundamentalists operating under the cloak of the Tea Party. The 2010 electorate was substantially older, whiter, and more religious than the American population as a whole, as well as wealthier, more Republican, and more conservative than the 2008 electorate. According to exit polls, about half of all midterm voters attended religious services weekly, a 25 percent increase over 2008. Forty-two percent of voters described themselves as conservative, a 31 percent increase over its share for the last midterm election.

In only a few states did the exit poll include questions about religious belief and views on hot-button issues, but the limited results were revealing. In Iowa, almost four in ten voters were evangelical or born-again. Iowa voters recalled three state Supreme Court justices who had ruled that it was unconstitutional to prohibit gay marriage. They had been mobilized to vote by a campaign bankrolled by hundreds of thousands of dollars from organizations and political action committees run by Newt Gingrich and former Christian Coalition leader Ralph Reed. They elected a Christian Right governor and ousted the incumbent Democrat, Chet Culver. (Culver's father had met a similar fate in 1980, when sexual fundamentalists had been mobilized by Phyllis Schlafly's Eagle Forum to defeat a referendum on the ERA and to elect Charles Grassley to his first term in the

U.S. Senate.) Indiana, another heartland state, had gone for Obama in 2008 with a turnout of 59 percent. In 2010, Republicans picked up two seats in the House and the contested U.S. Senate seat, with a lackluster midterm turnout and 40 percent of all voters saying they identified with the Christian Right.

Rebranding seemed to have served the Republican Party and the sexual fundamentalists well. The Tea Party enabled Republicans to score an upset, despite the fact that 53 percent of midterm voters viewed the GOP negatively. The sexual counterrevolutionaries' adoption of the freedom-loving, small-government, fiscal-discipline frame likewise enabled them to sail under the radar among less informed voters. The one-quarter of voters who had a neutral opinion about the Tea Party favored Republican candidates. Although only a third of Tea Party affiliated candidates won their races, almost half of the eighty-seven Republican freshmen elected to the 112th Congress were Tea Partiers. Almost a third of them had been endorsed by Palin.

The Tea Party accomplished one other momentous feat: it induced the Democrats to overreact and ignore the voters who had put them in office. Intimidated by the exaggerated and misleading coverage of the Tea Party, the typical Democratic candidates typically pitched their message to potential Tea Party voters and ignored the Democratic base. These anxious candidates also prevailed upon the Democratic-controlled Congress to put off difficult votes. With Democrats in control of both houses of Congress and the presidency for the first time since 1994, Democrats never passed a budget. Some Democrats were terrified that allowing the Bush tax breaks for the wealthy to expire would give Republicans an opportunity to accuse them in campaign ads of raising taxes. The surviving Democrats would have many occasions over the next year to rue that evasion.

The response from ordinary Democratic voters, especially the newest ones, was collective demoralization. Forty million fewer Americans voted in 2010 than in 2008. In key swing states that had gone Democratic in the presidential election, such as Virginia, Ohio, Michigan, and Pennsylvania, midterm turnout fell. The so-called Obama-surge voters, the new voters who had carried the Democrats to a resounding victory in 2008, mostly stayed home. In 2008, voters under the age of 30 had made up a record 18 percent of the electorate and had outnumbered seniors. Youth turnout plunged 50 percent between 2008 and 2010; seniors made up a larger share of the electorate than they had since 1992. Turnout by unmarried women and African Americans plunged too. Among Obama's surge voters, only Latinos showed up in force, spurred by an outbreak of anti-immigrant extremism in the Republican Party.

Young voters, a survey for Rock the Vote (RTV) revealed, were angry about the bank bailout and concerned that corporations had too much control. They had watched in disbelief as Democrats had failed to pass the DREAM Act, which would have allowed college students and veterans who had been brought to the country illegally as young children to become naturalized citizens. They were unhappy that DADT hadn't been repealed. "The elections themselves just felt irrelevant to young people," RTV director Heather Smith told me. "Young voters felt that the Tea Party had no impact on them; they knew little about what it stood for." On the Democrats' strategy, Smith ventured, "It's like having a party and if you invite all the old white people to come, it's not a big surprise when this highly diverse group of young people doesn't come knocking on the door."

Yet in states where Democrats had gotten out the message about how far right Tea Party Republicans were on subjects ranging from Social Security to abortion and immigration, Democrats won. Tea Party Republicans who were the subject of extensive media coverage of their cultural extremism, such as Ken Buck of Colorado, Carl Paladino of New York, Linda McMahon of Connecticut, and Miller, O'Donnell, and Angle, all lost. In Colorado, antiabortion forces tried to relitigate a 2008 initiative defining a fertilized egg, "from the moment of conception," as a person. Buck favored it, a fact that Democratic Senate candidate Michael Bennet was pleased to publicize. The initiative was defeated with 71 percent of the vote; Bennet won with a staggering 17-point gender gap. The issue of legal abortion also redounded to the benefit of Democrats in Nevada, Washington, and California, as well as contributed to Murkowski's historic write-in victory against Miller. An unusually high turnout made the difference in some very close races. In Washington State, turnout hit a four-decade high, and Patty Murray held on to her Senate seat in an election rated by all the experts as a toss-up. Turnout for Murray's election was six points higher than it had been in 1994, when the sexual counterrevolutionaries' stealth campaign had wiped out the state's Democratic congressional delegation and unseated the Speaker of the House. High turnout, particularly among Latino and African American voters, led to a Democratic sweep in the nation's most populous state. In the California matchup between a progressive female incumbent and a Palin-branded Mama Grizzly, Democratic Senator Barbara Boxer handily defeated Carly Fiorina. Another Republican businesswoman, Meg Whitman, was running for governor, but just 39 percent of Californian women voted for the two women on the Republican ticket. Similarly, Buck, Angle, Fiorina, and O'Donnell all won less than 40 percent of the women's vote in their contests.

Democratic victory in these populous and diverse states was powerful testimony that unmasking the sexual fundamentalists and embracing a culturally progressive platform was a recipe for success. But it was a strategy only rarely ventured in the midterm elections of 2010.

BY JOINING THE Tea Party as a silent partner, the sexual counterrevolutionaries had taken a page from an old playbook—the one that had ushered the GOP back into power in 1994 and in 2000. Rebranding themselves as freedom-loving, Constitution-revering Tea Partiers, dozens of certifiable sexual counterrevolutionaries passed into office largely undetected. Eighty-seven Republican freshmen were poised to enter the House, many of them political neophytes. Thirty-nine of them were formally affiliated with or endorsed by the Tea Party, more than doubling the membership of the House Tea Party caucus founded by Bachmann a few months earlier. Yet again, the sexual fundamentalists had put the Republican Party in power through stealth.

This time, however, the sexual fundamentalists had turned their pitchforks on the Republican establishment. In just nineteen months, almost every Republican cultural moderate up for election had been dispatched to the political graveyard. And every Republican left standing snapped to attention.

16

ENDGAME

THE 2010 MIDTERM elections infused the GOP with hope of capturing the White House in 2012, yet the apparent success of the Tea Party complicated the path to victory.

The presidential primary season opened with three Republicans in the lead: Mitt Romney, Mike Huckabee, and Sarah Palin. Romney was experienced at running a government and running for president, but not personally popular. Palin was popular but polarizing. Huckabee had experience and was also broadly popular.

Huckabee, in his 2008 presidential attempt, he had won the media's affection by playing the warm-hearted conservative populist while deflecting questions about his theocratic politics. But now his perch as a paid commentator for Fox News threatened to give wider play to some of the unusual views of the former governor and past president of the Arkansas Southern Baptist Convention. In February, Huckabee claimed gay marriage would lead to polygamy, essentially equated homosexuality with murder and stealing, and promised to use the constitutional powers of the presidency against "dysfunctional" families that lacked both a mother and a father. Then he said Obama was raised in Kenya, corrected himself, and explained what he meant was that the president had a "different world view" because of his exotic upbringing. "This is not a kid who grew up going to boy scout meetings and playing little league baseball in a small town." In March, Huckabee inveighed against an unmarried Natalie Portman for appearing in public "visibly pregnant" to accept her Oscar for Best Actress. "It's unfortunate that we glorify and glamorize the idea of out of wedlock children." Ultimately Huckabee decided not to run. Asked why by Reverend Pat Robertson, he answered, "the atmosphere right now is so toxic."

Huckabee's departure left the votes of the sexual fundamentalists available to be claimed by someone else. Palin appeared to be best positioned to step into the gap. Of the three early frontrunners, Palin emerged from the 2010 midterms with the most momentum. Only the Koch brothers and Dick Armey's FreedomWorks could claim more statistically significant wins than Palin. Resigning from her governorship seemed to have hurt her little with Republican voters. The governors of Iowa and South Carolina, in which two key early contests in the Republican primary took place, were especially beholden to Palin.

At the moment everyone expected her to pivot to a formal presidential run, Palin stumbled badly.

On Saturday January 8, Representative Gabrielle Giffords was holding a "Congress on Your Corner" at a supermarket in suburban Tucson when a man walked up and shot her point blank in the head. He then opened fire with a semi-automatic 9-millimeter pistol, killing six and wounding thirteen.

For months, Democrats, political observers, and Giffords herself had been calling on public figures to dial down their inflammatory political rhetoric. Six months earlier, Palin's SarahPAC had published an image of sniper cross-hairs over Giffords's district, metaphorically suggesting that Giffords be targeted for her vote in favor of health care reform. Although reporting about the shooter Jared Lee Loughner revealed in the following days that he was mentally deranged, many people gave voice that day to their anger and fear that the shooting had been politically motivated and encouraged by the toxic political environment. Palin and her cross-hairs map were singled out, as were Glenn Beck and Sharron Angle, the defeated

Senate candidate who had talked of "second amendment solutions."
That weekend the map was pulled from Palin's sites. Palin issued a
statement condemning the shooting and sending her support to the
families of the victims.

Four days later, the House delayed its planned vote on H.R. 2,
"Repealing the Job-Killing Health Care Act," to pass a resolution
condemning the attack and honoring Giffords. Later that day, President Obama spoke in Tucson at a memorial service for the victims.
Obama detailed the life stories of the six people killed, quoted liberally from scripture, and called on Americans to transcend partisanship—"to listen to each other more carefully, to sharpen our instincts
for empathy and remind ourselves of all the ways that our hopes and
dreams are bound together."

That same morning, Palin released a video made in her state-of-
the-art home television studio. Seated in front of a stone fireplace
with a large flag at her side, she offered her sympathy to the victims' families yet spent the better portion of the nearly eight-minute
video casting herself as the aggrieved victim. Uninterrupted by the
cheers of encouraging fans and her trademark quips, Palin's speech
presented a stark and discordant vision of unfounded resentment and
paranoia. "Especially within hours of a tragedy unfolding," Palin
said, "journalists and pundits should not manufacture a blood libel
that serves only to incite the very hatred and violence that they pur-
port to condemn. That is reprehensible." Most observers found it
reprehensible that Palin equated the criticism she experienced as a
public official to a "blood libel," the anti-Semitic superstition that
had triggered deadly attacks on Jews in medieval Europe. (Gabrielle
Giffords happens to be Jewish.) Palin went on to pledge defiance to
her critics. "We will not be stopped from celebrating the greatness
of our country and our foundational freedoms by those who mock
its greatness by being intolerant of differing opinion and seeking to
muzzle dissent with shrill cries of imagined insults."

The Republican establishment took advantage of Palin's self-
dramatization to strike. Insider Beltway publications like *Politico*
ran anonymously sourced articles about how the GOP was going to
stop her from becoming president. Karl Rove and others went public
with their doubts about her quality and viability as a candidate. Her

original cheerleader, Bill Kristol, said Palin "probably shouldn't be the Republican nominee for president." Palin scaled back her political speeches, her public appearances, and her social media posts. She continued, however, to give speeches to smaller church groups and conservative organizations. She traveled to Israel and India, two important American allies, keeping alive the speculation that she intended to run. Most pundits predicted she would not and surmised that she was just trying to cash in on her celebrity. Still, two out of three Republican and Republican-leaning independents, the people who voted in Republican primaries, viewed her favorably.

Romney steadily held a solid lead in most national polls of Republican voters. In any other year, the Republican establishment would have been delighted to run a man such as Romney against a Democrat. He positively exuded the aura of sane, respectable, corporate Republicanism. Here was a man who could rescue the nation from the economic abyss by applying the eternal wisdom of the rugged American capitalist. Born into an affluent family, he had also made a fortune at Bain Capital, a private equity firm, by buying other companies with borrowed money and dismantling them to make them profitable to the shareholders. He had even saved the 2002 Salt Lake City Winter Olympics from scandal and financial disaster. True, Romney was somewhat challenged on the charisma front. The *Huffington Post*'s daily D.C. wrap-up, HuffPost Hill, took to calling him the "Romneybot," as in "Algorithm-driven techno-human Mitt Romney, who would make history as our nation's first Mormon AND firewire-compatible president." Romney also seemed out of sync with the season's right-wing Tea Party populism. "My friend, corporations are people too," he declared with a cockeyed smile, sweating atop a hay bale at the Iowa State Fair.

In 2008, Romney had campaigned hard for the votes of the sexual fundamentalists by repudiating the beliefs he had told Massachusetts voters he held. For 2012, he positioned himself from the start for a general election run against Obama. Although he did not waver from his antiabortion and antigay vows to the base, he was ever so careful to keep a healthy distance from the movement's enthusiasts. Romney supported a constitutional amendment to ban gay marriage, said he would restore DADT, and was explicit that he hoped to see *Roe v. Wade* overturned by his Supreme Court appointees. But he refused to sign the Susan B. Anthony List PAC's antiabortion pledge, which would have committed him to applying an antiabortion litmus test to every one of his appointees, not just judges and Supreme Court nominees. He used the occasion of the Family Leader Pledge, sponsored by a powerful Iowa antigay activist, to denounce extremism. (The pledge, purportedly in defense of "traditional marriage," was as bizarre as it was extreme. Its original preamble claimed that African American children had been better off in slavery than they were today, because they had lived in intact families. Of course, the premise was empirically false and morally repugnant. It also demanded candidates pledge sexual loyalty to their spouse.) Indeed, Romney pivoted off the season's right-wing mania for pledges as a way to bolster his image as a sane Republican, just as George W. Bush had once cast himself as "a different kind of Republican" by throwing stage punches at the Christian Right.

Yet Romney's signature accomplishment as Massachusetts governor rendered him acutely vulnerable in the Republican primary. Romney had spearheaded a drive for universal health care, and the state's program had become the template for the 2010 Affordable Care Act, mandate and all. Antipathy to health care reform was one of the few issues that united the various factions of the Republican Right. Polls indicated that Romney had the best chance to beat Obama in the general election, but it was hard to fathom how the father of health care reform could prevail in the Republican primary.

Leading conservatives and establishment Republicans started to worry. So they embarked on a desperate courtship of those who seemed able to surmount the party's perennial dilemma—how to win the sexual fundamentalists in the primary and still appear credible to the mainstream voter in the general election. Rich Lowry, the editor of the conservative *National Review*, was particularly enamored of Mitch Daniels, the Indiana governor and one of the architects of George W. Bush's tax cuts. Daniels "seems temperamentally incapable of unseriousness; he is the anti-panderer . . . He's the kind of guy who makes you think, 'He should run for president—and probably won't.'" George Will lauded Daniels's "conservatism for grownups." Daniels had a year earlier famously called on his party to put "social issues" on hold to deal with the economic crisis. Nonetheless, while Daniels mulled over the idea of running, he became the first governor to sign a law defunding Planned Parenthood. Ultimately Daniels declined to run.

Perhaps Republican voters could settle for another former governor. On paper, Tim Pawlenty seemed well suited to mount a George W. Bush–style stealth campaign. Pawlenty was a born-again evangelical who opposed abortion, gay marriage, and the repeal of DADT. He had won two terms as governor of a Democratic-leaning state. He had cut taxes, ostensibly balanced the budget, and displayed an ability to work in a bipartisan fashion. But Pawlenty sorely lacked W's charisma—John McCain's team had passed him up for the vice presidential nomination because they thought he was too vanilla.

More fatally, even as Pawlenty campaigned to the right, he kept getting upstaged by the true believers. Likely Republican voters flocked to fringe candidates who were highly unlikely to be elected president. Herman Cain, former CEO, inspirational speaker for the Koch Brothers' Americans for Prosperity, associate Baptist minister, and talk radio host had never won an election but won the first GOP debate and briefly rose to the top of the polls. Cain, who was a cancer survivor, believed "my life was spared because God had something really big that he wanted me to do. And that's unfolding." The presidential candidate did not believe that the First Amendment's protection of freedom of religion did not apply to Muslims. "Islam combines church and state. They're using the church part of our First Amendment to infuse their morals in that community." At least the delirious real estate tycoon Donald Trump, who briefly surfed the Birther conspiracy to the top of the polls, retired to the haven of his reality TV show, utterly deflated by Obama's release of his birth certificate and the public's ephemeral surge of approval for the president after the Navy Seals raid that killed Osama Bin Laden.

"None of them are going to be president of the United States," Republican consultant Steve Schmidt predicted, speaking about Trump, Newt Gingrich, and Palin, who continued to intimate she was going to run. (Schmidt had played a key role in choosing Palin to be McCain's running mate but had long since changed his mind about her.) "None of them is going to be the Republican nominee. But you've had this theater of the absurd taking place over the course of much of the spring. In there somewhere is a serious campaign waiting to get started."

It is doubtful that Michele Bachmann, a woman much like Palin, was the one Schmidt had been waiting for.

IN DEFERENCE TO the theatrical sensibilities of his Tea Party freshmen, Speaker John Boehner instituted a new ritual to swear in the 112th Congress. On January 6, 2011, Representatives took turns reading aloud from the full text of the U.S. Constitution.

First on the Republicans' agenda was the repeal of the health care reform law. Next was the attempt to undo one hundred years of bipartisan progressive legislation. During every other economic downturn since the late 1930s, Democratic and Republican administrations alike had increased federal spending and run deficits in efforts to restore economic growth. No more. Budget cutting was the order of the day, while right-wing Republican fulminations against the Federal Reserve cowed the Fed into scaling back its efforts to stimulate economic growth with an expansionary monetary policy. Investing in America's crumbling infrastructure, a tried and true method of creating jobs while gaining long-term benefit? Republican governors rejected funding for high-speed rail. Environmental protection, long proven by economists to be fully compatible with economic growth and by scientists to have saved millions of lives? Efforts to defund and neuter the EPA, repeal environmental regulations, and open public lands to private exploitation took a backseat only to efforts to legislate labor unions and Planned Parenthood out of existence.

Any casual student of American history could tell you this was not your mother's Republican Party. Abraham Lincoln, besides saving the Union and issuing the Emancipation Proclamation, presided over the building of the Transcontinental Railroad. Dwight D. Eisenhower created the federal highway system, and Richard Nixon established the EPA and started Title X, the federally funded family planning program. George H. W. Bush established the first cap-and-trade program to reduce pollution. Ronald Reagan raised taxes to reduce the budget deficit created by his tax cuts, military spending, and a recession, and George W. Bush bailed out the American auto industry and the banks. Theodore Roosevelt was the first to set aside land in the Grand Canyon for a national park; his Republican heirs introduced a rider to the 2012 Interior Appropriations bill to fast-track uranium mining in the national forest bordering the majestic park.

The 112th Congress's first major partisan battle over the federal budget revealed how much of the change in the GOP could be laid at the doorstep of the sexual counterrevolution, currently doing business as the Tea Party. In early April 2011, House Republicans brought the U.S. government of the United States to the brink of shutting down over funding for Planned Parenthood, with the deceptive claim that they were stopping taxpayer dollars from funding abortion. Federal funding for abortion was of course already prohibited. The measure instead targeted $300 million in Title X funding, which provided states with matching funds for family planning and women's health services. Republican obstructionism was only breached after Democratic Senators Harry Reid and Charles Schumer went public that Republicans were holding the budget hostage over birth control and reproductive health services. Just 90 minutes before the government was to shut down for lack of funding, Republicans relented and voted for a budget that preserved the Title X funding. Boehner promised he would revisit the fight with a stand-alone bill.

A week later, Republicans tackled a few issues that more clearly affected Americans' economic well-being. On April 15, House Republicans voted unanimously for Wisconsin Representative Paul Ryan's budget, which would if implemented turn Medicare into a voucher system, raise taxes on the middle class, and cut in half the taxes paid by the richest one percent. The display of party unity, however, masked internal dissension. The Ryan plan had been so unpopular in polling and focus groups that veteran legislators and staffers for the National Republican Congressional Committee implored the leadership to forgo a vote. *Politico* reported that Boehner bulldozed ahead anyway, in order to "scratch the Tea Party itch." When House Republicans went home in late April and held town hall meetings, their constituents castigated them for undermining Medicare and refusing to raise taxes on the wealthy. Gallup found disapproval of the Republican Congress higher than it had been for the Democratic congress on the eve of the 2010 midterm. Negative views of the Tea Party had risen to an all-time high, with 57 percent of moderates holding an unfavorable view of the Tea Party. Undeterred, as soon as they returned to Washington Republicans voted to pass the "No Taxpayer Funding for Abortion Act".

A similar imperviousness to political reality and submission to the sexual fundamentalists gripped the states where the midterm elections had left Republicans in control of 29 governorships and 25 state legislatures. In Wisconsin, under the cover of a budget emergency, Republican Governor Scott Walker eliminated collective bargaining rights for teachers and other public employees. He also defunded Planned Parenthood, repealed the state's new "contraceptive equity" program to require insurers to cover birth control, and threw men out of the state family planning program. Texas, in the midst of a budget crisis, adopted a law requiring women seeking an abortion to undergo a sonogram and listen to a doctor read a state-prescribed description of the fetus. Governor Rick Perry had designated the bill an "emergency priority" to fast-track it. Republicans introduced hundreds of laws at the state and federal level. Ostensibly to limit abortion and end taxpayer funding for abortion, the laws in reality cut funding for birth control and reproductive health care, imposed a bevy of new regulations on doctors and private health insurers, and raised taxes on small businesses. Texas, which ranked third worst in teen pregnancy and worst in repeat teen pregnancy, reduced funding for family planning by two-thirds. Montana eliminated family planning funding altogether. Five states defunded Planned Parenthood's provision of reproductive health services. In the first six months of 2011, GOP-dominated states enacted 80 laws restricting abortion, a 347 percent increase in antiabortion legislation compared to the previous year.

So much for the Tea Party Republicans' promise to fix the economy and devote themselves to job creation. The Tea Party sexual counter-revolutionaries were playing a three-dimensional shell game, and the media kept getting played.

AS THE SUMMER boiled over in a record-breaking heat wave, 15 million Americans remained unemployed and economists began to warn there was a one-in-three chance the United States was heading into a double-dip recession. It seemed the only good news so far in 2011 was that Osama Bin Laden was dead.

Meanwhile, the United States stood on the precipice of default. Standard & Poor's, Moody's, the International Monetary Fund, and the world's leading economists warned that the credit rating of the United States would be downgraded without a vote in Congress to raise the statutory debt limit. Congress had uneventfully raised the debt limit 74 times since 1962. This time, however, Tea Party and freshmen Republicans were refusing to do so unless the deal included a balanced budget amendment, trillions of dollars in cuts, and no new revenues.

Clearly it was a moment for national leadership.

President Obama, having insisted seven months earlier that no sane elected official would dally with the nation's creditworthiness, offered a so-called Grand Bargain. Negotiated in secret with the Republican leadership and Reid, the deal was rumored to contain dramatic changes to Social Security and Medicare for the small price of closing some tax loopholes to bring in additional revenue. (Obama excluded House Minority Leader Nancy Pelosi from the talks. Word had it that she would demand too much and thus not be helpful.) Speaker John Boehner protested that his hands were tied, as many in his caucus believed "if we have enough chaos, we could force the Senate and the White House to accept a balanced budget amendment."

Seasoned politicians and economic leaders warned the novice legislators that they were endangering the stability of the global economy and the nation's credit rating with their maximalist posturing. Utah Senator Mike Lee, the insurgent Tea Party candidate who had knocked off one of the staunchest conservative incumbents in 2010, responded that he wanted America's "house to come down." Senator Rand Paul characterized a potential failure to raise the debt ceiling as "a temporary inconvenience." His father, GOP presidential candidate Ron Paul, mused that a U.S. Government default might be salutary: "Maybe people will say, 'hey, maybe they're serious!' And maybe it would be a positive." Palin, still playing coy about her presidential ambitions, took to Facebook on the eve of a critical House vote to urge members to vote no on raising the debt ceiling: "remember us 'little people'," the "commonsense patriots" who voted them into office. And "P.S. Everyone I talk to still believes in contested primaries." In the last week of July, as another round of negotiations broke down and the stock market turned in its worst week of the year on fears of default, Romney played it both ways, remaining mum about how he thought Republicans should vote while "applaud[ing] Speaker Boehner for standing firm against raising taxes when our nation can least afford them."

In such a moment it did not seem surprising when a writer for the liberal *New Yorker* suggested that the Republican Party had gone "raving mad." More surprising was the normally temperate, pro-business *New York Times* columnist Joe Nocera, who likened Tea Partiers to Jihadists. He apologized a few days later for his intemperance. When conservatives joined the chorus of lament, it was clear that a new low in American political dysfunction had been reached. Charles Krauthammer, a columnist on the Right, called out the holdouts for acting "counter-constitutional." McCain took to the floor of the Senate to denounce his House colleagues as "Tea Party Hobbits." He was reading, no less, from the ultraconservative editorial page of Rupert Murdoch's *Wall Street Journal*: "This is the kind of crack political thinking that turned Sharron Angle and Christine O'Donnell into GOP Senate nominees."

Just a few hours before the Treasury was projected to run out of funds to pay U.S. creditors, Congress voted to raise the debt ceiling. Republicans crowed about their victory. Boehner boasted that the deal gave him "98 percent of what I wanted." "I think some of our members may have thought the default issue was a hostage you might take a chance at shooting," Senate Minority leader Mitch McConnell told the *Washington Post*. "Most of us didn't think that. What we did learn is this—it's a hostage that's worth ransoming." Nearly a century of routine Congressional votes to raise the debt ceiling were over. McConnell, the top Republican in the U.S. Senate, promised that brinkmanship over the nation's debt would be his new normal.

Two days after Obama signed the debt ceiling agreement, all

the gains made in the major U.S. markets in 2011 were erased as the Dow Jones and most markets around the world dropped more than 4 percent. The next day, after the markets closed on Friday, Standard & Poor's announced that it was downgrading the U.S. from a AAA credit rating. The agency conceded that their initial estimate included a $2 trillion calculation error but went ahead anyway, citing their concern about America's broken political system. After Republicans took up the talking point "the Obama downgrade," an S&P director clarified that a main reason for the rating was the Republicans' cavalier attitude about default. "That a country even has such voices, albeit a minority, is something notable," he said. "This kind of rhetoric is not common amongst AAA sovereigns."

Asked for "one single word to describe your impression of the budget negotiations in Washington," Americans volunteered "crazy," "disgusting," "stupid," and "juvenile." Two-thirds of the American public called them "ridiculous." In the weeks after the debt ceiling crisis, polls registering record levels of dissatisfaction poured in from every major survey firm and every major news outlet. Obama's approval rating fell to its lowest level yet, but Congress and the GOP fared even worse. Approval of Congress plunged to an all-time low, while disapproval of the Republican Party rose to record highs.

The group that plummeted most in the public's esteem was the Tea Party. Reviewing extensive polling data for a revised edition of their book *American Grace*, the eminent political scientists David Campbell and Robert Putnam discovered that the Tea Party "ranks lower than any of the 23 other groups we asked about—lower than both Republicans and Democrats. It is even less popular than much maligned groups like 'atheists' and 'Muslims.'"

"Interestingly, one group that approaches it in unpopularity is the Christian Right." As Putnam and Campbell confirmed, there was little meaningful distinction between the Tea Party and the Christian Right. "The Tea Party's generals may say their overriding concern is a smaller government, but not their rank and file, who are more concerned about putting God in government." That was, according to Campbell and Putnam, why 40 percent of Americans in their survey viewed the Tea Party unfavorably. "It is precisely this infusion of religion into politics that Americans increasingly oppose.

While over the last five years Americans have become slightly more conservative economically, they have swung even further in opposition to mingling religion and politics. It thus makes sense that the Tea Party ranks alongside the Christian Right in unpopularity."

To many people, these findings about the Tea Party seemed counterintuitive. Those political activists who most wanted to interfere in the most intimate areas of private life did not seem to be the sort who would become impassioned about the size of government, debt, deficits, and monetary policy. Those issues seemed the province of the corporate elite and the doctrinaire libertarians, in other words, of what the Tea Party was conventionally thought to be.

How was this mystery to be explained? By the long-standing alliance between the sexual counterrevolution and other factions of the Right.

Since the late seventies, right-wing market fundamentalists had sought to attract voters to their cause by linking their economic policy goals to the cultural concerns of the grassroots sexual fundamentalists. That project originated in political calculation and was funded by special interests, yet it had been eased by the philosophical affinity between the two groups. Throughout American history, there have been Christians who believe that the traditional Christian virtues are the road to wealth, who interpret wealth as a sign of God's good favor and failure as the wages of sin, or who appreciate how the untrammeled competitive marketplace serves to forge Christian virtues of self-denial. As many a historian, sociologist, and economist have noted, capitalism and Protestantism are eminently compatible.

So when leaders of the New Right first approached middle-class, traditionalist, white fundamentalists in the run-up to Ronald Reagan's election, they were more or less preaching to the choir. Over the years, however, the balance of power in the Republican Party had substantially shifted. Reagan, for example, enacted many of the Right's economic wishes, but he essentially ignored the sexual fundamentalists' cultural agenda, prompting them to grouse that the president had his priorities wrong. Reagan, of course, prevailed in that contest of wills.

The Republicans' spectacular overreach throughout 2011 was proof that the establishment and conservative business interests had lost control to the sexual counterrevolutionaries. Neither Wall Street nor veteran Republican leaders desired a showdown over the debt ceiling. Business might not favor Democrats, higher taxes, or financial regulation, but in times of recession, they were pragmatic Keynesians and eager recipients of bailouts. They knew slashing the federal budget when the housing market remained depressed and unemployment was high would only further depress demand and stall a recovery. They could do the math to understand that the long-term federal deficit could not be reduced without more revenue.

By the Age of Obama, all of this pragmatic thinking was irrelevant to the sexual fundamentalists. They favored low taxes and less government, not just because it accorded with their individualism, but also because shrinking the federal government would deprive Democrats of the political means to impose science, sex education, gay marriage, gay civil rights, family planning, women's autonomy, and child care on the nation.

A few little-noticed eruptions of right-wing outrage during 2011's summer of delirium illustrate how the catchphrases of liberty, minimal government, and budget stringency served the sexual counterrevolutionaries' campaign to drag an unwilling nation back to a time when sex outside heterosexual marriage was risky, shameful, and even illegal.

"History should be honest," Governor Jerry Brown said as he signed a bill requiring California public schools to teach about the accomplishments of gay people. The law was motivated, in part, by an alarming wave of suicides by gay teens bullied by their peers, and even more, by a gruesome murder of a gay eighth-grader in his Oxnard, California, classroom by a 14-year-old classmate who claimed the murdered boy had come on to him. A few weeks after Brown signed the bill into law and one week after the resolution of the debt ceiling crisis, Phyllis Schlafly devoted her daily radio address to the new California law. Unsurprisingly, the veteran antigay agitator caricatured the bill, for example, by insinuating that its purpose was to convert first graders to a "gay lifestyle." She cast antigay teachers as victims of censorship and claimed the law violated parents' rights. She then sealed her case with exaggerated claims about excessive government spending, "the law will force taxpayers to replace textbooks and other school materials at a time when California is facing a massive fiscal crisis," and closed with a warning: "Parents you had better check in to what your state legislators, school boards, and school curriculum committees are deciding what to teach your children." Schlafly's 3-Minute Daily Radio Commentary, which she had been producing since the early days of the sexual counterrevolution, concluded with this announcement: "Here are at the Eagle Forum we continue to monitor the dangerous activities and liberal agendas of many school districts."

On August 1, the Obama administration issued regulations requiring private health insurers to cover the cost of contraceptives with no charge to the insured. (The power to issue this ruling derived from the health care reform law.) The administration was acting on the recommendation of medical experts that contraception qualified as preventive health care, and polls showed that 75 to 80 percent of Americans supported the policy. The lobbyists of the sexual counterrevolution quickly churned into action. In a piece published by the Fox News Opinion blog, Penny Nance, CEO of Concerned Women for America, not only condemned the birth control provision but also another regulation issued that day that required health insurers to cover the price of breast pumps. "You and I will pay more in premiums," she complained, while calling the measure "another very telling perk for working mothers." She then demanded the money be spent on tax credits, a proposal that, unlike the regulation, would in fact cost taxpayers money. But mostly she relied on Tea Party–esque appeals to liberty and small government. "Clearly, a government brazen enough to get involved in our most intimate mother-child relationship respects no boundaries in our lives. I'll say it: 'Uncle Sam, get out of our blouses and off our backs.'" CWA was still, of course, seeking to rewrite the U.S. Constitution to criminalize abortion and forever prohibit gay marriage.

Notwithstanding their patently contradictory stance about government interference in private life and their strategic use of Tea Party rhetoric, the sexual counterrevolutionaries in fact did believe that reducing the size and scope of government would in a practical sense serve their cultural objectives. Listening closely to them, however, reveals a different animating passion: hysteria about uncontrolled sex, women's in particular. "Why in the world would you encourage your daughters, and your granddaughters, and whoever else comes behind you to have unrestricted, unlimited sex anytime, anywhere, and that, somehow if you prevent pregnancy, that somehow you've helped them?" a spokeswoman for Family PAC said on Fox News in response to the ruling on insurance coverage. "I would submit to you that uncontrolled sexual behavior is what is harming our girls, not our lack of birth control."

Such views were not confined to the movement but were ably represented in the Republican Party. The day Representative Steve King voted against raising the debt ceiling, he asked to be recognized on the floor of the House. King started by attacking big government and defending the little guy: "We have people that are single, we have people that are past reproductive age, we have priests that are celibate. All of them, paying insurance premiums that cover contraceptives so that somebody else doesn't have to pay the full fare of that?" Never mind that this is the very essence of insurance, and every insured person could say the same about thousands of medical treatments they don't need or use. But King was soon suggesting that recreational sex, even among married men and women, was destroying American civilization. "And they've called it preventative medicine. Preventative medicine. Well if you applied that preventative medicine universally what you end up with is you've prevented a generation. Preventing babies from being born is not medicine. That's not—that's not constructive to our culture and our civilization. If we let our birth rate get down below replacement rate we're a dying civilization."

LIKE SO MAY other Tea Party sexual fundamentalists, Michele Bachmann appreciated the value of rebranding. In her carefully scripted announcement of her candidacy during a June Republican debate, Bachmann positioned herself as a champion of small government, personal liberty, and free enterprise. She had, in fact, been a devoted foot soldier in the shadow movement of sexual fundamentalists for thirty-five years, a zealous participant in almost every single cause of the sexual counterrevolution.

At the age of 20, Michele and her future husband Marcus Bachmann volunteered for the 1976 presidential campaign of the evangelical Jimmy Carter. But after seeing the antiabortion film, *What Happened to the Human Race*, made by the fundamentalist theologian Francis Schaeffer, the born-again couple turned against Carter. The Bachmanns were done with the Democratic party; Michele and Marcus volunteered for Ronald Reagan's 1980 presidential campaign. "We had new eyes that were opened up as we understood life now from a Biblical world view," Bachmann told Iowa voters on the campaign trail in 2011.

For the next two decades, Bachmann was a grassroots activist in the antiabortion and Christian home-schooling movements. She attended a Christian law school and helped out on a book that argued that America was founded as a Christian theocracy and that Christians must work to change American law to accord with the Bible. Marcus also devoted himself to advancing the sexual counterrevolution. He earned two graduate degrees in counseling, the first at Reverend Pat Robertson's Regent University, and focused both his thesis and his dissertation on the evil effects of child care. (Michele quit work and home-schooled their five children once Marcus was making enough money from his Christian counseling business.) Like thousands of other sexual fundamentalists, Bachmann first ran for elected office by injecting abortion politics into a school board election. Bachmann lost that race, but she joined a group of right-wing activists who massed at the 2000 Minnesota state Republican convention to overthrow the moderates in the party. Bachmann put herself forward as a candidate, beat an incumbent moderate Republican, and then won election to the state senate by promising to ban gay marriage—even though Minnesota already banned gay marriage. In 2006, she won a seat in the U.S. House, again running against gay marriage and abortion.

Bachmann quickly surged into second place in the 2012 GOP race with the support of Christian Right voters. But the more voters got to know about her, the less they liked. She and Marcus had simply spoken too freely on the public record to persuade ordinary Americans that they were anything other than Christian Right and antigay fanatics. Bachmann claimed to be a states' rights purist but swore she'd fight for a federal constitutional amendment that would end gay marriage in the states. She promised to restore DADT, regardless of what military commanders might think best for national security. Likewise she would make abortion illegal, even if the life of the mother was at stake. Just a year earlier, Marcus had been asked on talk radio about what to do with a teenager who might be experimenting with homosexuality. He answered, "I think you clearly say what is the understanding of God's word on homosexuality . . . We need to understand that barbarians need to be educated. They need to be disciplined." Just five years earlier, the woman who was putting herself forward to be America's first woman president had told voters she had become a tax lawyer because her husband told her to. "My husband said, 'Now you need to go and get a post-doctorate degree in tax law.' Tax law! I hate taxes—why should I go and do something like that? But the Lord says be submissive. Wives, you are to be submissive to your husbands. I was going to be faithful to what I felt God was calling me to do through my husband."

"Michele Bachmann says certain things that sound crazy to the general public," Frank Schaeffer, the son of the theologian who converted the Bachmanns to the politics of sexual counterrevolution, told journalist Michelle Goldberg. "But to anybody raised in the environment of the evangelical right wing, what she says makes perfect sense."

As Bachmann looked like she might ride the evangelical vote to the Republican nomination, serious Republicans became ever more anxious for a savior. They placed their hopes on Rick Perry, a brash native-born Texan who made the younger Bush look like the gentleman rancher he was. "There's a big hole in the Republican field," observed Doyle McManus, a Los Angeles Times columnist, "and it's made to order for a Southern governor who's conservative on social issues but not censorious, and who'd rather talk about cutting government spending and holding down taxes."

In other words, it was time to change the subject.

ON AUGUST 13, the sexual counterrevolutionaries lifted Bachmann to victory in the Iowa Straw Poll, a non-binding event but the first actual contest in the Republican race. Pawlenty, who had been banking on those Iowa evangelicals going his way, quit. "Came in third place behind Michele Bachmann and Ron Paul," he later explained to Stephen Colbert. "I think that's enough for any one person to endure."

That same day, Rick Perry went to South Carolina, the birthplace of the Confederacy, and announced that he was running for president before a gathering hosted by right-wing blogger and Tea Party enthusiast Erick Erickson.

Perry was the longest serving governor in the nation, but few voters outside of Texas had ever heard him speak, or for that matter, knew anything about what he stood for. The buzz that had intensified for several months around his potential candidacy guaranteed that his campaign rollout would win the news cycle with his preferred message that he was a proven job creator. Perry struck every Tea Party note in a pitch perfect tone. "I'll work every day to make Washington, D.C. as inconsequential in your life as I can."

A week earlier, Perry had been selling a different brand.

The morning after the S&P downgraded the nation's credit rating, Perry participated in The Response, an explicitly Christian prayer rally in Houston's Reliant Center. Governor Perry's invitation to the event, and his status as one of its "Leaders," had been prominently displayed on the event's website: "As a nation, we must come together and call upon Jesus to guide us through unprecedented struggles."

The Response was a family reunion of sorts for the sexual counterrevolution. The current generation of powerbrokers was well represented by Concerned Women for America's Penny Nance. "We are on the brink of moral and economic destruction," she preached from the stage. "We were founded as a nation of Christians, and as a nation of Christians we must now stand." (All the speeches were presented as prayers.) The rising Young Turks, such as the video guerrilla and antiabortion activist Lila Rose, were celebrated. Later in the day the M.C., Luis Cataldo of the International House of Prayer, brought to the stage "icons of the faith," including Focus on the Family's Christian ministry James and Shirley Dobson and Don Wildmon of the American Family Association. (AFA had just launched a boycott of Old Navy for selling items to benefit It Gets Better, a project created

to help gay teens emotionally survive bullying.) The day's parade
of luminaries included David Barton, the Christian fundamentalist
amateur historian, leader of the antigay WallBuilders, and past chair
of the Texas Republican Party; Tony Perkins of the Dobson-backed
Family Research Council; and Reverend John Hagee, who had in the
past called the Catholic Church the "whore of Babylon," preached
that Jews were not "spiritually alive," and suggested that Hitler
was sent by God to be a "hunter" of the Jews. (McCain had rejected
Hagee's endorsement in 2008; Hagee told his followers that he had
been personally asked by Perry to participate in The Response.)
Indeed, the idea for the prayer rally originated with Reverend James
Robison, the fire-and-brimstone–breathing Texas sexual fundamentalist who had shared a stage with Ronald Reagan in 1980 and later
condemned him for betraying the movement. Behind the scenes,
Robison had for months been quietly bringing dozens of pastors and
Christian Right leaders to meet with Perry as the governor contemplated a presidential bid.

When Perry took the stage at the prayer rally, standing at his side
was an African American preacher, C. L. Jackson, and Alice Patterson, a true heroine of the early sexual counterrevolution. Patterson
had run a chapter of Schlafly's Eagle Forum during Reagan's presidency and later served as the field director for the Texas Christian
Coalition, organizing over 130 chapters of the group in the three
years before George W. Bush's 1994 gubernatorial election. In 1996,
Patterson had resigned from the Christian Coalition in order to
devote herself to evangelizing for the New Apostolic Reformation, a
far-right, fringe sect of Pentecostalist biblical literalists, who believe
that Christians must take dominion over government. Patterson
had been disappointed, however, in the man she had once worked
to elect to the Texas governorship. In her book published the week
before the 2010 midterms, Patterson enumerated President Bush's
betrayals. He had "outraged evangelicals by stating that he believes
that Christians and Muslims worship the same god." He had failed
to act on his promise to advance a constitutional amendment banning gay marriage. And he had appointed "an open homosexual" to
office. Presumably, Perry would not fail her. The stakes could not be
higher, for Patterson was convinced that Satan actively controlled

the Democratic Party, via a "network of demonic principalities" led by the infamous Old Testament temptress. "Kissing the Baal for economic gain," Patterson wrote, "the shedding of innocent blood and sexual immorality comprise the Jezebel structure hiding behind the Democratic Party today." Standing before more than 30,000 Christians, Rick Perry hugged Patterson and thanked her and Jackson: "They have both been with me and prayed with me and supported me through the years."

"Get ready for a 'Holy War,'" David Brody, chief political correspondent at Pat Robertson's *Christian Broadcasting Network*, wrote the day after Perry's announcement and Bachmann's Iowa victory. "Bless their hearts. This should be interesting."

"And if Palin gets in (and my hunch is I think she will) then you may have to revive me with smelling salts since I will pass out from being delirious!"

"Is a title and a campaign too shackle-y?" Palin asked rhetorically on Fox News a few days before she announced she would not run for president and claimed she could be more effective campaigning for conservative candidates.

In fact, Perry had eclipsed her in the affections of the Republican base. As a debate marathon began after Labor Day, Perry had already attracted the sexual fundamentalist vote away from Bachmann and Palin and had cut significantly into Romney's support to become the frontrunner. In the governor's first national debate, the Republican audience erupted in spontaneous applause when the moderator noted that Perry had presided over a record number of executions. Perry's stock, however, quickly plunged. Five days later at the next debate, the candidates vied with each other about who could repeal Wall Street regulation and health care reform faster. The audience booed Perry after he defended providing instate tuition to illegal immigrants as the "American way;" they laughed and hooted, "Yeah!" to a question posed to Ron Paul, should society just let an uninsured man die?

Ten days later, a Fox News/Google debate featured crowd-sourced questions. Fox cut to a graphic of a world map and zoomed in on Iraq, where a soldier stood in his barracks and spoke into a computer camera.

"In 2010, when I was deployed to Iraq, I had to lie about who I was, because I'm a gay soldier, and I didn't want to lose my job. My question is, under one of your presidencies, do you intend to circumvent the progress that's been made for gay and lesbian soldiers in the military?"

On stage in Florida, down the road from Disney World, nine Republican presidential hopefuls stood mute as the sexual fundamentalists in the Republican base, the people on whom their ambitions rested, booed an American soldier serving his country in Iraq.

EPILOGUE

THE 2012 PRESIDENTIAL race and the actions of the 112th Congress have provided ample evidence that the Republican Party is in thrall to the sexual fundamentalists.

It cannot be emphasized enough that a serious candidate to be the presidential nominee of the Party of Lincoln speaks as if secession is a legal and legitimate option for a political party that hasn't gotten its way. It cannot be underscored enough that the Republican Party very nearly sent the world's oldest democracy and largest economy into default, only three months after it nearly shut down the government over birth control.

By any standard, this is insanity. Delirium. Still, it is a logical, historically understandable result of the sexual counterrevolution of the past forty years.

To borrow a line from Bill Clinton, the notion that today's Republican Party or the broader right-wing movement will call its sexual counterrevolutionaries to account and deal responsibly with the very real challenges facing our country is a fairy tale. The Republican Party offers voters not a choice, but rather echoes on a single theme. No matter who faces Barack Obama in the general election, one fundamental matter was long before decided. The 2012 Republican presidential nominee has made the causes of the sexual counterrevolution his own.

After Barack Obama's commanding election in 2008, it seemed that Republicans might have learned a lesson about the perils of cultural extremism. Some Republicans, such as General Colin Powell and former Homeland Security Secretary Tom Ridge, let it be known they were available to steer the Grand Old Party back into the mainstream. A few Republican politicians, such as Senators Olympia Snowe and Susan Collins, remained true to an earlier Republican Party of business, smaller government, personal liberty, and yes, women's rights. Jon Huntsman valiantly tried to gain traction in the 2012 field by affirming he believed the scientists on global warming and evolution. As the GOP leadership embraced the Tea Party and the far Right over the past three years, respected conservative intellectuals, including Andrew Sullivan, Christopher Buckley, and David Frum, engaged in wrenching struggles to drag their comrades back to the stable ground of sane conservatism. Instead, the Republican Party and the Right renewed its vows with the sexual fundamentalists.

There are not large numbers of American citizens clamoring to turn Medicare into a voucher system, as Congressional Republicans voted to do. Or who think, as Newt Gingrich does, that Social Security should be privatized. Or who see corporations as people in need of a break, as Mitt Romney would have it. Or who want to lower taxes on the wealthy, and raise them on the middle class, as Herman Cain would do. Republican politicians, right-wing leaders, and the top 1 percent know this. So they have ridden the riptide of sexual counterrevolution in order to get their lieutenants elected. Once upon a time, the men who led the Republican Party and the mainstream conservative movement were in control. But no more. They have left America at the mercy of their ground troops, the sexual fundamentalists.

THIS BOOK HAS told the story of how and why the sexual counterrevolution arose and its numerous political consequences. The sexual counterrevolution exerted a critical influence in shattering both political parties and in dividing Americans into warring ideological camps over matters of sex and culture. By inducing paralyzing division among Democrats and an ideological maximalism among Republicans, the sexual counterrevolution has been a prime culprit in America's self-destructive political dysfunction.

The impact of the sexual counterrevolution, however, goes well-beyond politics and government. This history matters because the sexual counterrevolution has also exacted an enormous toll on the lives and prospects of real Americans. About half of all Americans live in a community where it is perfectly legal to a fire a woman because she is a lesbian or refuse to rent an apartment to a man because he is gay. Only eighteen states provide a clear legal right to adoption for same-sex couples. Only seven states and the District of Columbia recognize same-sex marriage, yet even in these states, DOMA denies married gay couples the munificent economic benefits the government bestows on married straight couples.

Fifty years after the Equal Pay Act, forty years after the feminist revolution, and more than two decades after women started taking home the majority of college degrees, full-time women workers still make only 79 cents for every dollar earned by male workers. Women still perform the lion's share of housework and caring for children and elderly relatives, and many analysts think that the persistence of the gender wage gap, as well as the dearth of women at the highest levels of government and business, results less from outright discrimination than from the lack of government support for families. The victory of the sexual fundamentalists was so decisive against federal support for parental leave and public child care that now, even with roughly three out of four mothers in the workforce, these subjects are almost completely absent from our national political debate. The United States is one of only three countries in the world that does not provide universal paid maternity leave; almost every advanced nation generously subsidizes the cost of parenting preschool aged children.

American teenagers have the highest rate of pregnancy, abortion, and motherhood among advanced nations. This is not because they have more sex; it is rather due to the fact that they have less access to affordable birth control and medically accurate sex education.

WHILE THIS STATE of affairs can largely be chalked up to Republican design, Democrats have been complicit participants in America's bipartisan sexual counterrevolution. But something odd happened to the Democratic Party after its defeat in the 2010 midterm elections. It was hard to find anyone willing to blame cultural progressives, the heirs of the McGoverniks, for the loss. An exception was William

Galston, the Democratic Leadership Council's original family values advocate, who prophesied alone in the wilderness. Obama's hopes for reelection, Galston insisted in late 2010, would rest with the quintessential Reagan Democrats of the "heartland," conservative Ohioans, rather than with the progressives "on the Democratic periphery" in places like Colorado. By contrast, most Democratic strategists and analysts kept the focus where it belonged: on the economy. Stan Greenberg and James Carville's polling firm reviewed the election results and concluded that Reagan Democrats abandoned the party over the lack of jobs, nothing more, and advised that future victory depended on progressives. "Democrats can win by producing an electorate with presidential-year demographics—engagement of minorities and younger voters. Democrats cannot produce a sustainable majority without doing both." The old prescription, to run right on culture to capture culturally conservative populists, had expired.

A spurt of progressive policy-making by the lame-duck Congress in late 2010 also indicated that the Democratic Party was done with the tired battles of its own sexual counterrevolution. On Saturday December 18, 2010, the U.S. Senate voted 65 to 31 to repeal Don't Ask, Don't Tell, opening the way for gay, lesbian, bisexual, and transgendered Americans to serve openly in the armed forces. (A bill repealing DADT, sponsored and championed by Democratic representative and Iraq War veteran Patrick Murphy, had passed the House for the second time that year three days earlier.) After Republicans filibustered funds for troops in Afghanistan and Iraq in order to block DADT repeal, Democrat Kirsten Gillibrand, Independent Joe Lieberman, and Republican Susan Collins jointly led a risky effort to repeal DADT through a stand-alone bill. Every Democratic senator, the two Independents who caucused with the Democrats, and eight Republicans voted for repeal. Congress and the president had finally caught up to public opinion. Nearly eight in ten Americans favored repeal. On September 20, 2011, a new era of equality in the U.S. armed services began.

Even as Republicans ramped up their antiabortion rhetoric to distract attention from their effort to undermine access to birth control and women's health services, the Obama administration pushed ahead in a progressive direction. In February 2010, the Department of Health and

Human Services, led by Kathleen Sebelius, overturned a Bush administration midnight executive order that had allowed those who opposed birth control to defy medical science and claim it was abortion and then refuse to fill prescriptions for contraceptives and emergency contraception. Democrats also resisted Republican efforts to take away family planning funds from Planned Parenthood and other abortion providers. The administration later ruled, as we have seen, that health insurers had to cover contraception without charge. This too was in line with mainstream public opinion. Three-quarters of the public believed that insurers should cover birth control and that the government should subsidize its cost for low-income Americans; 57 percent opposed efforts to deny federal funds to medical providers who also performed abortions with their own funds.

Perhaps the most surprising post-2010 development was how rapidly the politics of gay marriage changed. In late February, Obama's Justice Department announced that it would not appeal two pending cases on the Defense of Marriage Act, as it had determined the law was unconstitutional. In March, California Senator Dianne Feinstein introduced legislation to repeal DOMA. In a case argued by the two opposing lawyers in *Bush v. Gore*, California's Prop 8 banning gay marriage had been ruled unconstitutional. (It was still proceeding through appeals at the time of this writing.) In New York, Democratic Governor Andrew Cuomo put his political reputation on the line to win same-sex marriage from the dysfunctional New York legislature. Employing the power of his bully pulpit, personal behind-closed-doors persuasion of moderate Republicans, and the leverage of Republican donors, Cuomo was able to persuade four moderate Republican state senators to vote for marriage equality.

CULTURAL PROGRESSIVISM IS the new American way. The nation has crossed the tipping point on gay marriage. A majority of all Americans now supports same-sex marriage. On abortion, Americans strongly favor upholding *Roe v. Wade* and strongly oppose the position of the Republican Party. Fully 62 percent think that abortion should be legal in the first three months of pregnancy, in which 89 percent of abortions occur; only 15 percent favor outlawing abortion in all circumstances. Americans have become less religious and less culturally conservative over the past forty years. Polling on birth control and sexual morality show that Americans unequivocally reject the sexual fundamentalists' attempt to take us back to a time when sex was stigmatized and only legitimate when confined within the traditional heterosexual marriage. The majority of Americans believe in the basic values underpinning a culturally progressive approach to matters of sex, gender, family, and culture: privacy, personal freedom, equality, and pluralism.

The sexual counterrevolutionaries are a minority, and demographic reality is running completely against them. The aging of the sexual fundamentalists and the flight of Americans from organized religion is every year shrinking the ranks of the sexual counterrevolution, while population growth is every year creating a more broadly progressive adult voting population. The sexual counterrevolution has persisted as long as it has by deceptive rebranding—most recently as the Tea Party—and by exploiting the many leverage points our system of government offers to well-organized and single-minded minority factions.

The anti-democratic behavior of Republican elected officials and the insurrectionist rhetoric of Republican presidential candidates, the Republican congressional leadership, and right-wing pundits and activists suggest they too know their days are numbered. Republicans are trying to write minority rule into the U.S. Constitution; the so-called balanced budget amendment contains a clause requiring a two-thirds vote in both Houses to pass any tax increase. Twelve Republican-dominated states have rewritten their laws to make it more difficult to vote and participate in campaigns; in seven more states, Democratic governors vetoed laws passed by Republican legislatures. Florida's law is so onerous that even the venerable League of Women Voters, which has conducted voter registration drives in the state for 70 years, said their organization would have to stop registering voters. "Good old-fashioned voter suppression" is how the League characterized the law's intent. The burden of these new measures falls disproportionately on Democratic-leaning and progressive demographic groups—the young, students, minorities, and low-income men and women. The laws tend to spare Republican-leaning voters from the intended voter purge. In Texas, student IDs are not valid for purposes of voter registration, but a permit for a concealed weapon is, courtesy of "emergency" legislation passed by the Republican legislature and signed by Perry. Suppressing the potential Democratic vote is also an important contributing motive in the GOP's refusal to consider comprehensive immigration reform. In a related move, Republicans are seeking to financially cripple the Democratic Party before the full force of demographic trends takes effect. Many of the recent state laws against labor unions strike at the ability of unions to use their own funds for political donations, donations that overwhelmingly go to the Democratic Party. This has little to do with democracy and choice, as the GOP maintains. Republicans want to repeal the Dodd-Frank Wall Street Reform and Consumer Protection Act, which gives shareholders the power to vote on executive pay, and have rebuffed the effort to give shareholders the right to vote on the political donations of publicly owned corporations.

THE SEXUAL COUNTERREVOLUTION has polarized our society, distorted our politics, distracted us from our priorities, broken our governing institutions, and denied opportunity and liberty to many Americans.

This is no way to run a country.

The good news is that there is a way out of our national political delirium. And it's quite straightforward.

When everyone commits to voting in every election and to staying moderately informed between elections about what politicians say and do, the sexual counterrevolution will end at the ballot box. The sexual fundamentalists are a small minority of the public, and they and their Republican partners cannot survive the scrutiny of an informed and active citizenry. In short, more democracy will go a long way toward ending our political dysfunction and restoring our national sanity.

There is a good chance that the Democratic Party can be an ally in a movement to bring America's politics into alignment with the majority's progressive cultural values. In recent years, Democrats have experienced their most impressive victories by embracing the nation's multiethnic diversity and progressive cultural values. That was one of the important lessons of Barack Obama's improbable victory, and as we have seen, this trend has been politically salient since

Bill Clinton's 1992 election. But the nature of party politics and the record of American history teach another important lesson. Progressivism will only prevail, both nationally and within the Democratic Party, if politicians can count on progressive voters showing up, staying active, and rewarding them for standing true to principle.

I do not mean to minimize how hard it will then be to address our real challenges—creating enough jobs in a highly competitive global economy, leaving our planet habitable for future generations, extricating our military from the Afghan quagmire and corporate money from our political system, among the most pressing on a far-too-long list of problems. Likewise, differences in political philosophy will never go away; Americans throughout our history have disagreed about the appropriate balance between liberty and equality, opportunity and security, individualism and community. But ending the sexual counterrevolution, by the eminently American method of majority rule, will remove an enormous obstacle to our ability to honestly confront the issues that really matter.

A generation of Americans was initiated into the messy business of politics through a euphoric mass movement. They were transported by a vision of possibility, that America was still a land of hope, opportunity, and freedom for everyone, that in their diversity they could unite to transform our country and fulfill that promise for each and all.

Yes We Can, they believed.

They weren't wrong. They just forgot that every movement for progress in America has been met by vehement resistance, by a counter-movement hell-bent on dragging America back to a less fair, less equal, and less free time.

America is a better place than we have seemed to be in our recent seasons of delirium. It is time to reaffirm that the moral arc of history bends toward justice. And to remember that the arc is long and that change is not given but won.

ACKNOWLEDGMENTS

I DON'T BELIEVE IN fate, but I do believe in luck, and mine struck when my path unexpectedly crossed Dan Smetanka's. Dan's devotion to the editor's craft, keen eye, and instinct for narrative shaped this into a far better book. His humor and great sensitivity to the care and feeding of authors rescued me from the occupational hazards involved in thinking about politics 24/7 in today's America. I am enormously grateful to Dan.

It has been a joy to be published by Counterpoint. Many thanks to Laura Mazer and Kelly Winton, who shepherded the manuscript through production with professionalism and grace; Lorna Garano and Liz Parker for launching this project into the marketplace; Norman MacAfee, my copyeditor, who saved me from several embarrassing errors; and to Charlie Winton and Jack Shoemaker, for preserving the best traditions of publishing. Many thanks also to my intrepid agent Jill Marr at Sandra Dijkstra Literary Agency.

Many friends and relatives shared their ideas and put up with my single-mindedness during the year and a half I spent working on this book. Paula A. Daniels, Torie Osborn, and Tracy Gray read multiple drafts of many chapters and offered brilliant editorial advice. It is hard to imagine how I would have completed this project without their wisdom, support, and encouragement.

My daughters Helena and Camille, both now teenagers, have reminded me every day of how much has changed for the better in America, and the very real human stakes involved in preserving freedom and equality in our nation. My stepchildren, Paloma,

Morgan, Isaac, and Daniel, all nearly adults when I entered their lives, welcomed me into their hearts and opened their minds to me and, in doing so, shaped my ideas about family in ways crucial to the evolution of this book.

Finally, I dedicate this book to my husband, Jonathan Parfrey, for his faith in me when I had lost it, for his unwavering conviction that this was a story that needed to be told, and for the transcendent joy of his company.

NOTES

Sources for the following types of information, unless otherwise noted, are:

NATIONAL ELECTION RESULTS

Official national election results are available from the U.S. House, Office of the Clerk, Statistics of the Presidential and Congressional Election, biennial. Results from every year since 1920 are accessible at http://clerk.house.gov/member_info/electionInfo/index.aspx

Another source for national elections results, complete with maps down to the county level, is *Dave Leip's Atlas of U.S. Presidential Elections*, at http://www.uselection atlas.org. Because the reader can more easily access and search Leip's website, specific references to national elections in this book come from Leip's website, unless otherwise noted.

The most reliable source for national level voting demographics, public opinion, and voter choice related to elections is the American National Election Studies (ANES) Guide to Public Opinion and Electoral Behavior (Ann Arbor: University of Michigan, Center for Political Studies). The ANES includes detailed surveys going back to 1948. Its website provides graphs and includes the demographic breakdown for most polled questions. Most scholarly analyses of elections cited in this book use the ANES as their source for data. That information can be accessed from this page: http://electionstudies.org/nesguide/nesguide.htm

I have used exit polls sparingly. They are, however, useful for issues specific to a particular election (for example, gay marriage or the Iraq War), for state-level opinion, and for the religious profile of actual voters. CNN.com's Election Center maintains a well-organized presentation of exit poll data, and I have used their site for all elections since 2000.

Additional information about voting demographics for elections prior to 2000 can be accessed at the U.S. Census Bureau, Historical Voting and Registration Reports: http://www.census.gov/population/www/socdemo/voting/past-voting.html

Turnout is notoriously difficult to measure. In surveys, Americans over-report their actual participation in elections. Historically turnout was calculated as a percentage of the voting-age population. More recently, the preferred measure is "voting-eligible" population, primarily because there are two large groups in the adult population ineligible to vote: immigrants and those disenfranchised because of a criminal conviction. The political scientist Michael McDonald has done the seminal research on this subject, and his website, The United States Election Project, maintains detailed tables accessible to the public. See http://elections.gmu.edu/voter_turnout.htm

GOVERNMENT

Supreme Court cases: Additional information about any case named here can be found by its case name at The Oyez Project, Illinois Institute of Technology Chicago–Kent College of Law. (www.oyez.org)

The Presidency: All presidential approval ratings, national party platforms, convention speeches, and presidential speeches, writings, and executive orders are accessible at The American Presidency Project, a project of Professors John Woolley and Gerhard Peters of the University of California, Santa Barbara (http://www.presidency.ucsb.edu/index.php).

Congress: The text of bills, roll call votes, and all other legislative activity are available at The Library of Congress, Thomas: http://thomas.loc.gov/home/thomas.php

PUBLIC OPINION SURVEYS

I have consulted four main sources for public opinion, two scholarly and two nonpartisan ones: the ANES, The General Social Survey (National Opinion Research Center, University of Chicago), The Pew Research Center for the People and the Press, and Gallup. All four make their data and reports publicly available, although the GSS site is quite difficult for the nonexpert to navigate and interpret. The GSS subject index is at http://www3.norc.org/GSS+Website/Browse+GSS+Variables/Subject+Index

Pew is particularly useful for insight into broader cultural and social views. I have used both their published analyses and their reports of results (http://people-press.org/). Gallup is particularly useful for election season political polling and approval ratings of public figures. (http://www.gallup.com/home.aspx)

When I have used surveys from ostensibly nonpartisan firms thought to have a partisan or ideological tilt in their research I have noted that in the text. I have used these sparingly.

VIDEOS

Videos easily found by a simple search on YouTube are not cited in the notes. Early or more obscure videos are cited with links.

Speeches given at party conventions or in Congress can be found in C-SPAN's video library at http://www.c-spanvideo.org/videoLibrary/

ABBREVIATIONS

AAP: Almanac of American Politics, by Michael Barone and Richard E. Cohen (National Journal Group), various years

ANES: The American National Election Studies (www.electionstudies.org). The ANES Guide to Public Opinion and Electoral Behavior. Ann Arbor: University of Michigan, Center for Political Studies

APP: The American Presidency Project, by John Woolley and Gerhard Peters, University of California, Santa Barbara

CSM: Christian Science Monitor

GSS: General Social Survey

HSUSA: Historical Statistics of the United States

LAT: Los Angeles Times

MMA: Media Matters for America

NORC: National Opinion Research Center, University of Chicago

NYRB: New York Review of Books

NYT: New York Times

Pew: The Pew Research Center for the People and the Press

TAP: The American Prospect

TNR: The New Republic

USCB: United States Census Bureau

WP: Washington Post

WSJ: Wall Street Journal

INTRODUCTION

1   *The officials testify*: Kevin Baron, "'DADT' Could Be History by End of Summer, Pentagon Says," *Stars and Stripes*, April 1, 2011.

1   *She has also called homosexuality*: Ryan Lizza, Jill Lawrence, "Michele Bachmann's Biblical Submissiveness," *Daily Beast,* July 10, 2011.

2   *On the campaign trail*: Jon Ward, "Primary Election 2012: Conservative Fears of Permanent Welfare State May Create Wild Ride," *Huffington Post*, May 8, 2011; William Petroski, "Santorum Calls Early Education Programs an Effort 'to Indoctrinate Your Children,'" *Des Moines Register*, August 2, 2011.

2   *"Glamorizes homosexual behavior"*: "American Family Association Goes to War with *Glee*," *Right Wing Watch*, May 9, 2011, http://www.rightwingwatch .org/content/american-family association-goes-war-glee; Peter J. Smith, "Dr. Jim Garlow: Biblical truth and sacrifice are the keys to renewing America," LifeSiteNews .com, June 7, 2011.

   Herman Cain: Trevor Persaud, "Herman Cain on Faith, Calling, and Presidential Aspirations," Christianity Today, March 21, 2011; The View, October 4, 2011; Piers Morgan, Oct 19, 2011.

2   *"It wasn't supposed to happen"*: Charles M. Blow, "Repeal, Restrict and Repress," *NYT*, February 11, 2011.

4   *"Constitutional right to be gay"*: Lloyd Grove, "Barry Goldwater's Left Turn," *WP*, July 28, 1994.

4   *Just 15 to 20 percent*: The Christian Right is made up of white traditionalist evangelicals (13 percent of the nation), Mormons, and a shifting percentage of religiously orthodox white Catholics. African Americans, despite high

levels of evangelicalism and cultural conservatism, remain overwhelmingly Democratic. Catholic Latinos also have not joined the Christian Right. Only evangelical Protestant Latinos have broken somewhat with Latinos' historical Democratic identification. Few non-Christians are part of the Christian Right, and for this reason I think it is a misnomer to call the movement the "religious right." On which evangelicals align with the Christian Right, see John Green, "American Religious Landscapes and Political Attitudes," Pew, September 9, 2004.

5   *Cultural progressivism*: These issues are usually included under the rubric of "social issues," and by extension, social liberals and social conservatives. The term "social issues" includes immigration and race. Since my purpose is to look at a narrower range of issues about sex, gender, sexuality, and family, I use the term "cultural," except in direct quotations, in place of "social."

7   *Fewer than a third*: These figures are from 1992 and are roughly accurate for today. Clyde Wilcox, *Onward Christian Soldiers? The Religious Right in American Politics* (Boulder: Westview Press, 1996), 142.

CHAPTER ONE

On sex, see John D'Emilio and Estelle B. Freedman, *Intimate Matters: A History of Sexuality in America* and Barbara Ehrenreich et al., *Re-Making Love: The Feminization of Sex*. On American family in the 1950s, see Elaine Tyler May, *Homeward Bound: American Families in the Cold War Era*; Stephanie Coontz, *Marriage, A History*; and *The Way We Never Were: American Families and the Nostalgia Trap*. On recent women's history and feminism, see Gail Collins, *When Everything Changed: The Amazing Journey of American Women from 1960 to the Present*; Ruth Rosen, *The World Split Open: How the Modern Women's Movement Changed America*; Mary Ryan, *Mysteries of Sex: Tracing Women and Men Through American History*; and Sara M. Evans, *Tidal Wave: How Women Changed America at Century's End*. On gay liberation, D'Emilio and Freedman. On marriage, Coontz. For historical data on the U.S. economy, see USCB. All statistics on sexual practices in this chapter are from T. Smith, "American Sexual Behavior." For additional statistics on women's work, education, and family, see Cynthia B. Costello, et al., *American Woman, 1999–2000* and *American Woman, 2003–2004*. My interpretation of the trends covered in this chapter has been influenced by all of these works, and only quotations and specific statistics are cited in this chapter.

9   *"I don't confess"*: John D'Emilio and Estelle B. Freedman, *Intimate Matters: A History of Sexuality in America* (New York: Harper & Row, 1988), 252.

9   *6 million American Women*: Stephanie Coontz, *Marriage, a History: From Obedience to Intimacy or How Love Conquered Marriage* (New York: Viking, 2005), 254.

      The true warriors in that revolution were young, single women: Barbara Ehrenreich, Elizabeth Hess, and Gloria Jacobs, *Re-Making Love: The Feminization of Sex (New York: Anchor, 1987)*.

11   *87 percent of American women believed that it was wrong*: Daniel Yankelovich, *How Changes in the Economy Are Reshaping American Values* (Washington, DC: Brookings Institution, 1994), 24.

      By the time girls born during the sexual revolution: Tom Smith, *American Sexual*

Behavior: Trends, Socio-Demographic Differences, and Risk Behavior, GSS Topical Report (Chicago: NORC, April 2003),Table 1.

12 *According to the economists Claudia Goldin and Lawrence Katz*: Claudia Goldin and Lawrence F. Katz, "The Power of the Pill: Oral Contraceptives and Women's Career and Marriage Decisions," *Journal of Political Economy* 110, no. 4 (2002): 767; Claudia Goldin and Lawrence F. Katz, "On the Pill: Changing the Course of Women's Education," *Milken Institute Review*, 2nd Quarter 2001, 767.

14 *Two-thirds of all white women*: Cynthia B Costello, Anne J. Stone, and Shari Miles, *The American Woman, 1999–2000* (New York: Norton, 1998), table 4-1, 264 (work); 186 (fertility); home ownership, USCB.
     "Sick," "neurotic," or "immoral": Coontz, *Marriage, a History*, 230.
     American women were grossly ill-prepared: *American Woman, 1999–2000*, 193.
     Mothers of the fifties were telling pollsters: Coontz, *Marriage, a History*, 251.
     Women flooded into the paid labor force: *The American Woman, 2003–2004* (New York: Palgrave Macmillan, 2003), 263.

15 *A typical middle-class mother*: See Economic Policy Institute analysis of work and gender, "Average hours have remained flat for married men, while married women have seen a significant increase," State of Working America, http://www .stateofworkingamerica.org/charts/view/161

17 *Many men, however, didn't quite appreciate*: Quotations in Rosen, *The World Split Open*, 72–73.

18 *Before, it was perfectly legal*: A young Ruth Bader Ginsburg argued the landmark *Reed v. Reed* (1971), overturning Idaho probate law favoring men as administrators of estates. On rape laws, see *Intimate Matters*, 214.

21 *The GLF's manifesto declared*: Quoted in ibid., 320–322.

CHAPTER TWO

23 *Party had been taken over by "abortionists"*: George Meany, "Address before the 16th Constitutional Convention of the United Steelworkers of America, Las Vegas, Nevada," September 18, 1972, Box 83, George Meany Memorial Archives.

24 *Indeed, only three presidential candidates*: James W. Ceaser and Daniel DiSalvo, "The Magnitude of the 2008 Democratic Victory: By the Numbers," *The Forum* 6, no. 4 (January 9, 2009): 3.

24 *"Lost the election at Miami"*: Bruce Miroff, *The Liberals' Moment: The McGovern Insurgency and the Identity Crisis of the Democratic Party* (Lawrence: University Press of Kansas, 2007), 83.

25 *When the Democratic candidates*: "A Future That Is Up for Grabs," *Time*, November 20, 1972.

25 *At the GOP convention*: *Nixonland: The Rise of a President and the Fracturing of America* (New York: Scribner, 2008), 716.

25 *"The Democratic Party is going to pay heavily"*: "The Vote: Splintering the Great Coalition," *Time*, November 20, 1972.

26 *Their behavior, he recounted, "was just bizarre"*: *The Liberals' Moment*, 204.

26 *Men kissed men in the aisles*: *Nixonland*, 689–699. The definitive history of the campaign, by Miroff, is highly sympathetic to McGovern and critical of

the so-called extremists. Another account of Democratic Party woes and its solution also uncritically recycles the death-by-McGovernik thesis, even as it acknowledges that the McGovern coalition is the basis for the Democrats' majority. John B. Judis and Ruy A. Teixeira, *The Emerging Democratic Majority* 2004 ed. (New York: Scribner, 2002).

26   *"The speculations were for a ranting mob"*: Cecil Smith, "TV Pros Chronicle Democratic Amateurs," *LAT*, July 12, 1972.

27   *Of the 3,100 delegates*: R.W. Apple, "Delegate Reforms Bring New Types to the Convention," *NYT*, July 9, 1972.

27   *"McGovern's legions"*: "The Battle for the Democracy Party," *Time*, July 17, 1972.

27   *"Struck many onlookers"*: R. W. Apple, "Convention Notes: Irate Leader of Ohio Bloc Says It's His 'Last Go at This'," *NYT*, July 12, 1972, 20.

27   *"Those who muttered about wild-haired 'freaks'"*: Nan Robertson, "Delegates' New Look: A Sparkling Fashion Show All Their Own," *NYT*, July 12, 1972; Marlene Cimons, "Womanpower Emerges in Miami Beach," *LAT*, July 11, 1972.

28   *"We're scared to death of him"*: Terry Robards, "McGovern's Views Alarm Big Donors," *NYT*, July 3, 1972.

29   *"It was madness"*: "The Campaign: The Confrontation of the Two Americas," *Time*, October 2, 1972.

29   *A Time report of the poll observed*: "The Nation: A Vote on Abortion," *Time*, September 4, 1972.

30   *Most reporters understood the more significant fault lines*: Bill Boyarsky, "McGovern Strives to Reconcile Party," *LAT*, July 12, 1972; "Platform Geared to Please Most Minorities but Not Businessmen," *LAT*, July 13, 1972; John Herbers, "Debate Runs Long," *NYT*, July 12, 1972, 1.

30   *Most voters had seen McGovern as a strong liberal*: "Nixon Moves Out to an Astonishing Lead," *Time*, October 2, 1972.

30   *The percentage of Democrats who viewed McGovern as a radical*: "Gallup Finds Nixon Continues to Lead Top 2 Democrats," *NYT*, July 3, 1972, 18; "The Nation: Alternate Democratic Visions," *Time*, July 3, 1972; *"Time* Citizens' Panel: The Voters Assess the Two Tickets," *Time*, August 21, 1972.

30   *A third of white conservatives*: Alan I. Abramowitz and Kyle L. Saunders, "Exploring the Bases of Partisanship in the American Electorate: Social Identity vs. Ideology," *Political Research Quarterly* 59, no. 2 (June 2006): 80.

31   *"Late September poll . . . couldn't help marveling"*: "Nixon Moves Out to an Astonishing Lead."

31   *"He comes on like a soft-spoken preacher*: "The Campaign: God May Be a Democrat: But the Vote Is for Nixon," *Time*, October 30, 1972; *The Liberals' Moment*, 193.

32   *Things got much worse for McGovern*: The assessment is in *Time*'s "After the Landslide: Nixon's Mandate," *Time*, November 20, 1972; the anecdote is in *The Liberals' Moment*.

32   *One of the most troubled souls*: For a brilliant take on Nixon's character, see Perlstein, *Nixonland*.

32   *George Meany held his own press conference*: Ibid., 687.

33   *Conspiracy to derail his candidacy*: This account draws on reporting by *Time* magazine, *The New York Times,* and *The Los Angeles Times.* See, in addition to

specific articles cited below, Bill Boyarsky, "New Plan to Stop McGovern Devised," *LAT*, July 9, 1972; Steven Roberts, "Pressures and Fears Unite 'Stop McGovern' Coalition," *NYT*, July 10, 1972.

33 *"It was the old politics"*: "Democrats: A Setback for McGovern," *Time*, July 10, 1972.

33 *McGovern survived a potentially fatal challenge*: California still had a winner-take-all primary, which McGovern had won. Humphrey, who had said earlier that he would not challenge the California system, decided after he lost that California was in violation of the new reform rules. (He didn't bother to challenge several other states that still used winner-take-all rules.) The key strategy of the Stop-McGovern conspirators was to work the credentials committee to win a proportional division of the California delegation. The difference would have left McGovern with a huge plurality at the convention, but one still about 200 votes short of the 1,509 needed to win the nomination on the first ballot. The pre-convention challenges went all the way to the Supreme Court, which sent it back to the party to work it out. The outcome was in doubt until late in the night on the first day of the convention.

34 *"the barons of labor"*: Tom Wicker, "New Breed and Old," *NYT*, July 13, 1972.

34 *in 1968*: For a vivid description of the 1968 convention, see *Nixonland*, 301–327.

35 *in the words of Gary Hart*: *The Liberals' Moment*, 42.

36 *Democratic women lobbied the commission*: McGovern resigned his chairmanship of the reform commission when he announced his candidacy—before the NWPC began its lobbying campaign.

36 *In a bid for women's votes*: *The Liberals' Moment*, 206.

37 *"the Barry Goldwater of the Left"*: Evans and Novak, "Anybody but McGovern," *WP*, April 6, 1972.

38 *Humphrey's radical-baiting*: "The Nation: Advantage to the Incumbent," *Time*, July 10, 1972.

38 *controlling more than 1,300 of the 1,509 delegates*: "Alternate Democratic Visions," *Time*.

38 *Meany engineered a vote*: "Labor: Sitting Out 1972," *Time*, September 11, 1972.

38 *Carter, with Daley, Meany, Jackson*: *The Liberals' Moment*, 262–263; "A Future That Is Up for Grabs."

38 *"didn't do squat"*: *The Liberals' Moment*, 199.

39 *The McGovernik extremists, in their view*: "A Future That Is Up for Grabs."

39 *Traditional Democratic groups . . . quarter of all Democratic votes*: Robert Axelrod et al., "Communications," *The American Political Science Review* 68, no. 2 (June 1974): 718.

40 *religious and ethnic voters*: For Catholics, McGovern's association with sexual radicals, and the false charge that he favored legalized abortion, was probably a factor in his poor showing among them. But Catholics, historically, liked Nixon. Republicans had made big inroads in the Catholic vote in 1952 and 1956, when Nixon was the vice presidential candidate—a fact obscured by Nixon's 1960 run against Kennedy, who became the first Catholic president. There were as yet no exit polls, and the ANES did not yet ask about abortion, so any conclusion is speculative.

41 *Voters felt more negative*: ANES, "Average Feelings Toward Presidential Candidates"; "Nixon Moves Out to an Astonishing Lead," *Time*.

41 *"second-class citizens"*: *The Liberals' Moment*, 189.

42 *"Men accustomed to viewing politics"*: "The Price of Change," *NYT*, July 9, 1972.

42 *"The Democratic Party has no historic choice"*: Anthony Lewis, "Whose Party Is It?" *NYT*, July 15, 1972.

43 *"We listened for three days"*: Meany, "Meany USW Address."

44 *two-thirds believed a woman's place*: ANES, "Equal Role for Women 1972–2004."

CHAPTER THREE

46 *Equal Rights Amendment*: This account of Schlafly and the anti-ERA campaign is based on *Phyllis Schlafly and Grassroots Conservatism: A Woman's Crusade* (Princeton: Princeton University Press, 2005); *For a "Christian America": A History of the Religious Right* (Amherst, NY: Prometheus Books, 2002); Catherine E. Rymph, *Republican Women: Feminism and Conservatism from Suffrage through the Rise of the New Right* (Chapel Hill: University of North Carolina Press, 2006); Donald T. Critchlow and Cynthia B. Stacheki, "The Equal Rights Amendment Reconsidered: Politics, Policy, and Social Mobilization in a Democracy," *Journal of Policy History* 20, no. 1 (2008): 157–176; Jane J. Mansbridge, *Why We Lost the ERA* (University of Chicago Press, 1986).

47 *Pseudo-conservatives*: Hofstadter, *The Paranoid Style in American Politics* (New York: Random House, 1952).

47 *"The nut fringe"*: Rymph, *Republican Women*, 179.

48 *Marched a thousand of her supporters*: Ibid., 186.

48 *when Gallup asked Americans*: Mansbridge, *Why We Lost the ERA*, 206.

49 *"They were all so awful"*: Brown, *For a "Christian America,"* 65.

49 *foremothers of the Christian Right*: On Hobbs's life and role, see ibid.

50 *"God created you"*: The Pink Sheet is partially reproduced in ibid., 40–42.

50 *"I never would have been able to write"*: Ibid., 41.

51 *Alabama chapter of STOP ERA wrote*: Critchlow, *Phyllis Schlafly*, 225.

51 *"Freedom to be a homemaker"*: Brown, *For a "Christian America,"* 93.

51 *"We, the wives and working women"*: Critchlow, *Phyllis Schlafly*, 224–225.

51 *"A Christian View of the ERA"*: Ibid., 235–236.

51 *Bunny Chambers*: Brown, *For a "Christian America,"* 86–87.

52 *A poem written by Beverly Findley*: Reprinted in ibid., 63.

53 *"Some being very shrill"*: Critchlow, *Phyllis Schlafly*, 238.

53 *called her a traitor to her sex*: Ibid., 226.

54 *real power of the anti-ERA campaign*: Brown, *For a "Christian America,"* 57.

54 *circulation for her monthly report*: Rymph, *Republican Women*, 215.

54 *Public opinion surveys confirm*: Brown, *For a "Christian America,"* 69–70.

55 *God made us different*: Mansbridge, *Why We Lost the ERA*, 175.

55 *In the mid-1970s*: William Martin, *With God on Our Side: The Rise of the Religious Right in America* (New York: Broadway Books, 2005), chaps. 4–5. Local campaigns against sex education began in the late sixties. They too were organized by religious women, in the most famous case in West Virginia, by the wife of a Church of Christ minister. Efforts to censor textbooks and return to the teaching of creationism were part of these campaigns as well.

55 *The session's most "radical" legislation*: "Richard Nixon: Veto of the Economic Opportunity Amendments of 1971," December 9, 1971, http://www.presidency.ucsb.edu/ws/index.php?pid=3251&st=&st1=

56 *Mondale's revised child-care bill*: Several sources, such as New Right leader Connie Marshner (in *With God on Our Side*) incorrectly date the mass anti–child care agitation to 1971. For a reliable account of the grassroots activism, see *For a "Christian America,"* 11–12, 52, 68–69. On the legislative challenges, see Walter Mondale, *The Good Fight: A Life in Liberal Politics* (New York: Scribner, 2010), 98–109.

56 *"Anti-family women's lib movement"*: Brown, *For a "Christian America,"* 52.

58 *excommunicate members who supported the ERA*: Sara M. Evans, *Tidal Wave: How Women Changed America at Century's End* (New York: Free Press, 2004), 173.

58 *First Lady Betty Ford*: Critchlow, *Phyllis Schlafly*, 233.

59 *Audiotapes mailed out*: Brown, *For a "Christian America,"* 106–107.

59 *National Women's Conference*: Ibid., 111–114; Critchlow, *Phyllis Schlafly*, 244–248; Martin, *With God on Our Side*, 165–167; Marjorie Spruill, "Rightward Bound"; Rymph, *Republican Women*, 227; Evans, *Tidal Wave*, 139–142.

63 *61 percent of white evangelicals*: Clyde Wilcox, *Onward Christian Soldiers? The Religious Right in American Politics* (Boulder: Westview Press, 1996), 107.

CHAPTER FOUR

65 *As the 1980 presidential election approached*: Andrew Busch, *Reagan's Victory: The Presidential Election of 1980 and the Rise of the Right* (Lawrence: University Press of Kansas, 2005), chap. 3. Unless otherwise noted, details of the 1980 primaries and general election come from *Reagan's Victory*.

67 *After Reagan came up 117 delegate votes short*: Donald T. Critchlow, *Phyllis Schlafly and Grassroots Conservatism: A Woman's Crusade* (Princeton: Princeton University Press, 2005), 242; William Martin, *With God on Our Side: The Rise of the Religious Right in America* (New York: Broadway Books, 2005), 206–209.

68 *Phyllis Schlafly observed*: Martin, *With God on Our Side*, 165.

69 *Carter had misrepresented himself*: David Skaggs and Calvin Van Taylor, *With God on Our Side: George W. Bush and the Rise of the Religious Right in America* (documentary film; First Run Features, 2005).

69 *convene a major conference on the family*: Leo P. Ribuffo, "Family Policy Past As Prologue; Jimmy Carter, the White House Conference on Families, and the Mobilization of the New Christian Right," *Review of Policy Research* 23, no. 2 (2006): 311–338.

70 *reached 18 million fundamentalist viewers*: Sara Diamond, *Not by Politics Alone: The Enduring Influence of the Christian Right* (New York: Guilford Press, 2000), 66.

70 *The Religious Roundtable*: Martin, *With God on Our Side*, 198–199.

71 *Reagan was the unrivaled favorite*: Lisa McGirr, *Suburban Warriors: The Origins of the New American Right* (Princeton: Princeton University Press, 2001).

71 *"I have here a copy of a report"*: YouTube—*Berkeley in the Sixties* (clip) 1990, http://www.youtube.com/watch?v=rGd_EsNCM4Y&feature=related

72 *Thanks to an infusion of cash*: Martin, *With God on Our Side*, 209.

72 *As the March 18 Illinois primary loomed*: Busch, *Reagan's Victory*, chap. 3.
72 *Reagan personally enlisted Schlafly*: Critchlow, *Phyllis Schlafly*, 268.
73 *Constitutional amendment banning abortion*: Schlafly's allies had inserted an anti-abortion plank in the 1976 platform also, but it included a clause recognizing legitimate differences within the party.
73 *To many Republican women*: Catherine E. Rymph, *Republican Women: Feminism and Conservatism from Suffrage through the Rise of the New Right* (Chapel Hill: University of North Carolina Press, 2006), 218–219, 227–230.
74 *So when the sexual counterrevolutionaries objected*: Ibid., 230; Martin, *With God on Our Side*, 214.
75 *Late August speech*: Martin, *With God on Our Side*, 216–217; Howell Raines, "Reagan Backs Evangelicals in Their Political Activities," *NYT*, August 23, 1980.
75 *Sandra Grogan Jeter and her mother*: For a *"Christian America": A History of the Religious Right* (Amherst, NY: Prometheus Books, 2002), 90.
76 *Christian Voice*: Diamond, *Not by Politics Alone*, 69; Sara Diamond, *Spiritual Warfare: The Politics of the Christian Right* (Cambridge, MA: South End Press, 1999), 62–63.
76 *"It's time for a change"*: The 1980 exit polls are reported on in Adam Clymer, "The Collapse of a Coalition," *NYT*, November 5, 1980.
76 *36 percent of voters answered that they didn't know*: ANES, "Liberal-Conservative Self-Identification."
76 *dissatisfaction with Carter's performance*: Jerome L. Himmelstein and James A. McRae, "Social Conservatism, New Republicans, and the 1980 Election," *The Public Opinion Quarterly* 48, no. 3 (Autumn 1984): 592–605.
77 *a record high of 49 percent*: ANES, "Power of the Federal Government, 1964–2000."
77 *Support for women having an equal role*: ANES, "Equal Role for Women (total)"; Jane J. Mansbridge, *Why We Lost the ERA* (Chicago: University of Chicago Press, 1986), 206–207 Table A1.
77 *attitudes toward gays*: Alan S. Yang, "Trends: Attitudes Toward Homosexuality," *The Public Opinion Quarterly* 61, no. 3 (Autumn 1997): 477–507.
77 *"gender gap"*: Later analysis also revealed a statistically significant gender gap in the 1972 election. The gender gap is typically calculated as the percentage of women minus the percentage of men voting for a candidate. A positive number means a candidate performed better among women voters than among men. A negative number indicates a better performance among men. Gender gaps can be calculated using either exit polls or the ANES surveys. Throughout the book, the number that I cite for the gender gap comes from Barbara Norrander's calculation of the gender gap from the ANES data set. In Lois Duke Whitaker, ed., *Voting the Gender Gap* (Champaign: University of Illinois Press, 2008), 27.
77 *Anderson voters*: Clymer, "The Collapse of a Coalition."
78 *fundamentalists and evangelicals swung sharply*: Clyde Wilcox, *Onward Christian Soldiers? The Religious Right in American Politics* (Boulder: Westview Press, 1996), 107.
78 *Evangelicals also played a critical role*: Critchlow, *Phyllis Schlafly*, 265.

78 *"People were reluctant"*: ibid., 266.
78 *"The rising tides of the Pro-Family Movement"*: ibid., 267.
78 *Only 10 percent of Americans shared that view*: ANES, "Abortion (1972–1980)."
78 *Abortion had not been on the original agenda*: Brown, *For a "Christian America,"* 124, 205–206; Martin, *With God on Our Side*, 156, 192–194.
79 *2012 GOP presidential candidate*: The film was one of the last two segments of a larger series titled "How Should We Then Live." I have not been able to determine if the Bachmanns viewed just that segment as part of Koop and Schaeffer's antiabortion tour, or if they saw the entire series through another venue. On Michele Bachmann see Chapter 16.
80 *an effective wedge issue*: Diamond, *Not by Politics Alone*, 66.
80 *Family Protection Act*: John D'Emilio and Estelle B. Freedman, *Intimate Matters: A History of Sexuality in America* (New York: Harper & Row, 1988), 349.
81 *"the husband is the head"*: Rebecca Klatch, *Women of the New Right* (Philadelphia: Temple University Press, 1988), 146.
81 *membership in NOW quadrupled*: Sara M. Evans, *Tidal Wave: How Women Changed America at Century's End* (New York: Free Press, 2004), 172.
81 *Feminists also had themselves to blame*: Mansbridge, *Why We Lost the ERA*.
82 *"I want to see women on a pedestal"*: Critchlow, *Phyllis Schlafly*, 251.
83 *"I can't believe it didn't pass"*: Klatch, *Women of the New Right*, 21.
83 *"elaborate scheme to devalue the blue collar man"*: Diamond, *Spiritual Warfare*, 109.
83 *Lottie Beth Hobbs*: Brown, *For a "Christian America,"* 66.
83 *Her pamphlets*: Cindy Horswell, "More Books Rejected As Censorship Effort Grows," *Houston Chronicle*, December 21, 1986; Dena Kleiman, "Parents' Groups Purging Schools of 'Humanist' Books," *NYT*, May 17, 1981; Brown, *For a "Christian America,"* 66.
83 *23 percent reduction*: Tax Policy Center, Urban Institute and Brookings Institution; U.S. Statistical Abstract, 1990.
84 *Reagan's liaison to the religious right*: Skaggs and Van Taylor, *With God on Our Side*.
84 *Schlafly quickly quashed that idea*: Critchlow, *Phyllis Schlafly*, 280–281.
85 *Many Christian Right leaders*: Martin, *With God on Our Side*, 227–230.
86 *"A man reaps what he sows"*: D'Emilio and Freedman, *Intimate Matters*, 354–355.
86 *"A little less research and a little more quarantine"*: Donald T. Critchlow, *The Conservative Ascendancy: How the GOP Right Made Political History* (Cambridge, MA: Harvard University Press, 2007), 217–218.
87 *Advice of a young White House lawyer*: Presidential Briefing Memo by John G. Roberts and Deborah K. Owen, September 13, 1985 posted on website "The Age of AIDS," PBS Frontline, http://www.pbs.org/wgbh/pages/frontline/aids/docs/robertsmemo.html#ixzz1OXfCNyNt
87 *In Britain*: Sean Wilentz, *The Age of Reagan: A History, 1974–2008* (New York: Harper, 2008), 186.
88 *LaHaye received a $1 million grant*: Diamond, *Not by Politics Alone*, 72.
88 *"If the mother does not do her duty"*: Susan Faludi, *Backlash: The Undeclared War Against American Women* (New York: Three Rivers Press, 2006), 275.
88 *The administration adopted an ideological test*: Wilentz, *The Age of Reagan*, 188–191. Quotation on 188.

89   *False myth of Reagan's overwhelming popularity*: Ibid., 278.

90   *Shift toward cultural progressivism*: GSS, Importance of Women's Rights Issue to You; ANES, Equal Role for Women, Legal Abortion; Alan S. Yang, "Trends: Attitudes Toward Homosexuality." There is a wide discrepancy in views about women's rights and opinions about feminism. Generally, by the mid-1980s Americans supported women's rights, but felt negative or indifferent toward feminism and feminists.

CHAPTER FIVE

92   *The roughly 30 men*: Stanley B. Greenberg, *Middle Class Dreams: Building the New American Majority* (New York: Crown, 1995), 298–299, note 14.

94   *"In liberalism {the Middle} saw a creed"*: E. J Dionne, *Why Americans Hate Politics* (New York: Simon & Schuster, 1991), 345.

95   *"supposedly disaffected group"*: Jerome L. Himmelstein and James A. McRae, "Social Conservatism, New Republicans, and the 1980 Election," *The Public Opinion Quarterly* 48, no. 3 (Autumn 1984): 604.

95   *Neither could Reagan's landslide reelection*: Robert S. Erikson, Thomas D. Lancaster, and David W. Romero, "Group Components of the Presidential Vote, 1952–1984," *The Journal of Politics* 51, no. 2 (May 1989): 342.

95   *wasn't a backlash*: Thomas J. Sugrue, *The Origins of the Urban Crisis: Race and Inequality in Postwar Detroit* (Princeton: Princeton University Press, 2005), 267–268.

96   *"Liberal fundamentalism"*: William Galston and Elaine Kamarck, "The Politics of Evasion: Democrats and the Presidency," *Progressive Policy Institute Blueprint*, September 1989.

96   *"family disintegration"*: William Galston and Elaine Kamarck, "America's Children, Still at Risk," *NYT*, November 19, 1990.

96   *"moral and cultural values"*: The DLC believed that the most electorally damaging liberal views Democrats held were on crime and welfare, and most of their energy went to those topics. Galston and Kamarck, "The Politics of Evasion."

97   *the DLC promised to clamp down*: "The New American Choice Resolution," adopted at the DLC Convention, Cleveland, Ohio, May 1, 1991.

97   *most DLC'ers were themselves culturally progressive*: Galston seems to be an exception. Into the 2000s, his writings continued to reject progressive gender policies and advance conservative solutions.

97   *In a scathing attack*: Robert Kuttner, "The Poverty of Neoliberalism," *TAP*, June 30, 1990.

98   *"To the extent that liberal positions"*: Robert Kuttner, *The Life of the Party* (New York: Penguin, 1988), 112.

99   *Greenberg penned emblematic expressions*: Stanley Greenberg, "From Crisis to Working Majority," *TAP*, September 21, 1991.

100 *Governor Bill Clinton*: "Interview with Stanley Bernard Greenberg," Diane D. Blair Papers (MC 1632), Special Collections, University of Arkansas Libraries, Fayetteville, December 10, 1992.

100 *"remain a secular party"*: Greenberg, "From Crisis to Working Majority."

101 *One of the George Bushes*: "A Tale of Two Bushes," *Time*, January 7, 1991, p. 20.

102 *federal funding of child care was wrong*: Robert F. McDonnell, "The Republican Party's Vision for the Family: The Compelling Issue for the Decade" (M.A., Virginia Beach, VA: Regent University, 1989), 39–40; Steven K. Wisensale, "The White House and Congress on Child Care and Family Leave Policy: From Carter to Clinton," *Policy Studies Journal* 25, no. 1 (March 1997): 75–86.

102 *When Bush invited a few gays and lesbians*: Gary Wills, "The Born-Again Republicans," *NYRB*, September 24, 1992.

103 *The Moral Majority*: Sara Diamond, *Not by Politics Alone: The Enduring Influence of the Christian Right* (New York: Guilford Press, 2000), 76.

104 *"We decided the days of kowtowing"*: David Skaggs and Calvin Van Taylor, *With God on Our Side: George W. Bush and the Rise of the Religious Right in America* (documentary film; First Run Features, 2005).

104 *"Pray that this doctor"*: Jeremy Campbell, "Doctors Carrying Guns in War over Abortions," *The Evening Standard*, February 3, 1992.

104 *more than a little encouragement from Terry*: "When Dissent Turns Violent," *St. Louis Post-Dispatch*, March 12, 1993, editorial.

105 *his preferred choice*: Jeffrey Toobin, *A Vast Conspiracy: The Real Story of the Sex Scandal That Nearly Brought Down a President* (New York: Simon & Schuster, 2000), 76.

106 *Protestors threw themselves*: Thomas Frank, *What's the Matter with Kansas? How Conservatives Won the Heart of America* (New York: Metropolitan Books, 2004), 90–95.

107 *They coached Thomas*: Garry Wills, "Thomas's Confirmation: The True Story," *NYRB*, February 2, 1995.

108 *For a decade, women had been told*: Susan Faludi, *Backlash: The Undeclared War Against American Women* (New York: Crown Publishers, 1991).

CHAPTER SIX

109 *On October 3, 1991*: The following account of the campaign is drawn from my review of national and local newspapers from the spring of 1991 to the summer of 1992 and interviews in the Diane Blair Papers.

111 *"was the most attractive political animal"*: Kenneth S. Baer, *Reinventing Democrats: The Politics of Liberalism from Reagan to Clinton* (Lawrence: University Press of Kansas, 2000), 163, 198.

111 *But to the Right*: Joe Conason and Gene Lyons, *The Hunting of the President: The Ten-Year Campaign to Destroy Bill and Hillary Clinton* (New York: St. Martin's Press, 2000), 67–72.

111 *"When you listen to the Clinton haters"*: Molly Ivins, *You Got to Dance with Them What Brung You* (New York: Vintage, 1999), xvii.

113 *Gail Sheehy portrayed Hillary*: Gail Sheehy, "What Hillary Wants," *Vanity Fair*, May 1, 1992.

114 *Both Bill and Hillary had resisted*: Carl Bernstein, *A Woman in Charge: The Life of Hillary Rodham Clinton* (New York: Knopf, 2007), 201; Sheehy, "What Hillary Wants."

114 *the expenditure of $100 million*: Haynes Johnson, *The Best of Times: America in the Clinton Years* (New York: Harcourt, 2004), 257.

115 *"I suppose I could have stayed home"*: Bernstein, *A Woman in Charge*, 206.

115 *"If the wife comes on looking too strong"*: Jennifer Stevenson and Barbara Hijek, "Running Mate," *St. Petersburg Times*, March 8, 1992.

115 *An internal campaign memo*: Bernstein, *A Woman in Charge*, 207.

116 *"One can detect the calculation"*: Sheehy, "What Hillary Wants."

116 *It was a perfectly reasonable concern*: For an example of this rational debate, see Richard Reeves, "Who Is Afraid of Hillary Clinton?," *The San Francisco Chronicle*, April 30, 1992, Editorial.

116 *"Legitimate questions have been raised"*: Editorial, "Hillary Pilloried," *CSM*, April 13, 1992.

117 *"She was great"*: Jeanne Freeman, "Hillary Clinton Drawing Rave Reviews," *The San Diego Union-Tribune*, February 26, 1992.

117 *"I'm proud of them"*: Jeffrey Schmalz, "The 1992 Campaign: Voters; A Spouse Who Grabs the Stage," *NYT*, April 28, 1992.

117 *"Political wives traditionally play"*: Robert Maynard, "Hillary Clinton Would Be a Novel Kind of First Lady," *The Dallas Morning News*, February 4, 1992.

117 *Lisa Caputo, Hillary's press secretary*: Interview with Lisa M. Caputo, Diane D. Blair Papers (MC 1632), Special Collections, University of Arkansas Libraries, Fayetteville, December 10, 1992.

117 *"I doubt she'll be the new Willie Horton"*: Amy Bayer, "Caution Now Hillary Clinton's Watchword," *The San Diego Union-Tribune*, April 28, 1992.

118 *"There is little doubt"*: Cal Thomas, "A Radical Feminist for President?," *St. Louis Post-Dispatch*, April 16, 1992.

118 *"a Jezebel"*: Virginia Culver, "Rescue Leader to 'Restoke' Anti-Abortion Movement," *Denver Post*, May 27, 1992.

118 *Roger Ailes*: Bayer, "Caution Now Hillary Clinton's Watchword."

118 *acting on advice of his chief of staff*: on Kristol's role, see David Brock, *Blinded by the Right: The Conscience of an Ex-Conservative* (New York: Crown, 2002), 56.

120 *"Your aunts say"*: "Profile: Randall Terry and His Operation Rescue," *NBC News: Today*, April 23, 1992.

121 *A Gallup poll*: "Abortion Support Stable 77 Pct. Disapprove of Wichita Protest," *St. Louis Post-Dispatch*, September 11, 1991.

122 *The party's embrace of progressive cultural values*: Some argue Clinton's call for welfare reform undercut every other program for women. It is a complex subject that is beyond the scope of this book. My view, however, is that the reform Clinton preferred had much to recommend it from a feminist perspective, and its defects derived from neoliberalism, not sexism.

123 *"the Democratic party is a feminist organization"*: Judi Hasson, "Female Candidates on Center Stage Tonight," *USA Today*, July 13, 1992.

123 *On the other side of the political divide*: Garry Wills, "The Born-Again Republicans," *NYRB*, September 24, 1992. Schlafly is quoted in Wills and in Jo Freeman, "Feminism vs. Family Values: Women at the 1992 Democratic and Republican Conventions," *PS: Political Science and Politics* 26, no. 1 (March 1993): 21–28.

124 *he had sent a fundraising letter*: Jurek Martin, "Republicans Resort to Fire and Brimstone," *Financial Times*, August 24, 1992.

124 *"Remember, not everyone joined the counterculture"*: "Marilyn Quayle—Republican National Convention Address," C-SPAN Video Library, http://www.c-spanvideo.org/program/31358-1

125 *Her husband's campaign manager*: Wills, "The Born-Again Republicans"; Brock, *Blinded by the Right*, 139.

125 *her travels prompted*: Margaret Carlson, Walter Shapiro, and Priscilla Painton, "All Eyes on Hillary," *Time*, September 14, 1992.

125 *One senior aide could claim*: Laurence I. Barrett, "Rot on the Right," *Time*, August 24, 1992; Laurence I. Barrett and Priscilla Painton, "After Willie Horton Are Gays Next?," *Time*, August 3, 1992.

126 *Schlafly had come to the convention*: Jo Freeman, "Feminism vs. Family Values," 22.

126 *Republican pro-choice women*: Catherine E. Rymph, *Republican Women: Feminism and Conservatism from Suffrage Through the Rise of the New Right* (Chapel Hill: University of North Carolina Press, 2006), 242.

127 *a Time/CNN poll*: Carlson, Shapiro, and Painton, "All Eyes on Hillary."

127 *political scientists reached a consensus*: Perot did draw votes disproportionately from Bush, according to exit polls, but not enough to offset Clinton's sizable margin over Bush. In a hypothetical two-way race, assuming all Perot voters would have voted, Clinton would still have won, but by a somewhat smaller margin than he did in the three-way contest. R. Michael Alvarez and Jonathan Nagler, "Economics, Issues and the Perot Candidacy: Voter Choice in the 1992 Presidential Election," *American Journal of Political Science* 39, no. 3 (August 1995): 714–744. In a different hypothetical scenario, adding the option for Perot voters to abstain from voting, Clinton's margin increases to a landslide 23 points. Dean Lacy and Barry C. Burden, "The Vote-Stealing and Turnout Effects of Ross Perot in the 1992 U.S. Presidential Election," *American Journal of Political Science* 43, no. 1 (January 1999): 233–255.

127 *The number one issue*: Alvarez and Nagler, "Economics, Issues and the Perot Candidacy."

128 *The issue of abortion*: Alan I. Abramowitz, "It's Abortion, Stupid: Policy Voting in the 1992 Presidential Election," *The Journal of Politics* 57, no. 1 (February 1995): 176–186.

128 *Support for legal abortion*: ANES, "Abortion (2), by Law 1980–2008.".

128 *Bush paid dearly*: Abramowitz, "It's Abortion, Stupid."

128 *The gender gap*: Based on ANES surveys, not exit polls, in Lois Duke Whitaker, ed., *Voting the Gender Gap* (Champaign: University of Illinois Press, 2008), 27.

128 *The cause of the gender gap*: Jeff Manza and Clem Brooks, "The Gender Gap in U.S. Presidential Elections: When? Why? Implications?" *American Journal of Sociology* 103, no. 5 (March 1, 1998): 1235–1266.

129 *Analyses of races involving women candidates*: Eric Plutzer and John F. Zipp, "Identity Politics, Partisanship, and Voting for Women Candidates," *The Public Opinion Quarterly* 60, no. 1 (Spring 1996): 30–57.

CHAPTER SEVEN

132 *"I didn't hear the whole convention"*: "Rich Bond—Right, but Late," *NYT*, February 2, 1993, editorial.

133 *"Moral imperialism"*: Gerry Braun, "Party Dissident Blames GOP Losses on Christian Coalition," *The San Diego Union-Tribune*, January 31, 1993.

133 *"Rich Bond is advocating political suicide"*: Richard L. Berke, "Political Memo: G.O.P. Seeks Identity and a Message," *NYT*, January 31, 1993.

133 *"Barely fill the average country club"*: Paul A. Gigot, "Why 'Moderates' Are the GOP's Lost Tribe," *WSJ*, December 18, 1992.

134 *"It's going to be hand-to-hand combat"*: David Foster, "Religious Right Vows 'Hand-to-Hand Combat' for Its Political Agenda," *Associated Press*, November 4, 1992.

134 *"That Clinton, who was always"*: Molly Ivins, *You Got to Dance with Them*

134 *What Brung You* (New York: Vintage, 1999), xvii.

134 *Personal and cultural conservatism*: Carl Bernstein, *A Woman in Charge: The Life of Hillary Rodham Clinton* (New York: Knopf, 2007).

134 *"As the icon of American womanhood"*: Margaret Carlson, "At the Center of Power," *Time*, May 10, 1993.

135 *"A captive of the radical left"*: Ibid.

135 *National Review columnist Florence King*: Florence King, "She," *National Review*, April 26, 1993.

135 *"has good ideas"*: George C. Church, "Are You Ready for the Cure?" *Time*, May 24, 1993.

135 *Shortly after Bill announced her role*: James M. Perry and Jeffrey H. Birnbaum, "'We' the President: New First Lady Shows Washington She, Too, Is Now at the Helm," *WSJ*, January 28, 1993.

136 *Hillary spent three days on Capitol Hill*: Bernstein, *A Woman in Charge*, 396.

136 *57 percent of those polled*: Michael Duffy, "Picture of Health," *Time* October 4, 1993.

136 *"Perhaps the most startling thing"*: James Carney, "Next Question," *Time*, October 11, 1993.

136 *"You are too strong"*: Haynes Johnson and David S. Broder, *The System: The American Way of Politics at the Breaking Point* (Boston: Little Brown & Co, 1996), 255.

137 *"a neanderthal fantasy"*: Bernstein, *A Woman in Charge*, 172.

137 *"I was astonished to see"*: David Brock, *Blinded by the Right: The Conscience of an Ex-Conservative* (New York: Crown, 2002), 169.

137 *"The most bizarre day"*: Quoted in Bernstein, *A Woman in Charge*, 364.

137 *"A sexually voracious sociopathic cipher"*: Brock, *Blinded by the Right*, 165.

138 *In March, a Time/CNN poll*: Nancy Gibbs, "The Trials of Hillary Clinton," *Time,* March 21, 1994.

138 *Hillary's favorability rating*: Hillary Clinton's historical approval rating can be found at Gallup.com.

138 *42 stories aired on network television*: Johnson and Broder, *The System*, 259.

139 *"I find it not an accident"*: "The Nightmares Before Christmas," *Time*, January 3, 1994.

139 *Among Clinton's Arkansas enemies*: Joe Conason and Gene Lyons, *The Hunting of the President: The Ten-Year Campaign to Destroy Bill and Hillary Clinton* (New York: St. Martin's Press, 2000).

140 *money and efforts of Peter W. Smith*: Ibid., 59–60.

140 *In 1993, Smith was tipped off*: Ibid., 338–339, 132–135.

140 *"get that goddamn guy out of the White House"*: Ibid., 111.

141 *The existence of the Arkansas Project remained secret*: Joe Conason and Murray Waas, "Richard Scaife Paid for Dirt on Clinton in 'Arkansas Project'," *The New York Observer*, February 8, 1998.

141 *Enamored of covert operations*: Conason and Lyons, *Hunting of the President*, 107–109.

141 *"The creation of the modern conservative movement"*: Robert G. Kaiser and Ira Chinoy, "Scaife: Funding Father of the Right," *WP*, May 2, 1999.
   "Clinton was the embodiment": Conason and Lyons, Hunting of the President, 109.

142 *Pat Robertson claimed*: Bill Geroux, "Wallets Voted, Robertson Says Evangelicals Stuck by Bush, Poll Shows," *The Richmond Times-Dispatch*, November 5, 1992.

142 *Ralph Reed*: Edwin J. Feulner, Jr., "The Blame Game Begins," *WSJ*, November 5, 1992.

142 *"While the more secular wings of the conservative movement"*: Brock, *Blinded by the Right*, 175–177, 216.

142 *They were already peddling*: Conason and Lyons, *Hunting of the President*, 136–139.

143 *The Clinton Chronicles*: Ibid., chap. 9.

143 *"The country has no morals"*: Nina Burleigh, "Clintonophobia!" *Time*, April 11, 1994.

143 *"While we grieve for him and his widow"*: "When Dissent Turns Violent," *St. Louis Post-Dispatch*, March 12, 1993, editorial.

144 *"slow everything down"*: Paul A. Gigot, "Why Liberals Really Hate Newtonian Politics," *WSJ*, October 22, 1993.

144 *"war without blood"*: Michael Schaller and George Rising, *The Republican Ascendancy: American Politics, 1968–2001* (Wheeling, IL: Harlan Davidson, 2002), 127.

145 *justly famous memo*: Bernstein, *A Woman in Charge*, 399.

145 *The collusion . . . homosexual communists*: Johnson and Broder, *The System*, 461–473; Jane Mayer, "Covert Operations," *The New Yorker*, August 20, 2010, 52.

CHAPTER EIGHT

148 *"It's the Russian Revolution in reverse"*: Howard Fineman, "Revenge of the Right," *Newsweek*, November 20, 1994.

149 *Subsequent analysis of the election results*: Contrary to anecdotal tales of the angry white male voter, which implied that Clinton had fallen from grace with the capricious Reagan Democrat of the hard-hit industrial areas, affluent women and conservative Southern men were the ones who shifted most decisively toward the GOP. Gary C. Jacobson, "The 1994 House Elections in Perspective," *Political Science Quarterly* 111, no. 2 (Summer 1996): 203–223; Jeffrey M. Stonecash and Mark D. Mariani, "Republican Gains in the House in the 1994 Elections: Class Polarization in American Politics," *Political Science Quarterly* 115, no. 1 (Spring 2000): 93–113.

149 *"The most important strategy for evangelicals"*: Reed's statement was widely quoted. This version is in Joan Lowy, "'Stealth' Christian Coalition Is Making Inroads in Politics," *Houston Chronicle*, January 3, 1993.

149 *"You don't know it's over"*: Sara Diamond, *Not by Politics Alone: The Enduring Influence of the Christian Right* (New York: Guilford Press, 2000), 78.

149 *In San Diego county*: Seth Mydans, "Evangelicals Gain with Covert Candidates," *NYT*, October 27, 1992.

150 *"You should never mention"*: Lowy, "'Stealth' Christian Coalition."

150 *two dozen state Republican parties*: Ibid.

150 *In Washington state*: Mydans, "Evangelicals Gain with Covert Candidates."

151 *Mobilization of the sexual fundamentalist voter*: Mark J. Rozell and Clyde Wilcox, *God at the Grass Roots: The Christian Right in the 1994 Elections* (Lanham, MD: Rowman & Littlefield, 1995).

151 *Of all the House seats picked up by the GOP*: Ibid., 16; Bryan Le Beau, "The Political Mobilization of the New Christian Right," http://are.as.wvu.edu/lebeau1.htm; Kimberly H. Conger, and John C. Green, "Spreading Out and Digging In: Christian Conservatives and State Republican Parties," *Campaigns & Elections* (February 2002): 58–65. Calculations by author from Conger and Green and reporting in *Congressional Quarterly.*

151 *"They were dancing"*: Sharon Schmickle, "Christian Conservatives Aim for Mainstream," Minneapolis-St. Paul *Star-Tribune,* October 31, 1994.

152 *His female opponent*: John F. Harris, "Far-Right Candidate Stirs Fears for Some in Va. GOP; But Loudoun Lawyer Who Seeks Lieutenant Governor's Job Attracts Passionate Following," *WP*, March 22, 1993.

152 *The strategists behind the Contract*: Garry Wills, "What Happened to the Revolution," *NYRB*, June 6, 1996.

152 *Swayed few voters*: Political scientists Jeffrey M. Stonecash and Mark D. Mariani present compelling evidence that the Contract's articulation of conservative economic themes was a factor in a shift among high-income voters from Clinton in '92 to the GOP in '94. (Health care reform and tax increases also soured high-income voters on Clinton.) They make the important point that high-income men *and women*, not economically strapped angry white men, were the vote switchers. Many House races were close, so these small numbers of voters made a difference. As we'll see throughout, the GOP can't win with only Christian Right voters. I would argue that the Contract's role in rebranding the GOP and masking the influence of the sexual fundamentalists in the party is consistent with these findings. (Stonecash and Mariani, "Republican Gains in the House in the 1994 Elections.")

153 *"You have been hearing"*: James Moore and Wayne Slater, *Bush's Brain: How Karl Rove Made George W. Bush Presidential* (New York: Wiley, 2004), 208–210.

153 *"There was clearly an organized Republican"*: Ibid., 210; Paul Alexander, *Machiavelli's Shadow: The Rise and Fall of Karl Rove* (New York: Rodale Books, 2008), 60.

154 *They openly doubted that George W.*: Nicholas Lemann, "The Redemption," *The New Yorker,* January 31, 2000.

154 *One of the most notorious casualties*: David Van Biema and Greg Aunapu, "Governors on the Run," *Time,* October 24, 1994, 44.

154 *In Texas*: Mark J Bruce, "Texas: The Emergence of the Christian Right," in *God at the Grass Roots*, 67–89.

156 *Pragmatist with bipartisan inclinations*: Richard Lacayo and Sam Allis, "They Can Multiply Without Dividing," *Time*, November 21, 1994, 66.

156 *"As Bush brothers go"*: Molly Ivins, "Shrubwhacked," *The Nation*, November 28, 1994.

156 *Voters who were registered but did not vote*: Martin P. Wattenberg and Craig

Leonard Brians, "Partisan Turnout Bias in Midterm Legislative Elections," *Legislative Studies Quarterly* 27, no. 3 (August 2002): 407–421.

156 *Clinton's missteps had alienated the moderate middle*: The more conservative version of the Middle America theory won important reinforcement from two brilliant defectors from the conservative movement, Garry Wills and Michael Lind. Unfortunately there is not space here to deal with them. See, especially, Lind's *Up from Conservatism* (New York: Free Press, 1997).

156 *"For President Clinton"*: Richard Lacayo, "After the Revolution," *Time*, November 28, 1994.

156 *Stan Greenberg insisted Clinton had failed*: Stanley B. Greenberg, *Dispatches from the War Room: In the Trenches with Five Extraordinary Leaders* (New York: Thomas Dunne Books, 2009), 103.

157 *"The racial and cultural polarization"*: See also Stanley Greenberg, "After the Republican Surge," *TAP*, September 21, 1995 and Greenberg, *Middle Class Dreams*, 276–277.

157 *"The group that holds the future"*: E. J. Dionne, *They Only Look Dead: Why Progressives Will Dominate the Next Political Era* (New York: Simon & Schuster, 1996), 66–68.

157 *Its members recoiled when Clinton*: Ibid., 115.

157 *"On questions of culture and morality"*: Ibid., 86.

158 *"Signaled cultural moderation"*: Robert Kuttner, "Up from 1994," *TAP*, December 1, 1994.

158 *"Democrats have always been out of sync"*: Jeff Faux, "A New Conversation: How to Rebuild the Democratic Party," *TAP*, March 21, 1995. For another variation on this theme, see Ruy A Teixeira and Joel Rogers, *America's Forgotten Majority: Why the White Working Class Still Matters* (New York: Basic Books, 2000).

159 *"A Left that was serious"*: *The Twilight of Common Dreams: Why America Is Wracked by Culture Wars* (New York: Holt, 1995), 34, 234.

160 *"Regardless of what any of us tells him"*: Robert B. Reich, *Locked in the Cabinet* (New York: Knopf, 1997), 261–262.

161 *"The enemy of normal Americans"*: Michael Schaller and George Rising, *The Republican Ascendancy: American Politics, 1968–2001* (Wheeling, IL: Harlan Davidson, Inc., 2002), 122, 127.

161 *"The Gestapo of government"*: Ibid., 132–133.

162 *Americans approved of Clinton's firmness*: Pew, "Retro-Politics: The Political Typology—Version 3.0," November 11, 1999; Gallup, "Gingrich an Unpopular Figure During His Tenure As Speaker," November 11, 1999.

162 *"Out of our pockets"*: Thomas B. Edsall, "Robertson Urges Christian Activists to Take Over GOP State Parties," *WP*, September 10, 1995; Robin Toner, "Right Hook: G.O.P.'s Libertarian Streak Becomes a Blur," *NYT*, February 25, 1996.

162 *"The flames of hedonism"*: Jerry Gray, "House Passes Bar to U.S. Sanction of Gay Marriage," *NYT*, July 13, 1996.

163 *The Clinton reelection campaign*: "Ad Touts Clinton's Opposing Gay Marriage," *NYT*, October 15, 1996.

163 *"was a feminist icon"*: David Brock, *Blinded by the Right: The Conscience of an Ex-Conservative* (New York: Crown, 2002), 271.

163 *he recounted in his memoir*: The book followed on his 1997 article revealing

the inner workings of the anti-Clinton conspiracy, "Confessions of a Right-Wing Hit Man," *Vanity Fair*, July 1997.)

164 *"Red meat"*: Brock, *Blinded by the Right*, 287, 284.

164 *The bottom line*: R. Michael Alvarez and Jonathan Nagler, "Economics, Entitlements, and Social Issues: Voter Choice in the 1996 Presidential Election," *American Journal of Political Science* 42, no. 4 (October 1998): 1349–1363.

165 *Voters who felt negatively toward fundamentalists*: Louis Bolce and Gerald de Maio, "The Anti-Christian Fundamentalist Factor in Contemporary Politics," *The Public Opinion Quarterly* 63, no. 4 (Winter 1999): 508–542. As in most studies of the Christian Right, this study examined white voters only.

<h2 style="text-align:center">CHAPTER NINE</h2>

For detailed and reliable analyses of the issues involved in the so-called Clinton scandals, see Jeffrey Toobin, *A Vast Conspiracy: The Real Story of the Sex Scandal That Nearly Brought Down a President* (New York: Simon & Schuster, 2000); Joe Conason and Gene Lyons, *The Hunting of the President: The Ten-Year Campaign to Destroy Bill and Hillary Clinton* (New York: St. Martin's Press, 2000); Haynes Johnson, *The Best of Times: America in the Clinton Years* (New York: Harcourt, 2004). The best brief history of the politics of Clinton's second term is Sean Wilentz, *The Age of Reagan* (New York: HarperCollins, 2008), chs.12, 13. Sanctions against Clinton were imposed by the judge in the Paula Jones case, who ruled him in contempt of court for lying about his relationship to Monica Lewinsky—information that only made it to that case because of the right-wing conspiracy.

169 *announced he was resigning*: Conason and Lyons, *The Hunting of the President*, 264–268.

169 *Scaife lost patience*: Ibid., 312–314.

169 *"unemployable and the obsessed"*: Toobin, *A Vast Conspiracy*, 189.

169 *Ewing and some like-minded colleagues*: Ibid., 190–193.

170 *Jones's lawyers resigned*: Ibid., 127.

170 *Carpenter-McMillan took charge*: Ibid., 136; Conason and Lyons, *The Hunting of the President*, 318–321.

172 *"Mr. President, if these allegations are true"*: Katharine Q. Seelye, "The President Under Fire: The Conservatives; Senator Urges Clinton to Quit If Sex Scenario Was a Reality," *NYT*, January 31, 1998.

172 *"'just sex'"*: Emory, "The Clinton Legacy," *Weekly Standard*, August 10, 1998

173 *Clinton had "defiled" the presidency*: Michiko Kakutani, "The Lewinsky Scandal as Presidential Decoder," *NYT*, October 20, 1998.

173 *child care ranked alongside child abuse*: William J. Bennett, *The Index of Leading Cultural Indicators: American Society at the End of the 20th Century* (New York: Broadway Books, 1999). The book was first published in 1994. Quotations are from the 1999 edition.

174 *Gingrich and Clinton*: Steven M. Gillon, *The Pact: Bill Clinton, Newt Gingrich, and the Rivalry That Defined a Generation* (New York: Oxford University Press, 2008).

174 *Gingrich's pollsters*: Johnson, *The Best of Times*, 395.

174 *Scaife and the Arkansas Project*: David Brock, "Confessions of a Right-Wing Hit Man," *Vanity Fair*, July 1997; Joe Conason and Murray Waas, "Richard Scaife Paid for Dirt on Clinton in 'Arkansas Project'," February 8, 1998.

175 *"We had worked so hard"*: Kaiser, "The Chronicle of Lieberman," *WP*, February 13, 1999.

176 *reporters trapped Democrats*: Eric Schmitt, "Many Democrats Concur with Rebuke to Clinton," *NYT*, September 5, 1998.

176 *Polls showed consistently*: See Gallup and Pew polls for 1998; Alan I. Abramowitz, "It's Monica, Stupid: The Impeachment Controversy and the 1998 Midterm Election," *Legislative Studies Quarterly* 26, no. 2 (May 2001): 211–226.

177 *Not since 1922*: Jacob S. Hacker and Paul Pierson, *Off Center: The Republican Revolution and the Erosion of American Democracy* (New Haven: Yale University Press, 2005), 74.

177 *Impeachment was the sole and most important issue*: Alan I. Abramowitz, "It's Monica, Stupid," 215.

178 *Starr testified*: Johnson, *The Best of Times*, 398–400.

178 *a New York Times poll reported*: Ibid., 409.

178 *"a small, intricately knit rightwing conspiracy"*: Conason and Lyons, *Hunting of the President*, 302.

179 *Clinton would have lost*: Clem Brooks, "Civil Rights Liberalism and the Suppression of a Republican Political Realignment in the United States, 1972 to 1996," *American Sociological Review* 65, no. 4 (August 2000): 483–505.

179 *Although southern white women*: Alan I. Abramowitz and Kyle L. Saunders, "Exploring the Bases of Partisanship in the American Electorate: Social Identity vs. Ideology," *Political Research Quarterly* 59, no. 2 (June 2006): 175–187.

179 *These gender gaps*: Karen Kaufmann, "Culture Wars, Secular Realignment, and the Gender Gap in Party Identification," *Political Behavior* 24, no. 3 (September 2002): 283-307.

180 *GOP drove its own voters away*: Clem Brooks and Jeff Manza, *Social Cleavages and Political Change: Voter Alignments and U.S. Party Coalitions* (New York: Oxford Univ. Press, 1999; Brooks, "Civil Rights Liberalism."

180 *Negative view of the Christian Right*: Louis Bolce and Gerald de Maio, "The Anti-Christian Fundamentalist Factor in Contemporary Politics," *The Public Opinion Quarterly* 63, no. 4 (Winter 1999): 508. The Christian Right is a white political movement, and because African American evangelicals vote overwhelmingly Democratic, scholarly studies of it almost always analyze white voters only.

180 *Concerned with the so-called decline of the family*: Clem Brooks, "Religious Influence and the Politics of Family Decline Concern: Trends, Sources, and U.S. Political Behavior," *American Sociological Review* 67, no. 2 (April 2002): 191–211.

180 *"intensely dislike fundamentalists"*: Bolce and de Maio, "The Anti-Christian Fundamentalist Factor in Contemporary Politics."

180 *By the late 1990s*: Brooks and Manza, *Social Cleavages and Political Change*.

181 *Class voting*: See particularly Larry M. Bartels, *Unequal Democracy: The*

Political Economy of the New Gilded Age (Princeton Univ. Press, 2008); Jeffrey M. Stonecash, *Class and Party in American Politics* (Boulder: Westview Press, 2000); Mark D. Brewer, "The Rise of Partisanship and the Expansion of Partisan Conflict within the American Electorate," *Political Research Quarterly* 58, no. 2 (June 2005): 219–229.

181 *Blue-collar middle-class men voted less Republican*: Brooks and Manza, *Social Cleavages and Political Change*, 78–80, 284.

182 *Demographic and cultural tipping point*: Tom Smith, "The Emerging 21st Century American Family" (Chicago: NORC, February 1999): USCB, Stat. Abstract, 2008, Tables 84, 1301.

183 *Sexual mores*: Tom Smith, "American Sexual Behavior: Trends, Socio-Demographic Differences, and Risk Behavior," GSS Topical Report (Chicago: NORC, April 2003), 42; Smith, "The Emerging 21st Century American Family"; USCB, Stat. Abs. 2008, table 97.

CHAPTER TEN

The following account of the 2000 campaign is drawn primarily from my review of national and local newspapers in the ProQuest and LexisNexis databases.

184 *"The fear among many party professionals"*: James Barnes, "Next Up: Gore vs. Bush?" *National Journal*, November 7, 1998.

185 *"perfectionist caucus"*: James Traub, "A Curse on the House, *NYT*, February 28, 1999.

185 *Paul Weyrich ventured*: David Von Drehle, "Social Conservatives' Ties to GOP Fraying: Weyrich's Disillusion 'Touched a Chord'," *NYT*, February 28, 1999.

185 *George W. Bush*: Nicholas Lemann, "The Redemption," *The New Yorker*, January 31, 2000; Molly Ivins and Lou Dubose, *Shrub: The Short but Happy Political Life of George W. Bush* (New York: Vintage, 2000); Burt Solomon, The Other, Softer, GOP," *National Journal*, February 20, 1999.

185 *"compassionate conservative philosophy"*: Barnes, "Next Up: Gore vs. Bush?"

186 *carefully honed Bush's image*: Terry Neal, "A Web of Bush Tickets," *WP*, May 14, 1999; Cokie and Steve Roberts, "Bush Faces Hurdles on Path to Top," June 18, 1999, *Times-Picayune* (New Orleans); Dan Balz, "Bush Shows a Shadow of Clintonism," *WP*, October 17, 1999; Gene Lyons, "How Bush Could Lose Presidency," *Arkansas Democrat-Gazette,* October 13, 1999; Howard Fineman and Matthew Cooper, "Back in the Amen Corner," *Newsweek*, March 22, 1999; Von Drehle, "Social Conservatives' Ties to GOP Fraying."

187 *the sexual counterrevolutionaries complained*: Robert Cohen, "Republican Right-wingers Stump for Forbes," *Times-Picayune*, November 28, 1999.

187 *"Dubya's skillful handling"*: Ivins and Dubose, *Shrub*.

188 *Older feminists:* Rebecca Traister, *Big Girls Don't Cry: The Election That Changed Everything for American Women* (New York: Free Press, 2010), 1.

189 *"the incredible stain"*: The exact quote is from a 2000 column by liberal *New York Times* columnist Bob Herbert. The sentiment of disgust, and its damage to Gore, was widespread. Bob Herbert, "Gore's Crucial Week," *NYT*, August 14, 2000.

189 *"I have always thought"*: Ronald Brownstein, "Impeachment Debate Could Tar Gore and GOP," *LAT*, February 5, 1999.

189 *when NBC News and the* Wall Street Journal *asked:* "Poll Readings," *National Journal*, March 27, 1999.

189 *In April, Pew reported*: Pew, "Clinton Fatigue Undermines Gore Poll Standing," April 17, 1999.

189 *"It is hard to find solid evidence"*: Gallup, "'Clinton Fatigue' Far from Epidemic Among Voters," October 21, 1999.

190 *A comprehensive, multi-year survey*: Pew, "Retro-Politics: The Political Typology—Version 3.0" (Pew, November 11, 1999).

191 *said the word conservative twelve times*: Benen, "God and Election 2000," *Church and State*, December 2000.

191 *Dobson issued a press release calling McCain*: Eric Gorski, "Dobson Keeps Low Profile in Presidential Race," *The Gazette*, February 28, 2000; "Falwell and Dobson Condemn Bauer Endorsement of McCain," *PR Newswire*, February 18, 2000.

191 *Pat Robertson dispatched Roberta Combs*: Benen, "God and Election 2000."

191 *Norquist's groups ran TV ads*: John Cassidy, "The Ringleader," *The New Yorker*, August 1, 2005.
    South Carolinian voters were deluged: Eric Pooley, "Read My Knuckles," *Time*, February 28, 2000.
    "Will moderates still buy": Pooley, "Read My Knuckles."

192 *McCain denounced Robertson and Falwell*: David Barstow, "The 2000 Campaign: The Arizona Senator," *NYT*, February 29, 2000.

192 *"We don't have to win the education debate"*: Bruni, "Bush Signaling a Readiness to Go His Own Way As an Unconventional Republican," *NYT*, April 3, 2000.

192 *The sexual fundamentalists publicly indulged Bush*: Elizabeth Drew, "Behind the Right's Disarray," *WP*, March 19, 2000; Berke, "Grand Old Pragmatists," *NYT*, April 22, 2000.

193 *"Jesus day"*: Benen, "God and Election 2000."

193 *General Colin Powell*: "Republicans Pitch Their Big Tent Powell," *Boston Globe*, August 1, 2000.

194 *"We thought at the end of the primaries"*: Katharine Q. Seelye, "Gore's Post-Primary Pace Worries Some Democrats," *NYT*, May 25, 2000.

194 *"pulled the mask off Bush"*: Helen Kennedy, "Veep: Primary Unmasked GOPers," *Daily News*, February 22, 2000.

194 *"Bush is trying to emulate"*: Berke, "Grand Old Pragmatists." Early in the race Al From was using Bush's centrist positioning for his own DLC purposes. See John A. Farrell, "GOP's Right Wing Could Face More Defections," *Boston Globe*, October 9 1999.

195 *centrist Democrats damned Gore with faint praise*: "Gore and Bush Toot the Reform Horn," *National Journal*, June 17, 2000.

195 *"The prevailing view"*: Jack W. Germond and Jules Witcover, "Hold Up on Gore Remake II," *National Journal*, June 3, 2000.

195 *Voters were confused*: Gallup, "Voters Generally Unaware of Bush-Gore Differences on Issues," June 5, 2000.

195 *"At a time when the electorate"*: Stanley B. Greenberg and Anna Greenberg, "Adding Values," *TAP*, August 2000.

196 *He opened his acceptance speech*: Benen, "God and Election 2000"; "Why Line Is Fading Between Politics and Piety," *CSM*, September 1, 2000.

197 *"Pretty much everyone in the White House"*: Victor Kirk, Richard E. Cohen, and David Baumann, "Lieberman: Pros and Cons," *National Journal*, August 12, 2000.

197 *Kohut*, "The Bright Line Gore Needs to Draw," *NYT*, August 14, 2000.

197 *the ironic headline*: Burt Solomon, "Militant Moderates," *National Journal*, 32:41:3144.

198 *To win Pennsylvania*: Jack Germond and Jules Witcover, "Bush's Pennsylvania Problem," *National Journal*, October 14, 2000.

198 *Gallup's final pre-election national poll*: Gallup, "Major Turning Points in 2000 Election," November 7, 2000.

199 *Conservative icon William Buckley*: "Is Pat Buchanan Anti-Semitic?" *Newsweek*, December 23, 1991.

199 *more than 2,000 unintentional votes for Buchanan*: Jonathan N. Wand et al., "The Butterfly Did It: The Aberrant Vote for Buchanan in Palm Beach County, Florida," *The American Political Science Review* 95, no. 4 (December 2001): 793–810.

199 *20 percent of ballots in predominantly African American areas*: Ford Fessenden and John M. Broder, "Examining the Vote: The Overview," *NYT*, November 12, 2001.

200 *the Republican D.C. staffers broke through the doors*: John Lantigua, "Miami's Rent-a-Riot," *Salon*, November 28, 2000.

200 *the results of the national vote*: The numbers here are from Leip's almanac, which tallies all valid votes certified by the states, often months after an election. Although there are more total votes in Leip's calculation, Gore's margin over Bush in the popular vote, roughly a half million votes and half a percentage point, was known the day after the election and did not change.

202 *Every vote that could be counted*: Fessenden and Broder, "Examining the Vote: The Overview."

202 *"I call on all Americans"*: Gore and Bush speeches available at APP.

203 *Never mind that Clinton's extramarital escapades*: The rate of extramarital affairs has dropped dramatically since the sexual revolution. Tom Smith, "American Sexual Behavior: Trends, Socio-Demographic Differences, and Risk Behavior," NORC, April 2003, 49.

203 *Gore lost white men*: Thomas Schaller, "So Long, White Boy," *Salon*, September 17, 2007.

203 *Greenberg asserted that Gore lost*: Stanley Greenberg and Robert Borosage, "Liberal Loss or Progressive Mandate?" *TAP*, April 22, 2001.

204 *"The idea that the Clinton record"*: Ruy Teixeira, "Lessons for Next Time," *TAP*, December 18, 2000.

204 *"the issues of gays in the military"*: Stanley B. Greenberg, *The Two Americas: Our Current Political Deadlock and How to Break It* (New York: St. Martin's Griffin, 2005), 20.

204 *Clinton could not have disagreed more*: Taylor Branch, *The Clinton Tapes: Wrestling History with the President* (New York: Simon & Schuster, 2009), 643.

205 *Academic experts had almost unanimously predicted*: Gerald M. Pomper, "The

2000 Presidential Election: Why Gore Lost," *Political Science Quarterly* 116, no. 2 (Summer 2001): 201–223.

205 *Clinton begged*: Branch, *The Clinton Tapes*, 641–645.

205 *Gore's strong performance*: Gary C. Jacobson, "A House and Senate Divided: The Clinton Legacy and the Congressional Elections of 2000," *Political Science Quarterly* 116, no. 1 (Spring 2001): 5–27; Lois Duke Whitaker, ed., *Voting the Gender Gap* (Champaign: University of Illinois Press, 2008), 152.

205 *Gore won the same percentage of white men*: Schaller, "So Long, White Boy."

206 *no statistically sound investigation*: One statistically sound regression conducted by political scientists explicitly states that their model cannot explain *why* these voters defected, because the exit poll did not include any questions that could be used to analyze causation. D. Sunshine Hillygus and Simon Jackman, "Voter Decision Making in Election 2000: Campaign Effects, Partisan Activation, and the Clinton Legacy," *American Journal of Political Science* 47, no. 4 (October 2003): 583–596.

206 *"Gore neglected to put the election"*: Pomper, "The 2000 Presidential Election," 212.

206 *apparently because Greenberg convinced him*: Branch, *The Clinton Tapes*, 643.

206 *the one-quarter of the electorate that credited Clinton*: Thomas J. Rudolph and J. Tobin Grant, "An Attributional Model of Economic Voting: Evidence from the 2000 Presidential Election," *Political Research Quarterly* 55, no. 4 (December 2002): 805–823.

206 *richest 1 percent*: "Two Men, Two Visions," *Time*, November 6, 2000.

206 *more effort to clarify the clear differences*: Pomper, "The 2000 Presidential Election"; Branch, *The Clinton Tapes*.

207 *The income gap*: Jeffrey M. Stonecash, "The Income Gap," *PS: Political Science and Politics* 39, no. 3 (July 2006): 461–465.

207 *Independents, whose views were very close to Democrats*: Pew, "Retro-Politics."

207 *Nader's vote was drawn*: Pomper, "The 2000 Presidential Election," 208, Table 1.

208 *if everyone had voted*: Emmett H. Buell, "Review: The 2000 Elections," *The Journal of Politics* 64, no. 2 (May 2002): 213, n20.

208 *Many potential Democratic voters*: The turnout by voting-age population was 50.4 percent. Calculated as voting-eligible population, turnout was slightly higher than the other recent lows of 1988 and 1996. But low turnout in those races was primarily due to the lack of competitiveness. Months before those elections, the winners were clear. Pomper, "The 2000 Presidential Election"; Branch, *The Clinton Tapes*, 643; *Voting and Registration in the Election of November 2000*, U.S. Census, February 2002.

209 *On Election Day, the sexual counterrevolutionaries*: Lyman A. Kellstedt, Corwin E. Smidt, James L. Guth, and John C. Green, "Cracks in the Monolith? Evangelicals and the 2000 Election," *Books & Culture: A Christian Review* 7, 3 (May/June 2001). Clinton had lost some of these states in 1996. Kimberly H. Conger and John C. Green, "Spreading Out and Digging In: Christian Conservatives and State Republican Parties," *Campaigns & Elections* (February 2002): 58–65.

209 *Denied that he supported Bush*: Ceci Connolly, "McCain Dislikes Attack Ad— Sort of," *WP*, January 7, 2000.

209 *"Bush went to every piece of my coalition"*: Cassidy, "The Ringleader" (on voter

lists); Norquist quoted in "Pumping Iron, Digging Gold, Pressing Flesh," *Newsweek*, November 20, 2000.

209 *Four out of five evangelicals*: Kellstedt et al., "Cracks in the Monolith?"

210 *"From the moment Ralph Reed clambered aboard"*: Howard Meyerson, "Gore's Mating Ritual," *TAP*, July 2000. (The article is misdated in the *TAP* online article archives.)

210 *A joint study by Pew's Project for Excellence*: "Convention Must Push Bush to the Center," *San Diego Union Tribune*, August 2, 2000.

210 *expose the workings of Bush's shell game*: The first quotation is from Dionne's June 20 column; the second is from "The GOP's Stealth Agenda," *WP*, October 27, 2000; and the third is from Berke, "Conservative Organizations: Some Quiet Support on Polarizing Topics," *NYT*, September 26, 2000.

211 *Falwell said to reporter Steve Benen*: Benen, "God and Election 2000."

211 *Bush received 28 percent of his total*: Buell, "Review: The 2000 Elections."

CHAPTER ELEVEN

213 *He governed as a pseudo-conservative*: Hofstadter, *The Paranoid Style in American Politics* (New York: Random House, 1952).

213 *Bush reversed himself*: Ron Suskind, *The Price of Loyalty: George W. Bush, the White House, and the Education of Paul O'Neill* (New York: Simon & Schuster, 2004), chaps. 2–4.

214 *"There are very large opportunities"*: Ibid., 131.

215 *A third of the $1.35 trillion, 10-year tax cut*: Paul Pierson and Jacob S. Hacker, *Winner-Take-All Politics: How Washington Made the Rich Richer—and Turned Its Back on the Middle Class* (New York: Simon & Schuster, 2010), 214.

216 *"When George W. Bush nominated"*: Lindsey Sobel, "About Face: Far from Unifying, Bush Coddles the Christian Right," *TAP*, January 26, 2001.

216 *The Family Research Council enthused*: David Skaggs and Calvin Van Taylor, *With God on Our Side: George W. Bush and the Rise of the Religious Right in America* (documentary film; First Run Features, 2005).

216 *The regulations prohibited teachers*: Heather Boonstra, "Advocates Call for a New Approach After the Era of 'Abstinence Only' Sex Education, *Guttmacher Policy Review* vol. 12, 1 (Winter 2009).

216 *"What became clear to me"*: Suskind, *The Price of Loyalty*, 130.

216 *the treasury department announced*: "U.S. to Borrow Billions to Cover Tax-Refund Checks," *Associated Press*, August 1, 2001.

216 *the CIA had briefed the president*: Ron Suskind, *The One-Percent Doctrine: Deep Inside America's Pursuit of Its Enemies Since 9/11* (New York: Simon & Schuster, 2006), 2.

217 *"I really believe that the pagans"*: Falwell and Robertson, *700 Club*, Sep. 13, 2011 http://www.youtube.com/watch?v=H-CAcdta_8I

218 *"I think God gave us"*: Skaggs and Van Taylor, *With God on Our Side*.

218 *One out of every fourteen Bush administration interns*: Michelle Goldberg, *Kingdom Coming: The Rise of Christian Nationalism* (W.W. Norton, 2007), 3.

218 *a third of all U.S. funding for AIDS prevention*: "Institute of Medicine: Abstinence Education Spending Requirement Hinders International Response to HIV/AIDS," *Guttmacher Policy Review*, Spring 2007,

219 *"social fundamentalists"*: Christine Todd Whitman, *It's My Party Too: The Battle for the Heart of the GOP and the Future of America* (New York: Penguin, 2006).

219 *"The breadth of the unhappiness"*: Franklin Foer, "The Grumblers," *The New Republic*, September 13, 2004.

220 *increased 37 percent*: AAP 2008, 22.

220 *But only 15 million Americans*: Barry T. Hirsch and David A. Macpherson, "Union Membership and Coverage Database from the Current Population Survey: Note," *Industrial and Labor Relations Review*, Vol. 56, No. 2, January 2003, pp. 349–54.

220 *Joan Blades and Wes Boyd*: Joan Blades, interview by author, January 25, 2011.

221 *the California Democratic party hosted*: http://www.gwu.edu/~action/2004/cdp0303/cdp0303main.html

223 *MoveOn had offered*: Blades interview.

224 *In the 2004 election cycle*: These figures are taken from the groups' websites and have not been independently verified. They are, however, consistent with the overall turnout numbers and with reporting about mobilization during the election.

224 *Young voters*: Heather Smith, interview by author, March 28, 2011.

225 *In Illinois, an obscure state senator*: David Remnick, *The Bridge: The Life and Rise of Barack Obama* (New York: Knopf, 2010), 376, 389.

225 *National Election Pool exit poll*: Results available at CNN.com Election 2004, http://www.cnn.com/ELECTION/2004/pages/results/states/US/P/00/epolls.0.html

226 *"Can the Democrats ever connect"*: The Chris Matthews Show, NBC, November 7, 2004.

226 *"don't believe that the Democrats"*: "Democrats and the God Gap," *LAT*, November 7, 2004.

226 *"Ours is not a right-wing country"*: Dionne, "Moderates Not Moralists," *WP*, November 9, 2004.

226 *"The question in effect asked"*: Gary Langer and Jon Cohen, "Voters and Values in the 2004 Election," *Public Opinion Quarterly* 69, no. 5 (January 1, 2005): 747.

226 *The issue of gay marriage*: Alan I. Abramowitz, "Terrorism, Gay Marriage, and Incumbency: Explaining the Republican Victory in the 2004 Presidential Election," *The Forum* 2, no. 4 (December 29, 2004). There is some disagreement among scholars about the value of gay marriage to GOP turnout. Nevertheless, nothing about these results indicates a conservative *shift* in the electorate, the main issue here.

227 *A rigorous study concluded that Latinos*: David L. Leal et al., "The Latino Vote in the 2004 Election," *PS: Political Science and Politics* 38, no. 1 (January 2005): 41–49.

227 *Bush's margin over 2000*: Langer and Cohen, "Voters and Values 2004."

227 *Lower-income supporters of the war*: Jeffrey M. Stonecash, "The Income Gap," *PS: Political Science and Politics* 39, no. 3 (July 2006): 461–465.

227 *women's different views on security*: Karen M. Kaufmann, "The Gender Gap," *PS: Political Science and Politics* 39, no. 3 (July 2006): 447–453.

228 *Nor did independents swing*: D. Sunshine Hillygus and Todd G. Shields, "Moral Issues and Voter Decision Making in the 2004 Presidential Election," *PS: Political Science and Politics* 38, no. 2 (April 2005): 201–209.

229 *"The trick never ages"*: Thomas Frank, *What's the Matter with Kansas? How Conservatives Won the Heart of America* (New York: Metropolitan Books, 2004), 7.

229 *"People getting their fundamental"*: All quotations in this paragraph from ibid., 243–245.

229 *implored Democrats to concede*: Stanley Greenberg and Anna Greenberg, "Contesting Values," *TAP*, March 5, 2004; Stanley B. Greenberg, *The Two Americas: Our Current Political Deadlock and How to Break It* (New York: St. Martin's Griffin, 2005).

230 *"have probably cost more Democrats"*: Carville and Begala, *Take It Back: Our Party, Our Country, Our Future* (New York: Simon & Schuster, 2006), 34.

230 *reprising their tales of betrayal*: Edsall, *Building Red America* (New York: Basic Books, 2006); Gitlin, *The Bulldozer and the Big Tent* (Wiley, 2007).

230 *Dean was running a religious voters office*: James L. Guth, "Religion in the 2008 Election," in Janet M. Box-Steffensmeier and Steven E. Schier, *The American Elections of 2008* (New York: Rowman & Littlefield, 2009), 120.

230 *"Shift the debate"*: Carville and Begala, *Take It Back*, 56.

231 *"Liberals made a series of fundamental mistakes"*: Eric Alterman, "Where Does American Liberalism Stand Today?" *TPMCafe*, May 19, 2008.

231 *"sported an outspoken foreign wife"*: Eric Alterman, *Why We're Liberals: A Political Handbook for Post Bush America* (New York: Viking, 2008), 55, emphasis added. Alterman thought it was a matter of principle to support gay marriage. Alterman included a respectful tip of the hat to Dinesh D'Souza (a Culture War pioneer who resurfaced in 2010 with his racist book, *The Roots of Obama's Rage*). Alterman praised D'Souza's insight that "the biggest victories of the cultural left in the past few decades have all been achieved undemocratically." Obscuring the real history of the social movements behind the sexual revolution, feminism, and gay rights, Alterman claimed that it was Supreme Court decisions which "had the effect of transforming not only abortion rights in America but also sexuality itself, and did so on the basis of an extremely convoluted and easily challenged legal reading." What were the cases involving "convoluted" reasoning? The same cases the right-wing sexual fundamentalists despised: *Griswold*—which decriminalized birth control for married couples by recognizing a constitutional right to privacy. *Loving*—which overruled bans on interracial marriage by recognizing marriage as one of the fundamental rights of a constitutional republic.

231 *"Working-class whites"*: Larry M. Bartels, "What's the Matter with What's the Matter with Kansas?," in *Annual Meeting*, presented at the American Political Science Association, Washington, D.C., 2005.

232 *reached a similar conclusion*: Teixeira and Abramowitz found that low-income, non–college-educated Democratic voters were somewhat more conservative than higher-income voters—the former still favored abortion rights at the 55 percent level—but their party identification was not particularly linked to their abortion views. "It does not appear that cultural issues like abortion have played a major—and certainly not *the* major—role in the decline

of Democratic identification among [lower-income and less educated] white voters," they explained. "The story of declining white working class support for the Democrats is, as we outlined earlier, far more complex than that." Ruy Teixeira and Alan Abramowitz, "The Decline of the White Working Class and the Rise of a Mass Upper Middle Class," Brookings Working Paper (Washington, DC: Brookings Institution and American Enterprise Institute, April 2008), 20. See also Thomas F. Schaller, *Whistling Past Dixie: How Democrats Can Win Without the South* (Simon & Schuster, 2006)

232 *"is a classic sucker's bet"*: Schaller, "So Long, White Boy," *Salon*, September 17, 2007; see also John B. Judis and Ruy A. Teixeira, *The Emerging Democratic Majority* (New York: Scribner, 2002; 2004 ed.).

232 *"I earned capital in this campaign"*: Presidential press conference, November 5, 2004.

233 *"man on dog" sex*: A transcript of the interview is in USATODAY.com: "Excerpt from Santorum interview," http://www.usatoday.com/news/washington/2003-04-23-santorum-excerpt_x.htm

233 *when President Bush rushed back*: Details and the timeline of the Schiavo case available from University of Miami, Ethics Programs, Schiavo Case, http://www6.miami.edu/ethics/schiavo/timeline.htm

233 *According to a CNN/ USA Today/ Gallup poll*: cited in "The Progressive Majority: Why a Conservative America Is a Myth," Campaign for America's Future and Media Matters, June 2007.

234 *The bill was sponsored:*" Stem Cell Research Enhancement Act of 2005": http://thomas.loc.gov/cgi-bin/bdquery/z?d109:HR00810:@@@R TK LAW

234 *when Hurricane Katrina made landfall*: "ThinkProgress Katrina Timeline," http://thinkprogress.org/katrina-timeline/. A hat tip to Markos Moulitsas and Jerome Armstrong for noting Bush's lack of urgency in *Crashing the Gate: Netroots, Grassroots, and the Rise of People-Powered Politics* (White River Junction, VT: Chelsea Green, 2006), 19.

235 *DeLay "actually cared about"*: Robin Toner, "A Partisan Leaves; Will an Era Follow Suit?" *NYT*, April 5, 2006.

235 *I wouldn't be surprised"*: quoted in *AAP* 2008, 119–121.

236 *Center-Right nation frame of reference*: "The Progressive Majority," 1–2.

237 *On the hot-button issues*: "The Progressive Majority," 2.

237 *"My belief is that the power of government"*: *AAP* 2008, 1666.

238 *Democrats gained almost no ground*: Guth, "Religion in the 2008 Election," 120.

238 *A look at who voted*. Exit polls, 2006.

239 *The annual survey of college freshmen*: Haynes Johnson and Dan Balz, *The Battle for America 2008: The Story of an Extraordinary Election* (New York: Viking, 2009), 64–65.

239 *A Pew Research Center survey*: Pew, A Portrait of "Generation Next," January 9, 2007.

CHAPTER TWELVE

240 *Mark Penn, Hillary's chief strategist*: Memo, Launch Strategy Thoughts, December 21, 2006 reprinted in Joshua Green, "The Front-Runner's Fall," *The Atlantic*, September 2008.

242 *"look like Facebook"*: David Plouffe, *The Audacity to Win: The Inside Story and Lessons of Barack Obama's Historic Victory* (New York: Viking, 2009), 114.

242 *Obama's "belief that the American people*: Ibid., 21.

242 *"is a function of math"*: Robert Boynton, "Demographics and Destiny," *NYT*, January 18, 2009.

243 *"The great conventional wisdom"*: Richard Wolffe, *Renegade: The Making of a President*, (New York: Crown, 2009), 70.

243 *"You are uniquely suited"*: Strategy memo by David Axelrod, November 28, 2006, discussed in Haynes Johnson and Dan Balz, *The Battle for America 2008: The Story of an Extraordinary Election* (New York: Viking, 2009), 29.

244 *an ABC News/Washington Post poll*: Ibid., 99.

245 *"this all-women's college"*: Ibid., 98.

245 *"Aren't you appalled"*: "Matthews Asked About Clinton Endorsers' 'Willingness' 'to Become Castratos in the Eunuch Chorus," MMA, December 17, 2007, http://mediamatters.org/research/200712180002

245 *"Hillary's loyal lieutenants"*: Jamison Foser, "MSNBC's Chris Matthews Problem," MMA, January 11, 2008, http://mediamatters.org/columns/ 20080 1110014

245 *McCain laughed and said*: YouTube: "How Do We Beat the Bitch, Extended Version," November 13, 2007, http://www.youtube.com/watch?v= WLQGWpRVA7o

246 *"I think men have a reason to be angry"*: "MSNBC's Carlson Invoked Lorena Bobbitt to Claim Clinton Is Tapping into Women's Anger Toward Men," MMA, November 1, 2007, http://mediamatters.org/research/200711020002?f=s _search

246 *Iowa's Democratic caucus*: AAP 2010, 577; Johnson and Balz, *The Battle for America 2008*, 125.

247 *Only 11 percent of Iowans under 30*: Iowa Democratic Caucus Entrance Poll, http://www.cnn.com/ELECTION/2008/primaries/results/epolls/#IADEM

248 *"It's not easy"*: YouTube: "Hillary Clinton Tears up During Campaign Stop," http://www.youtube.com/watch?v=6qgWH89qWks&feature=player _embedded#at=93

248 *Obama had to rebuke*: Wolffe, *Renegade*, 111.

249 *"Is it ironic"*: "Russert Suggests Irony in Women Identifying with 'Self-Avowed Feminist' Who Showed Emotion," MMA, January 19, 2008, http://mediamatters.org/research/200801190001

250 *They had crushed most other insurgents*: Philip Klinkner and Thomas Schaller, "LBJ's Revenge: The 2008 Election and the Rise of the Great Society Coalition," *The Forum* 6, no. 4 (January 9, 2009).

251 *"Strength has been the key"*: Penn to Interested Parties, memo, March 5, 2008, in Green, "The Front-Runner's Fall."

252 *"September 11 has replaced abortion"*: Thomas B. Edsall, "Why the GOP's Future Belongs to Rudy," *TNR (Online)*, May 14, 2007.

254 *crashed three Navy fighter*: Tim Dickinson, "Make-Believe Maverick," *Rolling Stone*, October 16, 2008.

254 *Romney had served as the highest-ranking*: Sheryl Gay Stolberg, "For Romney, A Role of Faith and Authority," *NYT*, October 15, 2011.

255 *That prompted comedian Jon Stewart*: David Remnick, *The Bridge: The Life and Rise of Barack Obama* (New York: Knopf, 2010), 545.

255 *Giuliani was the only one*: CNN/ YouTube debate, November 29, 2007.

256 *In the 2008 Republican caucus*: Iowa Caucus Entrance Polls, 2008, CNN.com.

256 *the Republican primary*: Republican primary results in Election Center 2008, CNN.com; James L. Guth, "Religion in the 2008 Election," in Janet M. Box-Steffensmeier and Steven E. Schier, *The American Elections of 2008* (New York: Rowman & Littlefield, 2009), 117–136.

257 *a third of white evangelicals*: Pew, "McCain's Support Soars. Democratic Race Tightens," February 3, 2008.

258 *Right-wing leaders*: Michael Grunwald, "The Right Fight," *Time*, February 18, 2008; Johnson and Balz, *The Battle for America 2008*, 285.

259 *campaign had consciously downplayed race*: Remnick, *The Bridge*, chap. 14.

260 *"And let's not forget"*: "On MSNBC, Reuters' Decker on Obama's Bowling," MMA, April 14, 2008, http://mediamatters.org/research/200804140008

260 *"Won't a single tape of Wright"*: Memo, March 30, Green, "The Front-Runner's Fall."

261 *With the delegates won on May 6*: Despite much Democratic hand-wringing in that last month, nothing happened during that time to negatively affect the general election. I attribute the near hysteria of the end of the primary to old Democratic habits of overreaction and the venting of pent-up emotion, rather to any deeper cause. Since the primary has been treated in many other books, it does not seem necessary to recount the events of the last month here. For a good treatment of it, see Johnson and Balz, *The Battle for America 2008*, chap. 16.

261 *"gave them something to believe in"* : Heather Smith interview.

CHAPTER THIRTEEN

266 *Five days before McCain*: The story of Palin's selection is told in Haynes Johnson and Dan Balz, *The Battle for America 2008: The Story of an Extraordinary Election* (New York: Viking, 2009), 328–331; John Heilemann and Mark Halperin, *Game Change: Obama and the Clintons, McCain and Palin, and the Race of a Lifetime* (New York: Harper, 2010), 355–361; Jane Mayer, "The Insiders," *The New Yorker*, Oct. 27, 2008.

268 *Obama's campaign manager*: David Plouffe, *The Audacity to Win: The Inside Story and Lessons of Barack Obama's Historic Victory* (New York: Viking, 2009), 307.

268 *"In just 38 hours"*: Schlafly, "The Republicans' Call to Arms," *Eagle Forum*, September 5, 2008.

269 *"That speech by Alaska Governor Sarah Palin"*: "Who Chose Sarah Palin," crooksandliars.com, August 31, 2008.

269 *"should be extremely reassuring"*: Sam Hananel, "Brownback, Social Conservatives Cheer Palin As Energizing Force," *AP*, August 29, 2008.

269 *"shot directly into the heart"*: Michael D. Shear and Juliet Eilperin, "With Palin on the Ticket, Evangelicals Are Energized," *WP*, September 1, 2008

269 *"our poster woman"*: Michelle Goldberg, "Palin and the Christian Right," *The Nation*, September 24, 2008.

269 *poster child for Alaska Right to Life*: Sarah Palin, *Going Rogue: An American Life* (New York: HarperCollins, 2009), 2–3.

270 *"Palin, who is a born-again"*: The incidents in this and the following two paragraphs are related in: William Yardley, "Palin Start: Politics Not As Usual," NYT, September 3, 2008; Goldberg, "Palin and the Christian Right"; Max Blumenthal, *Republican Gomorrah: Inside the Movement that Shattered the Party* (New York: Nation Books, 2009), 394; Joe McGinniss, *The Rogue: Searching for the Real Sarah Palin* (New York: Crown, 2011), 52–63. Although McGinniss has been criticized for using anonymous sources, this section on Palin's early political career is sourced to credible and named interviewees and accords with other credible reporting published during the 2008 campaign.

271 *Mayor Palin asked Wasilla's librarian*: This incident is one of many Palin denies through an evasive explanation that doesn't answer the actual charge. Her account in *Going Rogue* simply is not as credible as the reporting on the episode. For that, see Yardley, "Palin Start."

271 *she opposed "explicit sex-ed programs"*: "Eagle Forum Alaska: 2006 Gubernatorial Candidate Questionnaire," http://eagleforumalaska.blogspot.com/ 2008/ 09/ 2006 -gubernatorial-candidate.html

271 *a $1,200 bonus payment*: Yereth Rosen, "Outsiders' Guide to Understanding Alaska's Politics and Peculiarities," *CSM*, September 15, 2008.

272 *Governor Palin lent her support*: "Who Is Sarah Palin? Questions Abound," *WP*, September 3, 2008, editorial.

273 *That week 35 percent of all news*: Pew, "McCain's Image Improves, With Big Assist From Palin, September 10, 2008

273 *sexist treatment of both Palin and Hillary*: A lot has been written about the role of the media in the campaign. For the definitive treatment of sexism specifically, see Rebecca Traister, *Big Girls Don't Cry: The Election That Changed Everything for American Women* (New York: Free Press, 2010).

274 *"I think he would be aborting*: "McCain Poised to Flip on GOP Abortion Platform," ABC News, May 9, 2008.

274 *With Schlafly watching over*: David Kirkpatrick, "Wooing Conservatives Pays Off," *NYT*, September 3, 2008.

274 *"Really, we evacuated*: Collins, "Misery Loves Democrats," *NYT*, September 11, 2008.

274 Plouffe, *The Audacity to Win*, 313, 320.

275 *McCain's cynical play*: Greenberg Quinlan Rosner, Democracy Corps, "The Changing Presidential Race After the Conventions," September 15, 2008; Steinem, "Palin: Wrong Woman, Wrong Message," *LAT*, September 4, 2008.

275 *"a depression greater"*: As related by President Bush to ABC's Charles Gibson, quoted in Johnson and Balz, *The Battle for America 2008*, 346.

276 *Bush invited Obama*: Plouffe, *The Audacity to Win*, 340–341.

276 *At the Oval Office meeting*: Johnson and Balz, *The Battle for America 2008*, 348–349.

278 *interview with James Dobson*: Blumenthal, *Republican Gomorrah*, 305.

278 *in front of 8,000 supporters*: Dana Milbank, "44 - In Fla., Palin Goes for the Rough Stuff as Audience Boos Obama," *WP*, October 6, 2008, http://voices .washingtonpost.com/44/2008/10/in-fla-palin-goes-for-the-roug.html

279 *"Sit down, boy"*: Dana Milbank, "Unleashed, Palin Makes a Pit Bull Look Tame," *WP,* October 7, 2008, http://www.washingtonpost.com/wp-dyn/content/article/2008/10/06/AR2008100602935.html?referrer=emailarticle

279 *McCain, too, surfed the rage*: "McCain Does Nothing As Supporter Calls Obama a 'Terrorist'," AMERICAblog News, October 6, 2008, http://www. americablog .com/2008/10/mccain-does-nothing-as-crowd-member.html

279 *video posted from Bethlehem*: Dana Milbank, "Rage in the Town of Bethlehem," *WP,* October 9, 2008, http://www.washingtonpost.com/wp-dyn/content/article/2008/10/08/AR2008100803601_2.html?hpid=opinionsbox1

280 *"visceral" dislike for her*: Heather Smith, Interview by author, March 28, 2011.

280 *not qualified to be president*: Johnson and Balz, *The Battle for America 2008,* 360.

280 *Ecstatic celebrations erupted*: This description is based on an extensive review of election night coverage. The specific statements are from "As It Happened: US Election Reaction," *BBC,* November 4, 2008, sec. Americas, http://news.bbc .co.uk/2/hi/7700298.stm

281 *that Barack Hussein Obama*: Milbank, "Rage in the Town of Bethlehem."

281 *Obama won*: Vote totals and percentages are from Leip's Atlas; turnout from Michael McDonald, "Voter Turnout, 2008," *United States Election Project*; new voters in Obama's coalition from Philip Klinkner and Thomas Schaller, "LBJ's Revenge: The 2008 Election and the Rise of the Great Society Coalition," *The Forum* 6, no. 4 (January 9, 2009); on participation, see ANES, "Tried to Influence How Others Vote," http://www.electionstudies.org/nesguide/toptable/tab6b_1 .htm

282 *The coalition that elected Obama*: Klinkner and Schaller, "LBJ's Revenge"; Alan I. Abramowitz, *The Disappearing Center: Engaged Citizens, Polarization, and American Democracy* (New Haven: Yale University Press, 2010); Exit polls, President—Election Center 2008, CNN.com.

282 *expanding the pool of voters*: Lorraine Minnite, "First-Time Voters in the 2008 Election" (Washington, DC: Project Vote, April 2011); Abramowitz, *The Disappearing Center,* 131; Exit polls; Klinkner and Schaller, "LBJ's Revenge"; USCB, "Voting and Registration 2008", http://www.census.gov/hhes/www/socdemo/voting/index.html

283 *Women were also indispensable*: Klinkner and Schaller, "LBJ's Revenge"; Abramowitz, *The Disappearing Center,* 115. Hillary was responsible for some of these new voters. In response to Obama's unconventional primary campaign, she too put effort into registering and mobilizing new voters in the primary, who then voted for Obama in the general election. Obama did better among men than all recent Democrats, but that advantage came from young whites and minorities, not white men overall.

283 *Obama attracted voters whom pundits*: Exit polls.

283 *religious activists who considered themselves progressive*: John C. Green, Robert Jones, and Daniel Cox, "Faithful, Engaged, and Divergent: A Comparative Portrait of Conservative and Progressive Religious Activists in the 2008 Election and Beyond," Ray C. Bliss Institute of Applied Politics and Public Religion Research, September 2009.

284 *Outside the states of the South*: Abramowitz, *The Disappearing Center,* 117.

284 *voters who supported legal abortion*: Exit polls; ibid., 118.

284 *Prop 8* : This account of Prop 8 is based on Tim Dickinson, "Same-Sex Set-back," *Rolling Stone*, March 25, 2011, and anonymous interviews conducted by the author.

286 *Nine out of ten McCain-Palin voters*: Klinkner and Schaller, "LBJ's Revenge."

286 *Traditionalist white evangelicals*: Abramowitz, *The Disappearing Center*, 115.

286 *fastest growing demographic groups*: Klinkner and Schaller, "LBJ's Revenge," 5; Abramowitz, *The Disappearing Center*, chap. 6.

286 *There was compelling evidence*: The only counties where the 2008 GOP ticket outperformed Bush were in those with older native southern white majorities. Political scientist Alan Abramowitz reaches this conclusion after noting that Bush's unpopularity, plus the gravity of the recession, would have predicted a larger share of the white vote for Obama. The large disparity in the white vote between the Deep South and the Northeast and West also points to lingering racial prejudice. Abramowitz, *The Disappearing Center*, 115–116.

288 *Stan Greenberg wrote*: Greenberg, "Goodbye, Reagan Democrats," Greenberg Quinlan Rosner, November 11, 2008, http://www.greenbergresearch.com/index.php?ID=2288

CHAPTERS FOURTEEN–EPILOGUE

Notes and hyperlinks to sources for the remaining chapters can be found on the book's website at www.nancylcohen.com

ABOUT THE AUTHOR

Nancy L. Cohen is a historian and author. Her books include *The Reconstruction of American Liberalism, 1865-1914*. She is a contributor to *The Huffington Post* and her writing has appeared in the *Los Angeles Times*, the *Chicago Tribune*, the *Business History Review*, and elsewhere. She has taught history and American politics at Binghamton University, SUNY, and Cal State University Long Beach, and has held positions as a visiting scholar at UCLA and a senior policy analyst at LAANE. She lives in Los Angeles with her husband, two daughters and four stepchildren.